Gentle Reads

Recent Titles in the
Children's and Young Adult Literature Reference Series
Catherine Barr, Series Editor

Best Books for Children: Preschool through Grade 6. Eighth Edition
Catherine Barr and John T. Gillespie

The Newbery/Printz Companion: Booktalks and Related Materials
for Award Winners and Honor Books
John T. Gillespie and Corinne J. Naden

Books Kids Will Sit Still For 3: A Read-Aloud Guide
Judy Freeman

Classic Teenplots: A Booktalk Guide to Use with Readers Ages 12–18
John T. Gillespie and Corinne J. Naden

Best Books for Middle School and Junior High Readers: Grades 6–9.
Supplement to the First Edition
John T. Gillespie and Catherine Barr

Best Books for High School Readers: Grades 9–12. Supplement to the First Edition
John T. Gillespie and Catherine Barr

War and Peace: A Guide to Literature and New Media, Grades 4–8
Virginia A. Walter

Across Cultures: A Guide to Multicultural Literature for Children
Kathy East and Rebecca L. Thomas

Best Books for Children, Supplement to the 8th Edition: Preschool through Grade 6
Catherine Barr and John T. Gillespie

Best Books for Boys: A Resource for Educators
Matthew D. Zbaracki

Beyond Picture Books: Subject Access to Best Books for Beginning Readers
Barbara Barstow, Judith Riggle, and Leslie Molnar

A to Zoo: Subject Access to Children's Picture Books. Supplement to the 7th Edition
Carolyn W. Lima and Rebecca L. Thomas

Gentle Reads

Great Books to Warm Hearts and Lift Spirits, Grades 5-9

Deanna J. McDaniel

Children's and Young Adult Literature Reference
Catherine Barr, Series Editor

A Member of the Greenwood Publishing Group

Westport, Connecticut • London

Library of Congress Cataloging-in-Publication Data

McDaniel, Deanna.
  Gentle reads : great books to warm hearts and lift spirits, grades 5–9 / Deanna
J. McDaniel.
      p. cm. — (Children's and young adult literature reference)
  Includes bibliographical references and indexes.
  ISBN 978-1-59158-491-9 (alk. paper)
  1. Middle school students—Books and reading—United States. 2. Junior
high school students—Books and reading—United States. 3. Preteens—Books
and reading—United States. 4. Teenagers—Books and reading—United
States. 5. Young adult literature, American—Stories, plots, etc. 6. Conduct of
life—Juvenile literature—Bibliography. I. Title.
  Z1037.M133   2008
  028.5'5—dc22   2008018878

British Library Cataloguing in Publication Data is available.

Library of Congress Catalog Card Number: 2008018878
ISBN: 978-1-59158-491-4

First published in 2008

Libraries Unlimited, 88 Post Road West, Westport, CT 06881
A Member of the Greenwood Publishing Group, Inc.
www.lu.com

Printed in the United States of America

The paper used in this book complies with the
Permanent Paper Standard issued by the National
Information Standards Organization (Z39.48–1984).

10 9 8 7 6 5 4 3 2 1

Contents

Preface

In the 8/22/04 issue of the *New York Times Book Review,* an article appeared with the title "A Good Book Should Make You Cry." The premise of the article was that language arts teachers love depressing books and that the YA award winners are full of bad adults, drug addiction, mental illness, and other negative aspects of the world we live in.

Maybe it was turning fifty. Maybe it was having a daughter of my own right in the middle of the age range that we are talking about. Maybe, just maybe, it had to do with twenty-five years of running school libraries and sharing good books with lots of wonderful young adults. Regardless, my immediate reaction was: That can't be right. I can think of hundreds of books that are warm, funny, inspiring, heartwarming, and enjoyed by young people. Many of them are as good as the award-winning "problem novels," and teachers and librarians need to be aware of them. So when Editor Catherine Barr called me and said, "I think there's a book in this," I could only agree. When she asked me how many titles I thought I could come up with, I blithely replied, "Oh, I could easily think of 500 inspiring reads." 500! What was I thinking? But here they are.

We set the following criteria:

- All books should be published in the last ten years, in hopes that they would all still be easily available and readers might find new titles and authors that they were not aware of. Most of them are brand new, right off the press in the last year or so.
- The books would be appropriate for young people in grades 5 to 9.
- The books would be inspiring, heartwarming, or in some way lift the reader's spirits.
- The list would not be about censorship, but more about finding stories that exemplify good morals, leadership, courage, and nobility: all those

character traits that you want to expose young people to without preaching at them.

☞ The titles were located by consulting lists of award winners, issues of *School Library Journal* and *Booklist*, and Junior Library Guild catalogs. I also included books that I knew from my own experience flew off the shelves and into my readers' hands. And many were suggested by my students (and daughter) once they heard about my project.

The list covers genres that language arts teachers in my school do as units: general fiction (which includes the popular area of realistic fiction), mystery and detective stories, science fiction, fantasy, historical fiction, biography, and nonfiction. Also included are short stories, novels in verse, poetry, and picture books.

This book should be of use to many different kinds of readers. Book clubs will find this a helpful list of titles that will be a comfortable fit for young people in grades 5 through 9. Language arts teachers looking for themes of courage, honesty, goodness, and perseverance will find lots of treasures here. This book is also for all those people who ever asked me for a wonderful read that they can feel comfortable picking out for a young person.

From the tenderness of *Firegirl,* badly burned and just needing a friend, to the adventure of *Marooned,* Robert Selkirk's real-life experience surviving on an island by himself, readers will be captivated by these great stories.

Arranged by genres, the entries include full bibliographic information, annotation, and a description of why the book fits the criteria. Also included are major awards, and whether at press time it was an Accelerated Reader or Reading Counts title. Junior Library Guild selections are also noted. There are author, title, subject, and series indexes.

This book is dedicated to my daughter and husband, who read, laughed, and cried with me; to all the authors who wrote the wonderful books; to the Westerville Public Library, which delivered many of the books to me; and to all the people who thought I was knowledgeable enough to suggest a good book to them.

Happy reading!

Picture Books

1   **Hearne, Betsy.** *Seven Brave Women.*

Ill. by Bethanne Anderson. HarperCollins, 1997, ISBN 978-0-688-14503-3; 2006, pap., ISBN 978-0-06-079921-2. Unpaged • All ages

☞ ACCELERATED READER ☞ READING COUNTS

The author takes readers through seven generations of women in her family who showed courage without ever fighting, even in times of war. The story begins with the author's great-great-great-grandmother, who crossed the mountains from Switzerland and then the seas to America with two small children and a third one on the way. She went on to have seven more children and to make a good life for all of them. These women lived through the Revolutionary War, the Civil War, the War of 1812, World War I, and World War II.

Gentle Criteria: This is a simple picture book that will be enjoyed by all ages, demonstrating to readers that there are a million ways to be brave. A great classroom exercise would be to share a story and then have students tell their families' own stories of bravery. The women here all possess physical, intellectual, and spiritual strength. They are truly unsung heroes.

2   **McCully, Emily Arnold.** *Beautiful Warrior: The Legend of the Nun's Kung Fu.*

Ill. by author. Scholastic, 1998, ISBN 978-0-590-37487-3. 36p. • All ages

☞ ACCELERATED READER ☞ READING COUNTS

When Jingyong is born at the end of the Ming dynasty, her father doesn't want her to learn the idle pastimes that girls normally learn. Instead, he enrolls Jingyong in art, literature, music, medicine, and martial arts studies. She becomes an expert at martial arts. When Manchurian warriors separate her from her family, she goes to the Shaolin Monastery to ask for training. She passes their test by defeating a monk and they allow her to shave her head and join them, giving her the name Wu Mei. Meanwhile Mingyi Yang witnesses Wu Mei's abilities when she saves her from thieves. Soong Ling comes to Mingyi Yang's father's shop, saying if she won't marry him, he will destroy the shop. Mingyi Yang asks Wu Mei to fight Soong Ling for her. Wu Mei refuses but said she will teach Mingyi Yang to protect herself. Readers will be intrigued to find out whether Mingyi Yang is able to defeat the man who threatens her and her family.

Gentle Criteria: This book emphasizes that martial arts are the smallest part of kung fu. Kung fu includes lifelong study of history, philosophy, science, and art, along with the exercises. The philosophy is similar to that of teaching a man to fish versus giving a man a fish. Kung fu teaches the practitioner how to get in touch with—and take care of—himself. By mimicking the movements of animals and learning to study how nature works, the characters in this book become self-sufficient.

3   **McCutcheon, John.** *Christmas in the Trenches.*
Ill. by Henri Sorensen. Peachtree, 2006, ISBN 978-1-56145-374-0.
Unpaged • All ages
☙ ACCELERATED READER

Based on a real historical account, this story takes place on a battlefield in World War I. Soldiers on both sides are in their trenches on Christmas Eve, some no more than thirty yards apart. In the middle of the cold and darkness, a Christmas tree is brought out, and someone begins to sing "Silent Night" in German. Before long, both sides are singing, in their respective languages. Men who were trying to kill each other are suddenly singing together, playing soccer, and trying to bridge their language barrier. The Christmas Truce of 1914 is a real event that demonstrates peace can happen anywhere. The book includes historical end-notes, along with a CD of "Silent Night," sung in German and in English. The author has also included a song of his own about the event.

Gentle Criteria: This is a book that kids *and* adults will enjoy reading. A classroom discussion about what it takes to make lasting peace between countries could be launched with this book.

4   **McGill, Alice.** *Molly Bannaky.*
Ill. by Chris K. Soentpiet. Houghton Mifflin, 1999, ISBN 978-0-395-72287-9. 30p. • Grades 5–9
☙ ACCELERATED READER ☙ READING COUNTS

This is a short, beautifully illustrated book with detailed drawings. The story tells of a maid by the name of Molly Walsh who in 1683 spills another pail of milk. She had been warned that she could lose her life if she lost another of the Lord's possessions. She is sent to court and because she can read, she is sent to America to serve as an indentured servant for seven years. After her indentured term is up, she is given an ox, a wagon, a gun, and all the supplies she will need to start her own life. She buys a slave, whom she names Bannaky, to help bring in the farm harvest. Molly falls in love with Bannaky and marries him. Fortunately for her, the neighbors like Bannaky; otherwise she could have been turned into a slave as well. They have four daughters, and their eldest daughter Mary marries a slave named Robert Banneker. Their son is Benjamin, who grows up to be a scientist and mathematician.

Gentle Criteria: Besides the wonderful illustrations, this story shows the perseverance of the human spirit. Mary is able to endure slave-like labor for seven years to earn her freedom. Molly looks into Bannaky's proud eyes and sees the honor there. Bannaky is actually a prince from Africa, who was captured and sold into slavery. They both work hard to raise their children and make sure they can read. Molly's actions started the course of eventual freedom for the slaves because her grandson Benjamin wrote to Thomas Jefferson about those injustices.

5   **Muth, Jon J.** *Zen Shorts.*
Scholastic, 2005, ISBN 978-0-439-33911-7; pap., ISBN 978-0-439-78923-3. 35p. • All ages
⌐ ACCELERATED READER ⌐ READING COUNTS

Karl, Addy, and Michael are siblings who don't get along. One day they find a giant panda named Stillwater in their backyard. Karl visits the bear and complains about Michael. Stillwater then tells him the story of two monks who assisted an ungrateful young lady. The younger of the two monks finally spouted, "That woman was very selfish and rude; she didn't even say thank you!" The older monk replied, "I set the woman down hours ago. Why are you still carrying her?" Over the next days, each of the children visits the bear, and he tells each a traditional Zen story. They learn the hidden meaning behind these stories and all three siblings become friends.

Gentle Criteria: Zen shorts is a term for short meditations. Through a parable format, each child learns a valuable lesson. An agitated mind sees the world as though one is looking at the moon reflected in a disturbed body of water. By applying these messages, one can learn to lessen the agitation in one's mind and see the real world: the moon through the reflection in a still body of water. These "Zen shorts" allow the reader to let go of everyday irritations and focus on the good and gentle things in life—the things that matter most and keep our hearts warm.

ജ   CALDECOTT HONOR BOOK, 2006

Fiction

6 **Abbott, Tony.** *Firegirl.*

Little, Brown, 2006, ISBN 978-0-316-02271-2. 145p. • Grades 6–9

☞ Accelerated Reader ☞ Reading Counts ☞ Junior Library Guild

No one knows what to expect when Mrs. Tracy tells her seventh-grade class at St. Catherine's that Jessica Feeney will be joining them. "There is something you need to know about Jessica," she says. No one wants to face the terrible truth about Jessica. "Firegirl" they whisper, making up awful stories about how Jessica got burned in the fire, about how her skin melted. No one wants to look at her or hold her hand during morning prayer. The class is relieved on the days that Jessica is not at school because she is receiving treatment at the hospital. But Tom Bender is fed up with the way his friends talk about Jessica. One day Mrs. Tracy asks Tom to take Jessica her homework; when he goes to her house, he discovers how Jessica was burned. Tom risks his closest friendships by trying to befriend the firegirl. Jessica will change Tom's perspective of life forever, but will Tom be able to show Jessica he cares before it's too late?

Gentle Criteria: This book shows how a boy learns to befriend and accept someone who is very different, despite the fact that he may lose his other friendships.

7 **Alexander, Lloyd.** *Gypsy Rizka.*

Dutton, 1999, ISBN 978-0-525-46121-0; Penguin, 2000, pap., ISBN 978-0-14-130980-4. 195p. • Grades 5–7

☞ Accelerated Reader ☞ Reading Counts

Gypsy Rizka is an unwanted gypsy girl who lives at the edge of town. Her mother has died, and she waits patiently for her father's gypsy caravan to come and get her. In the meantime, however, she cleverly and quietly makes things right for the townspeople around her. She persuades a man to accept the flea bites he got at the inn, by telling him that he has kidnapped some of the town's world-famous fleas. She then gives the money he paid her to the laundress, who has accidentally spoiled a customer's garment and can't afford to make good the damage. She amusingly convinces two warring families to let their children marry. In the end, when she realizes her father is never coming back for her, the townspeople convince her that they cannot live without her and are her true family.

Gentle Criteria: Gypsy Rizka quietly helps people in need, often in amusing ways but always with their best interests at heart. Every town needs a Gypsy Rizka to watch over its people. The heartwarming love of the townspeople saves her in the end.

8   **Alvarez, Julia.** *Finding Miracles.*
Knopf, 2004, ISBN 978-0-375-92760-7. 264p. • Grades 7–9
⌐ ACCELERATED READER ⌐ READING COUNTS

Fifteen-year-old Milly has kept it a secret that she was adopted as a baby from a Third World country. But one day Pablo arrives at her school. His family has recently escaped from Milly's birth country. He asks Milly where she is from because she looks so much like the people in the village near his. Pablo inspires her to track down her birthplace. Milly ends up with no certain answers but a new understanding of the country in which she was born and its people. Some of the story lines cover the violence of revolution and people living for the moment in an uncertain world in which babies cannot always be provided for, but there is nothing graphic about this book.

Gentle Criteria: This is an inspiring book about people trying to do what is best for their families, for their country, and for the world. It is a story about the love between birth and adoptive families, and the story of a family that learns to appreciate a culture different from its own. Milly deals with the fact that she is adopted and learns about a Third World country where people are not free.

9   **Anderson, Janet S.** *The Monkey Tree.*
Dutton, 1998, ISBN 978-0-525-46032-9. 152p. • Grades 7–9
⌐ ACCELERATED READER ⌐ READING COUNTS

Susanna is afraid she has lost her ability in two very important areas—art and friendship. When her grandmother dies and her family moves into her grandmother's house, she discovers a reclusive great uncle whom her grandmother took care of for twenty years. His room is a work of art; everything in it is beautiful and perfectly arranged. She also meets Melody, a neighbor girl with more problems than Susanna will ever have. Between her great uncle and Melody, Susanna begins to see life outside herself. She learns that people can choose to overcome bad things, or they can succumb to them. Even Melody's father, who is rough and scary, helps Susanna's brother when he breaks his leg. And Susanna learns that her brother is just as scared of being a nobody and losing his girlfriend as Susanna is about losing her friends. The monkey tree that Susanna draws shows readers how everyone has to hang on to each other in order to live together in the world.

Gentle Criteria: This is a book for an older audience because it contains some bad language and deals with serious issues. The reclusive great uncle is obviously not well, and Melody's family is in a bad way. Even so, this is a book about living positively, about pushing ahead instead of giving up, and about the fact that everyone feels shaky about their lives at one time or another.

10   **Anderson, Laurie Halse.** *Fear of Falling.*
Gareth Stevens, 2003, ISBN 978-0-8368-3255-6; American Girl, 2001, pap., ISBN 978-1-58485-059-5. 105p. Series: Wild at Heart •
Grades 5–7
☞ ACCELERATED READER

David sees a new horse at Mr. Quinn's stables and finds out it belongs to his dad. His dad has returned to spend Thanksgiving with the family after years in Texas looking for work. David's dad made the Olympic horse jumping team, and David is full of pride when he watches his dad ride. David wonders why his dad still hasn't contacted his mom. When his dad gives him a jumping lesson, he pushes David too far, and the boy ends up falling. David can see his mother is angry but she just thanks his dad for getting David to the hospital. David overhears that his dad had been fired from his job in Texas. David believes that his dad did not come back to be closer to them but rather to use old acquaintances to find a job. Will his dad be able to convince David that he is really trying to be closer to his family?

Gentle Criteria: David isn't sure how he feels about hearing that his dad is coming back home for Thanksgiving. But once David sees him, his emotions get the best of him and he runs into his father's arms for a hug. However, David still doubts his father's devotion. Mr. Quinn helps David understand that his dad wants David and the family to be proud of him. This statement seems to be all that is necessary for David to give his dad another chance.

11   **Anderson, Laurie Halse.** *Fight for Life.*
Gareth Stevens, 2000, ISBN 978-0-8368-3256-3; Penguin, 2007, pap., ISBN 978-0-14-240862-9. 127p. Series: Wild at Heart • Grades 5–7
☞ ACCELERATED READER ☞ READING COUNTS

All Maggie wants to do is spend time caring for the animals in her grandmother's clinic. But she has been told she must improve her grades; and, worse, her preppy, privileged cousin is coming to stay. Maggie didn't think things could get any worse. But suddenly, the clinic is overwhelmed with sick puppies. Many of the puppies are malnourished, dehydrated, and have difficulty breathing. Maggie discovers were all bought at the same place—from a gruff man at a farmer's market. Suspecting that the man runs a puppy mill, and with the help of the volunteers, Maggie tracks the man down and gets the police involved. Maggie and the others care for the dogs and find them good homes, and the man who mistreated the puppies is arrested.

Gentle Criteria: Maggie serves as a good example for readers because she stands up for something she believes in and sees it through. Even though she didn't want to share the clinic, she learns to accept the help of the volunteers and to get along with her cousin Zoe. In the end, she also agrees to get help from a tutor so she can improve her grades while continuing to help out at the clinic.

12   Anderson, Laurie Halse. *Homeless.*
Gareth Stevens, 2000, ISBN 978-0-8368-3257-0; American Girl, pap., ISBN 978-1-58485-045-8. 130p. Series: Wild at Heart • Grades 5–7
☞ Accelerated Reader ☞ Reading Counts

When Sunita and her friends who help at the Wild at Heart veterinary clinic accidentally let one of the cats loose, they discover a feral cat colony near an empty railroad car. The neighbors want Animal Control to destroy the cats. Sunita and her friends convince the neighbors to approve the Treat, Vaccinate, Spay, and Release (TVSR) program instead of ending the cats' lives. Sunita saves two neighborhood children from a rabid raccoon, lifting her standing in the neighborhood even higher, and ensuring that the program continues successfully.

Gentle Criteria: This book is not only informative; it will also inspire readers to volunteer in their own communities. Rather than ending the lives of these feral cats, this program enables them to live as they have been without spreading disease or reproducing in an uncontrolled manner. Sunita and her friends make a difference in their world and show readers how they can do the same.

13   Anderson, Laurie Halse. *Manatee Blues.*
Gareth Stevens, 2000, ISBN 978-0-8368-3258-7; American Girl, pap., ISBN 978-1-58485-049-6. 111p. Series: Wild at Heart • Grades 5–7
☞ Accelerated Reader

Once again the volunteer crew from the Wild at Heart veterinary clinic aims to save an animal in trouble. This time Brenna is doing a school project on manatees, one of her favorite animals, and she gets to go to Florida to work in a rescue center along with friends Zoe and Maggie. Unfortunately, Brenna's quick temper and habit of leaping before she looks puts her in hot water more than once. The girls discover that the mission is in financial trouble and may not be able to help the manatees much longer. Will the three find a way to save the center and the manatees?

Gentle Criteria: Once again young people are sincerely interested in the fate of animals and seek to do good in the world. The adults around them promote this positive independence. Readers are educated about an endangered species and learn practical ways to get involved and help.

14   Anderson, Laurie Halse. *Say Good-Bye.*

Gareth Stevens, 2001, ISBN 978-0-8368-3259-4; American Girl, pap., ISBN 978-1-58485-051-9. 129p. Series: Wild at Heart • Grades 5–7

⌐ ACCELERATED READER ⌐ READING COUNTS

Zoe has been sent to live with her veterinarian grandmother, Dr. Mac, because her mother's soap opera has been canceled. Her cousin Maggie has lived with Dr. Mac since the death of her parents. Dr. Mac gives Zoe a rescued puppy that Zoe must train but Zoe at first doesn't understand why she can't just hire a dog walker and trainer like her neighbors in New York. Zoe goes with Jane to the hospital to see how Jane's well-trained dog Yum-Yum entertains children in the cancer ward. They notice a dark spot on Yum-Yum's mouth and, after an examination, learn that Yum-Yum has cancer too. Now Jane must decide whether to treat Yum-Yum's cancer.

Gentle Criteria: Zoe learns that raising and training a dog is a big responsibility that requires time and energy. Fortunately, her cousin Maggie has a lot of experience and helps her. This book is full of people trying to do their best for each other. Although Zoe finds it hard not being with her movie-star mom in Hollywood, she understands that she would see her mom very little anyway and that she is more secure with her grandma. Dr. Mac recognizes that Yum-Yum is a member of Jane's family, and lets her make her own decision about whether to treat her or put her down. After Yum-Yum dies, Zoe is determined to train her dog Sneakers as a tribute to Yum-Yum; Sneakers will also entertain the children in the cancer ward. The process of training Sneakers helps ease Jane's sorrow, and the trainee brings a smile to Emma, who is lonely and sick. This book is full of love on the part of both humans and animals; it includes a nice section that shows how companion dogs are used.

15   Anderson, Laurie Halse. *Storm Rescue.*

Gareth Stevens, 2003, ISBN 978-0-8368-3260-0. 105p. Series: Wild at Heart • Grades 5–7

⌐ ACCELERATED READER

Sunita and her friends volunteer at Dr. Mac's Wild at Heart veterinary clinic. Sunita is scared of the big animals. She is also afraid of water and has never learned to swim. Her parents tell her she must get over her fears. When all the animals at the clinic start behaving strangely, everyone knows something is about to happen. Hurricane Felix is headed right toward them! While the doctors are out on emergency runs, a Great Dane's owner calls and asks them to get his dog, which is outside in its kennel. Leaving Zoe behind to answer the phones, the others go to get the dog only to discover that he's in two feet of water and panicking. Maggie gives the dog the command to sit and he obeys. They rescue the

Great Dane, but on their way back to the clinic they see Mrs. Clark being evacuated from her home. She's worried about her diabetic cat. Can Sunita overcome her fear of water to help rescue Mrs. Clark's cat?

Gentle Criteria: The volunteer efforts of this group of kids set a great example for readers. Sunita listens to the advice of her friends and finally faces her fears of both big animals and of water. Sunita even gets the courage to pet the Great Dane. She also decides to take the positive step of signing up for swimming lessons.

16   Anderson, Laurie Halse. *Teacher's Pet.*
Gareth Stevens, 2003, ISBN 978-0-8368-3261-7; American Girl, 2001, pap., ISBN 978-1-58485-055-7. 132p. Series: Wild at Heart •
Grades 5–7
ACCELERATED READER

Maggie didn't do well in school last year, and she remembers the discussion she had with her grandmother about it. Now school is starting again, and it is the last place Maggie wants to go. When Maggie enters her science class she is thrilled to find a huge dog in the classroom. But the teacher, Mr. Carlson, tells her not to pet the dog because it is working. The teacher explains that he is blind, and Scout is his guide dog. Maggie's fears about school are realized when she scores poorly on her first quiz. She doesn't even take notes in class because she feels she is doomed. Maggie is surprised when Mr. Carlson holds her after class and asks why she hasn't taken any notes. When Maggie explains her learning difficulties, Mr. Carlson reassures her that there are people there to help her so she will not fail the class. Maggie and her grandmother meet with a counselor to learn what can be done to help her succeed. Mr. Carlson learns too that he has some studying to do if he is going to succeed with Scout.

Gentle Criteria: This book is a gentle read because it features the good examples of Mr. Carlson and Maggie, both of whom work hard to overcome their challenges. Mr. Carlson lost his sight just two years earlier to an eye disease, but he is making the necessary changes to continue doing what he loves: teaching. Maggie works hard to overcome her learning challenges rather than giving up. The story demonstrates how students and parents can work with teachers and guidance counselors to ensure that students receive the assistance they need to succeed.

17   Anderson, Laurie Halse. *Time to Fly.*
Gareth Stevens, 2003, ISBN 978-0-8368-3262-4; American Girl, 2002, pap., ISBN 978-1-58485-061-8. 113p. Series: Wild at Heart •
Grades 5–7
ACCELERATED READER

Zoe is living with her grandmother in Pennsylvania while her actress mother looks for work in Los Angeles. Zoe spots a parrot in the neighbor's backyard and soon discovers a whole tree full of parrots. Upon further investigation, she determines that two of the parrots are tame and have likely escaped from a smuggler's vehicle. It is about that time that Zoe's mother shows up and says she wants Zoe to move to Los Angeles with her. Although Zoe was upset when her mother left her at her grandmother's, now she's upset to have to leave her new friends. She also loves working at the Wild at Heart veterinary clinic. To make matters worse, her mom doesn't want Zoe to bring her dog. Who will win this struggle of wills?

Gentle Criteria: All moms must make tough decisions concerning their children. Zoe now realizes her mom initially made a good decision on Zoe's behalf. Zoe doesn't want to leave Pennsylvania for several reasons: her cousin Maggie has become the sister she never had, she loves living with her Gran and working with the other volunteers at the clinic, she loves having animals around, and most importantly, she feels needed—something she never felt living with her mom. She knows, however, that she should join her mom. This book teaches a lesson in family communication and cooperation.

18   Anderson, Laurie Halse. *Trapped.*
        Gareth Stevens, 2003, ISBN 978-0-86383-263-5; American Girl, 2001,
        pap., ISBN 978-1-58485-124-0. 113p. Series: Wild at Heart •
        Grades 5–7
        ☞ ACCELERATED READER

Brenna and her older brother Sage are all for animal rights; so much so that Sage has become a vegetarian. They go ballistic when they discover a dog in a trap. The dog's leg must be amputated. Sage and Brenna stake out the trap and confront Billy Connor when he arrives. Billy is defiant and says he's always trapped here. Brenna tells him it is illegal to trap on government property, and turns him in to the authorities. After reading in the newspaper that Billy has been fined, Brenna is determined to change his mind about trapping. When she goes to find Billy, he is about to shoot a trapped baby deer. Brenna rescues the fawn but not before getting into a fight with Billy. Later Brenna listens to Billy's side of the story; he traps animals because his family is poor and needs the food. Brenna has an idea that will solve Billy's money problems.

Gentle Criteria: This book does a good job of presenting both sides of a controversial issue. Brenna sets a good example because she does what most people do not: she listens to the other side of the story. Brenna's observation of Billy's talent with woodworking leads to finding him a job that saves the animals.

19   Anderson, Laurie Halse. *Trickster.*
        Gareth Stevens, 2003, ISBN 978-0-8368-3264-8; American Girl, 2000,
        pap., ISBN 978-1-58485-047-2. 124p. Series: Wild at Heart •
        Grades 5–7
        ☞ ACCELERATED READER

David and friends volunteer at Dr. Mac's veterinary clinic. Dr. Mac tells them they will be helping out with Mr. Quinn's horses, but David says he has had a disagreement with Mr. Quinn and can't go. Apparently David used to ride at the stables but got lost the last time and ended up at a shopping mall! Dr. Mac says she's cleared that up and David is welcome to come back and clean the stables in exchange for riding horses. When Mr. Quinn arrives with an injured horse named Trickster, David volunteers to care for it. David is walking the horse when he takes a shortcut to help a fellow rider, but he fails to tie Trickster properly. When the other horse bolts, Trickster takes off after him, injuring his leg even further. Is this new mistake the end of David's horse riding?

Gentle Criteria: Teens and adults can learn a lesson from David's shortcuts. David sweeps dust balls behind plants, dumps manure behind the utility shed, and is careless with an injured horse, but he learns that taking shortcuts often leads to problems. The caring adults in this story give David a second chance to prove himself and he finally realizes that he has to give 100 percent effort to be considered responsible.

20   Auch, M. J. *Wing Nut.*

Henry Holt, 2005, ISBN 978-0-8050-7531-1. 231p. • Grades 5–9
⮐ ACCELERATED READER ⮐ READING COUNTS

Grady and his mom, Lila, have been moving from place to place ever since Grady's dad died. They leave the commune in which they've been living because Lila is fed up with doing all the cooking and cleaning while the others spend their time philosophizing. When their car breaks down in western Pennsylvania, Grady and Lila stumble upon a job caring for Charlie, an old man whose son is afraid to leave him alone when he departs for Florida in two weeks. Charlie isn't about to let anyone help him until he figures out that Lila is only interested in staying around until she has enough money to fix her car. When Charlie tastes Lila's food, he decides maybe he has had enough of frozen dinners. Charlie hires Grady to help him with his blue martin nests and is happy to teach Grady about repairing engines. But when Grady frees sparrows from a trap and they break some of the blue martin eggs, will that be the end of their stay at the best place they've ever lived?

Gentle Criteria: Readers learn that although Charlie appears to be an independent old cuss who doesn't want help from anyone, he actually needs Grady and Lila in his life just as much as Grady and Lila need Charlie in theirs. Charlie is willing to homeschool Grady and will even incorporate their love for birds and cars into the curriculum. Grady and Lila finally have a home and a sense of security. All three begin to care about each other and form their own kind of family.

21   Avi. *The Christmas Rat.*

Atheneum, 2000, ISBN 978-0-689-83842-2; Simon & Schuster, 2002, pap., ISBN 978-0-689-83843-9. 135p. • Grades 5–7

☙ Accelerated Reader ☙ Reading Counts

Eleven-year-old Eric is alone and bored the week before Christmas. When a strange exterminator shows up intent on killing a rat, Eric discovers the true meaning of Christmas as he feels a growing sympathy for the rat.

Gentle Criteria: Although at first glance this book does not appear to be a gentle read, it is actually a clever story about an angel reminding a young boy what the Christmas season is really about, underlining his love for his family and his unwillingness for even a rat to be harmed at Christmastime.

22   Banks, Kate. *Dillon Dillon.*

Farrar, Straus & Giroux, 2002, ISBN 978-0-374-31786-7; 2005, pap., ISBN 978-0-374-41715-4. 150p. • Grades 5–7

☙ Accelerated Reader ☙ Reading Counts

Why in the world did Dillon Dillon's parents give him such a stupid name? They are not stupid people. On his birthday he finally asks them, and the answer turns his world upside down. How could he have guessed that the family he lives with is not his first family but his second? Dillon's older brother tells him that he remembers when Dillon came to their family, and how he thought Dillon was a gift. Dillon finds it all difficult to understand until he discovers a family of loons and watches the parents and their babies. When the mother and father loon are killed, Dillon recognizes that someone can take another person's child and care for and nurture that baby as their own.

Gentle Criteria: This gentle story about a boy finding his way back to his family says a great deal about what makes up a family. This book is about the love that parents have for their families, whether they be birth or adoptive parents. Dillon struggles to find connections between himself and his family and is rewarded with lots of love and understanding.

23   Baskin, Raleigh. *Basketball (or Something Like That).*

HarperCollins, 2005, ISBN 978-0-06-059611-8. 166p. • Grades 6–8

☙ Accelerated Reader

This author has done a great job of understanding a middle-schooler. This book shows a teen's viewpoint of organized sports, along with glimpses of what teens think of parents' my-child-deserves-to-play-more attitudes. The main characters give readers insight into their feelings. Jeremy, who was recently left with his grandmother, only feels comfortable on the basketball court. Nathan has an uncle who failed at professional sports, and his parents have made it clear that school is for learning and basketball is for fun. Hank's parents are such rabid fans that they don't notice that it is his sister Anabel who is the real athlete. And Anabel shows them all what place sports should have in their lives.

Gentle Criteria: This is a clever book about friendship and what really matters in life. Readers should be aware that there is some mild profanity throughout the book, but the language rings true, and the heartwarming, feel-good ending outweighs the bad language. When the four students end up in detention they form a bond that lasts them through the rest of their school years. Anabel loves her brother even though he picks on her; Jeremy realizes he doesn't need to run away from his grandmother to find the safe haven that he yearns for; and Hank sacrifices himself so that his friend Jeremy can get what he really deserves. These students teach an important lesson about sports, but also about friendship, love, and family. They will go far in life as happy, satisfied adults.

24   Bauer, Joan. *Backwater.*
Putnam, 1999, ISBN 978-0-399-23141-4; Penguin, 2005, pap., ISBN 978-0-14-240434-8. 185p. • Grades 7–9
⌢ ACCELERATED READER ⌢ READING COUNTS

Ivy's family is full of lawyers, and she has always felt like an oddball. She prefers to read history than to argue points of law. When she starts to research her family's history, she discovers an aunt whom no one talks about. She tracks down her aunt in a mountain wilderness and finds a kinship she has never felt. Along the way are many exciting moments: a tree crashes through the cabin, breaking her aunt's leg, and Ivy must take her on a sled in the middle of winter to the safety of the ranger's cabin; and her aunt's wolf leads Ivy safely across a partially frozen lake where she meets a ranger in training who becomes her first boyfriend. Best of all, she brings a disagreeable family together. She discovers that you can love people and still not want to be around them all the time.

Gentle Criteria: There are numerous quotable moments in this book about finding one's own strength. The wilderness guide Ivy hires to take her up the mountain states that her biggest irritation is when "smart, strong women convince themselves they're not tough enough to try." She also claims that her personal definition of freedom is not being afraid of the unknown. This book is about understanding your family history and finding hidden strengths within yourself.

25   Bauer, Joan. *Hope Was Here.*
Putnam, 2000, ISBN 978-0-399-23142-1; Penguin, 2005, pap., ISBN 978-0-14-240424-9. 186p. • Grades 7–9
⌢ ACCELERATED READER ⌢ READING COUNTS ⌢ JUNIOR LIBRARY GUILD

Hope is moving once again, and she doesn't expect to feel comfortable when she and her aunt relocate from Brooklyn to Wisconsin. They quickly become embroiled in the local diner owner's campaign for the corrupt mayor's job. The diner owner has leukemia, and the disease has made it very clear to him what is important in life. Hope learns that hope can make all kinds of things possible. This book features many wonderful small-town moments. When the mayor pulls up in front of the diner in a hearse to remind people that they don't want to vote for a dying man, the diner owner thanks him for reminding them that there is no time like the present to make a change. Although Hope's mother rarely shows up, her aunt gently reminds her that sometimes people just don't have the capability to love you like you need them to, but that doesn't mean they don't love you. Hope also manages to get the father she's been searching for.

Gentle Criteria: Tremendous hope is a constant part of this story. The diner owner's wish to do something good for his town intensifies once he is diagnosed with cancer. Hope's wish for stability and a father, her aunt's wish for happiness—and a good diner to run—Flo's wish for her infant daughter to develop normally, and the hope that the diner owner's cancer will go into remission are sustaining threads in this strong story about always doing one's best.

🐝 NEWBERY HONOR BOOK, 2001

26 Bauer, Joan. *Stand Tall.*
Putnam, 2002, ISBN 978-0-399-23473-6; Penguin, 2004, pap., ISBN 978-0-14-240148-4. 182p. • Grades 7–9
☞ ACCELERATED READER ☞ READING COUNTS ☞ JUNIOR LIBRARY GUILD

Tree is twelve years old and six feet three inches tall. His parents are in the process of getting a friendly divorce, but Tree still feels terrible. His grandfather, a Vietnam War veteran, has just lost part of his leg. In their own way, both feel as if they are recovering from war wounds. Tree's best friend Sophie must deal with the bullies at school. As Tree watches his grandfather do exercises to strengthen his leg, he wishes there were exercises to strengthen one's soul after a divorce. As they both get better, there are some light moments. For example, Tree's grandfather realizes he no longer has to match socks—a dreaded laundry task! When a flood wipes out most of the town, everyone helps each other in spite of their differences—even the town bullies.

Gentle Criteria: This story is a gentle read because it is full of hope and humor. When Sophie gets exasperated with the school bullies, her aunt reminds her that you can't beat people over the head with the truth. And although Tree's parents are unable to live together, they still love their children—and even each other—deeply. In the end, this story is about hope, love, and how to get along in the world.

27 Beam, Matt. *Getting to First Base with Danalda Chase.*
Dutton, 2007, ISBN 978-0-525-47578-1. 164p. • Grades 5–9
☞ ACCELERATED READER

Darcy knows everything there is to know about baseball but *nothing* about girls. Entering middle school, he finds that his friends are more interested in the opposite sex than in the most wonderful game in the world. When he decides to use his baseball knowledge to impress the girl of his choice, the results are not what he expected. So he trades baseball lessons for lessons from Kamna about girls and discovers that he has more in common with her than with the girl he thought he wanted. This author cleverly begins each chapter with a baseball term, and then relates it to what is going on in Darcy's life, often with a wry look at middle school life. Baseball fans and budding middle-school students will both enjoy this book.

Gentle Criteria: This is a real study in how to get along with all kinds of groups and cliques in school while still holding on to one's integrity. In this entertaining story, Darcy figures out a lot about life, love, family, and the place baseball has in his life.

28 **Birdsall, Jeanne.** *The Penderwicks: A Summer Tale of Four Sisters, Two Rabbits, and a Very Interesting Boy.*
Random House, 2005, ISBN 978-0-375-93143-7. 262p. • Grades 5–6
 ACCELERATED READER JUNIOR LIBRARY GUILD

When the Penderwicks—four motherless girls and their lovable but untrained dog Hound—lose the cottage that they usually rent for summer vacation, they grab another one sight unseen. It turns out to be the caretaker's cottage on the grounds of a beautiful mansion, complete with magnificent gardens. A young boy lives in the mansion and when they discover each other, much adventure follows: rabbits and dogs chasing across the manicured gardens just as the committee is about to judge them, a close escape with a bull for a little girl and her daisies, a rescue from military academy, a secret crush, and a fire in a kitchen. In the end, everyone is better for the experiences of a lovely summer.

Gentle Criteria: This book is reminiscent of *Little Women* and adults who share this book with children will be reminded of those wholesome stories. In the middle of the comical misadventures are a mother and son who finally get to know and understand each other, all with the help of the lovable Penderwicks. This book is filled with old-fashioned values.

29 **Birney, Betty G.** *The Seven Wonders of Sassafras Springs.*
Ill. by Matt Phelan. Atheneum, 2005, ISBN 978-0-689-87136-8; Simon & Schuster, 2007, pap., ISBN 978-1-4169-3489-9. 210p. • Grades 5–7
 ACCELERATED READER READING COUNTS

In the summer of 1923 Eban lives with his Pa and his Aunt Pretty on a farm in Sassafras Springs. Eban shares with his Pa the Seven Wonders of the World book he's reading and says he would like to see them someday. Pa tells Eban that if he can find seven wonders of the world right here in Sassafras Springs, he'll get to visit relatives in Colorado and see a huge mountain. Eban hurries through his daily chores so he has time to look for the wonders around Sassafras Springs. He starts at the house of the richest person in town and is shown pearls and gems, and even given chocolate, but he still doesn't consider these wonders. As he continues his search, he discovers ordinary objects with extraordinary stories that do indeed make them wonders in his mind. When his father receives a postcard saying his relatives are fighting influenza in Colorado, Eban worries he has done all this searching for nothing. Will he be stuck in this little town forever?

Gentle Criteria: This book points out how we tend to take the miraculous things around us for granted. By listening to the stories behind the seven wonders that Eban finds, we feel better about the world around us. One of the most amazing stories is the one about the saw fiddler who scares off swarming grasshoppers that would have destroyed the crops. Lastly, Eban agrees with his father that his Aunt Pretty is probably the most amazing wonder of all.

30   **Bledsoe, Lucy Jane.** *The Antarctic Scoop.*
        Holiday House, 2003, ISBN 978-0-8234-1792-6. 168p. • Grades 5–7
        ⌐ ACCELERATED READER

Victoria Von Woolf, science geek, is determined to stay true to herself. She can hardly believe it when she wins a science contest to travel to Antarctica and see a new telescope. For a moment it looks as if the prize will be given to the runner-up when Victoria is accused of computer sabotage at her school. But her science teacher fights for her to win this once-in-a-lifetime chance and succeeds. In Antarctica Victoria gets close enough to touch orcas. But then the runner-up in the contest informs her by e-mail that the company sponsoring her trip is planning to develop this wonderful continent—not to preserve it. The two of them join forces to reveal the scam.

Gentle Criteria: This is a great story for many reasons. Readers are informed that Antarctica is the only continent in the world full of scientists from many countries, all working toward the same goals. Victoria's wonderful teacher recognizes her love of science and finds a way to encourage it. The runner-up, Alexander the Great, knows he has found a kindred spirit in Victoria, and Victoria overcomes her shyness to make a new friend.

31   **Blume, Lesley M. M.** *Cornelia and the Audacious Escapades of the Somerset Sisters.*
        Random House, 2006, ISBN 978-0-375-93523-7. 264p. • Grades 5–8
        ⌐ ACCELERATED READER

Cornelia, the daughter of Lucy, a famous concert pianist, is often left alone with the hired help while her mother travels. Cornelia is lonely and ends up further alienating herself from prospective friends by using her advanced vocabulary. Her maid flounces off when Cornelia calls her names she doesn't understand. Then Cornelia meets her new next-door neighbor, Virginia Somerset, who is a famous writer and the first person to pay attention to Cornelia on her own merits. Cornelia visits Virginia in secret and hears wonderful tales about adventures

Virginia had with her sisters when she was younger. When Cornelia finds her mother visiting Virginia, she feels betrayed that her mother has invaded the secret world where she is admired for a change. Cornelia's mom explains that Virginia invited her to tell her what a wonderful child Cornelia is, and that Virginia is dying of cancer.

Gentle Criteria: It is great to see Cornelia come out of her shell when she befriends Virginia. The book points out how people perceive life differently. Cornelia assumes her mother left her behind because she didn't want her in the way. Lucy finally explains to Cornelia that she herself grew up traveling around the world and hated it. She wanted to spare Cornelia the same miserable childhood. Thus, this book illustrates how lots of hurt feelings can be avoided if people just communicate better.

32   **Bonk, John J.** *Dustin Grubbs: One Man Show.*
Little, Brown, 2005, ISBN 978-0-316-15636-3; 2006, pap., ISBN 978-0-316-15408-6. 243p. Series: Dustin Grubbs • Grades 5–8
⚘ ACCELERATED READER

Eleven-year-old Dustin Grubbs is keeping a secret from his mother: He's starring in the school play. Dustin doesn't want his mom to know because he's afraid it will upset her. His dad couldn't squelch his own desire for the stage and finally left the family for show business. Dustin's aunt tells him that his dad tried to stay in touch with him, but his mom sent the presents back and failed to pass on his messages. Dustin leaves a message for his dad, asking him to come to his acting debut. Will his father disappoint Dustin again? In a subplot, a child television actor moves into Dustin's class. Will he take Dustin's spot in the play?

Gentle Criteria: Dustin has a lot of emotions brewing inside and he often takes them out on his friends. But this is a realistic book for this age group because many kids experience similar circumstances. Middle-school students do not always know how to be friends: Dustin is not a good friend to Wally when he invites Hollywood Jeremy to his party instead, and he is not a good friend to Ellen when he tells her to get lost. But because they are his friends they help him out anyway when they see he is in trouble. Dustin realizes how important his friends are to him, and he starts giving back. He also realizes that his mother was trying to protect him from more heartache. Dustin undertakes the huge emotional risk of contacting his father. Many readers will relate to and learn from Dustin's situation and actions. And at the very end of the story, when his father makes the attempt to see him, readers will have a lump in their throats.

33   **Bonk, John J.** *Dustin Grubbs: Take Two.*
Little, Brown, 2006, ISBN 978-0-316-15637-0. 243p. Series: Dustin Grubbs • Grades 5–8
⚘ ACCELERATED READER

This is the sequel to *Dustin Grubs: One Man Show*. Dustin lives with his brother, aunt, mother, and grandmother. Dustin learns that the school is putting on a musical and expects to be chosen as the lead because of his previous success. Dustin has also established contact with his comedian father and plans a weekend visit with him in Chicago. During the visit, Dustin's father is called to audition for a national commercial. The casting company notices how perfect Dustin is for one of the roles and asks him to return for the final audition. Dustin is excited until he realizes his aunt is getting married on the same day as the final audition. Now he must make a difficult decision: whether to become like his dad, who went for the chance to hit it big, or to do the responsible thing and walk his aunt down the aisle.

Gentle Criteria: This author really knows how to capture teenage emotions. Dustin wears his feelings on his sleeve when he's dealing with his irritating neighbor, his bothersome brother, and the many others who so commonly annoy middle-school students. Although Dustin gets upset when he doesn't land the lead role in the musical, he still defends it when the town threatens to put a stop to the musical. Dustin even sacrifices a $1,000 reward he receives, donating it to the basketball team in an attempt to make peace between the feuding arts.

34   **Boyce, Frank Cottrell.** *Framed.*

HarperCollins, 2005, ISBN 978-0-06-073403-9. 306p. • Grades 5–8
⇍ Accelerated Reader ⇍ Reading Counts ⇍ Junior Library Guild

Dylan's family runs a service station in a very small town in Wales. When a bunch of trucks turn up, the whole town wonders what's going on. Dylan discovers that Lester, the stranger in charge of all the vans, is storing famous paintings in the abandoned mine to keep them safe from flooding in London. Dylan and his teacher convince Lester to share one masterpiece at a time with the town. What then happens in this gray and rainy town is amazing; the adults and children are deeply touched by the magnificent pieces of art. Daft Tom, upon seeing a still life, begins arranging all the storefronts in town with still-lifes of his own. Seeing "The Umbrella," brings Dylan's mother out of her depression, and she finds hundreds of umbrellas for the children to use. People start walking to school and sharing umbrellas, which changes the whole town both visually and socially. When Dylan's father is forced to go away to find work, Dylan, Daft Tom, and Dylan's sister Minnie decide they must steal a painting and turn it in for the reward money. The entire town becomes acquainted with the power of art, not just to make money but to change lives, in the process.

Gentle Criteria: It is exhilarating to see how great art can have such an uplifting effect. This story also shows how Dylan's family works together to keep the family business afloat.

35   **Boyce, Frank Cottrell.** *Millions.*
HarperCollins, 2004, ISBN 978-0-06-073330-8; Trans-Atlantic, pap.,
ISBN 978-0-330-43331-0. 247p. • Grades 5–8
☞ ACCELERATED READER ☞ READING COUNTS

Fourth-grader Damian Cunningham's mother has died, and he and his fifth-grade
brother are told they need to be good to help their father out. Damian goes to
extremes, striving to be excellent. He attends a Catholic school and has memo-
rized every saint. He can even recite what they did to become saints. He stuffs his
shirt with holly and sleeps on the floor at night to prove he is saint-worthy. He
creates a hermitage out of cardboard boxes because he thinks it will be more
saintly than his home. One night when he goes to his cardboard box by the railroad tracks to pray, a huge bag of pound notes lands near him. He is convinced
this money is from God. But Damian and Anthony, his brother, have only seventeen days before the money will become worthless because the euro is about to
become the official currency in England. What follows is exactly what one would
expect of kids this age—lots of pizza and toys. Damian wants to give the money
to the poor, but Anthony has other ideas. When Anthony gets on the Internet
and shows Damian that the money is stolen, things really start to unravel.

    Gentle Criteria: Whether Damian has a vivid imagination or events
truly did happen, saints appear and speak to Damian to guide him throughout
the story. Even at the end of the book when Damian is burning the money, his
mother appears, hugs him, and tells him he's doing a great job and that it is okay
to miss her. Damian tells his mother that Anthony says she is a saint, and he
wants to know what miracle she performed. She replies, "I made you."

❧ CARNEGIE MEDAL, 2004

36   **Bradley, Kimberly Brubaker.** *Halfway to the Sky.*
Random House, 2002, ISBN 978-0-385-90029-4; 2003, pap., ISBN
978-0-440-41830-6. 166p. • Grades 7–9
☞ ACCELERATED READER ☞ READING COUNTS

The day twelve-year-old Katahdin's older brother dies from muscular dystrophy
is also the day her father leaves, and the day her parents start the process of
divorce. Angry and grief-stricken, Katahdin decides to hike the 2,000-mile
Appalachian Trail alone. Her parents met on the trail, and she and her brother
are named for its beginning and end points. Katahdin saves her money, buys her
gear, leaves her mom a note, and sets off. When her mom catches up with her,
they decide to spend two months hiking to see how far they can go. Along the
way they become part of a community of hikers, all conquering the trail for their
own reasons. The trek enables Katahdin and her mom to begin to deal with the
turmoil in their lives. Katahdin also does some growing up and begins to look at
things from her parents' perspectives. They must also overcome the challenges of
snow, hypothermia, blistering heat—and most of all—love.

Gentle Criteria: Katahdin has a normal reaction to grief, the stress of years of helping care for a sick sibling, and anger over both her parents' divorce and her brother's death. What she discovers along the trail is her parents' love, and the fact that sometimes you just have to deal with what life serves you and accept the love and help of the people around you. You also have to draw on the strength within. When Katahdin's father's new wife hands their newborn baby to her, Katahdin finds hope in a difficult situation.

37 Bruchac, Joseph. *Eagle Song.*
Ill. by Dan Andreasen. Dial, 1997, ISBN 978-0-8037-1919-4; Penguin, 1999, pap., ISBN 978-0-14-130169-3. 80p. • Grades 5–8
⟿ ACCELERATED READER ⟿ READING COUNTS

Danny's family has moved to New York because the water in Akwesasne is so polluted from the Canadian factories that they can't fish there any longer. His mom has a job at the American Indian Community House in Manhattan. Danny's father is an iron worker, traveling around the country building sky-scrapers. When his father comes home between jobs for a week, Danny tells him that after two months at school, he still doesn't have any friends. Danny's father makes a point to visit his classroom and share with the students the story of Aionwahta and his song of peace. Aionwahta is the Iroquois name for Hiawatha, the Indian made famous by Longfellow's poem. When his people had forgotten how to live together in peace, Aionwahta traveled and talked to people to soothe them and make them forget their anger. Together with other leaders he healed the mind of Adodarhonh, created the Great League of Peace, wampum strings, the five nations, and threw the weapons of war away. To this day, the Iroquois believe that even bad people can be made good and become great lead-ers. Students become friendlier after the visit, and Danny visits an older Native American boy who has joined a gang. Will Danny's new message of peace help his friend understand that violence is not a solution to anything?

Gentle Criteria: This book presents a positive message in which Danny's father jumps right in to help his son make friends—an extremely important issue to this age group—and tries to win Danny's class over with humor and history, emphasizing that everyone should be proud of his heritage. The message is that sometimes it is more difficult to be friends than enemies. Afterward Danny marches right up to Tyrone and tells him he wants to be friends, or to at least stop the name calling and have peace between them. Tyrone agrees, shakes Danny's hand, and says "Peace."

38 Cassidy, Cathy. *Scarlett.*
Penguin, 2006, ISBN 978-0-670-06068-9. 261p. • Grades 5–8

Scarlett has been expelled from her fifth school since her father divorced her mother—this time for leading the students in a food fight! Now her mother is sending her to live with her father and his new wife, and Scarlett is furious. She hates her father and his wife. She believes all the bad things her mother said about her father and is determined to be as big a pain as she can. She walks out of school the first day and meets a gypsy boy on a horse. Her father arranges for Scarlett to be home-schooled, but she spends most of her time out in the woods secretly meeting the gypsy boy. He is her only friend. Her new stepsister idolizes Scarlett and wants to get her tongue pierced just like Scarlett's. When Scarlett refuses to help, her stepsister threatens to tell about the gypsy boy. Just when things are going well, will Scarlett cause a scene again?

Gentle Criteria: Most children today have experience with divorce—either in their own family or their friends' families. This is a great book for children who are dealing with divorce because it helps them to understand that they are not alone. Other children have the same feelings in this situation. Scarlett's story reveals her anger and resentment and demonstrates how one parent can influence a child against the other parent. Scarlett learns that her father has not stopped loving her, and she starts to cooperate when she finds out that he has kept all her treasures.

39   Cheaney, J. B. *The Middle of Somewhere*.
Knopf, 2007, ISBN 978-0-375-93790-3. 218p. • Grades 7–9

Veronica Sparks is reading *Seize the Way: Ten Weeks to SuperSize Your Life!* Veronica's mother is out of commission with a bad knee, and Veronica and her brother, who is afflicted with ADHD, find themselves accompanying their grandfather on a cross-country RV trip in search of wind-power-generating sources. The two soon find that spending twenty-four hours a day with their grandfather is very different from visiting him a few times a year. More than once he nearly takes them home. The fun is only beginning when Veronica wins a card game and the right to keep a stray dog. But it is her brother's quest to see Cannonball Paul shot out of a cannon that leads them on their biggest adventure. And when they think they have lost her little brother for good, it becomes clear just how much family means. Having a grandfather back in their life is just one of the benefits.

Gentle Criteria: This book is a gentle read because it demonstrates the natural love that grandparents have for their grandchildren—even when they hardly know each other. From the beginning we know that Veronica is a girl who is used to being in charge. Her brother Gee is difficult to love much of the time but when he is well-behaved, he is hard to resist. Their mother loves her father even though he wasn't there for her when she was little. She insists that he finally do the right thing for her kids when she can't take care of them herself. Pop gets fed up with Gee's ADHD in less than an hour but comes back and does the right thing, showing his love in a variety of ways. Every chapter begins with a quote from *Seize the Way*: "Every upside has a downside," "Periodically, try to step back and take a look at the big picture," "Always be ready to accept a certain amount of risk," and so forth.

40   Clark, Catherine. *Frozen Rodeo.*

> HarperCollins, 2003, ISBN 978-0-06-624008-4; 2004, pap., ISBN 978-0-06-447385-9. 287p. • Grades 7–9
>
> ☞ ACCELERATED READER ☞ READING COUNTS ☞ JUNIOR LIBRARY GUILD

Peggy Fleming Farrell is stuck in Lindville for the summer. After several unfortunate mishaps with her parents' car, they have confiscated her driver's license. She is sentenced to spending the summer riding the bus, and earning money to repay her parents. Working as a "coffee wench," babysitting her younger siblings, and becoming her pregnant mother's Lamaze coach is not her idea of a good time. But as the summer passes, Peggy discovers several truths: boyfriends are not always what they seem; sometimes it's okay to be stuck in a small town; and families can support and help each other. Stopping an attempted robbery, riding through the middle of the parade on her way to help her mom deliver her baby, and skating with her dad in his ice show are just some parts of Peggy's summer in a small town.

> **Gentle Criteria:** This is a typical teen story with kids hanging out and getting into minor trouble. The characters are all good kids trying to make their way through adolescence. Peggy's frustration with the town and her life is all part of this coming-of-age story. Her realization that she doesn't have to impress people allows her to see her family and her real friends in a different light.

41   Clements, Andrew. *Lunch Money.*

> Ill. by Brian Selznick. Simon & Schuster, 2005, ISBN 978-0-689-86683-8. 222p. • Grades 5–8
>
> ☞ ACCELERATED READER ☞ READING COUNTS

Greg Kenton loves to make money. He charges his brothers for making their beds. He shovels neighbors' driveways. He is always thinking of new ways to make money. His only problem in the world is his neighbor, Maura, who copies his ideas. When he sells lemonade for a quarter, Maura sells it for twenty cents. When Greg makes comic books to sell at school, Maura immediately copies him, causing a fight that ends all school sales. Then Maura notices that the schools allow companies to sell to kids. Greg, Maura, and their teacher, Mr. Z, approach the school board for permission to sell their comic books, and they reach a compromise.

> **Gentle Criteria:** This book is an entertaining feud between rivals Greg and Maura, with Greg's emotions running amok in typical teen fashion. It is a nice story that shows how Greg goes from being a greedy money-miser to someone who gives back to the community. This book also illustrates good examples of how kids can make and save money.

42   Clements, Andrew. *A Week in the Woods.*
Thorndike, 2003, ISBN 978-0-7862-5016-5; Aladdin, 2004, pap., ISBN
978-0-689-85802-4. 190p. • Grades 5–7
⌐ ACCELERATED READER ⌐ READING COUNTS

Mark is a rich kid who has everything. His parents have just bought another
house in New Hampshire, and they are making Mark move for the last three
months of the school year. Then they will enroll him in summer camp followed
by the prestigious Runyon Boarding Academy. To his teachers and classmates,
Mark appears to be a spoiled rich kid who has no intention of making new
friends for such a short time. His parents are out of town for weeks at a time, so
Mark explores the beautiful barn and woods around his new home. He realizes
he has not been giving the local kids a chance to become his friends. He tries to
be more welcoming—but is it too late? On the Week-in-the-Woods trip, the
highlight of the school year, Mark is caught with a friend's knife, and he takes
off into the woods. Can his teacher find him before something tragic happens?

Gentle Criteria: This book presents two interesting perspectives. Mark's
new teachers view him as a slacker; Mark finds school just plain boring. He
knows he'll only be there a short time, so why even try to make friends? Mark
finally realizes that what is important in life is time—his own time and how he
chooses to spend it. He learns that making friends is never a waste. In the end he
decides he would like to stay.

43   Codell, Esme Raji. *Sahara Special.*
Disney, 2003, ISBN 978-0-7868-2627-8; 2004, pap., ISBN 978-0-7868-
1611-8. 175p. • Grades 5–7
⌐ ACCELERATED READER ⌐ READING COUNTS ⌐ JUNIOR LIBRARY
GUILD

Although the classroom in this book is full of rough characters and some strong
language, the love that readers find here is truly heartwarming. Sahara's father
has left the family, and Sahara spends a year missing him and writing him letters
instead of doing her schoolwork. The letters are found and placed in her file, and
she is assigned to the special education class, where she acquires the unfortunate
nickname "Sahara Special." Sahara's mother knows nothing is wrong with her,
so she takes Sahara out of the special education class, telling the teacher if she
doesn't do the work, then she should fail the class. And Sahara does fail. She
believes she is doomed to experience the same unfortunate school year over
again until she meets the new fifth-grade teacher. Boring is a bad word in this
class. Everyone gets respect, and the students all learn how much this teacher
loves them. These students succeed in spite of themselves.

Gentle Criteria: This is a positive, heartwarming story about students who
are far from perfect—like their parents. But their new teacher has a way of making both students and parents understand just how special they are. She under-

stands that they really do try to succeed in school, and she has a surefire formula to ensure their success. All it takes is a special teacher who shows lots of love.

44   Codell, Esme Raji. *Vive la Paris.*

Hyperion, 2006, ISBN 978-0-7868-5124-9. 210p. • Grades 7–9

This is a companion volume to *Sahara Special*. Paris is Sahara's classmate. She is named Paris because her parents were planning a trip to that city when they found out they were expecting a baby. Rather than spending the money to travel there, they decided Paris would come to them. Paris's family is full of musical talent. Paris takes piano lessons from Mrs. Rosen, and her brother Michael accompanies her. Mrs. Rosen teaches Paris and Michael much, much more than the piano—she teaches them about love, forgiveness, and most of all how to look at life as if it is the way you want it to be. She gives Paris rose-colored glasses, so she can see life the way Mrs. Rosen sees it. Paris discovers that Mrs. Rosen was a spy in the Jewish Resistance during World War II, and that everyone in her family was killed in the camps except her and her mother. In the end, Mrs. Rosen leaves Paris money to get to Paris someday, but Paris finds an even better use for it.

Gentle Criteria: As in *Sahara Special*, this touching story contains some rough language and rough street characters. One of her brothers' girlfriends must move in with them because she is pregnant. But the point of this book is to look at life in a peaceful and hopeful way and to explore beyond what you see at first. Paris learns her older brother has made a commitment to God to be peaceful, and that the girl she hates the most—the neighborhood bully—has a very good reason to be so angry. And when Mrs. Rosen says "Goddamnit," it is not because she is a rough character but because she is short on patience due to her age and Holocaust experiences. Book clubs and classes will appreciate the themes of tolerance, forgiveness, and living at peace with one another.

45   Cole, Sheila. *The Canyon.*

HarperCollins, 2002, ISBN 978-0-06-029496-0. 146p. • Grades 5–8

☞ ACCELERATED READER

Zack gets mad when the Bowen Company decides to develop the canyon that San Ramon residents have used for years. At first, eleven-year-old Zack and his friend Trevor just remove the company's zoning stakes. Then Zack suggests letting the air out of a truck's tires, and Trevor smashes the windshield. Zack knows they have gone too far. Zack's older sister joins the protest by organizing a peaceful petition to get City Council to rescind the Bowen Company's building permit. Zack worries that his vandalism will be associated with the peaceful petition, jeopardizing its chances for success. So Zack decides to write an apology letter for his vandalism and to repay the damages by sending the Bowen Company his baseball card collection. Soon the whole country is sending baseball cards to the company in hopes of stopping the development. Will his ploy work, or will Zack be arrested for his bad judgment?

Gentle Criteria: Zack is an example of a kid who makes snap decisions. This story is refreshing because it details how Zack's parents take the correct steps to make Zack see that he must apologize and make restitution for his vandalism. Zack realizes that even if you make a wrong choice that does not mean you're a bad person for life. Zack also learns that he can fight for his cause, but he must do it in a peaceful, lawful manner.

46   Cooney, Caroline. *Hit the Road.*
Delacorte, 2006, ISBN 978-0-385-90174-1. 183p. • Grades 5–7

Teachers will enjoy sharing this gentle read with students. Brit thinks she can manage staying with her grandmother for two weeks during her parents' vacation. But what she doesn't know is that Nannie and her friends plan to kidnap one of their friends, have a lawyer rewrite her will so her good-for-nothing son won't inherit her five-million-dollar estate, and then proceed to their 65th college reunion. The wild ride begins when Brit, who has had her driver's license for exactly eleven days, learns that she is to be the driver. Brit finds out that she has a lot in common with these eighty-six-year-old women. More and more control of their lives has been taken from them as they have grown older—and now they're taking back that control! They are still young girls at heart, out to save their friend. Not only does Brit help "the girls" accomplish what they need to do in this wildly entertaining story, but she also learns a lot about family and what people will do out of love.

Gentle Criteria: This is a great story about what people do for each other in the name of love. A sixteen-year-old-girl finds out what she is really capable of while helping four elderly women.

47   Cooney, Caroline. *What Child Is This? A Christmas Story.*
Delacorte, 1997, ISBN 978-0-385-32317-8; Trafalgar, 2000, pap., ISBN 978-0-330-37053-0. 150p. • Grades 5–7
⌒ ACCELERATED READER ⌒ READING COUNTS

Katie is a foster child who wants only one thing for Christmas: a family. Allison, who recently lost a baby, has always longed for a family. Matt, a foster child in the same home as Katie, works at a restaurant where foster children's wishes for Christmas are hung on the tree for patrons to choose and make come true. Matt hangs Katie's wish for a family on the tree. Are there enough miracles to make this happen? Liz wants to experience a *real* Christmas, not one whose sole object is presents. When Liz's father tears up the star on the tree, saying that a family is simply too much for a foster child to ask for, the reader is disappointed. But the author's multiple story lines come together to produce a miracle for Katie and a warm and wonderful Christmas story.

Gentle Criteria: There is no read more gentle than a Christmas miracle story. This book expresses the wish in all of us for the warmth and love of people who care about us.

48   Cooper, Ilene. *Sam I Am.*

Scholastic, 2004, ISBN 978-0-439-43967-1; 2006, pap., ISBN 978-0-439-43968-8. 252p. • Grades 5–9

☞ ACCELERATED READER ☞ READING COUNTS

Sam is a twelve-year-old boy with a Christian mother and a Jewish father, neither of whom has made a big deal over the difference in their religions. Sam has a current events assignment to watch the news and observe how people around the world celebrate the holidays. But all he sees is fighting, and he wonders what it is about religion that makes people combative. When the dog knocks over the Hanukkah bush—his family's name for the Christmas tree—his parents seem to change their position. The situation goes from bad to worse when Hanukkah and Christmas Eve and the two warring grandmothers all arrive at the same time. Sam studies the Holocaust in school and realizes that he would have been persecuted just for having Jewish blood. Finally, Sam asks God some questions and realizes that maybe God is answering them; not with God's own voice but through other people. His sister, friends, parents, and grandparents all share with him things that help Sam make sense of what is needed in the world: more love.

Gentle Criteria: This book tries to answer the question of where God is and why he doesn't seem to be doing anything about conditions in the world. Through introspection, Sam discovers that it's up to people to make the world a better place. Sam dates the attractive Heather but is never comfortable around her as Avi is with his girlfriend. Finally, when Heather starts making fun of overweight people, Sam realizes that he needs to take a stand. In the end, when Sam's mother and father are in an accident, the whole family comes together. Sam realizes that, like snowflakes, everybody is unique and can love God in many different ways.

49   Corbett, Sue. *Free Baseball.*

Dutton, 2006, ISBN 978-0-525-47120-2. 152p. • Grades 5–9

☞ ACCELERATED READER ☞ READING COUNTS ☞ JUNIOR LIBRARY GUILD

Felix is the Cuban American son of a famous Cuban baseball player who enabled Felix and his mom to escape to America even though he had to stay behind. Felix's mother works extra hours to make ends meet. Felix wishes she didn't have to work so hard and keeps hoping his father will join them. He wins tickets for the semi-pro team's opening night but his mother makes him go with a baby-sitter because she has to work again. He punishes his mother by hiding in the baggage area of the visiting team's bus. He spends the night in the club house, is mistaken for the new ball boy, and soon becomes a lucky charm for the team. But the truth comes out, and his upset mother comes to retrieve him.

Gentle Criteria: This is a wonderful, feel-good story. Vic, the owner of the team, has lost his wife, and Felix's arrival helps him to move on with his own life. Vic convinces Felix's mom to become the team's office manager and provides her with a house to live in. He allows Felix to keep his job as ball boy. His mom finally tells Felix the story of how his dad gave up his space in the boat to the United States. His dad was willing to risk his baseball career so his child could have a better life.

50   Couloumbis, Audrey. *Getting Near to Baby.*
Scholastic, 1999, ISBN 978-0-439-23860-1; Putnam, 2001, pap., ISBN 978-0-698-11892-8. 211p. • Grades 5–9
☞ ACCELERATED READER ☞ READING COUNTS

Hard times have fallen on the Dean family. Willa's father must leave the family in search of work. Mrs. Dean borrows water from a carnival merchant for her baby, and the baby becomes ill and dies. The family is sinking in its sorrow when Aunt Patty arrives and suggests that she take the children for a while, until her sister recovers from her depression. At first, Willa is secretly happy. Her mom has been so engrossed in painting a picture of Baby with the angels that she hasn't been cooking or cleaning, and Little Sister has not spoken since the baby died. Then Willa finds out that living with Aunt Patty is stressful in its own way.

Gentle Criteria: Although Willa paints Aunt Patty as an overbearing tyrant who puts too much pressure on Little Sister to speak again, she is probably just what the family needs—although everyone must make adjustments. Aunt Patty and her husband, Uncle Hob, have never had children, and Willa and Little Sister aren't used to her strict rules. Uncle Hob's patience with the kids is touching, as is the scene when Little Sister finally speaks again. This is a great book about handling grief.
❧   NEWBERY HONOR BOOK, 2000

51   Creech, Sharon. *Bloomability.*
HarperCollins, 1998, ISBN 978-0-06-026994-4; 1999, pap., ISBN 978-0-06-440823-3. 273p. • Grades 6–8
☞ ACCELERATED READER ☞ READING COUNTS

When her sixteen-year-old sister gets married on the sly and subsequently has a baby, and her brother ends up in jail, thirteen-year-old Domenica—otherwise known as Dinnie—is sent to Switzerland to live with her aunt and uncle who run an international school. She is scared and angry over being sent away without her family, but she discovers that life offers many possibilities, or "bloomabilities." She is used to moving around a lot as her father searches for new opportunities, but here everybody is an outsider. Here everybody is from a different place: Spain, Saudi Arabia, Japan, and Italy, to name just a few. A student from Iraq tells about his country being bombed, and the students learn about the famine in Rwanda. They also learn about ethics and behavior, and when two students get caught in an avalanche during a ski trip, Dinnie realizes how much they all mean to her.

Gentle Criteria: This is a book about looking on the positive side of things and living a good life, no matter what country you are from. It is a book about getting rid of your prejudices about different countries and different peoples. There are lots and lots of possibilities for book club and/or classroom talks about ethics, prejudices, culture, and family.

52   **Creech, Sharon.** *Chasing Redbird.*

HarperCollins, 1997, ISBN 978-0-06-026988-3; 1998, pap., ISBN 978-0-06-440696-3. 261p. • Grades 5–7

🖙 ACCELERATED READER 🖙 READING COUNTS

Thirteen-year-old Zinny discovers a mysterious wilderness trail that begins on her family's farm and starts to clear it. The solitude of this task appeals to her because she lives in a small house with a large family and has very little time alone. As she works, she discovers unexpected family secrets, learns about herself, and finally starts to deal with the death of her beloved aunt. Added to the mix is Jake Boone, the boy who hopes to be Zinny's first boyfriend. Jake, formerly a skinny little kid, has just moved back to town and is now a broad-shouldered sixteen-year-old. There are some laugh-out-loud moments when Jake steals a dog and a car for Zinny in hopes of winning her affection.

Gentle Criteria: This is a great family story that reveals its members with all their love and idiosyncrasies. Death is part of this story as it is part of any family life, and Zinny's way of dealing with death is extremely touching.

53   **Creech, Sharon.** *Granny Torrelli Makes Soup.*

Ill. by Chris Raschka. HarperCollins, 2003, ISBN 978-0-06-029291-1; 2005, pap., ISBN 978-0-06-440960-5. 141p. • Grades 5–7

🖙 ACCELERATED READER 🖙 READING COUNTS 🖙 JUNIOR LIBRARY GUILD

Twelve-year-old Rosie and her best friend Bailey are in the middle of an argument. Granny Torrelli has the two help her make soup and pasta, all the while telling them stories that help the two true friends to make amends. Each chapter elicits another heartwarming memory, and Rosie is amazed by how much her friend's stories remind her of herself. Examples include when Rosie first learns that Bailey is blind, when Bailey's father leaves for good, and when Granny leaves Italy and never again speaks to her best friend Pardo—all stories told at just the right time to help two friends realize just how many good memories they share and why they are best friends in the first place.

Gentle Criteria: As usual, Creech brings her readers to both tears and laughter as they remember their own stories. Described herein is a young and tender friendship that may soon blossom into a romance. The reader understands that people can be angry with each other and still remain friends, but the best way to get over it is to remember the good memories that you share. This book features strong family and neighborhood ties and lots of good stories.

54   Creech, Sharon. *Replay.*
HarperCollins, 2005, ISBN 978-0-06-054020-3; 2007, pap., ISBN 978-0-06-054021-0. 180p. • Grades 5–7
ᴄ Accelerated Reader ᴄ Reading Counts

Leo, who is sometimes called Fog-boy because he is always daydreaming, often replays scenes in his head that show life working out the way he wants it to. When he finds his father's old journal, his perspective on his family begins to change. As each chapter unfolds, he learns more about the people in his life— why his father isn't the happy-go-lucky man he used to be; what happened to his aunt Rosario; how his best friend Ruby used to have a brother; and why his drama teacher wrote the play in which he is going to perform. Remembering his younger brother snuggling in bed with him like a warm bear cub, discovering his father's old tap shoes, and having his grandparents tell him about Rosario are just some of the gentle stories about this big family.

Gentle Criteria: Creech provides readers with another heartwarming tale that makes them stop and appreciate the people around them. This book is about the love felt within a big, rambunctious, noisy Italian family. Even though they don't always stop to listen to each other, their love remains a strong current. Leo discovers things about love, family, and friends that will sustain him for life.

55   Creech, Sharon. *Ruby Holler.*
HarperCollins, 2002, ISBN 978-0-06-027733-8; Scholastic, 2003, pap., ISBN 978-0-439-45808-5. 310p. • Grades 5–7
ᴄ Accelerated Reader ᴄ Reading Counts ᴄ Junior Library Guild

Thirteen-year-old twins Dallas and Florida have spent most of their lives in foster homes and orphanages. Most of their foster parents expected the twins to work for them. The twins never experienced the kind of love and caring that usually occurs in a family. When Tiller and Sairy take them home to Ruby Holler, the twins can't believe it: They don't have to do hard labor; they can run, skip, yell, get dirty, and climb trees like other kids. The twins are good for this elderly husband and wife whose own children are grown and long gone. Tiller becomes less cranky, and Sairy remembers how good it feels to cook for children. Life, overall, is better for everyone.

Gentle Criteria: One of Creech's more serious titles, this is a story about the love that usually exists in a family, the love between a brother and a sister, and the love between an old married couple. Love is what heals all of them and sustains them through the good and bad parts of life.

❧ CARNEGIE MEDAL, 2002

56 **Creech, Sharon.** *The Wanderer.*
HarperCollins, 2000, ISBN 978-0-06-027731-4; 2002, pap., ISBN 978-0-06-441032-8. 305p. • Grades 5–8
✑ ACCELERATED READER ✑ READING COUNTS ✑ JUNIOR LIBRARY GUILD

Sophie sets sail across the Atlantic with three uncles and two cousins for a visit with her grandfather, Bompie. The six must teach each other while they are sailing, and Sophie decides she will tell stories about Bompie when it is her turn to teach. The cousins are confused because Sophie is adopted and has never met Bompie. Through Sophie's journal and her cousin Cody's travel log readers get a glimpse of what is really going on in their minds and how they really feel about what is transpiring. Sophie endured many foster homes before she was adopted by the uncles' sister, and sometimes her stories sound like they are more about her than her grandfather. Will all of these people be able to get along on such a small boat? Will they make it safely across the ocean sailing in the patched-up *Wanderer*, and how will Sophie react when she finally meets Bompie? The cousins are dying to find out. They also want to know what happened to Sophie's parents, but the uncles will only say that Sophie can tell them if she wants them to know.

Gentle Criteria: Once again, Creech does an excellent job of plucking at the reader's heart strings. This story demonstrates that a person can act one way on the outside without revealing inner emotions. An example is a dream of Cody's that makes him worry that his dad is dead. He goes and pokes his dad, saying, "just checking." Although he doesn't tell his dad that he loves him, the reader knows Cody does by his actions.

❧ NEWBERY HONOR BOOK, 2001

57 **Cummings, Priscilla.** *A Face First.*
Dutton, 2001, ISBN 978-0-525-46522-5; Penguin, 2003, pap., ISBN 978-0-14-230247-7. 197p. • Grades 7–9
✑ ACCELERATED READER ✑ READING COUNTS

Twelve-year-old Kelley is burned so badly in a car accident that her life may never be normal. This story takes readers through the long process from the accident to her arrival at the hospital to painful skin grafts and reconstructive surgery. The author does a wonderful job of describing Kelley's emotions during weeks of physical pain, of isolation from family and friends, and anticipation of future surgeries. Kelley remembers that the accident was probably her mother's fault and wonders how she will forgive her. There are moments when Kelley wishes she had died in the fire, but as time progresses, she is able to move forward with her life.

Gentle Criteria: Kelley's progress is heart-wrenching but positive. The nurses who work with her take the time to visit her class and show the students what she is going through and what they can expect to see in the future. Her sister returns from France to tutor Kelley so that she can catch up with her schoolwork. When she starts to help a two-year-old burn victim, Kelley's emotional healing finally begins. She learns that her classmates care about her regardless of how she looks, and she finds a way to forgive her mom for the accident.

58   DeFelice, Cynthia. *Under the Same Sky.*

Farrar, Straus & Giroux, 2003, ISBN 978-0-374-38032-8; 2005, pap., ISBN 978-0-374-48065-3. 215p. • Grades 5–7

☞ Accelerated Reader ☞ Reading Counts

Joe desperately wants a motorbike, so his dad lets him work on the farm with the migrant laborers. Joe has no idea of the excitement—and danger—that he's about to experience. This book provides a realistic look at the life of these workers and why they choose to come to the United States—some legally and some illegally. Joe must make a choice when he discovers that three of his new friends have no immigration papers. Will he help them escape deportation? Joe quickly learns that he alone must live with the choices he makes.

Gentle Criteria: Joe finds that sometimes one must follow one's own conscience—or live with the consequences of not doing so. He also finds that there are times when it's impossible to find words for what is in your heart no matter what language you speak. Although there are no clear-cut answers here for the problems of illegal immigration, this story is full of good people (for the most part) who are trying to earn a living and help the people they care about.

59   DiCamillo, Kate. *Because of Winn-Dixie.*

Candlewick, 2004, ISBN 978-0-7636-2557-3; 2001, pap., ISBN 978-0-7636-1605-2. 182p. • Grades 5–7

☞ Accelerated Reader ☞ Reading Counts

Opal Buloni moves to the small town of Naomi, Florida, with her father, who is a preacher. Moving to a new town has made her miss her mother—who abandoned them when Opal was three years old. Then Opal finds a dog named Winn-Dixie and brings him home, reminding her father that he always says we should help those in need. A cast of uniquely southern small-town characters— Gloria Dump who is nearly blind; Miss Franny, the town librarian; and Otis, an ex-con, musician, and pet-store manager—help Opal grow closer to her father and discover a new kind of family.

Gentle Criteria: This story presents a positive message about the strength that people can draw from each other, rather than focusing on the mother who abandons her husband and three-year-old child. Opal comes to terms with her mother leaving, and her father realizes that his wife left the best part of her behind with him—their daughter Opal. Otis starts to share his music again, and even the ornery Dewberry boys show that they really are her friends when Opal's beloved dog goes missing. The characters in this story learn to accept each other's individuality, and that's what helps them to grow.

60   DiCamillo, Kate. *The Tiger Rising.*
Candlewick, 2001, ISBN 978-0-7636-0911-5; 2002, pap., ISBN 978-0-7636-1898-8. 116p. • Grades 5–9
⌐ Accelerated Reader ⌐ Reading Counts ⌐ Junior Library Guild

Rob Horton's mother has died and he now lives in the motel where his dad has taken a job. Rob bottles up all his feelings and tries to ignore the bullies at school. A strange girl named Sistine moves into the motel, and he admires the fact that she fights back when she's picked on. Rob tells Sistine about the tiger he's found caged up in the woods. (The owner of the motel bought the tiger as a tourist attraction but the children cannot accept this. The tiger is a metaphor for the feelings that the children are suppressing—Rob about his dead mother and Sistine about her absent father.) The children succeed in setting the tiger free. Each benefits as they fill the voids in their lives.

Gentle Criteria: This is a must-read for every adolescent. For kids who pick on others, this story can help them to understand how hurtful their behavior is. For kids who are being bullied, Rob and Sistine set good examples. Everybody needs a friend, and it's a delight to watch Rob and Sistine find each other. It is also touching when Rob reunites spiritually with his father after lashing out at him when his father shoots the tiger in order to save the two children.

61   DuPrau, Jeanne. *Car Trouble: A Novel.*
HarperCollins, 2005, ISBN 978-0-06-073674-3; 2006, pap., ISBN 978-0-06-073675-0. 288p. • Grades 7–9
⌐ Accelerated Reader

Duff Pringle, a seventeen-year-old computer whiz, has been offered a job, sight-unseen, in Silicon Valley. Instead of going to college, Duff buys a used car and leaves Virginia to drive to California seven days before he's to start work. After just three hours on the road, his car breaks down. Duff refuses to return home and feel like a loser, and relies on his wit to continue. At a hotel, he uses his computer to search for someone who needs him to drive a car to St. Louis. Along the way, Duff picks up a hitchhiker named Stu and finally has a real conversation with someone in person rather than through his computer. When they reach St. Louis, they meet sixteen-year-old Bonnie whose mother can't pay the fifty dollars Duff was promised to deliver the car, because she's in jail. So Bonnie allows Duff to drive her '57 Chevy to her aunt's house in Arizona because Bonnie can't drive and she doesn't want to stay with a social worker. What the trio doesn't know is that Bonnie's mom has called two thugs to track them down because there is a case of stolen money hidden in the car!

Gentle Criteria: Duff shares his feelings about how he was called names such as nerd and geek in high school and how such experiences left a bad taste in his mouth for education—one of the reasons he decided not to go to college. When he encounters scheming Stu and Bonnie, the daughter of a criminal, he develops friendships that he never thought he could have. As the story develops, Duff becomes more comfortable around others and begins to realize what is really important in life. Adults should note that the book contains a brief mention that Bonnie's aunt is gay and should deal with this fact accordingly when recommending this book to students.

62   **Eige, Lillian.** *Dangling.*

Atheneum, 2001, ISBN 978-0-689-83581-0; Simon & Schuster, 2003, pap., ISBN 978-0-689-86350-9. 166p. • Grades 5–9

☙ ACCELERATED READER ☙ READING COUNTS ☙ JUNIOR LIBRARY GUILD

While Ring and Ben's families enjoy a picnic at the park, Ring wades out into the water, goes under, and disappears. For the next three-quarters of the book, we see how Ben deals with the grieving process. Alternate chapters flip back to the past, describing the boys' budding friendship. Ben visits places where they used to hang out, and finds a Baby Ruth wrapper, the kind Ring loved, in a bird's nest. He starts to wonder if Ring is still alive. Ring is eventually found halfway across the country and returns home. Now Ben must deal with feelings of both relief and anger.

Gentle Criteria: Readers witness the developing friendship between the two boys and the two families. At the end of the book, Ring's past is revealed, and Ben can finally make sense of Ring's actions. Ring was a foster child. When his foster parents moved to another state for employment reasons, Ring went with them, defying the regulations. When Ring got a postcard from someone who tracked him down, he chose to run away rather than get his foster family in trouble. In the end, his foster parents make the adoption legal and all is right with the world.

63   **Ferber, Brenda A.** *Julia's Kitchen.*

Farrar, Straus & Giroux, 2006, ISBN 978-0-374-39932-0. 151p. • Grades 5–7

☙ ACCELERATED READER ☙ JUNIOR LIBRARY GUILD

When eleven-year-old Cara's mother and sister are killed in a house fire, Cara struggles—not only with the Jewish traditions and religion that are embedded in her family life—but with her relationship with her father who is confronting his own grief. Cara has difficulty with the concept of finding comfort in one's faith, because nothing is able to give her comfort. The Kaddish prayers mean nothing to her as she sits asking herself "why." Hebrew school feels strange because she is not sure she believes in God anymore. Marlee, Cara's best friend, helps by listening and understanding, but once Cara goes back to school Marlee thinks they should get back to their usual routine. Cara's memories of her mom's catering service, "Julia's Kitchen," eventually help her begin to cope with her grief. Along the way, Cara experiences some heartfelt questioning of God.

Gentle Criteria: This is a realistic depiction of a good family coping with tragedy. The comfort of the Jewish traditions and the support of Cara's family, even when they are not easy to be around, are a strong part of the story. When Cara finds a mezuzah in the box of things that survived the fire, she feels it is a message from God that he does exist. When she begins to bake with her mom's surviving recipes, readers know that she is starting to heal herself. Mrs. Block, the school social worker, is a wonderful adult role model who listens and allows Cara to grieve. And when Cara donates the profits from her baking to the fire department that tried to save her mother and sister, readers will have tears in their eyes.

64   Ferris, Jean. *Love Among the Walnuts.*

Harcourt, 1998, ISBN 978-0-15-201590-9. 216p. • Grades 5–9

☞ ACCELERATED READER ☞ READING COUNTS

This book is a delightfully zany read in which the good guys triumph in the end. Sandy has been raised in isolation by his wealthy and eccentric family. When his jealous uncles poison his parents—leaving them both in comas—Sandy must reach out for help. He hires a wacky private nurse named Sunnie. She helps him find Walnut Manor, an institution that takes care of those who can no longer cope with life. As Sunnie and Sandy care for the residents of Walnut Manor, they realize that no one can live successfully in isolation. Sunnie helps the residents of Walnut Manor understand that there is nothing wrong with them that a little tender loving care can't fix, and Sandy finds out there is a whole world out there that he knew nothing about. As they all grow together they are able to outwit Sandy's scheming uncles, as well as the relatives of the residents of Walnut Manor, culminating in a delightful ending.

Gentle Criteria: This is a good old-fashioned adventure with scheming villains and victorious good guys. Sandy learns that "anything that means anything comes straight from the heart, and always has."

65   Fleischman, Paul. *Seedfolks.*

HarperCollins, 1997, ISBN 978-0-06-027472-6; 1999, pap., ISBN 978-0-06-447207-4. 69p. • Grades 5–9

☞ ACCELERATED READER ☞ READING COUNTS

A little Japanese girl whose father died when she was just eight months old decides to plant some lima beans in a vacant lot near her house. She thinks that planting the beans will enable her farmer father's spirit to see her and get to know her. An elderly woman who has been watching the little girl from her window sees that the plants are dying, and she decides to help. Slowly but surely, people in the rundown neighborhood discover what is becoming a large garden, and they start to participate. A pregnant teen learns that she is actually part of the cycle of life and looks forward to the birth of her child; a young black man shows others that he is not someone to fear; a woman who has been robbed learns to trust people again; and an elderly man who had given up on life becomes active again. The garden helps thirteen people, all with very different stories, to discover what community can mean.

Gentle Criteria: The thirteen individuals in this story become stronger and better people through their wonderful experiences participating in a community garden. People who had never spoken to anyone in the community suddenly find themselves part of a family. The empowerment of creating a bountiful garden out of a vacant lot is like a miracle unfolding in the middle of a big city.

66   **Frederick, Heather Vogel.** *The Mother-Daughter Book Club.*

Simon & Schuster, 2007, ISBN 978-0-689-86412-4. 236p. • Grades 5–7
One phrase makes Emma Hawthorne cringe: "The other mothers and I got to talking after yoga class . . . ." That statement *never* means anything good. And so the mother-daughter book club was born. In Concord, Massachusetts, the hometown of Louisa May Alcott, four very different girls are thrust together—against their will—to read *Little Women*. Over the course of a year the girls and their mothers read the book, and along the way form unexpected bonds of friendship. The girls find inspiration in Louisa's words and in Jo March's actions. They learn to meet their individual challenges, such as taking the lead in a school musical; rebelling against "Are you wearing Nicole Patterson's hand-me-downs?" remarks; making the boys' hockey team; and turning down popularity in favor of true friendship. Follow these girls as they enter middle school and learn about themselves and each other through the mother-daughter book club.

Gentle Criteria: This is a prime example of a gentle read. Each of the girls faces and meets a worthy challenge. Megan forfeits popularity because of the way her former friends treat Jess, another member of the book club. Megan also finds the courage to tell her mom she wants to be a fashion designer, even though her mother wants her to go to Harvard and become an environmentalist or lawyer. Cassidy makes a compromise with her mom so that she can play hockey.

67   **Friedman, D. Dina.** *Playing Dad's Song.*

Farrar, Straus & Giroux, 2006, ISBN 978-0-374-37173-9. 131p. •
Grades 5–7

Gus Moskowitz would change everything about his life if he could. His father, killed in the World Trade Center attack, would still be alive. His mother would not be tired all the time. He would not be hiding under his blanket all the time. When his mother finally decides that Gus needs to stop moping and do something with himself, he begins taking oboe lessons. His sister talks him into trying out for the school play, which makes every part of him shake. But Gus discovers that he has a definite talent for composing, and he writes a song for the father he misses so much. More than just a story about grief, this is a story about a boy discovering who he really is.

Gentle Criteria: This is an inspirational story about people who continue on after sad events take place in their lives—simply because they know they must. In the process of discovering his music, Gus both matures and learns how to live with missing his father. This is a gentle story for children who have lost a parent.

68   Gauthier, Gail. *Happy Kid!*
Penguin, 2006, ISBN 978-0-399-24266-3. 230p. • Grades 5–9
∽ ACCELERATED READER

Kyle is entering seventh grade and is not a happy person. Last year, a screwdriver he made for a Father's Day present fell out of his backpack on the bus, and he was accused of carrying a weapon. The police were called, making him appear a criminal. Now Kyle just wants to keep a low profile. His mother, a family counselor, buys him a self-help book entitled *Happy Kid!* and offers to pay him a dollar per chapter to read it. Kyle soon realizes the book has a mind of its own—it only opens to pages that Kyle needs to apply to his life at a given moment. The book refuses to move to new pages until it feels Kyle is ready. This is a fascinating book about middle-school kids trying to fit in. It does include some minor profanity.

Gentle Criteria: Kyle has to find a way to make the kids realize he's not dangerous; he's just another kid. The first chapter he turns to in *Happy Kid!* tells him to say hello to everyone. As Kyle continues to learn pearls of wisdom from the book, he eventually regains his old self-confidence and is able to pass the book on to someone else who needs it. This thoughtful book will give readers tips on how to get along in the world.

69   Giff, Patricia Reilly. *All the Way Home.*
Random House, 2001, ISBN 978-0-385-90021-8; 2003, pap., ISBN 978-0-440-41182-6. 169p. • Grades 5–8
∽ ACCELERATED READER ∽ READING COUNTS ∽ JUNIOR LIBRARY GUILD

Brick's family's orchard is destroyed by a fire, causing Brick's parents to leave their Windy Hill farm to find work elsewhere. They decide to send Brick to stay with his mom's friend Loretta, who lives in Brooklyn. Brick's mom and Loretta worked together as nurses near Windy Hill years before, caring for polio patients; Loretta adopted Mariel, a girl suffering from the disease. It's not long before Brick and Mariel become friends. Both have a desire to return to Windy Hill. Brick wants to help his elderly former neighbor bring in the apple harvest, and Mariel wants to see the green curtains she remembers as a baby and to find information about her mother. Brick and Mariel take off for the farm, determined to save the apples. Once Mariel is on a ladder, she realizes that the curtains she remembers were actually the leaves from the apple trees. She finds a farmer who remembers her mother, and more harvesters arrive just in time to save the apple harvest.

Gentle Criteria: Readers will be heartbroken when they read about Brick's family separating so they can find work. It is touching that Brick is so determined to help with the apple harvest. Brick is rewarded for his kind deed when his neighbor sets aside a huge orchard for Brick to have in the future. And what Mariel learns about her mother during this trip is certain to evoke tears.

70   Hannigan, Katherine. *Ida B.: And Her Plans to Maximize Fun, Avoid Disaster, and (Possibly) Save the World.*
HarperCollins, 2004, ISBN 978-0-06-073025-3. 246p. • Grades 5–7
⌒ ACCELERATED READER ⌒ JUNIOR LIBRARY GUILD

Ida B. is not your average fourth-grader. She's full of life and overflowing with ideas, plans, and hopes. She also likes to know what's happening and she *does not* like surprises. So when her parents send her to public school for the first time in her life, Ida B. is angry. She doesn't understand why her parents stopped home-schooling her and sold their land, or why her Mama got sick. Ida B. decides to start hating life, threatening in the process to destroy her parents' love and her peers' respect. Can she earn back that care, respect, and love?

Gentle Criteria: Ida B. is refreshing; she is a little girl who loves life and is full of energy. This book shows that the world is not a bad place with some good things in it, but rather, it is a good place with a few bad things in it. Besides, Ida B. always says, "There are too many things to think about in this world besides what I'm going to have for lunch."

71   Harkrader, L. D. *Airball: My Life in Briefs.*
Roaring Brook, 2005, ISBN 978-1-59643-060-0. 198p. • Grades 5–8
⌒ ACCELERATED READER ⌒ READING COUNTS ⌒ JUNIOR LIBRARY GUILD

Kirby lives in a small town with a population of three hundred. He has no plans to try out for the basketball team until he hears that the team will get to go to a Jayhawks game and meet the famous pro player Brett McGrew. Why does the opportunity to meet Brett McGrew appeal to Kirby? Because he's been collecting evidence that suggests the famous player is his father. But the team must win its first basketball game and what worries Kirby is that the team hasn't won a game in two years! Coach Armstrong, however, has a plan. He hands out "invisible shorts" that will make them play better. It works! They all focus on basket-ball and play together as a team. Will Kirby get to the game and have the courage to ask Brett if he's his father?

Gentle Criteria: Lots of humor makes this book a fun read. Kirby lives with his grandmother and the reader never learns where Kirby's mother is, but assumes that she has passed away. In the end, Kirby does find out who is father is, but it's not whom he expects. As Kirby says, "Sometimes the thing you want most in the world really does want you back."

72   **Hartnett, Sonya.** *The Silver Donkey.*
Ill. by Don Powers. Candlewick, 2006, ISBN 978-0-7636-2937-3. 266p.
• Grades 5–9
☞ ACCELERATED READER ☞ READING COUNTS ☞ JUNIOR LIBRARY
GUILD

This fable of peace will be read on many different levels. During the Great War, four English children discover a soldier sleeping in the woods and decide to help him. All the soldier wants is to make it back home across the Channel. As the children get to know him and attempt to help him, the soldier shares four short allegorical stories of peace with them, all centered on the silver donkey that he carries as a good luck charm. One story is about the donkey who carried the baby Jesus to Bethlehem; one story is about the donkey who convinced the sky to let the rains come by being willing to suffer rather than watch the suffering of others; one is about a donkey who carried wounded soldiers to safety; and the last is about how the soldier's younger brother discovered the donkey in the first place. All are tender tales about peace prevailing. The tales are not too didactic and could be used not only as examples of allegory, but also for a discussion on the power of peace.

Gentle Criteria: Gentle is exactly the right word for this tender tale. Although peace and goodness do not always win, they are always the right choice.

73   **Hill, Kirkpatrick.** *Do Not Pass Go.*
Margaret K. McElderry Books, 2007, ISBN 978-1-4169-1400-6. 229p. •
Grades 5–9
☞ ACCELERATED READER ☞ READING COUNTS ☞ JUNIOR LIBRARY
GUILD

Deet lives with his mother, father, and two younger sisters. They are having a hard time making ends meet, so Deet's father has taken on two jobs. To stay awake, his dad starts taking drugs, gets arrested, and is now in jail, which embar-rasses Deet. Deet's mom has to take a job as a waitress, and Deet has to babysit his sisters. Deet's English assignment is to select a quote and write about its possi-ble meaning. Deet finds quotes related to his father's being in jail, and the assign-ment helps him to express his feelings. Deet gets to know some of the other visitors at the jail, and he soon realizes that circumstances can land normal people in jail. Both the visitors and the inmates look and act just like ordinary people, dispelling some stereotypes that Deet holds in his heart. The big, arrogant basketball star of whom Deet was so wary at school tells Deet he has a brother in jail, but his mom will not let him visit. A shy, quiet girl Deet has noticed at school visits her brother in jail. This book discusses various crimes and contains some mild profanity.

Gentle Criteria: This is a good book to share with students who may have similar family situations, proving that one can cope if one has supportive people around. Deet is ashamed that his first thought was about his own embarrassment at school rather than what was happening to his gentle, cheerful dad. But he soon finds out who his friends are and that there are many other kids in similar situations. Deet's supporters are these kids, fellow jail visitors, and his English teacher, who writes wonderful comments on his homework. Deet realizes what a loving family he has, and that people sometimes make mistakes even when their intentions are good. Deet's dad observes, after getting to know his cellmates, that it is a wonder so many are able to stay *out* of jail with all the hardships they endure. At the end of the book, Deet knows that jail is not the end of the world. His dad's drug problem is over and they have found many new and old friends. His family has found out what it is made of, and it is positive stuff indeed!

74   Hobbs, Valerie. *Carolina Crow Girl.*
Farrar, Straus & Giroux, 1999, ISBN 978-0-374-31153-7; Penguin, 2000, pap., ISBN 978-0-14-130976-7. 138p. • Grades 5–9
ᴄ Accelerated Reader ᴄ Reading Counts

Eleven-year-old Carolina has been traveling around the United States in a converted bus with her mother Melanie and sister Trinity. They move every few months, following Red, who is Trinity's dad but not Carolina's, as he changes jobs. Carolina tries to fit in at new schools, but her family's poverty makes this difficult. When they park their bus on what they believe is vacant land, Carolina meets Stefan, whose family owns the property. Stefan lost his sister in an accident, and his mother yearns to have another daughter. Stefan is confined to a wheelchair, and his mom is very protective of him. When Stefan's mom suggests to Melanie that Carolina live with them, Carolina must decide if she wants to enjoy a comfortable lifestyle or stay with her family.

Gentle Criteria: This book shows the love and compassion people have for children—sometimes for quite different reasons. Is Melanie willing to leave Carolina with Stefan's family because she loves her and wants something better for her, or because she wants to make her own life easier? Does Stefan's mom want to adopt Carolina because she is a compassionate person or because she wants to make Carolina her lost daughter? Readers learn the answers to these questions by the end of the book.

75   Hobbs, Valerie. *Defiance.*

Farrar, Straus & Giroux, 2005, ISBN 978-0-374-30847-6. 116p. •
Grades 5–7

∾ ACCELERATED READER ∾ READING COUNTS ∾ JUNIOR LIBRARY
GUILD

Toby Steiner is like every other eleven-year-old boy with one exception: He has cancer and has just finished a horrific course of treatment. When he discovers a new lump while on vacation, he decides not to tell his parents. He simply cannot face another round of chemotherapy; he is tired of being sick and angry about being fussed over constantly. He meets an elderly woman named Pearl and her cow Blossom, and these two begin to change the way Toby looks at life. Above Pearl's door a sign reads: "Whoever steals my freedom takes my life." Pearl is also tired of being fussed over; her children believe a 94-year-old woman (famous poet or not) should not be living alone. Toby helps with work around the farm, and in the process gets to know both Pearl and Blossom very well.

Gentle Criteria: This is an uplifting story about accepting what cannot be changed, but knowing when to fight. Pearl tells Toby that tears are a relief and a blessing, and sometimes life just isn't fair. The relationships—both the good and bad—are especially real, and the parents are two people doing the best they can. In the end, Blossom the cow is fondly remembered, Pearl begins to write poetry again, and Toby decides to continue treatment after all and fight for his life.

76   Hobbs, Valerie. *Sheep.*

Farrar, Straus & Giroux, 2006, ISBN 978-0-374-36777-0. 115p. •
Grades 5–7

∾ ACCELERATED READER ∾ READING COUNTS

Through a series of misfortunes, a border collie discovers what really matters in life: a place to bed down; warm food in your belly; honest work; good company; and, most importantly, the knowledge that you made a difference. When the sheep ranch where he grew up is destroyed by fire, this young dog finds himself without a home. He goes through a series of owners, both good and bad, until he encounters a young boy who needs him even more than he does. He finds a way to help this lonely boy find the family that both of them so desperately need.

Gentle Criteria: Although some of the dog's owners are truly terrible, this is still a heartwarming story. The Goat Man imparts words of wisdom to this bright dog as they travel down the road. The family that saves him from the pound does not understand that he is not made to be a house dog, but they mean well. The two robbers that befriend him are not good people in the eyes of the world, but they take care of him. The circus man is the worst owner, but when the dog escapes and finds the lonely boy, he discovers a way to make everything right with the world.

77   Hobbs, Valerie. *Stefan's Story.*

Farrar, Straus & Giroux, 2003, ISBN 978-0-374-37240-8; Price Stern Sloan, 2007, pap., ISBN 978-0-8431-2523-8. 165p. • Grades 5–9

✑ ACCELERATED READER ✑ READING COUNTS

In this sequel to *Carolina Crow Girl*, Stefan visits Carolina two years later. Carolina's mother is getting married and Stefan is going to attend the wedding, hang out with his best friend Carolina, and enjoy Oregon. When a huge forest company threatens to chop down an old-growth forest, Stefan and Carolina try to organize people to stop it. But what can two teens do to stop a huge corporation? The town is divided between the lumberjacks and the fishermen who know that excessive foresting will kill off the fish. Stefan no longer thinks of Carolina as just a friend, but Carolina is receiving a lot of attention from a new boy in town. How can Stefan compete with someone who is not in a wheelchair? Can the two save the forests, and who will Carolina choose?

Gentle Criteria: In *Carolina Crow Girl*, readers saw things from Carolina's perspective. In Stefan's story, however, readers now learn how he feels about Carolina. She is Stefan's best friend, but he also now has romantic feelings for her. Stefan struggles with his feelings as he watches Carolina dance with her new friend at the wedding. Will long-time friendship win out in the end?

78   Hobbs, Will. *Wild Man Island.*

HarperCollins, 2002, ISBN 978-0-06-029810-4; 2003, pap., ISBN 978-0-380-73310-1. 184p. • Grades 5–8

✑ ACCELERATED READER ✑ READING COUNTS ✑ JUNIOR LIBRARY GUILD

Andy is on a kayaking trip in Alaska. No one in the group knows that he is close to the place where his father died nine years before. Early in the morning on the day his group is to return home, Andy sneaks away in his kayak and finds the spot where his father died. On his return trip, a storm hits and sea lions charge his kayak, capsizing it. Andy is washed down the straits to Admiralty Island. He eats raw mussels but then goes into shock. He appears doomed until a hermit finds him. Having a grizzly bear sit down beside him, meeting a wolf pack, being thrown off his boat by the wake of a cruise ship, and discovering a prehistoric skeleton are just a few of the exciting moments that Andy experiences while making his way back to civilization.

Gentle Criteria: Andy comes from a strong family. His father left him a legacy of scientific work, and his mother has made sure that he is not helpless—that he knows how to survive on his own. This exciting story of survival—with the touching element of convincing the hermit that he has much more to offer the world—is a very readable tale.

79   Holt, Kimberly Willis. *Part of Me.*

Henry Holt, 2006, ISBN 978-0-8050-6360-8. 208p. • Grades 5–9

This book covers four generations of Rose's family. When her husband leaves in 1939 Rose's mom moves her family to New Orleans to stay with Rose's grandfather. Rose lies about her age and becomes the driver of the library bookmobile. She then marries a man who used to visit the bookmobile on a weekly basis. The story then focuses on Rose's son, Merle Henry, whose main activity is trapping and whose reading material consists of *Old Yeller*. Merle's daughter Annabeth is then discussed, in 1973; she longs for a fairy-tale life but finds her school years anything but a fairy tale. Annabeth's thirteen-year-old son Kyle, however, discovers a love of books after trying to solve a mystery. Harry Potter books are disappearing from the library, so he reads one to see why anyone would bother and finds himself captivated. At the end of the book, all living members gather to celebrate Rose's published book, *Books on the Bayou*.

Gentle Criteria: The story material is clean, and the reader can easily relate to the emotions of the characters. Although every other generation is slow to appreciate the love of books, both Merle Henry and Kyle do eventually discover them. Readers also come away with a sense of what part reading played in the lives of the different generations. Just as the title suggests, each character demonstrates how reading became "a part of me."

80   **Horvath, Polly.** *Everything on a Waffle.*
       Farrar, Straus & Giroux, 2001, ISBN 978-0-374-32236-6; 2004, pap.,
       ISBN 978-0-374-42208-0. 149p. • Grades 5–7
       ◟ ACCELERATED READER ◟ READING COUNTS

Readers will empathize with Primrose; everyone else is sure that her parents have died at sea in a terrible storm, but Primrose knows—just *knows*—deep in her heart that they are still alive. Being a possibly orphaned eleven-year-old leads Primrose through several adventures during which she meets many colorful characters, all the while holding steadfastly to the belief that her parents are still alive. In the end, of course, Primrose proves right. Each chapter ends with a recipe from one of the characters in the book, along with Primrose's observations about people and life.

Gentle Criteria: This is a heartwarming story of a young girl's faith even when all signs point to the contrary. The characters are not all completely good, but they all have their reasons for being the way they are, as Primrose so aptly points out.

81   **Hussey, Charmian.** *The Valley of Secrets.*
       Simon & Schuster, 2003, ISBN 978-0-689-87862-6; 2006, pap., ISBN
       978-1-4169-0015-3. 382p. • Grades 5–9
       ◟ ACCELERATED READER

This is a clever and well-researched story that includes lots of information about the rain forests of the Amazon. Stephen is an orphan who learns that his late great-uncle has left him an estate in Cornwall, England. The will stipulates that in order to inherit, Stephen must not make any changes—not to the grounds, the house, or anything else he finds there. When he starts living on the estate, Stephen makes many discoveries. He reads his great-uncle's journal of his travels through the Amazon, and he wonders at the strange people, animals, and plants living on the estate. Are the two related? Stephen eventually finds there the family he has always craved. This is a great book to use with a classroom unit about the Amazon. The author has included an extensive listing of species, resources, and bibliography.

Gentle Criteria: Stephen is a tender soul who wants nothing more than a warm and loving place to lay his head. When he inherits the Lansbury Estate he has high hopes. He does find the love and caring that he is looking for, but not in the ways he expected. Again and again this story makes the point that it is the goodness within people that matters most. The Amazon Indians' harmony with nature attracts him and he realizes it will be a great loss if it is destroyed. This is a wonderful story about the riches and pharmacology of the Amazon, along with the riches of finding family and kindred spirits.

82   Ingold, Jeanette. *Mountain Solo.*
Harcourt, 2003, ISBN 978-0-15-202670-7; 2005, pap., ISBN 978-0-15-205358-1. 309p. • Grades 5–9
☞ Accelerated Reader ☞ Reading Counts

This book features two stories. The modern-day story is about Tess who is a child prodigy on the violin. Her parents disagree over the amount of time Tess should spending practicing. When Tess's mother takes her to New York to pursue a career playing the violin, Tess's father stays in Montana, and her parents eventually divorce. Tess messes up during a concert and returns home to her father to take a break from the stress. Her father's new wife is researching the homestead of Frederick Bottner, a violinist who lived in the Montana mountains. Bottner's tough but happy life forms the second story in this book. By studying the past and examining her own choices, Tess finally decides what course she wants to follow.

Gentle Criteria: This book gives great insight into the challenges and sacrifices facing a child prodigy. Her father supported her desire to play the violin and didn't interfere as long as Tess was happy, but her parents' marriage is sacrificed to Tess's career. Through researching the historical violinist, Tess realizes why she performed so poorly at the concert. This is a good book to show children what goes into a career of performance at a young age.

83   Jennings, Richard W. *The Great Whale of Kansas.*
Houghton Mifflin, 2001, ISBN 978-0-618-10228-0. 150p. • Grades 5–8
☞ Accelerated Reader ☞ Reading Counts ☞ Junior Library Guild

Eleven-year-old Kevin unearths a gigantic prehistoric fossil of an unknown creature. The fossil expert says it could not possibly be the whale that it appears to be because mammals did not exist at that time. She says it is a fake and accuses Kevin of being a fossil artist. Kevin's science teacher comes to his rescue and gives the expert a piece that has been carbon-dated. To Kevin's astonishment, the people who believe that he faked the fossil are angry because the fossil is in fact real. Kevin's aunt, a lawyer, raises the issue of a long-forgotten treaty that gave the Native Americans rights to whale hunting. She emphasizes to the judge that this is the relic of the last known whale in Kansas and that the Native Americans have the rights to it. In a lovely ceremony, the whale is returned to its original resting place.

Gentle Criteria: This gently amusing novel has many layers to it. Kevin has to rise above all the people who want to treat his fossil find as the latest fad. He must also believe in himself when the experts say he is wrong. His Native American friend Tom White Cloud reminds him what is truly important in life. The whale's remains are returned to the earth where they rightfully belong. Respect, honor, and belief in oneself are strong themes in this amusing story.

84   Jennings, Richard W. *My Life of Crime.*
Houghton Mifflin, 2002, ISBN 978-0-618-21433-4. 145p. • Grades 5–7
   ACCELERATED READER   READING COUNTS   JUNIOR LIBRARY GUILD

When Fowler discovers a poor, bedraggled parrot in a classroom, he decides he must steal it—even though stealing is definitely wrong. What ensues is a multitude of mishaps, one leading to another, with Fowler constantly afraid he will get caught. This is a clever and entertaining story about doing the right thing—even though doing so sometimes has disastrous consequences.

Gentle Criteria: Readers will be much amused by Fowler and his clumsy attempts to save a poor bird from expiring in the classroom. With good intentions but a guilty heart, Fowler is certain to generate both empathy and hilarity in readers.

85   Jones, Jennifer B. *The (Short) Story of My Life.*
Walker, 2004, ISBN 978-0-8027-8905-1. 194p. • Grades 5–7
   ACCELERATED READER

Michael Jordan, who is *not* named after the famous basketball player, is the shortest sixth-grader in his middle school. Tired of being the butt of jokes and determined to make his new school year positive, Michael is pleased when an attractive eighth-grade girl takes an interest in him. Unfortunately, the school bully is also interested in the same girl. Michael's journal correspondence with a wonderful English teacher helps him to find other ways to stand tall. When the bully is stuck in a dangerous spot, and Michael is the only one small enough to get to him, Michael feels as tall as any kid in the school. This book is a great middle-school story because it is both amusing and realistic.

Gentle Criteria: A great teacher, a young hero, and a bully who learns to ask for help are the rich ingredients that combine to convey a positive message that what some see as weaknesses can prove to be strengths. An inspiring and entertaining book.

86   **Jones, Kimberly K.** *Sand Dollar Summer.*
Margaret K. McElderry Books, 2006, ISBN 978-1-4169-0362-8. 206p. • Grades 7–9
⌒ ACCELERATED READER ⌒ READING COUNTS

Twelve-year-old Lise spends the summer in a dilapidated beach cottage with her mother, who is recuperating from a car accident, and her mute younger brother. When she meets some of her mother's childhood friends, she begins to see another side of her mother's life. She understands the strength that her mother possessed to leave the place she loved to make a better life for her children. When a hurricane hits, Lise discovers just how much the people in her life love and care for her and the lengths to which they will go to protect her. She also learns a new concept: Her mother also needs her.

Gentle Criteria: Although the book contains some profanity, it portrays people who have high standards. Lise discovers that she has her mother's strength of spirit. Many good people are featured, from the taxi driver who refuses payment for driving them to the hospital to Indian Ben, who reminds Lise that a certain amount of trust and courage is required to live in this world.

87   **Jung, Reinhardt.** *Bambert's Book of Missing Stories.*
Knopf, 1998, ISBN 978-0-375-92997-7; Random House, 2006, pap., ISBN 978-0-440-42045-3. 124p. • Grades 5–9
⌒ ACCELERATED READER ⌒ READING COUNTS ⌒ JUNIOR LIBRARY GUILD

Bambert is a recluse who lives by himself on the top floor of a building that he owns. He is a dwarf, and has endured many painful operations to try to improve his condition. On the first floor of his building lives a semi-retired grocer who supplies provisions so that Bambert rarely has to make the journey downstairs. Bambert is a beautiful writer. One day he decides to send eleven of his stories off by hot-air balloon to seek their own settings. He hopes that each will make its way to a different place and will be sent back to him. One package contains nothing but blank pages, with the idea that a new story will be created. One by one the stories do return, and Bambert is able to set them in a time and place. But how is this happening? Bambert doesn't realize that friends are helping him. When Bambert loses his struggle with death, the final book is put together in a wonderful tribute to him.

Gentle Criteria: All of these stories feature noble people—children who save a whale; a princess who only wants to know what truth is; a child who helps the prisoners escape with a shaft of light. And the love and respect that Bambert's neighbor shows right up to the end is a wonderful tribute to the power of goodness and friendship.

88 Key, Watt. *Alabama Moon.*

Farrar, Straus & Giroux, 2006, ISBN 978-0-374-30184-2. 294p. • Grades 7–9

☞ READING COUNTS

Moon has lived in the wilderness with his father all his life, and his story provides great insight into the difficulties of such a life. When his father dies, Moon is brought to the jail and then taken to an orphanage. Moon tells everyone he's headed for Alaska because his dad told him the government will leave a person alone in Alaska. No one believes him until he escapes and takes the other orphans with him. This is a truly entertaining story about how hard it is to acclimate to new surroundings when people have preconceived ideas about you.

Gentle Criteria: This book contains instances of bullying and some profanity, so adults should consider these elements when using this book with students. Moon clings to the beliefs that his father has taught him. He even believes he can communicate with the dead by writing and then burning the paper. But the more people Moon meets, the more he starts to question the things his father taught him. Moon also realizes that he doesn't want to be alone anymore. As he develops friendships, he understands that his father's hatred of the government and desire for isolation was due to the injustices he encountered in the Vietnam War. This is an excellent story to demonstrate how someone can be misjudged.

89 LaFaye, A. *Strawberry Hill.*

Simon & Schuster, 1999, ISBN 978-0-689-82441-8; 2000, pap., ISBN 978-0-689-82961-1. 272p. • Grades 7–9

☞ ACCELERATED READER

A few swear words and driving a car while underage to an R-rated movie make this book a little edgier than most, but the themes run strong and true. Raleia wants to be transported back in time to when things were old-fashioned and graceful and the world was gentler. She especially wants to replace her hippie parents with a standard, follow-the-rules couple. Her mother lost a baby when it was just a few days old and now has another one on the way. It is up to Raleia and her younger brother to fend for themselves. When Raleia makes a tentative friendship with the old man in the graceful mansion on the hill, she thinks she has found what she is looking for. Little does she know that he is dealing with his own disappointments and tragedies. Long ago, In the town of Tidal where her family is spending the summer, a giant tidal wave killed many of the residents; this is just one of the historical events that Raleia discovers as the summer wears on.

Gentle Criteria: Raleia discovers that her parents have their own reasons for being the free spirits they are. She also discovers that they love her just as deeply and fiercely as any of her friends' "boring old normal parents," with their groundings and rules. Ian Rutherford and Raleia are kindred spirits who prefer their solitude but like to have somebody to share with when they feel like it. This book is about recognizing real love and realizing that it is important to live in the present.

90   Lieberg, Carolyn. *West with Hopeless.*

Dutton, 2004, ISBN 978-0-525-47194-3. 180p. • Grades 5–9

⌐ ACCELERATED READER

Carin doesn't trust her older half-sister Hope at all. Carin usually flies to Reno in the summer to stay with her dad, but this year Hope is driving her. Carin thinks Hope is up to her old tricks when they crash a reunion picnic and help themselves to the food. And she fears Hope has really lost it when she uses a car wash to take a shower. But then it's Carin who does something foolish when Hope takes a nap just a few miles from their destination. Carin decides to drive and ends up getting them lost and out of gas with no money. Will a miracle occur that gets Carin to her dad and Hope to her dream-job interview?

Gentle Criteria: Teens with step-siblings will identify with this story of half-sisters. Although readers don't know what poor choices Hope has made in the past, Hope proves that she has Carin's best interests at heart when their trip takes a difficult turn. It's a heartwarming story in which two rivals become true sisters.

91   Lin, Grace. *The Year of the Dog.*

Little, Brown, 2006, ISBN 978-0-316-06000-4; 2007, pap., ISBN 978-0-316-06002-8. 134p. • Grades 5–7

⌐ ACCELERATED READER ⌐ READING COUNTS

This book follows a year in the life of Grace Lin and her family. It is the Year of the Dog, the year that Grace Lin is supposed to figure out what she wants to do with her life, and the year that she should find a good friend. Grace meets another Chinese girl who moves to her school, and they become best friends. Grace enters a science fair, thinking science might be her talent in life, but she doesn't win. She then participates in a school play, but even that doesn't seem to be her talent. Then Grace takes part in a writing contest with twenty thousand other entries from across the country; the entries won't be judged until the end of the year, so she has to wait to learn whether writing is her talent. The year is almost over and Grace still hasn't figured out her life's talent—until she hears over the loud speaker that she has won fourth place and four hundred dollars in the writing contest. Now she feels she has finally found her goal.

Gentle Criteria: This book gives great insight into the culture of Chinese Americans. Their unique holidays and customs are explained, and Grace's mother shares stories from her childhood, giving readers real insight into what her life was like growing up in China. This is a gentle story that can help readers to understand a different culture.

92   Littman, Sarah Darer. *Confessions of a Closet Catholic.*
Dutton, 2005, ISBN 978-0-525-47365-7; Penguin, 2006, pap., ISBN 978-0-14-240597-0. 193p. • Grades 5–7
⤺ ACCELERATED READER

Justine Silver is Jewish, but she doesn't know what that means to her. One set of grandparents survived the Holocaust and keeps a kosher house; her other grandparents are more relaxed about tradition but still consider themselves practicing Jews. Justine, whose best friend is Catholic, decides to try her friend's faith for a while, a trial that has its own repercussions. But it is Bubbe, her father's mother, who shows Justine that it is okay to try different things and learn about different beliefs. She tells Justine that knowledge makes people tolerant and questioning is a sign of intelligence. Justine's faith is put to the test when Bubbe becomes ill.

Gentle Criteria: This is a novel about tolerance and understanding, and its promotion of intelligent questioning is the best part of the book. Justine realizes that it is the act of praying that makes her feel better, and that it does not matter to whose God she is praying. When she tells her mother how she really feels, she learns how much her mother really loves her. Both the rabbi and the priest tell her that she needs to change her image of God from being an enforcer to a loving God with open arms. It's a positive story for readers who are exploring the issue of faith.

93   Lombard, Jenny. *Drita My Homegirl.*
Putnam, 2006, ISBN 978-0-399-24380-6. 135p. • Grades 5–7
⤺ ACCELERATED READER ⤺ READING COUNTS

Drita's father has been in New York for the past year, saving money to send for the family back in Kosovo. When the family finally arrives in New York, Drita's mom is emotionally distraught, not knowing whether her cousin has made it out of the war-torn country. Drita goes to school but doesn't know any English. She meets Maxie, whose mother died in a car accident three years ago; now Maxie just seems to get into trouble all the time. She hasn't even told her classmates about her mom's death. For her rudeness, Maxie's teacher assigns her to write a report on Kosovo and suggests that she ask Drita questions about her native land. As Drita and Maxie get to know each other, they form a strong friendship that helps to fill a gap in each of their lives.

Gentle Criteria: This book gives firsthand insight into how hard it is to move to a new country and learn the language. Readers will have compassion when they learn what immigrants go through to acclimate to a new country, and they may contemplate what they would do in a similar situation. This story can move students to reach out to befriend and help immigrant students in their classes.

94   **Look, Lenore.** *Ruby Lu, Empress of Everything.*
Ill. by Anne Wilsdorf. Atheneum, 2006, ISBN 978-0-689-86460-5; Simon & Schuster, 2007, pap., ISBN 978-1-4169-5003-5. 164p. • Grades 5–6
☞ ACCELERATED READER ☞ READING COUNTS

Ruby Lu is having the best time until Chinese relatives move into her household. Ruby gets a lot of attention when she brings her deaf cousin Flying Duck, one of the immigrants, to school with her. Then her mom's saying that, "A wonder only lasts nine days," seems to come true. Suddenly, Ruby is sick of her cousin and tired of everyone using chopsticks, and she hates doing crafts after school with Flying Duck. Then her little brother sticks a couple of magnets up his nose and stops breathing. Flying Duck sucks them out of his nose and saves Oscar's life. Ruby Lu is once again thankful for Flying Duck. Ruby Lu and Flying Duck must go to summer school because of problems with homework (a note was pinned to each of their shirts, but Ruby Lu took them off and hid them in her book bag, an act she may regret).

Gentle Criteria: This book shows in typical fashion the excitement of having foreign guests in their home. It also points out how that novelty can soon wear off. This is a delightful read in which a young girl learns to deal with having a deaf housemate and no longer being the center of attention. Ruby Lu also teaches readers how to have objectives by creating a list of things she wants to accomplish during the summer.

95   **Lowry, Lois.** *Stay! Keeper's Story.*
Houghton Mifflin, 1997, ISBN 978-0-395-87048-8; Random House, 1999, pap., ISBN 978-0-440-41524-4. 127p. • Grades 5–9
☞ ACCELERATED READER ☞ READING COUNTS

The higher reading level of this slim book will surprise some readers, but the story will entertain all types of readers. Keeper, who does not like to be called "the Dog," relates the story of his life. After being born behind a high-class French restaurant with only the best of food, Keeper is left by his mother to take up residence with a kindly homeless man. Keeper enjoys the smells of the homeless man and lives a good life with him until the man gets sick. Keeper is a born poet and contributes his poetry throughout the book. A photographer discovers his sneer, and soon Keeper is a famous model, sneering through all kinds of commercials. He quickly becomes bored with this life and escapes one day to find residence with a young farm girl. Life is especially good when he finds his sister Wispy, who has taken up residence in his place at the photographer's. When he saves the farm girl from his deadly enemy Scar, his picture as an intelligent, heroic, and handsome dog is complete.

Gentle Criteria: This is an entertaining look at a dog's life through the animal's eyes. Why, he says, do humans insist on thinking that dogs want dog food instead of human food? The kindly souls Keeper comes across restore one's faith in humans, and Keeper himself is everything dog owners yearn for—loyal, intelligent, and obedient.

96 **Lubar, David.** *Sleeping Freshmen Never Lie.*
Dutton, 2005, ISBN 978-0-525-47311-4. 279p. • Grades 7–9
☞ ACCELERATED READER ☞ READING COUNTS

Scott is a freshman in high school when he finds out that his mom is going to have a baby boy. Scott decides to keep a journal so he can remember everything he wants to tell his new brother. Scott is infatuated with Jill, a girl he has known since kindergarten. Scott does everything he can to get close to Jill. He joins the newspaper staff but then finds out she is only a guest editor. He runs for Student Council because he hears Jill is running, but he is elected and she isn't. He joins the stage crew of a play that Jill tries out for, but she doesn't get the role! Scott shares all these failed attempts in his journal for his yet-to-be-born brother. Scott also writes about making new friends because his old friends are going off in different directions with their own endeavors. Students of this age group who have similar feelings about family, love, and life will relate to the events of Scott's life.

Gentle Criteria: Although this is a nice story overall, it does deal with the attempted suicide of one of the characters, so adults should consider this aspect when recommending the book to students. Keeping a journal is a good method for students to express their feelings, and students easily relate to Scott's journal entries. Scott feels like such a nobody, but Jill perceives him as someone who really has his act together. Jill is impressed that Scott is on the newspaper, the Student Council, and part of the drama crew, unaware that Scott did all those things just to have the chance to be closer to her.

97 **Lupica, Mike.** *Heat.*
Philomel, 2006, ISBN 978-0-399-24301-1. 220p. • Grades 5–7
☞ ACCELERATED READER ☞ READING COUNTS ☞ JUNIOR LIBRARY GUILD

This book is written by the author of *Travel Team* (2004). Michael Arroyo and his team are on the way to play in the Little League World Series. But will his family secrets prevent this from happening? This is a touching story and an exciting read about baseball. The "official people" as Michael and his brother call them, do not know that the boys' father died of a heart attack. Michael's brother will turn eighteen in just a few months, and they plan to keep their father's death a secret until then so they will not be placed in foster care. Another problem is Michael's missing birth certificate, lost in the boat trip from Cuba. The opposing team claims that Michael must be older than he says. Now Michael must give proof of his age before he can play.

Gentle Criteria: There are many wonderful moments in this book. There is the mysterious girl who stands by the fence and watches them play, wanting to be part of the gang. There is the neighbor who Michael saves from a mugger and who does her best to keep them safe from social workers. There is the social worker who knows something is not right and quietly makes sure that Michael and his brother are okay. The people around Michael and his brother are strong and supportive souls.

98   McCaughrean, Geraldine. *Cyrano.*

Harcourt, 2006, ISBN 978-0-15-205805-0. 128p. • Grades 7–9

This book is a retelling of the well-known *Cyrano de Bergerac* for young adults. Cyrano knows that Roxanne can never love someone as ugly as he, even though he loves her deeply and truly. He discovers that Roxanne is in love with Christian, a soldier under his command, and promises to protect Christian for her. When they go into battle and Christian cannot write to Roxanne, Cyrano writes to her for Christian. Although Cyrano thinks Christian has a space "as large as an empty library" in his head, Cyrano is determined that Roxanne will get what she wants. Cyrano's letters are so moving that Roxanne comes to the battlefield and witnesses Christian's death. Ah, but then Cyrano cannot sully Christian's death by telling her the truth. It is not until many years later, on the day of Cyrano's death, that Roxanne learns the truth. This is definitely a tale of unrequited love.

Gentle Criteria: Although mistaken, this is a tale of true love. Cyrano will do anything for the Roxanne he loves so much. All he wants is for her to be happy. He is willing to sacrifice his own joy for the sake of another's memory. He is also a man of uncompromised ethics, and says and lives what he means to his dying day.

99   McKay, Hilary. *Caddy Ever After.*

Margaret K. McElderry Books, 2006, ISBN 978-1-4169-0930-9. 218p. • Grades 6–8

⌒ ACCELERATED READER

This sequel to *Permanent Rose* (see below) is another entertaining story about the English Casson family. Four separate stories, each told by a different sibling—Saffy, Indigo, Rose, and Caddy—describe life in the year leading up to Caddy's wedding—or what was supposed to be a wedding. Rose tells of a humiliation at school, and how she and the teacher, in a most amusing way, made everything better. Indigo tells a wonderful story about how he made the school dance better for everyone, especially for Sarah who is in a wheelchair—even if they did end up spreading the flu around! Saffy tells of a troublemaking balloon and how the Casson family makes good use of it, and Caddy gives her own perspective on the events leading up to her non-wedding. This story presents the Casson family at its best and most amusing!

Gentle Criteria: Once again the Casson family warms readers' hearts. The siblings often stumble into trouble—but with the best intentions. Sarah's mother does not trust Saffy one bit, but when Sarah becomes very ill, she tells Saffy to please come visit. Nobody can go from miserable to happy as fast as the lovable Rose. Indigo is a quiet boy who lives in a world of his own, except when help is needed. And when Caddy finds the *real thing*—love—and it is not her fiancée, her father does not moan about all the money spent but says as long as she is happy it is all for the best. They encourage the guests to eat the cake—even though there was no wedding!

100 **McKay, Hilary.** *Indigo's Star.*
Margaret K. McElderry Books, 2003, ISBN 978-0-689-86563-3; Simon & Schuster, 2006, pap., ISBN 978-1-4169-1403-7. 265p. • Grades 6–8
☞ ACCELERATED READER ☞ READING COUNTS ☞ JUNIOR LIBRARY GUILD

This book is a sequel to *Saffy's Angel* (see below). Saffy's brother Indigo has been out of school for almost an entire term due to a bout of mononucleosis. His sister Rose is the only one who knows that Indigo is dreading returning to school because of the bullies who dunked his head in the toilet before he got sick. Rose's perspective on bullies is this: You can't be disgusting to people just because they annoy you. Millions of people annoy her, but she just has to put up with them. When Indigo returns to school, he discovers a new ally in Tom, a visitor from America. Tom doesn't tolerate the bullying even though he is much smaller than the bullies. Tom is angry with his father who has remarried and has a new child. Indigo's father is also drifting away from his family to create a new life of his own. As the story progresses, Tom and Indigo help each other with both the bullies and their family situations. They realize that parents are only human and that they can deal effectively with bullies.

Gentle Criteria: Both boys' families are going through major changes, but they all love each other deeply. Even though Rose thinks her father is absent from the family way too much, when she really needs him, he comes to her rescue. Tom is angry that he is no longer an only child, but he realizes that he still loves his father deeply. All the adults in this story are helping their children to be good, strong, caring individuals.

101 **McKay, Hilary.** *Permanent Rose.*
Margaret K. McElderry Books, 2005, ISBN 978-1-4169-0372-7; Simon & Schuster, 2006, pap., ISBN 978-1-4169-2804-1. 234p. • Grades 6–8
☞ ACCELERATED READER ☞ READING COUNTS ☞ JUNIOR LIBRARY GUILD

Saffy, Rose's adopted sister and cousin, is trying to find out who her father is, and Rose is trying to get in touch with their friend Tom, who has returned to the United States. Rose has been shoplifting; David, Tom and Indigo's old enemy, is trying to make up for his past deeds and be friends with Indigo, and he realizes what Rose is doing. David used to be a bully, and it is now important to him to help Rose before she gets into trouble. Caddy, Saffy's oldest sister, loses her engagement ring, and David is sure that Rose stole it. With many mishaps along the way, David tries to set things right. Rose, in her eagerness to track down Tom, inadvertently discovers who Saffy's father is. Will this unsavory secret be the end of this happy-go-lucky family?

Gentle Criteria: This entertaining book is a nice sequel to *Indigo's Star*. Although adults may question whether this is truly a gentle read when they learn that Saffy's real father is also her uncle, they should consider that this book does not dwell on this fact. The story focuses on Rose and her unshakable faith that everything will turn out for the best. This family has lots of ups and downs, and their only dependable asset is their love for each other. Even David the former thug turns out well, thanks to his involvement with this wonderful, zany family. Their problems do not diminish their love.

102   McKay, Hilary. *Saffy's Angel.*

Margaret K. McElderry Books, 2001, ISBN 978-0-689-84933-6; Simon & Schuster, 2006, pap., ISBN 978-0-689-84934-3. 152p. • Grades 6–8
⌒ ACCELERATED READER ⌒ READING COUNTS ⌒ JUNIOR LIBRARY GUILD

Saffy has always felt the odd one out in her artistic family. When she discovers she is adopted, this reinforces all her feelings of not belonging. Her grandfather dies, and attached to his will is a terse note about Saffy's angel. Saffy has a dim memory of a garden in Italy and a stone angel, and she sets out to find it with Sarah, who is confined to a wheelchair; Michael, a driving instructor; and Rose, Indigo, and Cadmium, her adoptive siblings. In the process, Saffy discovers that she really is more a part of this family than she ever thought possible. Getting nose studs at the mall, breeding guinea pigs, and rappelling down the side of the house are all everyday occurrences in this family.

Gentle Criteria: This book speaks to the essence of what really makes up a family—people who love and care about each other. Saffy's family is full of free spirits, but they all manage, in their own ways, to show Saffy how much they love her. Deeply touching, as well as entertaining and amusing, this book will prompt readers to find McKay's other books about Saffy and her siblings.

103   Malcolm, Jahnna N. *Perfect Strangers.*

Simon & Schuster, 2005, ISBN 978-1-4177-2038-5; pap., ISBN 978-0-689-87221-1. 217p. Series: Love Letters • Grades 7–9
⌒ ACCELERATED READER

Madison finds out that her archenemy Jeremy is running against her for school president. Three years ago Jeremy cruelly told her that she won the Homecoming Attendant spot for freshmen. Madison was totally embarrassed when she ran out to the float but was turned away. Madison has fallen in love with her anonymous pen-pal, Blue. As Madison and Blue get to know each other better through their letters, readers will anxiously anticipate new revelations. An added twist is the third presidential candidate, Reed, who shares information with Madison that changes how she's viewed her life for the past three years.

Gentle Criteria: This book shows how students often go through school life knowing classmates only superficially. Each of the main characters has a specific group of friends and doesn't associate with the other cliques. When Madison participates in the Heart-to-Heart anonymous writing exercise, she finds a pen-pal with whom she can share her innermost feelings and someone to whom she is attracted.

104 Many, Paul. *These Are the Rules.*
Walker, 1997, ISBN 978-0-8027-8619-7; St. Martin's, pap., ISBN 978-0-8027-8620-3. 149p. • Grades 7–9
☞ ACCELERATED READER ☞ READING COUNTS

Colm thought his father's connections would help him get a job in the city. But he discovers that not only is his dad not dependable, but his parents are also separated and heading toward divorce. Summer for Colm now means spending weeks in a cottage so crummy that the toilet can only be flushed once a day. Along the way, however, he learns some rules of life that will stick with him forever. Rules that explain why his dad is the way he is, how his parents really do love each other and their kids, and who his real friends are. Each chapter illustrates one of Colm's "rules of life" —Rule 1: Be prepared for surprises; Rule 2: Keep your eyes on the stars, but don't be surprised if you step on a banana peel; and so forth. The last rule is the most telling of all: Rule 12: There are no rules.

Gentle Criteria: This book should be recommended to mature readers because of the language, but it is a great story about a young man who is figuring out life. As he matures, he is able to understand the actions—or lack of action—of his family and friends. Although attracted to a good-looking but shallow girl, he learns the value of having a real relationship. And although she is often unable to get along with his father, it is Colm's mother who paves the way for father and son to reach a compromise. This is another positive book about people who love each other despite everything that happens in their lives.

105 Marcum, Lance. *The Cottonmouth Club.*
Farrar, Straus & Giroux, 2005, ISBN 978-0-374-31562-7. 328p. • Grades 7–9
☞ ACCELERATED READER

Soon to be twelve years old, Mitch has his summer all planned out—sleepovers, bike rides, and horror movie marathons with his best friend Tick. But his mother has other plans that include two months in the Louisiana bayou country with relatives he hasn't seen in years. From encounters with raging bulls and cottonmouth snakes to some major pranks along the way, Mitch finds out that he is a stronger person than he thinks, and there is nothing quite like being part of a family.

Gentle Criteria: Although this story includes moments where there could have been profanity, such words are always prefaced (rather amusingly) with remarks like "Oh shoot—only without the o's." This is a family story depicting real teen boys who get into trouble but end up the better for it.

106   Martin, Ann M. *A Dog's Life.*
   Scholastic, 2005, ISBN 978-0-439-71559-1; 2007, pap., ISBN 978-0-439-71700-7. 182p. • Grades 5–9
   ⌐ ACCELERATED READER ⌐ READING COUNTS

This is a tender story of a stray dog and her journeys as she searches for food and comfort. She and her brother live with their mother in a shed. Their days as puppies living with their mother are warm and tender. In one scene, a mother fox has not returned to feed her kits, so the mother dog feeds them as she is still nursing. The two pups wander out on their own and one is picked up as a pet, but Squirrel is left to forage on her own. Throughout her long life she is sometimes picked up as a pet and sometimes abandoned. She learns to avoid desperately hungry dogs in packs, and mostly avoids humans as well. She learns to fend for herself with the help of kind people who take pity on her. Then she meets Susan, an elderly woman who convinces her to come inside her house and get warm. In the end the two old females—one a dog and one a human—discover how much they need each other.

Gentle Criteria: Although there are humans who abandon the dogs along the way, this is a story of kindly people and a dog that never gives up hope searching for a good home.

107   Mass, Wendy. *Jeremy Fink and the Meaning of Life.*
   Little, Brown, 2006, ISBN 978-0-316-05829-2. 289p. • Grades 5–9
   ⌐ ACCELERATED READER ⌐ READING COUNTS ⌐ JUNIOR LIBRARY GUILD

Jeremy will turn thirteen in a month. A box arrives in the mail from his father who passed away four years ago. The box has writing on it that says, "The Meaning of Life for Jeremy Fink to open on his 13th Birthday." The box requires four keys to open it, but there are no keys, and opening the box by force might damage its contents. So Jeremy and his best friend and neighbor start looking for keys that might work. They begin at flea markets and end up breaking into the office of the lawyer who last had the keys. They get caught and are sentenced to do community service. Thinking they may never get the box opened, they begin asking everyone they meet what the meaning of life is. Some of the answers they get are quite profound, but none matches the message inside the box.

Gentle Criteria: This book really should be required reading for all teens. It makes the reader stop and take a realistic look at his own life. Jeremy's father writes that two wolves reside in each of us. One is anger, envy, sorrow, regret, and greed, while the other is joy, peace, love, hope, and kindness. Which one will win? The one that is fed. This book contains great wisdom that every reader can apply. Readers will need tissues when the box is finally opened.

108   Mass, Wendy. *A Mango-Shaped Space.*

Little, Brown, 2003, ISBN 978-0-316-52388-2; 2005, pap., ISBN 978-0-316-05825-4. 219p. • Grades 7–9

☞ ACCELERATED READER ☞ READING COUNTS

This is a realistic fiction story about synesthesia, a condition in which the visual cortex of the brain is activated when the auditory cortex is stimulated. One sense causes another sense to be stimulated in individuals who have this condition. For example, hearing music may cause them to see colors, or tasting certain foods may cause them to feel sensation in their hands. In this story, thirteen-year-old Mia finally tells her family that she has been experiencing synesthesia all her life. Doctors help her with this condition, but she must learn to manage her life, and especially her education, around it. Interwoven into this story of challenges and coping are the deaths of her grandfather and her cat Mango. Her best friend Jenna's mother has also died, but she still has a strong influence on the girls. This story is both touching and educational. Good friendships and competent adults help Mia cope with a condition that has made her life very difficult. Along the way are boyfriends, first kisses, parties, and best friends.

Gentle Criteria: This is a fascinating book that will be enjoyed on many levels by readers. Mia's love for her grandfather and her belief that his soul lingers on in her cat Mango make it especially heart wrenching when her cat dies. Mia's best friend Jenna's mother has passed away, but she left Mia's mother presents to pass on to Jenna every year on her birthday. And her grandmother, whom she never knew, leaves her a legacy that takes her completely by surprise.

109   Matthews, L. S. *Fish.*

Random House, 2004, ISBN 978-0-385-90217-5; 2006, pap., ISBN 978-0-440-42021-7. 183p. • Grades 5–9

☞ ACCELERATED READER ☞ READING COUNTS

Tiger's parents have been giving medical aid to the villagers. The country is threatened with war and the fighting is headed toward them, so they pack up and head for the border and a safer country. Before leaving, Tiger finds a fish helplessly floundering in a dried-up mud hole. His mom lets him put the fish in a pot that he ties to the donkey. Their guide leads them to the border, but they are not permitted through. They must go through a mountain pass to reach the border. When they get stuck in mud crossing a river and lose the fish pot, they put the fish in a water bottle. They encounter dangerous rebels who plan to use

Tiger and his family as hostages. They barely escape, and now the water bottle is cracked. They are running out of options for getting the fish to safety.

Gentle Criteria: Tiger grows up quickly living in an impoverished village where his parents treat the starving and war-injured population. He always makes new refugees feel welcome, but even he notices that some are too shocked to join in. The reader might find it ludicrous that Tiger takes on the responsibility of transporting a fish safely across the mountain. But as the mountain guide said, "You are who you are, so of course you'll do what you do." Meaning: Like his father, Tiger has a caring heart.

110　Mazer, Harry. *The Wild Kid.*
Simon & Schuster, 1998, ISBN 978-0-689-80751-0; 2000, pap., ISBN 978-0-689-82289-6. 103p. • Grades 5–9
☞ Accelerated Reader ☞ Reading Counts

Twelve-year-old Sammy has Down syndrome. When Sammy says a naughty word about his mom's boyfriend, they make him stay out on the front porch until he is ready to apologize. He doesn't want to apologize, so he gets on his bike and rides to the grocery store. He forgets to lock his bike and sees someone steal it. He chases after the thief, and then hitches a ride on a truck without the driver's knowledge. When the truck driver hears him, he chases him off the truck, and Sammy crawls under a guard rail and slides down a steep hill. Sammy is now face to face with K-man, who ties him up. K-man has been in foster homes and has decided he would rather live on his own in the wilderness than go back to foster care. If he lets Sammy go, Sammy might tell, and K-man might be sent back to foster care. What will he do with Sammy?

Gentle Criteria: Sammy's mother tries to emphasize appropriate behavior by giving him a time-out on the porch. She would probably have reconsidered her strategy had she known Sammy was going to disappear for thirteen days. Although K-man is rough around the edges, he needs Sammy as much as Sammy needs him. The fact that K-man ends up caring for Sammy more each day proves that everyone needs companionship.

111　Meehl, Brian. *Out of Patience.*
Random House, 2006, ISBN 978-0-385-90320-2. 292p. • Grades 7–9
☞ Accelerated Reader ☞ Reading Counts ☞ Junior Library Guild

Jake wants nothing more than to get out of Patience, Kansas, but his father's dream is to open the first ATM (American Toilet Museum) in Kansas. A curse involving a toilet plunger and a map to riches has kept his family there for generations. Reminiscent of Louis Sachar's *Holes* (1998), this is both a modern-day story and a family legend from the 1800s. When his father finds the Plunger of Destiny on eBay and buys it, it looks as if the family curse has sprung to life. Interwoven in this story are amusing toilet history facts, twin tornadoes, small-town baseball, the first flushable toilet in Kansas, buried treasure, and much more. Along the way Jake learns that life isn't worth anything without a dream, but sometimes— instead of looking at the horizon—you only need to look under your nose to see what's right in front of you. These small-town people know that even good people do bad things sometimes, but if they band together—even with twin tornadoes spewing manure all over—their town can turn into a gold mine!

Gentle Criteria: Lots of positive themes exist in this book. Friendship, family, and small-town support all work together to bring about the happy ending in this humorous story.

112   Mills, Claudia. *Alex Ryan, Stop That!*
Farrar, Straus & Giroux, 2003, ISBN 978-0-374-34655-3; Disney, 2004, pap., ISBN 978-0-7868-5118-8. 152p. • Grades 5–8
ᕭ ACCELERATED READER ᕭ READING COUNTS ᕭ JUNIOR LIBRARY GUILD

Alex Ryan seems to open his mouth and automatically insert his foot. He can't keep from saying the wrong thing to Marcia, the girl he has a crush on. When Alex's dad embarrasses him during a field trip meeting, Alex reacts by pointing out Marcia's pimple, causing her to run from the room in tears. Alex's dad seeks attention at school events just as Alex seeks attention at school with his smart-mouth comments. During the camping trip Alex scares Marcia with his rattle and she runs into the woods, falls, and breaks her ankle. Alex and another friend must splint Marcia's ankle and carry her back to camp. Will Alex confess to his role in the injury or keep quiet as his father, from a lawyer's perspective, encourages him to do?

Gentle Criteria: This author knows how teens think. What makes this a gentle read is that Alex ignores his father's advice to keep silent about Marcia's accident. When Marcia's father wants to know why Alex does such pointless things like throwing toilet paper all over their trees and scaring her with a snake rattle, Alex says, "To show that I like her."

113   Mills, Claudia. *Lizzie at Last.*
Farrar, Straus & Giroux, 2000, ISBN 978-0-374-34659-1; Disney, 2002, pap., ISBN 978-0-7868-1672-9. 151p. • Grades 5–7
ᕭ ACCELERATED READER ᕭ READING COUNTS ᕭ JUNIOR LIBRARY GUILD

Lizzie spends seventh grade trying to figure out whether it is more important to be popular or smart and unique. Changing her thrift-store vintage look for outfits from the Gap, dumbing-down her responses in class, and giggling like Marcia are all things that work to make her popular, but they don't sit well with Lizzie. Lizzie used to write poetry, but now she finds she can't write a word. And

Ethan, her secret crush, is disgusted when he can't depend on her math abilities. Nothing is working out as she planned. She doesn't want to be "Lizzie the Lizard" anymore, but she is not happy this way either. Struggling to find out who she really wants to be, Lizzie realizes that people like people who feel good about themselves. It's okay to feel unsure as long as it doesn't keep you from trying new things. When she discovers that her new friend Allison would also rather practice music than go to the football game, Lizzie is on her way to being herself again.

Gentle Criteria: Lizzie goes through typical middle-school worries about fitting in and figuring out who she really wants to be. When she hides from her father because a classmate makes fun of him, she is ashamed for not standing up for him. She becomes tired of trying to fit in, and wears her beloved white dress to the dance to suit herself. She finds that a nerd isn't a thing you are, it's a thing other people call you. Her writing ability returns when she is once again true to herself.

114   Mills, Claudia. *Makeovers by Marcia.*

Farrar, Straus & Giroux, 2005, ISBN 978-0-374-34654-6. 149p. •
Grades 5–7

☞ ACCELERATED READER ☞ READING COUNTS ☞ JUNIOR LIBRARY GUILD

Marcia is about to enter eighth grade. She is pretty and popular, and her biggest worry is the five pounds she gained over the summer because of a broken ankle. Alex Ryan, the boy she hopes will invite her to the school dance, caused the broken ankle when he scared her with a snake rattle. Marcia dreads the eighth-grade social studies class assignment because it is a service learning project at a local nursing home. Marcia can't imagine what she has in common with a bunch of old people who are getting ready to die. Little does she know that her talent with beauty and makeup will make her one of the most popular students at the nursing home. She begins to see the inner beauty that comes from many years of life, and she stops worrying so much about her own shallow problems. The crankiest old lady there is the one who gets Alex to invite Marcia to the dance!

Gentle Criteria: This book is a sequel to *Lizzie at Last* (see above). Marcia's art teacher presses her to do more than draw shallow beauties. Her French teacher, when confronted with an unflattering picture that Marcia has drawn of her, merely tells her that it is a good likeness but not a kind one. When Marcia draws the elderly people as they look but with their inner beauty shining, both teachers have accomplished their goal. And when Marcia chooses to stay by Mavis's side in the intensive care unit rather than go to the dance with Alex, she proves she has matured in her thinking. This is a gentle read about real beauty and making the right choices.

115 Morgan, Clay. *The Boy Who Spoke Dog.*

Dutton, 2003, ISBN 978-0-525-47159-2; Penguin, 2005, pap., ISBN 978-0-14-240343-3. 166p. • Grades 5–9

⌐ ACCELERATED READER ⌐ READING COUNTS

Jack is an orphan who has been selected by a ship's captain to become a cook's assistant. During a horrible storm, the captain calls for Jack to be thrown overboard with a life preserver, so he will survive if the ship wrecks. Jack washes up on shore and is soon befriended by a bunch of sheep dogs. This book is amazing to read. The sheep dogs have conversations, and the old wise one has told the sheep dogs all about humans. Fortunately for Jack, the sheep dogs protect him from a group of wild dogs called the Fangos. As Jack becomes more and more accustomed to the sheep dogs, he also becomes more and more like them. When Jack is finally rescued, will he remember that he is still human, or has he became too much of a dog to remember his human roots?

Gentle Criteria: This book gives insight into the sheep dogs. They are noble dogs that would never kill sheep. Their mission is to protect. Of course, they are carnivorous but they only eat sheep already killed by the Fangos. Even Jack notices the irony in this situation. The book deals with Jack's efforts to keep up hope that he will be rescued, but the reader understands when he finally accepts his situation and is happy to remain there with his dogs.

116 Morgan, Nicola. *Chicken Friend.*

Candlewick, 2005, ISBN 978-0-7636-2735-5. 148p. • Grades 5–8

⌐ ACCELERATED READER

Becca's parents have taken her and her two brothers out of public school and are now home-schooling them. They've moved out to the country so that her mother has more room for her inventions, and her father is less distracted with his writing. Becca's home-school project is to learn everything she can about chickens because they will soon be raising chickens on their farm. Becca is desperate for friends, and when two rough looking girls her age show up, Mel and Jazz, she goes to extremes to accommodate them. But Becca has a real crisis within because she knows she really isn't like Mel and Jazz, but she feels pressured to act like them. When Mel and Jazz talk her into having a birthday party, things really get out of hand. A small fire breaks out and her little brother Beech almost drowns getting water from the stream to put out the fire. And some boys bring booze to the party, leaving Becca with a lot of explaining to do.

Gentle Criteria: This book shows the peer pressure that challenges many young people. After the barn burns down, Becca realizes that she did all the wrong things just by not being herself. She learns that she should have stood up to Mel and Jazz, avoiding the serious problems that occurred. She also realizes that Mel and Jazz will have to accept her for who she is, otherwise, they aren't true friends.

117   Morgenstern, Susie Hoch. *Secret Letters from 0 to 10.*
Viking, 1998, ISBN 978-0-670-88007-2; Penguin, 2000, pap., ISBN
978-0-14-130819-7. 137p. • Grades 5–9
☞ ACCELERATED READER ☞ READING COUNTS

Ten-year-old Ernest leads a colorless life in Paris with his grandmother and her
friend Germaine. His father left him when he was one day old. Then Victoria
moves into the neighborhood and changes his life. She immediately announces
that they will marry someday and becomes his best friend. She takes him to her
house (full of her 13 siblings), comes over to his house so he can help her catch
up with her schoolwork, and makes Ernest begin to talk to people. Ernest discovers a book with his father's picture under the author's name. Has he finally
discovered where his father is? Will Victoria's family be able to decode the letter
he has from his grandfather? Readers will have fun watching rambunctious Victoria's family change Ernest's life and will be happily satisfied with the ending.

   Gentle Criteria: The messages in this book are great ones. It is never too
late to learn to live, to forgive, and to become a part of life. When Germaine has
a heart attack and Ernest's grandmother says she does not have the strength to
take care of everything, Ernest simply looks at her and says, "then we'll share
mine." When his father begs his forgiveness, he gladly gives it. As Ernest and
Victoria agree, nobody is the same as everybody else, and everybody is the same
as everybody else. Everyone has love to share, and sharing it can be wonderful!

118   Morpurgo, Michael. *Kensuke's Kingdom.*
Scholastic, 1999, ISBN 978-0-439-38202-1; 2004, pap., ISBN 978-0-
439-59181-2. 164p. • Grades 5–9
☞ ACCELERATED READER ☞ READING COUNTS ☞ JUNIOR LIBRARY
GUILD

When Michael's parents lose their jobs at the brick factory, they take their sever-
ance pay, sell their car, and buy a boat to sail around the world. Between Aus-
tralia and Japan, Michael and his dog are swept out to sea and end up on an
island. When Michael and his dog are thirsty and hungry, water and dried fish
mysteriously appear. Now Michael knows he's not alone. When he builds a fire
hoping for rescue, a Japanese man runs out shouting "Dameda," and stamps out
the fire. He also draws the island in the sand and shows Michael where his half
of the island is and to stay on it. When the man tells him not to go swimming,
Michael defies him, unaware he is being warned him about jellyfish in the water.
Michael gets stung, but the man rescues him and nurses him back to health.
They become friends, but can Michael convince him to leave the island and
search for his family?

   Gentle Criteria: Kensuke, the Japanese man, teaches Michael how to
paint, and in return Michael teaches the former Navy doctor how to speak English. Kensuke is certain that all of Nagasaki was destroyed, so he has no reason to

leave the island. Kensuke says that a bad boat comes to the island to shoot adult gibbon monkeys and take their young, so he must stay to protect them. But he finally understands Michael's desire to return home and prepares a bonfire to alert rescuers. The ending of this book is very emotional.

119   Napoli, Donna Jo. *North.*
HarperCollins, 2004, ISBN 978-0-06-057988-3; 2006, pap., ISBN 978-0-06-057989-0. 344p. • Grades 5–7
⟳ ACCELERATED READER ⟳ READING COUNTS

Great adventure! Twelve-year-old Alvin travels by himself without anyone's permission to the Arctic Circle. Alvin lives in Washington, D.C., with his over-protective mother. His personal hero is Matthew Henson, the African American explorer who went to the North Pole with Admiral Peary. When his mother refuses to even let him walk to school by himself, and his teacher starts talking about primary research, Alvin decides to go to the North Pole. He takes the train from Washington, D.C., to New York, from New York to Toronto, from Toronto to Winnipeg, and on up to the Arctic Circle. Along each leg of the journey he meets a stranger who is willing to help him. He almost freezes to death on a freight train but saves himself with plastic wrap, sleeps in an igloo, survives being lost in a blizzard, rides on a dog sled, eats walrus stew, and learns how much he is capable of. There are some major themes here about learning to live in the world, about needing other people, and about what a journey life is.

Gentle Criteria: In this survival story Alvin learns how much we all need other people. Love for the world, the need for other people, and what is truly important in life are all major themes in this book.

120   Nolan, Han. *A Face in Every Window.*
Harcourt, 1999, ISBN 978-0-15-201915-0; Penguin, 2001, pap., ISBN 978-0-14-131218-7. 264p. • Grades 7–9
⟳ ACCELERATED READER ⟳ READING COUNTS

JP's grandma Mary always took care of the family, and when she dies, the family begins to unravel. JP's mildly retarded father and sickly mother are now in charge. When his mom wins a large farmhouse in a contest and allows all of the community's misfits to move in, life becomes chaotic. Although JP's safe haven is now gone, he learns to get along with all kinds of different characters and grasps what is really important in life.

Gentle Criteria: This story is a gentle read about tolerance, acceptance, and love. JP finds the good in people, but more importantly finds the good in himself. Although some of the misfits in the book are of questionable character to the community (a former drug user, an abused child, a gay couple, and others), JP finds they all have redeeming qualities. He comes to care for them as part of his extended family.

121   Nye, Naomi Shihab. *Habibi: A Novel.*
Simon & Schuster, 1997, ISBN 978-0-689-80149-5; 1999, pap., ISBN
978-0-689-82523-1. 259p. • Grades 7–9
⁓ ACCELERATED READER ⁓ READING COUNTS

This is a story of friendship between enemies. Fourteen-year-old Liyana Abboud
and her family move from St. Louis to Jerusalem, where her Palestinian father
was born. They find life there very different after the freedom of the United
States. Brought up to believe that all religions have good points, and that the
world is full of good people just waiting to be met, Liyana has a hard time dealing with the anger all around her. But she and her brother manage to make
friends anyway—with a brother and sister from the refugee camp, with the
Armenians at their school, and with all of the Palestinian relatives they meet.
When young romance kindles between Liyana and a Jewish boy, the family's
beliefs of equality and peace are put to the test with positive results.

   Gentle Criteria: There are some bad moments in this realistic book. A
Jew tells Liyana that she should not be conversing with Armenians; her father, a
doctor, is put in jail for a day for trying to help a wounded refugee; and Liyana is
not positive that her father's family will welcome her boyfriend with open arms.
But this family's belief that all religions have their shining moments and that all
people are worth meeting makes the world a more positive place.

122   O'Connor, Barbara. *How to Steal a Dog.*
Farrar, Straus & Giroux, 2007, ISBN 978-0-374-33497-0. 170p. •
Grades 5–7

Move over, Opal Buloni. Here is a dog story in the style of *Because of Winn-
Dixie* (entry 59) that will change the way the world looks at itself. Georgina's
family has fallen upon hard times. Her father has left the family, and her mother
can't pay the rent. They are forced to live in their car while her mother works
two jobs. Georgina must take care of her little brother and get them to school
and back, all without letting anyone know they no longer live at their old
address. When Georgina sees a reward sign offering five hundred dollars for a
missing dog, she gets the idea of stealing a dog and then collecting the reward
that would surely be offered. But the big house she steals the dog from is not
what she thinks, and the people she meets along the way show her that the trail
she leaves behind is more important than the path ahead.

   Gentle Criteria: This is a heartwarming and sympathetic portrayal of a
young girl who is trying to make a decent life for her family. Just as Opal tries to
find the best in people, Georgina makes observations about the people she comes
in contact with and debates whether her efforts to steal a dog are really making
lives better or not. Georgina knows stealing is not right. This story is about her
path toward figuring out what is more important—her bad situation or conduct-
ing a moral life. She reminds herself constantly of the Aesop fable that teaches
there is always someone worse off than you are.

123   O'Dell, Kathleen. *Agnes Parker . . . Girl in Progress.*

Dial, 2003, ISBN 978-0-8037-2648-2; Penguin, 2004, pap., ISBN 978-0-14-240228-3. 157p. • Grades 5–7

⁕ ACCELERATED READER

As Agnes enters sixth grade, she is determined to become a better version of the old Agnes, someone who stands up for herself, especially to that bully Niedermeyer. When Agnes gets glasses, and a new boy enters her class, life looks rosier. Agnes learns that she doesn't have to let people bully her and that she can make friends all on her own. Agnes slowly makes friends with Joe, who recently lost his mother to cancer. She starts to see other people's problems: Joe's, her classmate Pat Marie's, and even Niedermeyer's. When she reads a private note from Joe's book bag, she almost loses the friend she has worked so hard to make. Will the better Agnes be able to make things right? Readers will cheer Agnes on as she learns from a gruff teacher that good people respect other's feelings.

Gentle Criteria: Two main themes here are how to deal effectively with a bully and how to be a good friend. Mrs. Libonati, although gruff, gives her students lots of support. Agnes quietly stands up for the loneliest student in class by anonymously leaving the teacher a note. And Agnes meets someone with whom she can argue and have differences of opinion and still remain friends.

124   **Park, Linda Sue.** *Project Mulberry.*

Clarion, 2005, ISBN 978-0-618-47786-9. 225p. • Grades 5–7

⁕ ACCELERATED READER ⁕ READING COUNTS ⁕ JUNIOR LIBRARY GUILD

Julia and her best friend Patrick have been friends for years. They have done projects together and now want to win a blue ribbon at the state fair. When Julia's mother suggests they raise silkworms to produce silk thread, Patrick thinks it is a great idea but Julia doesn't. How can Julia tell Patrick that raising silkworms is too Korean for her? Julia is sensitive about her Korean American background; she wants to blend in, not emphasize her differences. Additionally, the only available mulberry tree (which the worms need) belongs to an African American man, and Julie's mother is prejudiced against black people, perhaps from her experiences with American soldiers in Korea. This is a subtle story about what it really means to be an American. A unique feature is the conversations between author and main character at the end of chapter about how the story is developing. They provide both insight and humor.

Gentle Criteria: This book is a treasure trove of themes, including prejudice, friendship, ethnic heritage, and science projects. It is a story about real friendship, and how friendship transcends barriers such as ethnicity and disagreements. Two good friends learn to work out their problems in a positive way.

125   Parkinson, Siobhan. *Something Invisible.*
Roaring Brook, 2006, ISBN 978-1-59643-123-2; Gardners Books, pap.,
ISBN 978-0-14-131883-7. 156p. • Grades 5–7
☞ ACCELERATED READER ☞ JUNIOR LIBRARY GUILD

Jake, an only child, and Stella, who comes from a huge family, become good
friends. Jake's mother is expecting a baby, which takes up all her attention, and
Jake is left to his own devices. He slowly finds himself being absorbed into Stella's family, a new experience for him as he has always been something of a loner.
Despite their many differences, the two become fast friends. When tragedy
strikes one of Stella's siblings, Jake takes the blame. Because he had the baby
Daisy in his arms, he hesitated to step in the way of the car and pull Joanne to
safety. How will he ever forgive himself?

Gentle Criteria: Jake learns how to love people even when you don't like
what they do; how to forgive people when they hurt you, and—most of all—how
to forgive yourself. The real gentleness of this story lies in everyone's love for
Jake, their forgiveness, and the ways in which they help him to forgive himself.

126   Patron, Susan. *The Higher Power of Lucky.*
Ill. by Matt Phelan. Atheneum, 2006, ISBN 978-1-4169-0194-5. 134p. •
Grades 5–7
☞ ACCELERATED READER ☞ READING COUNTS ☞ JUNIOR LIBRARY
GUILD

Lucky's father never wanted children, so when Lucky's mother dies from a
downed electrical line, he sends for his first wife to come take care of her.
Brigitte becomes Lucky's guardian, and they live in three connected trailers in
the desert. Lucky tries to figure out how to achieve her higher purpose because
she is afraid Brigitte will leave her and go back to France. Lucky decides that if
she runs away, Brigitte will miss her and adopt her. But on the day that Lucky
plans to leave, a five-year-old boy from town runs away, and she finds and cares
for him. They camp out in a cave, and Lucky worries what Brigitte will do
when she finds her.

Gentle Criteria: This book does contain some strong references, which
adults will want to consider before recommending the book to students. The
story presents a good lesson: family members need to keep lines of communication open and to avoid making assumptions. Lucky assumes that Brigitte plans to
abandon her because she sees a packed suitcase. But if Lucky had asked Brigitte,
she would have found out that Brigitte was taking Lucky to visit a judge so that
she could adopt Lucky.
🎗 NEWBERY MEDAL, 2007

127   Pattison, Caroline Rennie. *The Whole, Entire, Complete Truth.*
Dundurn Press, 2005, pap., ISBN 978-1-55002-583-5. 220p. •
Grades 7–9

When Sarah Martin's father moves her family to the country to get away from the hustle of the big city, she expects only boredom and grief over the loss of her friends. The last thing she expects is that her one new friend will lead her right into the middle of a crime ring. Now she is busy compiling a report to her detective father explaining how and why her disobedience helped him solve his big case. Bear poachers, new friends, boy–girl crushes, horse-riding lessons, and undercover officers are just a few of the exciting elements in this page-turner. Book clubs and classes will want to do their own research into the issue of bear poaching, but more than anything, they will want to find out who the bad guys are—and they are not who readers might expect. It's a great suspense and adventure story in which no one gets seriously hurt—not even the bears.

Gentle Criteria: One of the best parts of this book is Sarah's report to her father, with her side notes about her annoying, egomaniacal older brother (who she would protect from any harm). This is a story in which both adults and teenagers put themselves in possible danger to do the right thing—and the good guys win. Teenagers will relate to Sarah's frustration over being considered a mere child, and to her involvement in a just cause.

128 **Paulsen, Gary.** *Molly McGinty Has a Really Good Day.*

Random House, 2004, ISBN 978-0-385-90911-2; 2006, pap., ISBN 978-0-440-41482-7. 105p. • Grades 7–9

ᔰ Accelerated Reader ᔰ Reading Counts ᔰ Junior Library Guild

Molly McGinty, the most organized seventh-grader in the world, finds her life coming apart when she loses the notebook that keeps her together, and her unpredictable grandmother comes to spend the day with her at school. She gets a black eye, loses her clothes, and has an entire lunch tray spilled on her. Her grandmother teaches one of her classes, gets sent to the principal's office, makes friends with the detention set, and starts a conversation with Molly's secret crush. What an altogether stressful day! But the most important thing that happens to Molly is that she realizes she can get through the day without her notebook, that it is okay to go with the flow, and that every crazy thing her grandmother does is because she loves Molly. This is a satisfying, crazy, humorous family story.

Gentle Criteria: Molly, trying desperately to control her own and her grandmother's chaotic lives, discovers the strong thread of love coming from her grandmother that holds their life together. As is typical of a seventh-grader, she is totally embarrassed by her crazy grandmother while all her friends adore her and wish they could live with her. Each chapter begins with a wonderful thought from Molly's notebook, such as "Achievement, success and high levels of effectiveness are not determined by your genes" and "Misery is optional." Good words indeed.

129   **Paulsen, Gary.** *The Schernoff Discoveries.*
Delacorte, 1997, ISBN 978-0-385-32194-5; Random House, 1998, pap., ISBN 978-0-440-41463-6. 103p. • Grades 5–8
☞ ACCELERATED READER ☞ READING COUNTS

Fourteen-year-old Harold Schernoff is an intelligent nerd who believes there is a formula for everything. He talks his friend Gary into following his lead throughout the book, from enrolling in Home Economics class in order to meet girls, to learning how to ski, to becoming cool. There are real insights into the clumsiness of adolescence as these two stumble through life's amusing lessons.

Gentle Criteria: Author Paulsen is impressive in his ability to say things like, "the guy said nine words that he hasn't heard since listening to a drunk bowler," and get the idea across without saying the offending words. He raises many common teen issues, such as bullying and the opposite sex, and it all comes across in a humorous fashion.

130   **Pearsall, Shelley.** *All of the Above.*
Ill. by Javaka Steptoe. Little, Brown, 2006, ISBN 978-0-316-11524-7. 234p. • Grades 5–9

Mr. Collins is a math teacher at Washington Middle School who is at his wits' end thinking of a way to get his students excited about math. So he starts a math club that will attempt to break the world's record for building the largest tetrahedron (made up of 16,384 pieces). James Harris III joins after facing a choice between math club and detention. Rhondell joins because she thinks it will help her get into college. Sharice joins because she usually wanders the streets until her foster mother gets home, and it's better than sitting in the library. The club members soon form an extended family. When the tetrahedron is destroyed before completion, their parents help them to find the will to finish what they started.

Gentle Criteria: This book is based on a true story. It illustrates how underprivileged students work together and ignore the low expectations that others have of them. By spending time together, they learn much more than math—they learn to care about each other. Rhondell's concern leads Sharice to move to a loving foster home. James Harris III realizes that working on something constructive is better than hanging out with his brother's criminal friends.

131   **Perkins, Lynne Rae.** *Criss Cross.*
HarperCollins, 2005, ISBN 978-0-06-009273-3. 337p. • Grades 7–9
☞ ACCELERATED READER ☞ READING COUNTS ☞ JUNIOR LIBRARY GUILD

Debbie wants something good to happen to her. Hector feels unfinished and wants to *be* something. Lenny wants to change the childhood version his friends have of him. This is a story of teens living in and passing through a small town, their lives intersecting and failing to intersect on different occasions. They dream, mature, and search for love and a more grown-up life.

Gentle Criteria: This book is a sequel to *All Alone in the Universe* (1999). All of the teens in this story are trying to do a good job of growing up and becoming better people. Debbie tries to please her mom while clothes shopping, even though she dislikes her choices. Hector begins to take guitar lessons after seeing another side of his sister. The story is fresh, heartwarming, funny, and wry at times, with drawings and side comments. All of the teens make discoveries about themselves and other people that help them to mature.

🐝 NEWBERY MEDAL, 2006

132   Perkins, Mitali. *Monsoon Summer.*
Random House, 2004, ISBN 978-0-385-90147-5; 2006, pap., ISBN 978-0-440-23840-9. 257p. • Grades 7–9
⟿ ACCELERATED READER ⟿ READING COUNTS

Jazz finds out that her family is going to spend the summer in India. Jazz's mother wants to work at the orphanage that took care of her when she was abandoned as a baby. Her mother plans to help the orphanage open a center for pregnant women. Jazz has no interest in helping. And going means she will have to leave the business she runs with her best friend, with whom she is secretly in love. But as the summer unfolds, Jazz discovers many positive things—that she is considered beautiful in India even though this is not the case in America; that she has the same heart as her mother as she discovers how good it feels to give of oneself; and that her best friend also has feelings for her that he has kept secret. This is a wonderful novel about discovering oneself, other cultures, and what real beauty means.

Gentle Criteria: All the characters in this story are positive people. The issue of helping those who are less fortunate is addressed without being preachy. There is a trend now in many schools towards service learning, where each student in the school must volunteer a specified number of hours at a local organization as a way of giving back to the community. This book is a good way to promote the reasons behind service learning.

133   Peterson, P. J. *Rising Water.*
Simon & Schuster, 2002, ISBN 978-0-689-84148-4; 2003, pap., ISBN 978-0-689-86356-1. 120p. • Grades 5–9
⟿ ACCELERATED READER ⟿ READING COUNTS ⟿ JUNIOR LIBRARY GUILD

Kevin's father is always busy at night and Kevin is bored—so bored that he borrows an elderly man's car night after night, using his hidden magnetic key. When caught, instead of being sent to juvenile detention, Kevin is sent to work at an animal shelter. Siblings Luke and Tracy try to show him the ropes. Tracy sees Kevin as a project—just like some of the animals—and thinks maybe she can straighten him out. While on a rescue mission during a flood, the three teens must rely on each other when they encounter robbers. Luke is taken prisoner, and Tracy and Kevin must repair a broken boat if they are to have any chance of saving him.

Gentle Criteria: The reader gains insight into how teens think about themselves and others while reading Kevin's and Tracy's thoughts. Tracy and Luke are role models who risk their safety to rescue animals without expecting any monetary compensation. By the end of the book, their actions have influenced Kevin to change his behavior.

134   Philbrick, Rodman. *The Young Man and the Sea.*
Blue Sky, 2004, ISBN 978-0-439-36829-2; Scholastic, 2005, pap., ISBN 978-0-439-36830-8. 192p. • Grades 5–9
☞ ACCELERATED READER ☞ READING COUNTS ☞ JUNIOR LIBRARY GUILD

Skiffy's mother has died, and his father hasn't worked since her death, preferring to drown his sorrows in beer. To make matters worse, their boat, *The Mary Rose*, needs repairs. The only way Skiffy can raise the money is by catching a bluefin tuna. He sets off in his tiny skiff and soon finds himself in a mighty battle. Readers will be glued to the pages when the tuna pulls him under. Skiffy's disappearance brings his dad out of his stupor and reminds him that he needs to attend to his son's physical and emotional needs.

Gentle Criteria: Skiffy still hears his mother's advice in his head. When he decides to hunt the tuna, he remembers her three rules: think smart, speak true, and never give up. Rule three comes in handy when he gets tangled in his fishing line and is pulled underwater. Skiffy has put himself in this dangerous situation because he's determined to keep his promise to his mother to take care of his dad.

135   Ritter, John H. *The Boy Who Saved Baseball.*
Philomel, 2003, ISBN 978-0-399-23622-8; Penguin, 2005, pap., ISBN 978-0-14-240286-3. 216p. • Grades 5–7
☞ ACCELERATED READER ☞ READING COUNTS

The city of Dillontown is poised on the edge of change. Will it rush ahead into the future and let developers change it into just another cookie-cutter town, or will it hold onto its unique heritage and find another way to survive? The pressure is on when the man who holds the town's future in his hands hangs the decision on the local youth baseball game. Old town prophecies, baseball legends, and small-town characters abound in this entertaining story.

Gentle Criteria: Baseball fans young and old will enjoy this book. Not only is this a story about bringing back old traditions such as small-town baseball, but it is also a story about a community coming together and supporting each other. It promises a feel-good ending.

136   Rodowsky, Colby. *Not Quite a Stranger.*
Farrar, Straus & Giroux, 2003, ISBN 978-0-374-35548-7. 181p. •
Grades 7–9
⌒ ACCELERATED READER ⌒ READING COUNTS ⌒ JUNIOR LIBRARY GUILD

When Zach's mother dies, she leaves him information to find his father—who thought she gave Zach up for adoption. There is no mistaking the physical similarities between Zach and his father, and Zach is immediately welcomed into the lives of his father and his wife. Zach now has step-siblings. Brian is thrilled to have a big brother; Tottie, on the other hand, is angry and disappointed with her perfect father—how could he have done something like this? She also doesn't like losing her position as the oldest child. Alternating chapters told by Zach and Tottie reveal the fear, discomfort, and anger that the two young people feel. Zach is angry that his father was not there for him—even though he had no way of knowing Zach had not been given up for adoption—and that his new family shows no interest in his mom.

   Gentle Criteria: This book presents a realistic look at good people finding their way toward loving each other. Readers will be touched when Zach finally calls his father "Dad" instead of "the doctor." His father and new step-mom believe in doing the right thing and welcome Zach into their home. When Tottie confesses to Zach how she first felt about him, Zach is also able to share his anger with her, and they come to terms with each other. Readers are assured that this family will make it because it is full of love and acceptance.

137   Rodowsky, Colby. *That Fernhill Summer.*
Farrar, Straus & Giroux, 2006, ISBN 978-0-374-37442-6. 169p. •
Grades 5–9
⌒ ACCELERATED READER

Thirteen-year-old Kiara knows her father's side of the family very well, but her mother has always been silent about her family. If asked, she turns a funny color and refuses to speak. So it comes as a big surprise when Kiara is rushed off to visit the dying grandmother she has never known. She meets aunts, uncles, and cousins she didn't know she had. The biggest surprise occurs when grandmother Zenobia awakens from her coma. The three cousins decide to spend the summer with their ailing grandmother and get to know this cantankerous old woman. Kiara learns more about the family rift that kept her apart from these relatives. She wonders if it has to do with the fact that all her cousins are white while she is half black, but finds that it is much more complex. There is no trite, happy ending here, but a story of a family that learns to understand and accept.

Gentle Criteria: This is a warm story about a family coming to terms with itself. Zenobia, a difficult woman, loves her family although she refuses to show this in the ways they want. Thrown together, the cousins get to know each other and their heritage. Although the reader keeps expecting the racial makeup of Kiara's family to be the big problem, it actually has nothing to do with the rift in Zenobia's family. Instead, the break was caused by a daughter who wanted to make her own way in life.

138   Salisbury, Graham. *Lord of the Deep.*

Delacorte, 2001, ISBN 978-0-385-90013-3; 2003, pap., ISBN 978-0-385-72918-5. 182p. • Grades 5–9

☞ ACCELERATED READER ☞ READING COUNTS

Mikey's mom's new husband Bill is perfect. He is the Lord of the Deep. He takes people on chartered fishing trips, and Mikey is now old enough to help. Mikey soaks up every word Bill says, learning the trade so he can run his own boat when he grows up. But when Bill's charter guests talk down to him and toss their beer bottles into the ocean, Mikey wonders why Bill puts up with their bad behavior. To top it off, they plan to take credit for a fish that Mikey hooked—and Bill expects him to go along with it! Breaking this rule would bring lots of extra business to his step-dad as well as the promise of triple pay on tomorrow's outing. Will Mikey stick to his own rules and refuse to sign the record registration form, or will he understand that sometimes rules need to be broken? Can Mikey understand Bill's point of view that he has a family to feed?

Gentle Criteria: Mikey says he liked Bill from the start because he was the only boyfriend of his mother's who paid attention to him. Bill even took Mikey for a guys-only boat ride. Mikey also adores his step-brother, Billy Jay, who is blind. When Bill lets a charter crew bend the rules, Mikey must make an adult decision balancing putting food on the table against holding on to one's pride.

139   Schlitz, Laura Amy. *A Drowned Maiden's Hair: A Melodrama.*

Candlewick, 2006, ISBN 978-0-7636-2930-4. 389p. • Grades 5–9

☞ ACCELERATED READER ☞ JUNIOR LIBRARY GUILD

Maud is an orphan who is adopted by three old ladies who want to use her in their flim-flam operation scamming the grieving. Maud likes Hyacinth and follows her directions in return for occasional conditional love. She soon finds out that Hyacinth is actually training her to deceive people during seances. During a seance in which they are tricking Mrs. Lambert, the house catches fire. Anna, the deaf and dumb maid, is the only one who tries to go back in to save Maud. Maud then tells Mrs. Lambert about the scam. After initial anger, Mrs. Lambert helps Anna heal, and they both go and retrieve Maud once again from the orphanage. Maud has finally found someone who loves her for herself.

Gentle Criteria: When Maud first meets Anna, otherwise known as Muffet, she is appalled by the noises Anna makes and her dragging step when she walks. But Maud spends a lot of time with Anna, helps her learn to read, and comes to realize that Anna cares for her and that she loves Anna. It is great to see Maud move from revulsion to love.

140   Schmidt, Gary D. *First Boy.*
   Henry Holt, 2005, ISBN 978-0-8050-7859-6. 197p. • Grades 5–9
   ☞ Accelerated Reader ☞ Reading Counts ☞ Junior Library Guild

When both his grandparents die, fourteen-year-old Cooper Jewett is left to run the dairy farm that he loves. With the help of neighbors, he might be able to make a go of it. But the workload is heavy and there are strange events that seem linked to his past. He looks through his grandfather's files and finds a birth certificate with his parents' names blacked out. When a large black limo starts to follow him, and the President of the United States has her men detain him, Cooper starts to question whose "first boy" he really is.

   Gentle Criteria: Although there are unpleasant events in this book, such as the death of his grandparents who are his only guardians, and some bad-tempered bodyguards, this is a down-to-earth story about a boy, the people who love him, and their love for the New Hampshire countryside and farming. Simple, old-fashioned love and down-to-earth values triumph in this uplifting story about finding out where your real home is.

141   Schumacher, Julie. *Grass Angel.*
   Delacorte, 2004, ISBN 978-0-385-90163-5; Random House, 2005, pap., ISBN 978-0-440-41923-5. 196p. • Grades 5–9
   ☞ Accelerated Reader ☞ Reading Counts ☞ Junior Library Guild

Frances and Everett live alone with their mother, Anna, who is an English teacher. Their father died a few years before. Their mother attends different churches, looking for something that is missing in her life. Frances's Aunt Blue doesn't get along with Anna and visits every Sunday while Anna is at church. When Anna decides to spend the summer at an Oregon spiritual retreat with Everett, Frances decides to stay with Aunt Blue. At day camp, some boys tell Frances that her mother has joined a cult, and Frances worries she will never return. Then Everett runs away and everyone joins forces to find him. His escapade opens the lines of communication and turns out to be the best thing he could have done to bond the whole family.

   Gentle Criteria: This is a story of a family trying to move forward while dealing with loss. Frances and her brother lie awake at night trying to remember their dad. Anna is searching to fill the void left by the death of her husband. And, like any teen, Frances lets her imagination gets the best of her. Fortunately, she has an aunt who can guide her through rocky times. Her aunt is empathetic and flexible. When Frances seeks information about the religious retreat her mom is attending, a librarian comments that religion's purpose is to help us make sense of what we can't understand. Frances also has good friends who help her understand why her mother would abandon her for a summer to attend a religious retreat. Frances finds out that sometimes life gives us things we can't plan for or argue our way out of, so we take comfort where we can. Powerful stuff indeed.

142   Schwartz, Virginia Frances. *4 Kids in 5E and 1 Crazy Year.*
Holiday House, 2006, ISBN 978-0-8234-1946-3. 265p. • Grades 5–7
⌐ ACCELERATED READER

This is the story of one inspiring year in a New York City classroom. The mayor has stopped funding for reading teachers, so parents and teachers rally to provide one more teacher for the students who need extra help. In the classroom of this great teacher, hope becomes a reality. Reminiscent of Codell's *Sahara Special* (entry 43), this book shows the tremendous possibilities that are waiting to be found in each student. As each character makes observations about the other, readers learn that all of these children are bright but face many problems. As Willie so eloquently observes, "Writers write to untangle the knots in their hearts." This class becomes a family as they help each other learn to read and write.

Gentle Criteria: Although each character has his own set of family problems, each also has a strong adult at home who wants nothing but the best for him. Watching the characters grow, both educationally and emotionally, will warm readers' hearts. Teachers might find this a useful book to explore the personality of their own classes with students. Resources included.

143   Shafer, Audrey. *The Mailbox.*
Delacorte, 2006, ISBN 978-0-385-90361-5. 178p. • Grades 5–9
⌐ ACCELERATED READER ⌐ READING COUNTS ⌐ JUNIOR LIBRARY GUILD

Gabe was in and out of foster care all his life until his long-lost uncle was found. He loves living with his uncle. But one day he comes home from school to find his uncle dead. He doesn't want to return to foster care, so he pretends his uncle is still alive. This isn't hard to do as his Vietnam veteran uncle was such a grump that most people left him alone. Then Gabe returns home to find his uncle's body is missing. There is a note saying, "I will keep your secret." Gabe is scared until he arrives home the following day and finds a dog. Gabe continues his secret life and his letters to the writer of the note until someone finally discovers his uncle's body. Will Gabe be returned to foster care? This is a book that shares a lot of emotion.

Gentle Criteria: Smitty, the note writer, is also a reclusive Vietnam veteran. He served with Gabe's uncle during the war and now works for a funeral home. It was Smitty who removed Gabe's uncle's body. Gabe finds out that there are many people who care for him and want to help him. Readers' hearts will be warmed when Gabe ends up with someone who needs him as much as he needs a real home.

144   Shearer, Alex. *Sea Legs.*

Simon & Schuster, 2003, ISBN 978-0-689-87143-6; 2006, pap., ISBN 978-0-689-87144-3. 309p. • Grades 5–7

⌒ Accelerated Reader ⌒ Reading Counts ⌒ Junior Library Guild

Twin brothers Clive and Eric are tired of their father leaving to work on luxurious cruise ships for weeks at a time while they are forced to stay home with their boring grandparents. They decide to stow away on the ship and succeed in enjoying two adventurous weeks aboard the luxury liner—seeing the pyramids of Egypt, outwitting pirates, saving lives, and recovering valuables—all the while evading their father

Gentle Criteria: Clive and Eric experience a physical and emotional journey. Although they are tired of their father being away, by the end of the adventure they understand his attraction to the sea. When they encounter pirates and are in a position to save a man's life, they remind themselves that this is real life and that you don't get to replay it, just as they can't bring their mother's life back. How their father manages to end up working closer to home is the best part of all.

145   Shulman, Polly. *Enthusiasm.*

Putnam, 2006, ISBN 978-0-399-24389-9. 198p. • Grades 7–9

⌒ Accelerated Reader

This author is oh so clever! Shulman has taken Jane Austen's *Pride and Prejudice* and adapted it as an entertaining story about two high school girls seeking love and adventure. Ashleigh, Miss Enthusiasm, is always immersing her unsuspecting best friend Julie in her latest craze. In this case, it's Jane Austen. Ashleigh decides they should crash the annual formal dance at the local boys' prep school. There they meet two boys and confusion ensues about who really loves whom. After many mishaps and misunderstandings, true love reigns supreme. Readers looking for a light and entertaining romance will find it herein.

Gentle Criteria: This is a light story about two teen girls looking for their first kiss and true love. In an underlying story line Julie comes to understand why her parents divorced, and she gets to know her stepmother better. The parents in this story do discuss birth control when they see their daughter beginning to date. Book clubs and English teachers will have fun pointing out the similarities between Jane Austen's book, this story, and real life!

146   Smith, Greg Leitich. *Ninjas, Piranhas, and Galileo.*

Little, Brown, 2003, ISBN 978-0-316-77854-1; 2005, pap., ISBN 978-0-316-01181-5. 179p. • Grades 5–7

This book is a romantic comedy with underlying themes about honor and family. Shohei, Elias, and Honoria have been a trio for years. Honoria has a crush on Shohei. When she enlists Elias's help to get Shohei interested in her romantically, she doesn't realize that Elias has a crush on her. What is Elias to do except be a good friend and help her get together with Shohei? In the meantime, Elias has convinced Shohei to team up with him on the important science fair project. When he decides to simply duplicate his older, idolized brother's project, he realizes that his brother faked the results. Will he admit what his brother did, and let his friend know? Will Honoria ever realize who it is that really cares for her? It's a light story filled with fun, as well as providing a good exercise in how to make decisions in life.

Gentle Criteria: This is a tender story about three good friends entering the stage of their lives where they want more than just friendship. These three smart friends make the right decisions but not without some entertaining angst along the way.

147 Sonnenblick, Jordan. *Drums, Girls and Dangerous Pie.*
Scholastic, 2006, ISBN 978-0-439-75519-1; pap., ISBN 978-0-439-75520-7. 273p. • Grades 7–9

When Steven's younger brother is diagnosed with leukemia, he has a hard time dealing with his emotions. He goes through the typical stages: bargaining, anger, and depression. He also has some wonderful people in his life who help him and his family. His counselor teaches him to deal with the things in life that he *can* change. His drum teacher offers him free lessons when Steven says he can no longer afford to pay because of his brother's extraordinary medical expenses. The All-City Band finds out about his brother's illness and stages a benefit concert that earns $30,000 for Steven's family. A friend helps Steven to understand that the most important thing he can do for his brother is to be there for him. Readers see Steven become a strong young man.

Gentle Criteria: This is a story of love and support within a family, a peer group, and caring outside adults. It also includes many humorous moments. Teachers, friends, neighbors, and relatives all stand by Steven and his family. The best part of the story is watching Steven become the man he is meant to be. He learns who his real friends are, and he learns to take responsibility for what he is able to do.

148 Spinelli, Jerry. *Eggs.*
Little, Brown, 2007, ISBN 978-0-316-16646-1. 220p. • Grades 5–9
While on an Easter egg hunt, David discovers an egg on top of a buried girl's body. Since his mother recently died, he's not too shocked by what he finds, but

when he sees the same girl at the library the next day, he screams! It turns out she was just having some fun. Nine-year-old David and thirteen-year-old Primrose are from broken homes. David's mother slipped on a wet floor at work and died. Primrose's mother is a fortune teller and doesn't know where her father is. Although David and Primrose fight like brother and sister, they depend on each other to get through the sorrow they feel in their lives. As time passes and they grow closer, they are able to move toward the future.

Gentle Criteria: This is a great book for kids whose lives are not perfect; they will appreciate seeing how the characters in this book cope. When David talks about the voices of his grandma, father, Primrose, and John, he states that all of their words for a thousand years cannot fill the hole left by his mother, but they can raise a loving fence around it so he doesn't keep falling in. It's a touching book that shows how tough it is for kids to cope when they're missing a loved one.

149   Stanley, Diane. *A Time Apart.*
HarperCollins, 1999, ISBN 978-0-688-16997-8; 2001, pap., ISBN 978-0-380-81030-7. 263p. • Grades 7–9
⌒ ACCELERATED READER ⌒ READING COUNTS ⌒ JUNIOR LIBRARY GUILD

When Ginny's mother finds out she has cancer and must undergo months of treatment, she decides to send Ginny to visit her father in London. Not only is her father someone Ginny has rarely seen, he is also now overseeing an Iron Age archaeological experiment. This means that Ginny is to be plucked from her comfortable home to live in a straw-thatch hut, a community under one roof. Over the months they grow close, and Ginny learns that everyone has wounds they carry around, and that sometimes laughter can ease your grief. Battling rats, using urine to set dye, and watching livestock being butchered all change her perspective on life. When she escapes to go see her mother, she learns how much her father cares for her and still cares about her mother.

Gentle Criteria: Not only is this a fascinating story about how Iron Age people lived, but it is also a look at how people have grown so used to modern conveniences. Ginny experiences the love of her father and she learns that she is capable of being self-sufficient. Her father's respect for her cooking and pottery making in an Iron Age situation is a maturing and gratifying experience.

150   Swallow, Pamela Curtis. *It Only Looks Easy.*
Henry Holt, 2003, ISBN 978-0-7613-2866-7. 168p. • Grades 5–9
⌒ ACCELERATED READER ⌒ READING COUNTS

Kat Randall has high hopes for seventh grade, but before the first day is over the year appears to be ruined. Her beloved dog Cheddar is hit by a car driven by a confused elderly woman with Alzheimer's. Kat is so worried about her dog that she leaves school without permission, takes a bike that doesn't belong to her, and rides to the vet's office. While she is checking on her dog the bike is stolen. Now what is she going to do? In trouble with her parents, with the owner of the bike, and with the police, things quickly go from bad to worse. More bikes are stolen and Kat is the prime suspect. When she befriends the woman with Alzheimer's and a pesky girl named Grace, things start to turn around, and Kat discovers that it only looks easy for everyone else.

Gentle Criteria: Kat's one bad decision has lasting consequences. She observes that when people think you are a juvenile delinquent it's like having slime all over your name. Her dad tells her that it is up to her to pull her reputation out of the sewer. Lessons about reputation, doing the right thing, and finding out who your real friends are run through this book.

151   Tarshis, Lauren. *Emma-Jean Lazarus Fell Out of a Tree.*
Dial, 2007, ISBN 978-0-8037-3164-6. 199p. • Grades 5–7
☞ JUNIOR LIBRARY GUILD

Emma-Jean takes after her logical father, who recently passed away, and she has trouble understanding her emotional, irrational classmates. When she comes upon Colleen sobbing in the bathroom, Emma-Jean surprises herself by offering assistance. Although her logical solution solves the problem, it is not without consequences. When Will's teacher accuses him of stealing candy, she once again solves the problem, writing a letter to Will's uncle's dealership about the problems his teacher is having with his car. Emma-Jean can clearly see the solutions to other people's problems but not the emotions behind them. She allows herself to cry twice a year, once on her father's birthday and once on the anniversary of his death. When her mother gently tells her how her birth gave her father the freedom to connect with other people, Emma begins to understand. But it is when Vakram's mother mends her precious quilt that Emma really begins to heal and understand that it is her relationships with other people that will bring joy to her life.

Gentle Criteria: This book will take readers by surprise and bring them to tears. Emma-Jean's father's has a favorite quote from famous mathematician and logician Poincaré: "It is by logic that we prove, but it is in our hearts that we discover life's possibilities." Emma finds out that she is more like other people than she thinks. A priest tells her that when people annoy him, he goes out of his way to do something nice for them, and it ends up brightening his world. Emma finally admits to herself that she will always be without her father, and she begins to allow herself to heal.

152   Tashjian, Janet. *The Gospel According to Larry.*
Henry Holt, 2001, ISBN 978-0-8050-6378-3; Random House, 2003, pap., ISBN 978-0-440-23792-1. 227p. • Grades 7–9
☞ ACCELERATED READER ☞ READING COUNTS ☞ JUNIOR LIBRARY GUILD

Josh wants to make a difference in the world. He starts a Web site and publishes sermons under the fake name of Larry. Josh uses his sermons to express his unconfessed feelings for Beth and to bash his stepfather's work in advertising. At one point, the famous rock group U2 notices his Web site and puts on a huge concert in support of his beliefs. Josh is ecstatic—he now feels he is making a change in the world. Unfortunately, his secret identity is eventually revealed and his stepdad is livid. Beth is also upset with him, and his life is thrown into the spotlight of a media circus. Josh finally realizes that he has expressed his mental thoughts but not his heartfelt thoughts, so he fakes his own death and then writes a book that describes his feelings. This is so that he can move forward with changing the world one life at a time instead of all at once.

Gentle Criteria: This book is a gentle read because Josh's stepfather remembers Josh's mom by visiting her grave. Josh remembers his mom by visiting the makeup counter at Bloomingdale's, one of her favorite places to shop. He sits there, remembers her by the smells, and talks to her. He accepts whatever the next person says as his mother's response. When he hears a shopper say, "I could just kill myself," Josh realizes what he must do. He must fake his own death so the media circus will end and he can get on with his life. He's finally realized that one should change the world by starting with oneself.

153   Timberlake, Amy. *That Girl Lucy Moon.*

Hyperion, 2006, ISBN 978-0-7868-5298-7. 294p. • Grades 5–8
⤐ ACCELERATED READER ⤐ READING COUNTS

In elementary school, Lucy Moon was a force to behold. She wore a woven hemp hat to support Third World workers and stuffed anti-hunting literature in lunches sold at the bakery. Now rich old lady Wiggins has put a fence around the town's only sledding hill. Lucy, now in middle school, starts a postcard campaign to get Mrs. Wiggins to remove the fence, but she ends up getting detention, a lot of students in trouble, and retribution from her classmates. To make matters worse, her mother has decided to go on the road with her photography job and leave Lucy with her dad, whom she feels she barely knows. As a result of all the stress, Lucy starts losing her passion for life. The whole town notices something isn't right. The students start wearing hats in support of Lucy, and her friends and dad try to cheer her up. The passionate Lucy is back and ready to take on the battle to reclaim the sledding hill. This time, she is not alone in her crusade.

Gentle Criteria: Adults should read this book before recommending it. Mature parts include Lucy describing what the kids in junior high are doing— "When teachers turn their backs, notes about who likes whom traveled palm to palm, and books with dog-eared pages describing people 'doing it' were read under the lips of desks." Lucy Moon, through her steadfast fight for just causes, changes the way students act, teaching them through example how to question authority.

154 **Tolan, Stephanie S.** *Listen!*

HarperCollins, 2006, ISBN 978-0-06-057936-4. 197p. • Grades 5–8

⌒ ACCELERATED READER

Charley is having a rough life; her mother died in a plane crash two years ago. Nine months ago, Charley was in a car accident. Her friends were fine, but Charley ended up in a coma and is now learning to walk again. Her father has lost patience and insists that she go outside and practice walking so she'll be ready to go back to school in the fall. While walking, Charley comes across a skinny, shy dog she names Coyote. She sees something in his eyes and feels that she can tame the wild beast. The two walk every day along with the neighbor's dog. After forty days of baby steps and buckets of liver, Coyote finally lets Charley touch him. She realizes that Coyote has done as much for her as she has done for him. She learns that she has to get on with life and trust in people.

Gentle Criteria: Charley has not visited the wooded area where her mother died. While walking Coyote, however, she is forced to go that way because Coyote avoids roads. Charley finally understands what her mother meant by the word "Listen." Charley sees the beauty of the forest through her mother's eyes, and she takes time to listen to what's going on around her, hearing the insects, the wind, and the pitter-patter of the rain drops. Coyote helps Charley get over her anger at the loss of her mother.

155 **Tolan, Stephanie S.** *Surviving the Applewhites.*

HarperCollins, 2002, ISBN 978-0-06-623603-2; 2004, pap., ISBN 978-0-06-441044-1. 216p. • Grades 6–8

⌒ ACCELERATED READER ⌒ READING COUNTS ⌒ JUNIOR LIBRARY GUILD

Jake is sent to the Applewhite family's Creative Academy as a last resort after he is expelled from school for starting a fire and his parents end up in jail. Jake doesn't know how to act with the free-spirited Applewhites, who pay no attention to his black clothes, body piercings, and spiked hair. Destiny, the youngest, tries to emulate Jake with amusing consequences. Jake quickly finds out that there is nothing he can do to shock this bunch. As the grandfather kindly tells him, the parrot has a worse vocabulary than Jake—and in four or five languages. Aunt Lucille calls him a radiant light being, something no one else has ever called him. Jake concludes that his spiked hair is too much trouble to keep, and his black clothes are too hot. A production of the "Sound of Music" helps Jake find what brings joy to his heart, and this wonderfully amusing story comes to a heart-warming finish.

Gentle Criteria: This is a story about accepting differences. Jake is a person who needs the space and time to find out who he is, and the Applewhites provide this. When Jake starts to accept who he really is, he finds life has some great things in store.

🐾 NEWBERY HONOR BOOK, 2003

156 Umansky, Kaye. *The Silver Spoon of Solomon Snow.*

Candlewick, 2004, ISBN 978-0-7636-2792-8. 289p. Series: Solomon Snow • Grades 5–8

ᔐ Accelerated Reader ᔐ Reading Counts ᔐ Junior Library Guild

This is the first book in the Solomon Snow series. Ten-year-old Solomon Snow discovers that his parents found him on their doorstep with a silver spoon in his mouth bearing the initials V. I. P. He sets off to town to find the pawnshop and reclaim his inheritance. He is joined by another poor neighbor, Prudence, who wants a ride to town to get her book published. They bump into a spoiled circus brat named Prodigy, who has the charming ability to talk people into giving her rides, sweets, and money when she sings. The three are captured by a lady who plans to sell them. But a chimney sweep, Freddy, whom they've befriended, crawls down the chimney and saves them. They trace Solomon's silver spoon to an orphanage and set off to find Solomon's parents. However, when they show the parents the silver spoon, the parents run right past Solomon and hug Freddy. Solomon doesn't understand why they're hugging the wrong boy. This story offers an interesting and surprising ending.

Gentle Criteria: Solomon's parents are poor laundry workers, but Solomon has always had good manners and is always polite. Solomon teams up with abrupt Prudence, spoiled Prodigy, and smelly Freddy, but finds they all have positive characteristics that enable them to help one another. Circus-trained Prodigy can charm the socks off of anyone. Well-read Prudence can predict what will happen based on books she's read, and Solomon can keep the peace when the others argue. A feel-good story where the evil deeds are all corrected.

157 Van Draanen, Wendelin. *Flipped.*

Random House, 2001, ISBN 978-0-375-91174-3; 2003, pap., ISBN 978-0-375-82544-6. 212p. • Grades 5–7

ᔐ Accelerated Reader ᔐ Reading Counts

In this charming romance, two eighth-graders tell, in alternating chapters, how they feel about each other. Julianna has been head-over-heels in love with Bryce since the second grade. Now she has become disillusioned with him. Bryce, on the other hand, has finally noticed how wonderful Julianna is. This is a wonderfully entertaining example of how two people can think they know everything about each other but have no idea how the other person really feels.

Gentle Criteria: This is an entertaining book that language arts teachers can use to show viewpoint or voice. The alternating chapters show in gentle ways how people fail to communicate with each other. The romance is innocent, with both characters realizing that there is more to a real relationship than just good looks and infatuation.

158   Vega, Denise. *Click Here.*

Little, Brown, 2005, ISBN 978-0-316-98560-4; pap., ISBN 978-0-316-98559-8. 215p. • Grades 5–9

ACCELERATED READER   READING COUNTS

Erin Swift has only one friend, the popular Jillian Hennessey. Erin is upset beyond words when she realizes their junior high schedules are different. Erin describes all her problems at school in her computer blog. One problem is that she feels like she always has to accommodate Jillian. Another is that she has met Mark and wants to keep him away from Jillian. She is also dueling with Serena; Serena calls Erin Pinocchio and Jillian her puppet master. When Erin accidentally switches her diary disk with her school Intranet disk, everyone reads her blog. Now she has a lot of apologizing to do, hoping that her friends will forgive what she wrote about them.

Gentle Criteria: This author keeps it real by discussing issues that kids talk about, like breast size and name calling, without including bad language and without going beyond kissing. The story does a good job of showing the emotions of students this age and describing the daily ups and downs they face.

159   Vejjajiva, Jane. *The Happiness of Kati.*

Atheneum, 2003, ISBN 978-1-4169-1788-5. 139p. • Grades 5–7

ACCELERATED READER   READING COUNTS   JUNIOR LIBRARY GUILD

A strong young girl spends the last few weeks of her mother's life with her. Her mother has been battling Lou Gehrig's disease. When Kati arrives at her failing mother's house, she simply opens the car door and "lets her heart lead the way." As each chapter unfolds, she comes to understand why her mother has not been able to take care of her for the last five years. Her mother has decided not to be put on a respirator so that she can communicate with her loved ones to the last minute. This strong family provides its own hospice care for Kati's mother, each taking turns caring for her. They are not afraid to cry, and they allow Kati to do the same. The question of who Kati's father is and where he lives hangs in the air but is never discussed. When her mother leaves that information, along with many specially prepared memories for her to keep, Kati makes an unusual decision that will surprise everyone.

Gentle Criteria: This is a story of a strong loving family that decides to care for their loved one through the last days of her life. They give Kati the love and support that she needs to get through her mother's death and to hold her together in the future. Readers will learn about Lou Gehrig's disease, the stages of dying and of grief, and what the deep love and support of a family means.

160 Warner, Sally. *Sort of Forever.*

Random House, 1998, ISBN 978-0-679-98648-5; 1999, pap., ISBN 978-0-375-80207-2. 136p. • Grades 5–8

ᔆ ACCELERATED READER ᔆ READING COUNTS

Twelve-year-olds Cady and Nana have been friends practically since they were babies. Cady has always relied on Nana to be the leader, the adventurous one. Things change when Nana gets cancer and is no longer the strong leader. Cady, grieving for the Nana she used to know, must now be the funny, creative leader and must keep Nana going. Cady has to come to terms with her fear and anger and learn to set it aside. The story goes through Nana's hospice care and her death, and is very matter-of-fact about what the last stage of cancer is like. Cady and her family provide support to Nana and her family and realize that their wonderful memories of Nana will see them through once she is gone. One of the best memories is a toilet-papering escapade with wheelchair-bound Nana wearing her mother's extravagant hat.

Gentle Criteria: Nana had always been the strong one, easing the way for Cady. Now Cady must not only make her own way at school but must try to be a strong, good friend to Nana at home. This is a moving story about friendship and how to hold onto it in the midst of change. Nana is dearly loved, and will always be in the hearts of those who knew her.

161 Weeks, Sarah. *So B. It.*

HarperCollins, 2004, ISBN 978-0-06-623623-0; 2005, pap., ISBN 978-0-06-441047-2. 243p. • Grades 7–9

ᔆ ACCELERATED READER ᔆ READING COUNTS

Heidi It has lived all her life with a mother who speaks only twenty-three words and an agoraphobic neighbor who is afraid to leave her apartment. When Heidi's luck with the slot machines lands her some money, she buys a bus ticket to Liberty, New York, where she hopes to find her origins and perhaps more of her family. On her journey, Heidi discovers that if all you care about is the past, you will never catch up with the present.

Gentle Criteria: This story is about a girl's inspiring determination and her journey to find the true meaning of love.

162 Wiles, Deborah. *Each Little Bird That Sings.*

Harcourt, 2005, ISBN 978-0-15-205113-6; 2006, pap., ISBN 978-0-15-205657-5. 247p. • Grades 5–8

ᔆ ACCELERATED READER ᔆ READING COUNTS ᔆ JUNIOR LIBRARY GUILD

Comfort's best friend, Declaration, spent the summer with her grandmother and has come back to town a changed person. Declaration is trying to act like a lady now. Comfort's family runs a funeral home, and Comfort has attended 248 funerals. When her aunt dies, Comfort and Declaration are talked into caring for Peach, a toddler who Comfort swears ruined her uncle's funeral with his antics and vomiting. Then, when Peach climbs up into the casket with Aunt Florentine, Comfort is incensed that she has to care for the brat. While walking to the graveyard, Declaration says some hateful things about death to little Peach and scares him into the Oak Grove. When Comfort sides with Peach, Declaration leaves, and Comfort, Peach, and their dog, Dismay, are caught in a sudden flash flood. Comfort chooses to save her cousin over her beloved dog when a choice has to be made.

Gentle Criteria: Comfort displays the emotions all adolescents seem to have, especially when they have to care for unruly toddlers. Comfort is also at odds with her best friend, Declaration, who is trying to figure out where she fits in this world. When push comes to shove, however, it is refreshing to see that Comfort will stand by her little cousin and not only protect him from an insensitive Declaration, but also do whatever is necessary to save him from drowning.

163   Wiles, Deborah. *Love, Ruby Lavender.*
Harcourt, 2001, ISBN 978-0-15-202314-0; 2002, pap., ISBN 978-0-15-204568-5. 188p. • Grades 5–7
☞ Accelerated Reader

Ruby Lavender is forced to spend a summer without her favorite people when her grandfather dies in a car accident and her grandmother goes to Hawaii to spend time with her new grandchild. Ruby must deal with both the fear that the accident was partly her fault, and with her anger and grief. Told with alternating letters between the chapters, this book has a wonderful southern feel. Root-beer floats, raising chicks, and a new teacher moving into town all help Ruby come to terms with her life.

Gentle Criteria: Strong family characters—her grandmother, her now-dead grandfather, and her mother, who is the first female extension agent in her county—support and love this little girl.

164   Wittlinger, Ellen. *Gracie's Girl.*
Simon & Schuster, 2000, ISBN 978-0-689-82249-0; 2002, pap., ISBN 978-0-689-84960-2. 186p. • Grades 5–7
☞ Accelerated Reader ☞ Junior Library Guild

Bess is getting ready to enter middle school, and she is intent on making the right friends and getting on the popularity track at school. But her experiences at the shelter where her parents volunteer teach her that there are more important things in life than being popular. She knows that many people are just one step away from being in the position of these homeless people. An elderly woman named Gracie is the key to these realizations. When Bess and her brother and friends try to help Gracie survive, they have to face very real problems.

Gentle Criteria: Suburban teens reach beyond their privileged environments to help people who are less fortunate and they all become better people for their experiences.

165 Wolfson, Jill. *What I Call Life.*

Henry Holt, 2005, ISBN 978-0-8050-7669-1. 270p. • Grades 7–9
☞ ACCELERATED READER ☞ READING COUNTS ☞ JUNIOR LIBRARY GUILD

Cal Lavender likes her life just fine even if she does take care of her mom more than her mom takes care of her. When her mentally ill mom has an episode in the public library, Cal is whisked away to foster care. She passes the days waiting for the people in charge to agree that her mom is once again capable of looking after her. While waiting, she learns from the Knitting Lady's stories and from the other girls in foster care that family can mean many things and that everyone has a different story.

Gentle Criteria: Although there are some sad stories in this book (one girl is left in a bathroom as a newborn), it is truly about what family means. It is also about accepting people for who they are. The more the characters find out about the underlying reasons for poor actions, the more understanding they become.

166 Woods, Ron. *The Hero.*

Random House, 2002, ISBN 978-0-375-90612-1; 2003, pap., ISBN 978-0-440-22978-0. 215p. • Grades 5–8
☞ ACCELERATED READER ☞ READING COUNTS

Jamie and his older cousin Jerry build a raft. Jamie's parents caution them about not taking it down the river with its wild current. Of course, the two don't listen and end up on the river with the raft out of control. What's worse, they allow Dennis Leeper to come along. Dennis is desperate for friends and Jerry feels sorry for him. When tragedy occurs, Jamie is left to find a way to keep peace in the town. This is a fast-paced story that readers won't be able to put down.

Gentle Criteria: As Jamie's mother says, you can wish things were different but that doesn't change a thing. What has happened has already happened. Life has a way of showing what we are made of. This book reveals many ways in which one can define heroism. Is it trying to save someone in the water? Is it telling a lie to stop a grief-stricken father from lashing out? Or is it just quietly trying to get along in a small town? Adults can prompt many kinds of conversations with this book!

167 Wyss, Thelma. *Ten Miles from Winnemucca.*

HarperCollins, 2002, ISBN 978-0-06-029784-8. 129p. • Grades 5–8
☞ ACCELERATED READER ☞ READING COUNTS ☞ JUNIOR LIBRARY GUILD

Martin's father died when he was five years old. Eleven years later, his mom marries a rich man in Seattle, and Martin insists on driving his Jeep there. Shortly after arriving in Seattle, his mother leaves for a European honeymoon. Meanwhile, his stepbrother has thrown all of his clothes out the bedroom window and told him to get lost. Martin makes a hasty, immature decision to drive back to Winnemucca, Nevada, and runs out of gas and money in Red Rock, Idaho. Rather than admit defeat, he gets a job at a burger joint, enrolls in school, and lives out of his Jeep. He meets another student, Deantha Dragon, who decides that Martin will be her boyfriend. Martin makes it on his own in this small town until his mother returns from her honeymoon.

Gentle Criteria: Like so many impulsive teens, Martin makes a decision that could easily have put him in harm's way. The positive aspect of this story is that Martin doesn't belabor the bad things that happen to him, but rather works on a solution. He gets a job, enrolls in school, and even makes a few friends. He keeps remembering positive things from his past, and he knows he just has to persevere until his mom gets back; then everything will be all right.

168   **Yee, Lisa. *Millicent Min, Girl Genius.***
Arthur A. Levine, 2003, ISBN 978-0-439-42519-3; Scholastic, 2005, pap., ISBN 978-0-439-77131-3. 248p. • Grades 6–8
☞ ACCELERATED READER

Millicent Min is a child prodigy who has trouble making friends because she never hesitates to show how smart she is. Her parents reluctantly agree to let her take a college course, during which she discovers that college students can be as silly as her middle-school friends. She is sent against her will to a volleyball camp where she decides not to let anyone know how smart she is. But at the camp she begins to understand that in many ways she is just like everyone else—unsure and unsophisticated.

Gentle Criteria: Readers will laugh at Millicent's attempts to get through middle school. This is a story about every middle-school student's attempt to fit in; in this case it's the unique problems of a child who has a high I.Q. Companion books include *Stanford Wong Flunks Big-Time* and *So Totally Emily Ebers* (see below).

169   **Yee, Lisa. *So Totally Emily Ebers.***
Arthur A. Levine, 2007, ISBN 978-0-439-83847-4. 280p. • Grades 6–9
☞ ACCELERATED READER ☞ READING COUNTS

This companion book to *Millicent Min, Girl Genius* (see above) and *Stanford Wong Flunks Big-Time* (see below) deals with Emily Ebers's life and point of view. Emily's parents have decided to divorce. Her mother is an award-winning journalist and her father is an aging rock star with dreams of revitalizing his music career. Emily's mother researches the best places in America to raise children, and she and Emily move to the town where Millicent Min and Stanford Wong live. The story is told in the form of letters that Emily writes to her dad, letters never sent because she has no address for him. Emily is nervous about being in a new place and is glad to make a friend in Millicent. Little does she know how smart Millicent is, a fact that Millicent keeps secret but that is bound to be discovered because Millicent is tutoring Stanford. Emily and Stanford are attracted to each other and of course the last thing Stanford wants Emily to find out is that he needs tutoring.

Gentle Criteria: Although a little edgy at times, and although it deals with Emily's anger at her mother for taking her away from her father, this story is actually about love and forgiveness. Emily forgives her mother for the hard times, Millicent for lying because she thought it was the only way to keep Emily for a friend, and Stanford for being ashamed of needing tutoring. But best of all, she forgives her wayward father when she tells him that she loves him and hopes he will get together with her regardless of what is going on in his life.

170   Yee, Lisa. *Stanford Wong Flunks Big-Time.*
Scholastic, 2005, ISBN 978-0-439-62247-9; 2007, pap., ISBN 978-0-439-62248-6. 304p. • Grades 6–9
☞ ACCELERATED READER ☞ READING COUNTS ☞ JUNIOR LIBRARY GUILD

Stanford Wong, basketball star, flunked sixth-grade English, and now his plans to attend summer basketball camp are in ruins. While Millicent Min is being told she has to play volleyball, Stanford is being told he has to attend summer school and be tutored by Millicent. Many other things are going on in Stanford's life— his grandmother (his favorite knitting buddy) is being sent to a nursing home, he falls in love for the first time, and he starts to figure out who his real friends are. Believe it or not, he even finds a book that he likes! His grandmother's feelings of uselessness, Stanford's feelings of failure as a student, and Millicent's feelings of failure as an athlete are nicely juxtaposed.

Gentle Criteria: This is a story about dealing positively with life's ups and downs. Stanford finds out that in the end teammates don't let each other down, that his parents love each other deeply in spite of their difficulties, and that the nursing home is the best place for his grandmother. Fans will want to be sure to read companion volumes *Millicent Min, Girl Genius* and *So Totally Emily Ebers* (see above). Teachers will want to use these books as examples of point of view.

Historical Fiction

171   Alexander, Lloyd. *The Gawgon and the Boy.*

Dutton, 2001, ISBN 978-0-525-46677-2; Penguin, 2003, pap., ISBN 978-0-14-250000-2. 199p. • Grades 5–7

⌒ ACCELERATED READER ⌒ READING COUNTS

In Depression-era Philadelphia, David is recovering from pneumonia, and the doctor will not allow him to go back to school. His mother arranges for his Great-Aunt Annie—whom David calls the "Gawgon" after the mythological monster—to tutor him. David soon finds out that there is more to the Gawgon than he suspected. She sees him for who he is, not just another child to be ignored. Interspersed among accounts of the Gawgon's inspiring lessons are wonderful stories written by David in which the Gawgon and political and historical figures they are studying are the main characters.

Gentle Criteria: Criteria: This is a book full of family love and caring as well as a good description of the Depression era. The characters help each other in small ways. Because of his illness, David gets to know a great aunt who secretly harbors a soft spot for him.

172   Avi. *Midnight Magic.*

Scholastic, 1999, ISBN 978-0-590-36035-7; 2004, pap., ISBN 978-0-439-24219-6. 249p. • Grades 5–7

⌒ ACCELERATED READER ⌒ READING COUNTS

Set in the Renaissance period, this clever ghost story is actually a tongue-in-cheek look at superstitions and the gullible people who subscribe to them. It is midnight, and Fabrizio is laying out tarot cards to foretell his and his master's futures. Death is the last card, and an immediate knock on the door frightens Fabrizio beyond words. It is a courier from the king, looking for Fabrizio's master, Mangus the Magician. Magic is currently illegal, but a magician is apparently what the king needs—a ghost is haunting the royal princess—and so off they go. Mangus, a calm follower of reason and facts, manages to free the princess, discover the truth, and uncover the wrongdoers in the palace. As Mangus says, "The only thing more fearful than what we know is what we don't know."

Gentle Criteria: Fabrizio is devoted to the man who has been like a father to him, so he goes with him to the castle and becomes the magician's eyes and ears. This cleverly constructed drama points out the damage that fear and ignorance can cause, while poking fun at those most susceptible to it. Reason persists above ignorance. As the book points out, "to be found guilty by those whose only evidence is fear is but a judgment on their own fears."

173   Ayres, Katherine. *North by Night: A Story of the Underground Railroad.*
Delacorte, 1998, ISBN 978-0-385-32564-6; Random House, 2000, pap., ISBN 978-0-440-22747-2. 176p. • Grades 5–9
☞ ACCELERATED READER ☞ READING COUNTS

This is the journal of Lucy, a sixteen-year-old girl living in Ohio whose family is part of the Underground Railroad. Lucy has always been aware of the "Wild Canada geese" her family has assisted to freedom. The year Lucy turns sixteen she becomes actively involved when her neighbor hides an entire family of runaway slaves, one who is pregnant. If they are caught, Lucy's family and her neighbor will be severely punished under the recently enacted Fugitive Slave laws. To further complicate matters, Lucy is trying to decide between two suitors—one who is also involved in helping slaves, the other not—when a slave family heading north needs help. Pregnant Cass is left behind and dies in childbirth. So Lucy sets off to smuggle Cass's baby to Canada to freedom. Will she make it, or will the slave catchers overtake her and the baby? And whom will Lucy choose to make a life with?

Gentle Criteria: This is a noble story of Quaker and Presbyterian families, farmers in Ohio, risking their livelihoods to help slaves escape to Canada. Those recommending this book should know that Cass is pregnant with her master's baby, and she runs away because his wife mistreats her.

174   Banks, Sara Harrell. *Under the Shadow of Wings.*
Atheneum, 1997, ISBN 978-0-689-81207-1; Simon & Schuster, 1999, pap., ISBN 978-0-689-82436-4. 147p. • Grades 5–9
☞ ACCELERATED READER ☞ READING COUNTS

Set during World War II, this is a touching family story. When Tatnall and her cousin Obie were little, Tatnall contracted measles and then gave them to Obie. Tatnall recuperated, but Obie was not so lucky and is now brain-impaired and lame. Now at age eleven, Tatnall is not sure she always wants Obie around. At the same time, Obie becomes increasingly resentful as he sees himself being left behind, both physically and emotionally. When Obie contracts pneumonia and dies, it is Tatnall who feels responsible. Lots of historical background gives readers a sense of what life was like on the homefront.

Gentle Criteria: This is a warm, small-town story in which people gather around each other in times of trouble. In the end, Tatnall believes that Obie has forgiven her, and she and her friend Bubba release their kites in honor of Obie, who never wanted to do anything but fly.

175   **Beard, Darleen Bailey.** *The Babbs Switch Story.*
Farrar, Straus & Giroux, 2002, ISBN 978-0-374-30475-1. 166p. •
Grades 5–9
☞ ACCELERATED READER ☞ READING COUNTS

It is 1924 in Babbs Switch, Oklahoma, and this story is based on a historical event. Ruthie has just found a kitten smothered to death by her mentally disabled sister Daphne. Daphne doesn't know any better; she just squeezes too tight sometimes. Then Daphne nearly suffocates a neighbor's child, and her family worries about repercussions. Ruthie is not allowed to sing the solo at the Christmas program. Fire breaks out during the pageant, and there is a mad rush for the single door in the schoolhouse. Will Ruthie's family make it out alive?

Gentle Criteria: In a refreshing twist it is Daphne who is the hero of the fire—she rescues the very child she nearly smothered. The whole town changes its opinion of Daphne and honors her for her bravery.

176   **Blackwood, Gary.** *The Shakespeare Stealer.*
Dutton, 1998, ISBN 978-0-525-45863-0; Penguin, 2000, pap., ISBN 978-0-14-130595-0. 216p. • Grades 5–7
☞ ACCELERATED READER ☞ READING COUNTS

Fourteen-year-old Widge is sent to work for Shakespeare and steal his scripts. This book is an excellent introduction to Elizabethan England as Widge expresses awe at all of the sights and sounds around him. This is also a story about a young boy who learns the true meaning of loyalty.

Gentle Criteria: This is the story about Widge making his way in life and finding out what is truly important: good and loyal friends.

177   **Blackwood, Gary.** *Shakespeare's Scribe.*
Dutton, 2000, ISBN 978-0-525-46444-0; Penguin, 2002, pap., ISBN 978-0-14-230066-4. 265p. • Grades 5–7
☞ ACCELERATED READER ☞ READING COUNTS

This book is a sequel to *The Shakespeare Stealer* (see above). When the Queen of England closes down the theater because of the plague, Shakespeare's troupe is forced to take to the road. When William's arm is broken, Widge, an apprentice, is called on to serve not only as actor but as scribe. During this period, Widge returns to his hometown and discovers information about his mother and father. When Jamie Redshaw, Widge's supposed father, shows his thieving side, Widge must decide between family and friends.

Gentle Criteria: Many characters reinforce the message that it is not who you are or where you are from that matters—what matters is what you have become.

178   Blos, Joan W. *Letters from the Corrugated Castle: A Novel of Gold Rush California, 1850–1852.*
Atheneum, 2007, ISBN 978-0-689-87077-4. 310p. • Grades 5–9

The third and final book in a geographical trilogy that began with *A Gathering of Days: A New England Girl's Journal, 1830–1832* and *Brothers of the Heart: A Story of the Old Northwest, 1837–1838.* Thirteen-year-old Eldora lives with the people she calls Aunt and Uncle. They have recently moved from Massachusetts to San Francisco, a rapidly growing city because of the Gold Rush. Uncle believes he can start a new school there, modeled after the principles of idealistic educator Bronson Alcott. Eldora's mother, long believed dead, suddenly contacts her, and Eldora must make some choices. Can she have the fairy-tale life she always dreamed of? What about the two people who have been the only family she has ever known? She meets up with Luke who is traveling with his father and determined to get rich working at the gold mines. Through their letters, we see two young people making their way toward adulthood during a very turbulent time in our country's history.

Gentle Criteria: Both Eldora and Luke see injustice and prejudice around them, and they try to make life better but sometimes with dire consequences. Eldora and Luke both learn to understand the people who love them: Eldora with her long-lost mother and the kind and loving people who took her in as a baby, and Luke with his father who does not understand his need for adventure but who supports his dreams.

179   Bruchac, Joseph. *The Arrow Over the Door.*
Ill. by James Watling. Dial, 1998, ISBN 978-0-8037-2078-7; Penguin, 2002, pap., ISBN 978-0-14-130571-4. 89p. • Grades 5–7
☞ ACCELERATED READER ☞ READING COUNTS

Based on a real incident that took place during the Revolutionary War, this is a story of peace. It is told in alternating chapters by a young Quaker boy and an Abenaki Indian boy. The British requested that the Abenaki join them in fighting the Americans. The Quakers do not want to fight anyone. Samuel, the Quaker boy, has endured mockery because he is not fighting. Stands Straight, the Abenaki boy, does not understand why his people want to help the white people because Stands Straight's mother and brother were killed by white people. The Abenaki decide to investigate further. They come upon the Quakers in the middle of a meeting with only peace and friendship on their minds. The handshake of peace is passed around the room. The Abenaki decide not to help the British fight against these peaceful people, placing an arrow over each door to identify them as friends.

Gentle Criteria: Many sad things happened to the Native Americans as the British and the Americans both tried to claim lands that belonged to the Native American tribes. This story has been handed down by both Quakers and Native Americans as an example of peace and living in harmony with God and nature. In the author's note at the end, Bruchac says that the story demonstrates that a true commitment to peace can transcend race and culture, and that we can all walk the way of peace.

180   Bruchac, Joseph. *Sacajawea: The Story of Bird Woman and the Lewis and Clark Expedition.*

Harcourt, 2000, ISBN 978-0-15-202234-1; Scholastic, 2001, pap., ISBN 978-0-439-28068-6. 199p. • Grades 5–9

⌐ ACCELERATED READER

This is a fictionalized account of Sacajawea and her journey with the explorers Lewis and Clark as a girl of sixteen, already newly married and pregnant. Sacajawea had earlier been captured by another tribe and taken away from her family. When she and her husband, the French trapper Charbonneau, meet up with Lewis and Clark, she cannot believe her good fortune. She will be able to travel back to her family and their tribe. The story is told in alternating chapters—by Sacajawea to her son, and by Clark to her son. Each chapter by Sacajawea is prefaced by an Indian legend describing peace and tolerance. Each chapter by Clark is prefaced by an entry from his journal describing the journey to discover new things and forge peace with the Native American tribes. Frozen buffalo floating downriver and hearing the "voice" of the Rocky Mountains are just some of the wonders they encounter while discovering new lands, creating new trade routes, and trying to make friends and show goodwill to all the people they meet along the way.

Gentle Criteria: Parts of this story are intense. There is some arguing with warring tribes, and there are fights with grizzly bears, but the intent of the journey is to forge new relationships and blaze new trails. Both Sacajawea and Clark seek to illustrate to her son the importance of honor in all things. Sacajawea is an admirable and strong woman, and she admonishes her son never to behave in a manner that will result in dishonor. The Shoshone tribe shares food with the members of the expedition even when they are starving themselves.

181   Burandt, Harriet, and Shelley Dale. *Tales from the Homeplace: Adventures of a Texas Farm Girl.*

Henry Holt, 1997, ISBN 978-0-8050-5075-2; Random House, 1999, pap., ISBN 978-0-440-41494-0. 154p. • Grades 5–9

⌐ ACCELERATED READER ⌐ READING COUNTS

The authors created this book to show how stories are passed down from generation to generation. The authors tell readers that we all have family stories—they have merely written theirs down. This book will encourage readers to create their own collections of family stories—some funny, some sad, some tragic. In the first chapter, Irene discovers that the one thing she didn't bother to bring to the creek is the only thing she needs—the shotgun. She realizes this when she sees the panther on the other side, trying to decide which of her younger siblings it wants for lunch! Another time when her brother tries to scare them all, a hole is shot in the wall by the very same shotgun—but no one's going to tell who did it. There are diamondback rattlers in the outhouse, prickly pear cactus at the bottom of a fall, and a hurricane that blows clothes off and then tars and feathers its victims. These stories all make for entertaining reading.

Gentle Criteria: These stories are all about families that care deeply for their members, in bad times and good. Irene's father buys a racehorse to please her mother. Jimmy, always teasing Irene, goes right to her house and tells her it's his fault the mules took off and Irene ended up sitting in a bunch of prickly pear cactus. Every problem is balanced by a good-natured and loving person who is ready to help.

182   Cheaney, J. B. *My Friend the Enemy.*
Knopf, 2005, ISBN 978-0-375-91432-4; Random House, 2007, pap., ISBN 978-0-440-42102-3. 266p. • Grades 7–9
⌒ ACCELERATED READER

During World War II, twelve-year-old Hazel discovers a young Japanese boy being hidden by her neighbors long after the local Japanese have been rounded up and taken to internment camps. To complicate matters further, the people hiding the boy are the future in-laws of her older sister. Hazel becomes friends with the boy, and this friendship and other events slowly change her assumptions about the war. Classrooms and book clubs alike will find this a good title for sparking discussions. What is a friend? What is an enemy?

Gentle Criteria: Loyalty, love, and friendship are present in this book. Hazel knows nothing about the Japanese except for the war hype. When she finally makes friends with an American-born Japanese, she has to realign everything she believed.

183   Choldenko, Gennifer. *Al Capone Does My Shirts: A Novel.*
Putnam, 2004, ISBN 978-0-399-23861-1; Penguin, 2006, pap., ISBN 978-0-14-240370-9. 228p. • Grades 5–7
⌒ ACCELERATED READER ⌒ READING COUNTS ⌒ JUNIOR LIBRARY GUILD

It is 1935, and Moose's father has just taken a job as a guard at Alcatraz Prison so that Moose's sister can go to a special school for children with autism. This means the family will live on the island where the convicts are housed. Even though Moose is angry that he's moving away from his friends, he knows it's not fair for him to be mad at his sister, who cannot help how she is. Moose is uneasy about living next door to some of the country's worst convicts, including Al Capone and Machine Gun Kelly, and he's suspicious of the food his father brings home from the prison dining room. As time passes, Moose realizes the prison is actually a very boring place, and the inmates are just people. In between all this, of course, are escapades with the pretty but bossy prison warden's daughter and adventures such as selling laundry that famous inmates have washed and catching baseballs that the convicts accidentally hit out of the pen. This story offers a taste of history.

Gentle Criteria: I like the way this book shows that people and life are not black and white. Al Capone may be in prison for doing terrible things, but he is the man who opened the first soup kitchen in Chicago. Moose's sister may drive him crazy with all of her special problems—and embarrass him as only a budding teenager can be embarrassed—but Moose knows he is important in her life. This is a real family story about people going through hard times and doing what is best for each other.

✿   NEWBERY HONOR BOOK, 2005

184   Clark, Clara Gillow. *Hattie on Her Way.*
Candlewick, 2005, ISBN 978-0-7636-2286-2. 177p. • Grades 5–9
⌐ ACCELERATED READER

This book is the sequel to *Hill Hawk Hattie* (see below). Pa has left Hattie at her grandmother's to receive the manners and schooling he cannot give her. But manners and schooling are not all Hattie must tolerate. Rumors about her missing grandfather, and small bones and keys found in the garden, lead Hattie to wonder just what happened in this house. Why did her mother say she could never return? Once again this is a real taste of society in the late 1800s, when mental illness was little understood and rarely discussed. As the story moves on, Hattie finds that her cantankerous grandmother is a more understanding soul than she imagined, and that the society matrons are not the people that they appear to be. In the end, Hattie discovers that it was her rough-edged father who saved her mother from more pain, and that her grandmother deserves some tender loving care after spending years taking care of her grandfather, now housed in an insane asylum.

Gentle Criteria: Hattie learns the hard way that polite society is sometimes a harder life than rafting down the Delaware River. She has to find the moral courage and stamina to figure out which are the really good people in her life. Hattie comes to love and understand all the members of her family, despite their weaknesses, and to stand by them.

185   Clark, Clara Gillow. *Hill Hawk Hattie.*

Candlewick, 2003, ISBN 978-0-7636-1963-3; 2004, pap., ISBN 978-0-7636-2559-7. 159p. • Grades 5–9

⌐ ACCELERATED READER ⌐ READING COUNTS

When Ma dies, eleven-year-old Hattie and her father are angry—angry at Ma for dying, angry at the world, angry with each other. Hattie's father no longer calls her his girl. When he tells her to dress as a boy and come work with him on the river, she does not know what to think. As he teaches her to raft down the river, readers are given a real slice of the late 1800s on the Delaware and the dangers of logging. When they witness a boy drowning, Hattie realizes how safe her father has kept her.

Gentle Criteria: These are two angry people suffering loss. They are very much alike and must learn to come to terms with each other. Hattie eventually realizes that her father has her best interests at hear. He is taking her down the river to stay with her grandmother; he wants her to go to school and learn the things that women need to know—and then return to him. Her father has only wanted what is best for her all along.

186   Couloumbis, Audrey. *Maude March on the Run: Or, Trouble Is Her Middle Name.*

Random House, 2007, ISBN 978-0-375-93246-5; pap., ISBN 978-0-375-83248-2. 309p. • Grades

⌐ ACCELERATED READER ⌐ JUNIOR LIBRARY GUILD

Readers who enjoyed *The Misadventures of Maude March* (see below) will want to read its sequel. Once again, Maude and Sallie find that you can't always believe what you read in the papers. Just as the girls are settling into regular, clean living, Maude is arrested by people who haven't heard that she is on her way to being cleared of the charges against her. Harden takes off to warn Uncle Arlen of trouble coming his way, and Maude and Sallie break out of jail to meet up with him. On the way are many adventures. More than one woman is posing as "Mad Maude March" and getting away with all kinds of crimes—at the innocent Maude's expense. They encounter more than one desperado, a caravan of brides looking for husbands, and the writer of the thriller novels that Sallie adores. Can the writer produce a book that will clear Maude's name in the vast wasteland known as public opinion? Readers will have fun identifying how the media then could be just as guilty as the media today in muddying the waters. What fun!

Gentle Criteria: This is a good old-fashioned western tale with no more violence than an earlobe getting shot off by mistake—and then the victim faints dead away at the sight of blood. Readers will cheer the gumption and cleverness of the women. Family sticks by family, and sometimes the bad guys just need another chance and a new place to live—something that was possible in the Old West.

187 Couloumbis, Audrey. *The Misadventures of Maude March: Or, Trouble Rides a Fast Horse.*

Random House, 2005, ISBN 978-0-375-93245-8; pap., ISBN 978-0-375-83247-5. 295p. • Grades 5–8

ᕽ Accelerated Reader ᕽ Reading Counts ᕽ Junior Library Guild

In this novel of the Wild West, eleven-year-old Sallie and her older sister Maude have been living with their deceased mother's sister. But Aunt Ruthie is shot when they are out shopping one day and Maude and Sallie, now orphans, are sent to live with Reverend Peasley and his family. After a brief, unhappy stay there, the girls take a couple of horses and head toward Independence, Missouri, in search of their only other living relative, Uncle Arlen On the trail they meet up with Joe Harden, who shot Aunt Ruthie. He explains that the shooting was an accident. When they bump into Joe later, he's robbing a bank and the newspapers report that "Wild Girl" Maude stole the horses and robbed the bank. This book tells the true story of what happened to Sallie and Maude on their journey to Independence, Missouri—a very different version from that published in the newspapers.

Gentle Criteria: Although two people are killed in this book, both are accidental shootings. Joe Harden takes on the responsibility of escorting these two orphan girls to their uncle because he feels responsible for their predicament. Along the way his feelings change from those of responsibility to true caring.

188 Cullen, Lynn. *Nelly in the Wilderness.*

HarperCollins, 2002, ISBN 978-0-06-029134-1. 184p. • Grades 5–8

ᕽ Accelerated Reader

Nelly and Cornelius's father just ups and leaves after their mother dies in the wilderness of Indiana in 1821—at least, that's how it feels. Nelly and Cornelius had to care for themselves for weeks not knowing if their dad had abandoned them. When he returns, he brings a new wife. Nelly and Cornelius promise each other they will not make it easy for her, hoping she will tire of frontier life and go back home. As stubborn Nelly continues to be standoffish with her new stepmother, the new Mrs. Chapman continues to show only kindness toward the children. When Nelly is bitten by a rattlesnake, it is her stepmother Margery who nurses her back to health. Cornelius and Nelly can't believe it when Margery suggests that Father sell his traps and begin full-time farming. When pregnant Margery goes off to help the Indians who are dying of measles, she contracts them as well. Will Margery survive childbirth? If she doesn't, has Nelly learned enough from her two moms to keep the family going?

Gentle Criteria: It is sad to see how Cornelius and Nelly are so against having a new mother, but it is uplifting to see their father finally confess that he remarried because he missed their mother so. What is also uplifting is the unconditional love that Margery shows the children, knowing full well the shenanigans they've been up to. Nelly finally understands at the end when Margery says that we all have to do what is right.

189   Cushman, Karen. *Matilda Bone.*

Clarion, 2000, ISBN 978-0-395-88156-9; Random House, 2002, pap., ISBN 978-0-440-41822-1. 167p. • Grades 5–7

☞ ACCELERATED READER ☞ READING COUNTS

Set in England, this novel is a vivid description of what medicine was like in the Middle Ages. When fourteen-year-old Matilda's father dies, Father Leufredus takes her to the bonesetter's to be an apprentice. Matilda has never learned anything except prayer and Latin. She does not know how to cook, clean, go to the market, or anything else useful. When she arrives at the house of Peg, the bonesetter, she is sure that she is better than anybody else there, and she hopes it will not be long before the priest comes back to get her. When she asks the bonesetter why she does not call on the saints to help heal, Peg's reply is that God gave her the brains and the capability to do it herself. Matilda begins to understand what worthwhile learning really is. When she asks the saints for help, they give her no pity. In the meantime she learns about setting bones, leeches, herbal remedies, bloodletting, and most of all, the value of friendship.

Gentle Criteria: Matilda's biggest need, though she does not realize it, is to find someone who loves and cares for her—something that she has never known. Although fascinating in its historical aspects, this is really a story about Matilda learning to love and be loved. In the end, it is her friendships with people that sustain her and make her life worthwhile.

190   Cushman, Karen. *Rodzina.*

Houghton Mifflin, 2003, ISBN 978-0-618-13351-2; Random House, 2005, pap., ISBN 978-0-440-41993-8. 215p. • Grades 7–9

☞ ACCELERATED READER ☞ READING COUNTS

This is a heartwarming—though rough—story of the orphan trains that transported children to the West during the mid-nineteenth century. Rodzina's family has come all the way from Poland to live in the freedom of America. One by one she has lost them all, and now she is being placed on an orphan train. Rodzina is big and tough, and the female doctor in charge is just as crusty. Rodzina is deeply afraid that she will be given away as a servant. But as the train rumbles on, and she and the crusty doctor tend to the other children, they find common ground and begin to share hope for both of their futures.

Gentle Criteria: Rodzina and the doctor, each in her own way, fiercely protect the children who are in their charge. Rodzina and the doctor have both experienced the love and care of a family, and they understand that it is what everyone really wants. An intelligent, self-assured woman like the doctor is just what Rodzina needs, and it is a wonderful thing when they recognize the kindred spirit in each other.

191 Denenberg, Barry. *Mirror, Mirror on the Wall: The Diary of Bess Brennan.*

Scholastic, 2002, ISBN 978-0-439-19446-4. 139p. Series: Dear America • Grades 5–9

✎ ACCELERATED READER ✎ READING COUNTS

In 1932, Bess Brennan is sledding one winter day and nearly collides with a boy who is trying to tease her by coming too close. In avoiding him, Bess runs into a tree, detaching her retinas. Despite multiple surgeries, she quickly loses her sight. Her mother is determined to keep her safe at home and to make sure nothing else happens to her, but her uncle looks farther ahead and knows she must be able to take care of herself. He persuades her mother to send her to the Perkins School for the Blind, where she lives during the week and comes home on the weekends. At first Bess is angry and scared, but gradually she realizes that her uncle is right as she makes friends and learns to become independent. When she has to introduce herself to the girls at the school, their teacher makes each tell her best and worst quality. Bess's are loyalty and stubbornness. Readers will see how both traits serve her well on her journey to independence.

Gentle Criteria: Although Bess has experienced a terribly tragedy, there is no time for her to feel sorry for herself, and she is not the only one who has suffered. Margaret Bourke-White, their commencement speaker, tells them to meet life's challenges head on, to open doors and stride right through. This story is set during the Great Depression, and Bess's family takes people in and helps out wherever they can. This story is about looking beyond yourself and seeing what you can do to help the world.

192 Erdrich, Louise. *The Birchbark House.*

Hyperion, 1999, ISBN 978-0-7868-2241-6; Disney, 2002, pap., ISBN 978-0-7868-1454-1. 244p. • Grades 5–9

✎ ACCELERATED READER ✎ READING COUNTS

A group of Native American men come across a lone baby on an island but are too superstitious to pick her up. One of the men tells a brave woman named Tallow, who retrieves this lone survivor of a smallpox outbreak. This book tells the story of this baby girl, Omakayas, and describes the daily life of the Ojibwa Indian tribe. At seven years old, Omakayas is learning to become a healer and acquiring the gift of dreams that will help the tribe read the future. During the winter, when they are starving, her adoptive grandmother has a dream that tells her exactly where Deydey can find a deer to shoot for food. Her dream saves all of their lives. Then a smallpox epidemic, brought by the white man, sickens the whole family. Omakayas's previous exposure allows her to nurse all of them back to health, except, sadly, for her little brother.

Gentle Criteria: This book is a gentle read even though Omakayas's baby brother dies during the smallpox epidemic, because it shows the love the members of the tribe have for each other.

193   **Erdrich, Louise.** *The Game of Silence.*

HarperCollins, 2005, ISBN 978-0-06-029790-9; 2006, pap., ISBN 978-0-06-441029-8. 256p. • Grades 5–9

⌐ ACCELERATED READER ⌐ READING COUNTS

A sequel to *The Birchbark House*. Nine-year-old Omakayas and her family live with their tribe on Lake Superior in the year 1850. She has lost a baby brother to disease but finds another when a group of starving Indians arrive with an orphaned child. They tell stories of how the white men are breaking their promises of payment to the Indians and plan to force them to move west. Two Ojibwas are sent to see if this is true. The story describes the Indians' daily chores, giving readers real insight into what life was like for them. Omakayas has a special gift of being able to dream the future. She dreams of her father and the preacher trapped on an island in winter, and is able to tell the rescue party where to find them. The children play a silence game while their parents meet to discuss serious tribal matters. This game serves them well when they canoe through strange rivers in enemy territory.

Gentle Criteria: Through the characters and the story, the author shows readers what life was like for the Ojibwa tribe—how they hunted, how they cleaned fish and game, how they traded, how they practiced their religion, and much more. Omakayas's brother Pinch annoys her just as siblings do today. One gets a true sense of the love and concern that the tribe's members share for each other and their willingness to help others in need.

194   **Fleischman, Sid.** *Bandit's Moon.*

Ill. by Jos. A. Smith. Greenwillow, 1998, ISBN 978-0-688-15830-9; Random House, 2000, pap., ISBN 978-0-440-41586-2. 136p. • Grades 5–7

⌐ ACCELERATED READER ⌐ READING COUNTS

This book is the second of the California Gold Rush Novels, a trilogy that includes *The Giant Rat of Sumatra* (see below) and *By the Great Horn Spoon* (1988). Based on a real outlaw, this is the story of Annyrose Smith who travels with Joaquin Murieta and his band of outlaws during the 1800s California Gold Rush. When Annyrose gets hurt, her brother travels on without her, leaving her with the terrible O. O. Mary. Joaquin rescues her from O. O.'s clutches, and she travels with him in hopes of catching up with her brother. Joaquin willingly takes her along so that she can teach him to read. Annyrose observes Joaquin's desire for revenge against the Yankees, who have recently acquired California and Texas in the war. As she continually points out the foolishness of this, he begins to call her daughter—because of her nagging. He outwits the people he robs—and even those who try to rob him—without hurting anyone. Humorous incidents abound in this story: One time they get held up by someone claiming to be Joaquin! The book includes notes about the real outlaw at the end.

Gentle Criteria: Annyrose's observations are pointed and accurate. As she observes both Americans and Mexicans lumping each other into stereotypes, she points out that one should not judge all Mexicans by the behavior of one Mexican, and the same with Americans. Joaquin's response is to hang signs around people's necks, so that the bad can be recognized from the good. Annyrose asks Joaquin where the honor is in mistreating people who have done nothing to you. How much vengeance is enough? Goodness is the only answer.

195   Fleischman, Sid. *The Giant Rat of Sumatra: Or, Pirates Galore.*
Ill. by John Hendrix. HarperCollins, 2005, ISBN 978-0-06-074239-3; 2006, pap., ISBN 978-0-06-074240-9. 194p. • Grades 5–7
ACCELERATED READER ✑ READING COUNTS

This is the third book in a trilogy that includes *Bandit's Moon* (see above). In the year 1846, twelve-year-old Shipwreck goes to sea as cabin boy on a sailing ship. The ship subsequently sinks and Shipwreck is the lone survivor—saved by a pirate ship. He soon finds that the pirates are no worse than many of the cutthroats he knew in Boston. The captain is bound for San Diego, and plans to make this his last voyage. Soon there will be no room for ships such as his. And war is breaking out between Mexico and the United States. The captain is returning to San Diego to take revenge for earlier misdeeds and to reclaim the love of his life. He takes Shipwreck along with him. As the ex-pirate begins to make improvements in the village he lives in, Shipwreck sees another side of him. This book is full of great characters—Senorita Wildcat; the bandit Oliviana, who finds missing emeralds but returns them; Captain Gallows, who is really just a soft-hearted orphan; and Siciliano, who repents of his bad ways.

Gentle Criteria: This is a great adventure story full of dashing characters, none of whom are quite what they seem. Shipwreck's observation that the pirates are no worse than the cutthroats he knew in Boston is an accurate one. As the layers of the story unfold, readers see why the characters chose their paths, and how they really yearn for the safe, warm comfort of a loving family.

196   Frederick, Heather Vogel. *The Education of Patience Goodspeed.*
Simon & Schuster, 2004, ISBN 978-0-689-86411-7; 2006, pap., ISBN 978-1-4169-1394-8. 314p. • Grades 5–7
ACCELERATED READER

The sequel to *The Voyage of Patience Goodspeed* (see below), this is an entertaining historical novel about women with spirit. In 1836 Patience is once again on the whaling ship with her father and her younger brother Tad. This time, her beloved Aunt Anne and the silly Fanny Starbucks are along for the ride. More adventures quickly ensue. Fanny longs for land, so father obliges and puts them on a beautiful beach for a picnic. When cannibals arrive, it is Patience who cleverly rescues the group, but this incident is enough to convince her father that the ship is no place for Patience and her younger brother. Patience is enrolled in a missionary school to learn the graces of a young woman with the help of her Aunt Anne. Patience does manage to teach the girls mathematics while she struggles with stitchery. Along the way she learns that navigating the heart can be just as tricky as navigating the seas, and that people are not always what they seem.

Gentle Criteria: This story is based on a real school in Hawaii. It has much to say about learning about the world, appreciating what different cultures have to offer each other, and not judging other people before you get to know them. Patience discovers that the Fanny she thinks she despises is actually a simple, sunshiny soul who brings out the best in people. When she delivers Mrs. Wiggins's baby, this miracle-of-life experience profoundly affects Patience. She finds that the Hawaiian people, while different, offer a fascinating culture to those who care to share it. Patience's quick wit and big heart often get her in trouble but, in the end, usually help to save the day.

197　Frederick, Heather Vogel. *The Voyage of Patience Goodspeed.*
Simon & Schuster, 2002, ISBN 978-0-689-84851-3; 2004, pap., ISBN 978-0-689-84869-8. 219p. • Grades 5–7
⌒ ACCELERATED READER ⌒ READING COUNTS

The year is 1835; after the death of their mother, Patience and her brother Thaddeus learn that they will be joining their father on a whaling trip—a voyage that could last three years. Unwillingly, Patience and her brother join the crew aboard the ship and experience the reality of a whaling voyage. With her quick wits and mathematical skills, Patience is able to help her father regain the ship after a mutiny. This is the tale of a strong girl who saves the day.

Gentle Criteria: This is a good old-fashioned adventure story with a female as the heroine. Many true historical incidents are woven into the tale. The story is both uplifting and exciting to read. Whaling terms and recipes are included at the end of the book.

198　Frost, Helen. *The Braid.*
Farrar, Straus & Giroux, 2006, ISBN 978-0-374-30962-6. 95p. • Grades 7–9
⌒ ACCELERATED READER

The Braid is an amazing novel set in the mid-eighteenth century. In alternating narrative and poems, Helen Frost has written a story about two sisters separated by tragic circumstances, who keep each other in their hearts with a braid woven from their hair. When they are forced to leave their island in western Scotland, most of the family emigrates to Canada. But Sarah chooses to stay behind with her grandmother. Tragedy strikes on the voyage to Canada, and only Sarah's mother, sister Jeannie, and baby brother survive. The sisters have no way to stay in touch. Holding onto their braids, each sister makes her way in the world. Despite many hardships along the way, they do find each other in the end. Portrayed here are two strong female characters who hold onto their love for each other. The author has braided poems together to make a beautifully braided story of love, hardship, and hope.

Gentle Criteria: This book is a more mature read. Two characters, Sarah and Murdo, express their sorrow and love for each other physically, knowing it may lead to the making of a new life. When it does, Sarah lives the life of a shamed woman, but there are still people ready to help. Jeannie struggles when her family expects her to take Sarah's place as eldest in the family, but she rises to the challenge. A captain with food on his ship sees people starving and feeds them even though he cannot pay the bank for the provisions.

199   Giff, Patricia Reilly. *Maggie's Door.*
Random House, 2003, ISBN 978-0-385-90095-9; 2005, pap., ISBN 978-0-440-41581-7. 158p. • Grades 5–9
⌒ Accelerated Reader ⌒ Reading Counts

Maggie's Door is the sequel to *Nory Ryan's Song* (see below). In the midst of the Great Potato Famine in Ireland, Nory and her friend Sean make their way separately to the ship they hope will carry them to New York. All that is between them and starvation is the hope that they can get to the ship, survive the journey, and find their families in Brooklyn. Amid people desperately clinging to life as they slowly starve, each makes friends and manages to survive. That they find each other on the ship is itself a miracle. Now will they make it to America? Rough seas, storms, and sickness stand in their way. If they do get there, will they find their families safe and sound? Readers will follow this story closely, knowing it is based on true stories.

Gentle Criteria: This book is a gentle read on many levels. Nory and Sean both have strong survival skills and a deep and abiding love for each other and their families. Nory, trained to be a healer, is intent on doing good even when it may compromise her own survival. When she and Sean finally meet up with their loved ones in America, every reader will be moved to tears. Book clubs and teachers will find strong themes of family, resilience, and goodness.

200   Giff, Patricia Reilly. *Nory Ryan's Song.*
Delacorte, 2000, ISBN 978-0-385-32141-9; Random House, 2002, pap., ISBN 978-0-440-41829-0. 148p. • Grades 5–9
⌒ Accelerated Reader ⌒ Reading Counts

This book is a wonderful period piece about the Great Potato Famine in Ireland in 1845. Twelve-year-old Nory Ryan's family's life has always been filled with hard work. The English technically own the land that her family has lived on for generations, and her family uses the money from the potato crop to pay the rent. When blight hits the potato crops, they have no money. The English take the animals to cover the rent and the family has no eggs or milk to live on. Nory watches her family and neighbors slowly starve to death amid the fields filled with rotten potatoes. This strong young girl finds a way to keep her loved ones alive, and to get them on their way to America, but not without dangerous and breathtaking moments. Historical notes are included at the end.

Gentle Criteria: Nory helps others out even when doing so leaves her nothing for herself. When there is only one ticket for America, she gives it to her younger brother who is nearly starved; she knows he will die if he stays. When she gets a chance at a ticket for herself, she still offers to stay and look after Anna, who has cared for her and her brother. This is a story of fighting for survival for those you love—and winning.

201   Giff, Patricia Reilly. *Water Street.*

Random House, 2006, ISBN 978-0-385-90097-3. 164p. • Grades 5–9

☞ ACCELERATED READER

The sequel to *Maggie's Door* (see above), this is a book about strong families working through hard times. It is now 1875. Bird Mallon is in eighth grade and lives on Water Street in Brooklyn. She can see the amazing bridge being built. Each person in her family has dreams: her brother for a farm of his own; her sister for her own family to raise; and Bird to become a healer like her mother, Nory. Then there is Thomas who lives upstairs and wants nothing more than to write and to be part of Nory's family. When Bird's brother Hugh is arrested and Bird finds healing more than she can face, it is her friendship with Thomas that gets her through. In the end, Bird does what she can to make her family's dreams come true, and they do the same for her. Fans of *Nory Ryan's Song* and *Maggie's Door* will especially want to read this book about Nory and Sean's daughter.

Gentle Criteria: Bird's mother Nory tells her that nothing is impossible, but that sometimes the getting there can be awfully hard. These are people who are not afraid to do what's necessary to fulfill their dreams and the dreams of the people they love.

202   Giff, Patricia Reilly. *Willow Run.*

Wendy Lamb Books, 2005, ISBN 978-0-385-90096-6; Random House, 2007, pap., ISBN 978-0-440-23801-0. 149p. • Grades 5–9

☞ ACCELERATED READER ☞ READING COUNTS ☞ JUNIOR LIBRARY GUILD

This is a companion book to *Lily's Crossing* (1997). Margaret (Meggie) Dillon's life is turned upside down by World War II. Her older brother Eddie has enlisted. Her father has a new job building airplanes in Michigan, and they're moving there, leaving her grandfather behind. He is a German immigrant who fought for the United States in World War I. In Willow Run, Meggie meets children from all walks of life while living in the factory complex. When Meggie realizes how much having a father at home means to a little girl, she sends her grandfather the money to come be with them even though it will be crowded. He will make her mom smile while they are waiting for her brother, who is missing in action.

Gentle Criteria: Meggie meets many people who remind her that life is not easy. When her grandfather shows her his medal from World War I, he says he doesn't love it because he got it for bravery—but because it reminds him that he can still be brave when he needs to.

203   Goodman, Joan Elizabeth. *Hope's Crossing.*
Houghton Mifflin, 1998, ISBN 978-0-395-86195-0; Penguin, 1999, pap., ISBN 978-0-698-11807-2. 212p. • Grades 5–9
⌒ ACCELERATED READER ⌒ READING COUNTS

Thirteen-year-old Hope is living through the Revolutionary War with her patriot family. Tories come to kidnap her father but he is away on a mission for General Washington. Incensed, they kidnap Hope instead and she becomes a servant in one of the kidnapper's homes. The kidnapper's ill-treated mother-in-law, Mother Thomas, and Hope believe in different causes but Mother Thomas draws the line when there is talk of Hope being sold. The two plot their escape, and along the way Hope is able to see both sides of the issue.

Gentle Criteria: This exciting historical novel is about people finding out that they can be friends with their enemies. War or no war, Mother Thomas is not about to do anything as immoral as selling a young girl.

204   Goodman, Joan Elizabeth. *Peregrine.*
Houghton Mifflin, 2000, ISBN 978-0-395-97729-3. 222p. • Grades 6–9
⌒ ACCELERATED READER ⌒ READING COUNTS

In this sequel to *The Winter Hare* (1996) fifteen-year-old Lady Edith's husband and child have died. She's afraid the king will demand that she marry Sir Runcival, a man she despises, so she goes on a journey to Jerusalem to escape him. She travels with her monk brother, other monks, a few soldiers, her page, and Dame Joan, her assistant. While traveling through the Dark Forest, a strange girl named Rhiannon runs up to Lady Edith, asking her to save her. Dame Joan is sure Rhiannon is a witch. Having recently lost her own child, Lady Edith eagerly accepts the responsibility of caring for another. As they travel, readers get glimpses of all the beautiful buildings they pass. Lady Edith's brother is an artist who is drawing beautiful scrolls in the pope's honor. Lady Edith is hoping to ask the pope for a decree saying she need not marry Sir Runcival. Will reaching her destiny finally rid Lady Edith of her nightmares of Sir Runcival and the loss of her child?

Gentle Criteria: This book gives great insight into the mindset of the people in the year 1144. Lady Edith's religious upbringing makes her think God will somehow answer her prayers. She believes that Rhiannon was sent by God to guide her to find the answers she seeks. Lady Edith is searching for a future of happiness in a world where men determine a woman's fate. In Jerusalem, Lady

Edith finally grieves for her lost child. Widowed, she can now choose what she wants to do with the rest of her life. She decides to go find Will Belet, her first love.

205　Graff, Nancy Price. *Taking Wing.*
　　　Clarion, 2005, ISBN 978-0-618-53591-0. 211p. • Grades 5–9
　　　☞ Accelerated Reader

This title refers both to Gus's father, who is training to be a fighter pilot, and to the orphaned ducks Gus is caring for. Gus is staying with his grandparents while his mom is recovering from tuberculosis and his dad is in the armed services. Gus took on the job of incubating the duck eggs and hopes to raise healthy ducks. An impoverished French Canadian named Louise walks two miles just to see the baby ducks, and she and Gus become friends. We get a great sense of the patriotism of the time—people working in victory gardens, donating scrap metal for weapons, going without sugar and meat, and volunteering to be spotters watching for enemy planes. We also get insight into prejudice against French Canadian Catholics.

　　　Gentle Criteria: This is an insightful book describing the early 1940s in Vermont. Gus visits Louise at her rundown farm and notices children with little clothing or food. Gus learns that Louise's father had rickets and is determined not to allow the same thing to happen to Louise. He takes all his money and even steals a little from his grandma's money jar so he can buy vitamins for Louise.

206　Gray, Dianne E. *Holding Up the Earth.*
　　　Houghton Mifflin, 2000, ISBN 978-0-618-00703-5; 2006, pap., ISBN 978-0-618-73747-5. 210p. • Grades 7–9
　　　☞ Accelerated Reader ☞ Reading Counts

This is an intergenerational story about strong women and the land and people they love. Hope has been shuffled between foster homes since her mother died in a car accident eight years ago. Hope is afraid to let go of her mother, even though she must to move forward with her life and have a chance to be happy again. She ends up with Sarah, who takes her to Nebraska for the summer, to the family farm where Sarah grew up. There Hope meets Sarah's mother, Anna, and she reads the letters and journals of the women who have spent time on the farm: Abigail, whose father first homesteaded the land; Rebecca, a young hired girl who saves a family; Anna, who saves the farm and an old woman's dream of returning to the meadow; and Sarah, who has good reasons for her fears. In the end, Hope learns that she doesn't have to let go of the mother she loves; she can lay her to rest in this place she has come to love.

　　　Gentle Criteria: This book should be recommended to older readers because it includes discussions about body parts that are maturing, and a father who is abusive (although he is helped with his problem). This is a story about women who stand firm for their beliefs. Sarah and her mother will do anything to prevent a missile silo being placed on the meadow that their family has loved for generations. Hope learns to love both the animals and the women of this place she has come to call home. Especially touching is the scene when Hope's mother's ashes mix in with the earth of the meadow.

207   Gray, Dianne E. *Together Apart.*
  Houghton Mifflin, 2002, ISBN 978-0-618-18721-8. 193p. • Grades 5–9
  ⌒ ACCELERATED READER

Isaac and Hannah survived the Great Blizzard of 1888 and have much to be thankful for. Unlike the children in the schoolhouse who died when the roof caved in, the two found a haystack and kept each other warm through the storm. Now Isaac has run away from a cruel stepfather, and Hannah's father cannot forgive her for spending the night alone in a haystack with Isaac. They both find a home with Eliza, the judge's widow, and begin to work for her, thinking they have finally found a safe haven. The three of them begin printing the *Women's Gazette,* a forward-thinking newsletter, and open up the Resting Room, where farm women can come while they wait for their husbands to do business in town. At a time when women could not vote, they are able to improve many people's lives.

  Gentle Criteria: Hannah, Isaac, and Eliza all know firsthand what inequality means, and they do everything in their power to change the times. In the Resting Room there is a sign that says, "Every woman, regardless of family circumstance, nationality, or creed will be welcomed and shown the highest and equal regard." These three special people live their lives by this creed, and do what they can to make the world a kinder, gentler place for all.

208   Gray, Dianne E. *Tomorrow, the River.*
  Houghton Mifflin, 2006, ISBN 978-0-618-56329-6. 233p. • Grades 5–9

In June 1896 fourteen-year-old Megan Barnett joins her older sister's family for the summer. They are taking a steamboat up the Mississippi River. Full of adventure, Megan's summer proves to be far more exciting than she imagined. Best of all she gets a chance to be a riverboat captain, discovers her amazing talent for still photography, and meets her future husband. What more could a young girl ask for? This is a wonderfully entertaining piece about the time when women were just beginning to feel the possibilities that awaited them. Megan is well on her way to becoming her own woman. A surprise letter at the end ensures that Megan will be able to make her way in the world as she desires.

  Gentle Criteria: Megan not only single-handedly outwits the bad guys, but she also finds the best in people whom others find unsavory. When she is reduced to cooking mussels all day in order to earn her wage back home, she makes the best of it. Her discerning eye not only fuels her talent for photography, but enables her to look beyond the obvious and see what is really residing in people's hearts. Readers will want a sequel to this book.

209   Gregory, Kristina. *Across the Wide and Lonesome Prairie: The Oregon Trail Diary of Hattie Campbell.*

Scholastic, 2003, ISBN 978-0-439-55508-1. 164p. Series: Dear America • Grades 5–9

ACCELERATED READER   READING COUNTS

When Hattie Campbell's uncle's coffin falls in the river, the steamboat captain offers to take the family to any destination they choose. Just like that, Hattie's father decides they will head to the beginning of the Oregon Trail and set out to make a new life. No one could be more surprised that they will leave in ten days. As they travel in their covered wagon, they face many challenges, including the birth of new life; the death of loved ones; the loss of livestock; eating "skeeter cakes" made of mosquito-laden batter; and discovering meat swarming with maggots. Hattie's mother must even leave her dead sister's things halfway along the trail because the trunk is too much for their tired oxen to carry. Hattie records all these events as she leaves the only home she has ever known.

Gentle Criteria: Hattie and her family remain strong through all the hardships they face. Hattie discovers that a woman is stealing, and she is furious. The wagon train allows the thief to continue traveling with them, but they shun her from most activities. At the Christmas party in Oregon, Hattie realizes how lonely this poor woman is and gives her a gift, inviting her to join the activities.

210   Griffin, Adele. *Hannah, Divided.*

Disney, 2002, ISBN 978-0-7868-2664-3; 2004, pap., ISBN 978-0-7868-1727-6. 264p. • Grades 5–7

ACCELERATED READER   READING COUNTS

Thirteen-year-old Hannah is a genius at math in this novel set in 1934 in rural Pennsylvania. When Mrs. Teddy Sweet from Philadelphia is scheduled to visit Hannah's town, everyone hopes she will give them the money needed to repair the schoolhouse. Instead, Mrs. Sweet discovers Hannah's math talents and offers her the chance to come to Philadelphia, live with her, and study for a scholarship to a school for rich girls. Two subplots deal with Hannah's compulsive behavior and her reading problems. When she is nervous, she taps out number rhythms to calm herself. This, combined with her reading problems, makes developing friendships difficult. As Hannah sorts out her new school and city life, she finds that all it takes is one friend to make the world shrink to a comfortable size. Joe, another scholarship student, helps Hannah see that all she needs to know is how to open doors of opportunity, and she will eventually find success.

Gentle Criteria: This is a story about how people who have few resources can find success. The people in this story are real and honest. Hannah's family would prefer that she just stay home and work on the farm, but they would never stand in her way. Hannah learns that sometimes she just needs to open her mind to both friendships and opportunities—and they will come.

211   Gundisch, Karin. *How I Became an American.*
Trans. by James Skofield. Cricket, 2001, ISBN 978-0-8126-4875-1. 120p. • Grades 5–9
◠ ACCELERATED READER ◠ READING COUNTS

In the early twentieth century, a wonderful teacher tells ten-year-old Johann—Johnny—to write down how he became an American. Life has been full of adventure from the moment his father decided to leave Europe and find a job at the steel mills in Youngstown, Ohio. Some fathers who left for America were never heard from again, but Johnny's father is no such man. First he sent the funds for Johnny's older brother Peter to join him; then, finally, the rest of the family set out. The voyage was not pleasant, and the baby died not long after the family arrived. As he writes his story, Johnny ponders what makes an American, and at what point they will become Americans, not just immigrants from another country. New food, new smells, new rules—all these are challenges and some of his family adapt better than others. The author's note at the end gives more information about the more than five million immigrants who came from Eastern and Southeastern Europe to make America their home.

Gentle Criteria: Johnny's family is intent on making a better life. They are willing to endure hardships and a new land to make sure their family has a better life.

212   Hale, Marian. *Dark Water Rising.*
Henry Holt, 2006, ISBN 978-0-8050-7585-4. 233p. • Grades 5–9
◠ ACCELERATED READER

Historical characters are combined with fictional ones to tell a spell-binding story of the Galveston flood of 1900. Seth's family has moved to Galveston so that he can get a good education. But Seth has other plans—he wants to follow in his father's footsteps and become a carpenter. So Seth is excited when he gets the chance to work as a carpenter before school starts. After a few days on the job, a powerful hurricane hits. He sees people drowning, houses demolished, and many acts of bravery. Seth later says he will always remember the ghosts when he sees black water, but now it is time for everyone to heal and move on. Marian Hale provides pictures and statistics and describes race relations in 1900.

Gentle Criteria: A book that describing such huge loss of life is difficult to consider a gentle read, but this story is a testament to the human spirit. We see how people like Seth and his African American coworker Josiah struggled through mud, waist-high water, and floating debris to find loved ones and rescue people along the way. We witness characters like Aunt Julia and Ella Rose who have lost loved ones but still put aside their sorrow to help care for the survivors.

213   Hale, Marian. *The Truth About Sparrows.*
Henry Holt, 2004, ISBN 978-0-8050-7584-7; Feiwel and Friends, 2007, pap., ISBN 978-0-312-37133-3. 260p. • Grades 5–9
☞ ACCELERATED READER ☞ READING COUNTS

It is Depression-era Missouri, and twelve-year-old Sadie and her best friend Wilma have just discovered that both their families have lost everything and must move to find work to survive. Sadie's family is going to Texas, and Wilma's to California. They swear to remain best friends forever. In Texas, Sadie is sure she is nothing like the other poor people living in tarpaper shacks. Her father, disabled since childhood, somehow manages to maintain his independence and convince everyone else that there is nothing wrong with him. With thirteen million men out of work, it doesn't much matter who you used to be. What is important is what you have—or don't have—right now. Between hurricanes and drought, Sadie finally realizes that the goodness in people shines through-you just have to look for it.

Gentle Criteria: When Sadie finally looks beyond herself and her misery to make friends, she finds them. When Sadie and Dollie deliver Sadie's sister, she realizes that she loves and depends on these people she disdained. At the end, when Sadie discovers a note from Elijah Haines and a cedar bird made just for her, she realizes how much difference you can make by helping those in need, sometimes in just the nick of time.

214   Hansen, Joyce. *I Thought My Soul Would Rise and Fly: The Diary of Patsy, A Freed Girl.*
Scholastic, 1997, ISBN 978-0-590-84913-5. 197p. Series: Dear America • Grades 5–9
☞ ACCELERATED READER ☞ READING COUNTS

Patsy's diary begins as a cruel joke. It is given to her by Charles and Annie, the children she used to care for. What Annie and Charles don't know, however, is that by playing school and keeping copies of newspapers, the stuttering, limping Patsy has secretly taught herself to read and write. Soon after this, the slaves are officially freed, although at first it seems little has changed. Then slowly families leave and the freed slaves demand pay and privileges, such as a share of the crops and a chance at schooling. But time passes and a teacher never comes. One day Patsy surprises everyone by reading aloud from a book, and they appoint her their schoolteacher. Along the way, Patsy—a girl who has no idea who her family is or where she came from—forms bonds of friendship that she never had the courage to seek.

Gentle Criteria: This book is a gentle read because it shows that even though the slaves are required to work hard all day, they still make time to learn to read and write. The adults even form a union and regularly discuss topics like politics and freedom to better educate themselves about their options and their futures.

🐝 CORETTA SCOTT KING AUTHOR HONOR BOOK, 1998

215 Harlow, Joan Hiatt. *Joshua's Song.*
Margaret K. McElderry Books, 2001, ISBN 978-0-689-84119-4; Simon & Schuster, 2003, pap., ISBN 978-0-689-85542-9. 176p. • Grades 5–9
☞ ACCELERATED READER ☞ READING COUNTS

This book is based on a fascinating moment in Boston's history. It is the year 1919 and Joshua's father has just passed away in the great influenza epidemic. At the same time Josh, a soloist for the Boston Boy's Choir, is let go from the choir because his voice is changing. When he is asked to sing at his father's funeral, Josh cannot bring himself to do it. Their financial situation forces his mother to take in boarders and Josh to quit school and look for a job. He becomes a newsboy and discovers a new side of Boston, encountering Charlie and his gang. Then disaster strikes in the form of a giant explosion. Josh and Charlie join forces to save the victims, and Josh discovers that his voice can still soothe a friend's dying mother.

Gentle Criteria: Josh's good soul makes him friends right away, even on the rough streets of Boston. He succeeds quickly because he is bright and knows how to get along. He speaks his mind about the need for improvements to the tenements. But it is when Charlie, the biggest bully, sides with Josh during the crisis that we are reminded that everyone has goodness in his heart and is capable of great things. Historical notes give facts about the Great Molasses Flood.

216 Harlow, Joan Hiatt. *Midnight Rider.*
Margaret K. McElderry Books, 2005, ISBN 978-0-689-87009-5; Simon & Schuster, 2006, pap., ISBN 978-0-689-87010-1. 404p. • Grades 7–9
☞ ACCELERATED READER

This story takes place in Boston at the beginning of the Revolutionary War. Fourteen-year-old Hannah Andrews ends up in the thick of things when her parents die and she is left in the care of her aunt. Her aunt quickly sells her off as an indentured servant to Governor Thomas Gage. Hannah then makes friends with people loyal to the patriots' cause. She becomes a spy and easily passes unsuspected. Hannah has the ability to mimic other people's voices, and this talent serves her well when she dresses as a boy and delivers messages from the governor's house to the patriots. Secret tunnels, narrow escapes on horseback, invisible ink, and double agents, including the governor's own wife, are all featured in this story based on real people and events.

Gentle Criteria: The characters in this book are willing to fight for what they believe in. The governor is portrayed as a good man who wants to save everybody from the war that is coming. When Hannah sees that her friend Will is going to be tried for crimes she committed, she confesses, knowing she is risking death. Mrs. Gage saves the children by reasoning with her husband. Students studying this era will get a real taste of how war impacted individuals.

217   Hesse, Karen. *A Light in the Storm: The Civil War Diary of Amelia Martin.*

Scholastic, 2003, ISBN 978-0-439-55535-7. 169p. Series: Dear America • Grades 5–9

☞ ACCELERATED READER

Just before the Civil War, Amelia Martin moves to the new lighthouse on Fenwick Island, Delaware, with her mother and father. Her father lost his previous position because he helped fugitive slaves; now he is assistant caretaker of the light. Amelia compares her mother and father to the country itself: They too are in violent disagreement over the issue of slavery. As Amelia sees a boat full of slaves trying to flee, she comes around to her father's way of thinking. But not everybody in her town agrees, and when the country erupts in war she is not surprised, merely disheartened. Amelia makes sure the light is burning bright in the lighthouse, and the actions of their good friends and neighbors—the Hales and solitary Oda Lee—offset the unpleasant incidents with slave catchers and looters.

Gentle Criteria: This book is filled with people who believe in doing the right thing, even if this involves personal suffering. Amelia's father steadfastly believes in abolition, and he calmly and quietly works to make that happen. The rambunctious Hales, with their large brood of children, are always there to help with a smile on their face. Oda Lee, while scavenging the carcasses of wrecked ships, silently helps those fleeing slavery. The author includes many historical notes at the end.

218   Holm, Jennifer L. *Boston Jane: An Adventure.*

HarperCollins, 2001, ISBN 978-0-06-028739-9; Scholastic, pap., ISBN 978-0-06-440849-3. 272p. • Grades 5–9

☞ ACCELERATED READER ☞ READING COUNTS

Twelve-year-old Jane lives with her surgeon father and their housekeeper; her mom died during childbirth. She is a bit of a tomboy, happy hanging out with boys and throwing manure at passing carriages. When her father takes William on as an intern, he suggests that Jane go to a finishing school to learn how to become a lady. William leaves for the Northwest and writes letters to Jane until she's fifteen. He then asks her to marry him. Against her father's wishes, Jane sets sail for Oregon. Her maid unfortunately dies during the journey, and once she arrives William is not there. Jane desperately tries to behave like a lady, but circumstances force her to bend those ladylike rules. She's soon bartering with Indians to get the supplies she needs and sewing people's torn clothes to do her part to pay for room and board. She meets a captain, and if it weren't for William, she would fall in love with him. William returns and Jane finds that he has taken an Indian wife. What will Jane do now?

Gentle Criteria: This book paints an accurate picture of the West in frontier days. Lots of real characters and events are featured. It is refreshing that Jane's physician father prefers a woman who can think and speak her mind over the meek kind of women groomed at the schools of etiquette. Jane realizes that her father prefers the real Jane, not the submissive one William wants.

219   Holm, Jennifer L. *Our Only May Amelia.*
HarperCollins, 1999, ISBN 978-0-06-028354-4; 2001, pap., ISBN 978-0-06-440856-1. 253p. • Grades 5–7
☞ ACCELERATED READER ☞ READING COUNTS

May Amelia lives with her Finnish parents and seven brothers in the wilds of Washington state. She continually proves the adage "To err is human." Her parents are overly protective and insist that one of her brothers accompany her all the time. She still manages to fall out of a boat in November and to be treed by a mother bear after she pets the cubs. When her grandma moves in and blames May Amelia for the death of her newborn sibling, she runs off to live with an aunt in Astoria. She has many adventures there but returns to the Nasel River on her grandmother's death. Then she comes to grips with the fact that she really does belong in this 1900s Washington wilderness. As she says, "After all, I am the only May Amelia we have."

Gentle Criteria: This book gives a good account of early settlement life in the wilds of Washington and in the port town of Astoria. The character of May Amelia is based on the journal of the author's great-aunt. May Amelia has plenty of burdens—mostly having to wait on the men and put up with their teasing, which at her age she takes as just meanness—but readers watch her persevere and continue to make unwise choices that she fortunately survives.

☙   NEWBERY HONOR BOOK, 2000

220   Holman, Sheri. *Sondok: Princess of the Moons and Stars, Korea, A.D. 595.*
Scholastic, 2002, ISBN 978-0-439-16586-0. 187p. Series: Royal Diaries • Grades 5–9
☞ ACCELERATED READER ☞ READING COUNTS

Sondok is the eldest princess in her ruling line in the year 595 A.D. She writes notes to her dead grandmother, putting them in an ancestor jar. These missives reveal interesting beliefs and practices of the time—for example, they clean the house thoroughly before the New Year, and then refrain from cleaning for the first five days of the year so that they don't sweep away their good luck. Sondok is destined to become the ruler when her father dies. She loves astronomy and wants to learn to read the stars so they can guide her in making decisions for the whole kingdom. When her childhood friend Chajang decides to leave her father's employ and enter a monastery, her father orders Chajang's death. Sondok pleads with her father to spare him. Many of the characters are figures from history.

Gentle Criteria: This book gives great insight into everyday life in Silla (now South Korea). Sondok was a forerunner of women's rights, trying to learn about science and mathematics as they pertained to astrology. Once she became ruler, she built a stargazing platform with 365 stones that is still in existence today. Her willingness to plead with her father for the life of Chajang served her well, as she married him after her father's death.

221   Holt, Kimberly Willis. *Dancing in Cadillac Light.*
Putnam, 2001, ISBN 978-0-399-23402-6; Penguin, 2002, pap., ISBN 978-0-698-11970-3. 167p. • Grades 5–7
☞ ACCELERATED READER ☞ READING COUNTS ☞ JUNIOR LIBRARY GUILD

The year is 1968, and eleven-year-old Jaynell Lambert's grandmother has died. Her grandfather moves into their house and Jaynell learns many things. She visits the cemetery with her grandfather and gets to know the history of the tombstones; she learns that her grandfather used to be a very different person when her mother and aunt were children; and she learns that her grandfather is a quiet man who does a good deed without telling anyone about it. When he buys an emerald green 1962 Cadillac, things start to change, but it is what happens after he has a heart attack and dies in the car that really changes everybody's lives, especially for the Pickens family. Along with this tender story are many moments from the sixties, most notably the walk on the moon by astronaut Neil Armstrong in 1968.

Gentle Criteria: This is a story about family love, but also about helping those in need and about how people can change. Grandpa stops his drinking when he sees his girls come home from school barefoot and embarrassed. When he is able, he helps to save the Pickens family from the fate that almost befell him.

222   Holt, Kimberly Willis. *My Louisiana Sky.*
Henry Holt, 1998, ISBN 978-0-8050-5251-0; Random House, 2000, pap., ISBN 978-0-440-41570-1. 200p. • Grades 5–7
☞ ACCELERATED READER ☞ READING COUNTS

Growing up in Louisiana in the 1950s, Tiger Ann must deal with her stern grandmother and her mentally deficient parents. She is at the age when any child is embarrassed by her parents, but Tiger Ann finds hers especially difficult. When Tiger Ann tries to talk to her grandmother about this, her grandmother reminds her that her momma's love for her is simple and sure, just like her mind. After her grandmother dies from a heart attack, Tiger Ann has a choice: she can go with her glamorous aunt and enjoy poodle skirts, Elvis, and running water; or she can stay home and take care of the people she loves. When she learns a family secret about why her momma is the way she is, she looks at things differently.

In the meantime, she experiences her first kiss, her first haircut, and a newfound respect for her slow father when he saves the flower nursery from a hurricane.

Gentle Criteria: What a great family story! Tiger Ann is a typical teen making her way through those years when teens want to distance themselves from their parents. But her process is especially complicated by her feelings of responsibility and love for two people who are not able to take care of themselves. In the end she realizes what is most important in life.

223   Holub, Josef. *The Robber and Me.*
Trans. by Elisabeth D. Crawford. Henry Holt, 1997, ISBN 978-0-8050-5599-3; Random House, 1999, pap., ISBN 978-0-440-41540-4. 213p. • Grades 7–9

☞ ACCELERATED READER ☞ READING COUNTS

Boniface Schroll is abandoned in the middle of the forest by the man who is supposed to be taking him to his uncle the mayor—his only living relative. A mysterious man in a big black hat rescues him and drops him off at his uncle's doorstep. Boniface lives in a harsh world—Germany in the late 1800s. The mayor is a stern man, in charge of morals as well as crime. However, lovable Fredericka is his maid. When a man is jailed for singing a song on Sunday that doesn't include the Lord's name, Boniface decides to steal his uncle's key and free the man, but Fredericka keeps him so busy that he does not have a chance. Someone does let the poor man out of jail, and all readers are told is that Fredericka has a smile on her face.

Gentle Criteria: This book is about morals. It is appropriate for an older audience because of some of its frankness (one woman is jailed for fornication). The story, told with old-fashioned humor and love for family, is about doing the right thing, even though the people in charge do not see what it is. Readers understand that Boniface's uncle, though stern, loves him dearly. The robber is simply a man in difficult straits trying to provide for his family. The local townspeople manage to outwit those in charge more than once, and they end up taking care of things the right way.

☙ MILDRED L. BATCHELDER AWARD, 1998

224   Hopkinson, Deborah. *Into the Firestorm: A Novel of San Francisco, 1906.*
Knopf, 2006, ISBN 978-0-375-93652-4. 200p. • Grades 5–7

This book is based on the San Francisco earthquake. Eleven-year-old Nick Dray, a cotton picker from Texas, escapes the orphanage he was sent to when his grandmother died and heads for San Francisco, a place his teacher has told him is the "Paris of the Pacific." Weary and homeless, he roams the streets until a kind storekeeper takes him in. When the storekeeper must leave town on business, he asks Nick to keep an eye on things. Then the earthquake hits. Nick vows that he will not walk away from the people who need him as so many people in his life have done. He manages to save Mr. Pat's store, helps save the block from burning by becoming part of a bucket brigade, and leads his pregnant neighbor and her daughter to safety in Golden Gate Park. This book is based on true stories.

Gentle Criteria: Nick is a young hero. He finds a home and people to love and sticks by them in a crisis. This is an inspiring read.

225   Hostetter, Joyce Moyer. *Blue.*
Boyds Mills, 2006, ISBN 978-1-59078-389-4. 197p. • Grades 5–7

The year is 1944. Thirteen-year-old Ann Fay's father tells her that she will have to be the "man of the house" as he goes away to war. Then her youngest sibling Bobby contracts polio and dies. It is up to Ann Fay to help her mother through this difficult time, keep the garden going, and make certain that everyone is taken care of. Her good neighbor Junior proves to be a pillar of strength in many ways, but especially when he helps her build a casket for her brother. When Ann Fay herself contracts polio, she draws on even more strength to deal with her illness and her therapy. She finds that other people who have been through hard times are good at giving comfort and help. This story provides an excellent slice of history, with information about the war, President Roosevelt, the polio epidemic of 1944, and the Hickory polio hospital.

Gentle Criteria: This book is full of strong people who share that strength with those in need, such as the neighbor who has lost two sons but is still there to help those in need.

226   Hunt, L. J. *The Abernathy Boys.*
HarperCollins, 2004, ISBN 978-0-06-029259-1. 199p. • Grades 5–7
⌒ ACCELERATED READER ⌒ JUNIOR LIBRARY GUILD

Bud Abernathy, age nine, and his brother Temp, age five, set out on horses to see the West in the year 1909. Their mother is dead and their father, a U.S. Marshal, gives them permission to make the journey and see for themselves all the wild places he has told them about. The boys cross the Texas caprock, a large area that the early explorers called "the Great American Desert." They eat dinner with a band of outlaws, defend themselves against a pack of wolves, and catch one of the famed "vinegaroons," a scorpion-like creature. The most amazing part of the story is that it is all true.

Gentle Criteria: This is an interesting story of a father who allows two very young sons to go on an adventure. Temp loves and adores his older brother Bud, and will follow Bud anywhere. The friendly outlaws they encounter shadow the two boys through what they know is the worst part of the trip—even though the boys' father is out to catch them. This was a time when people automatically helped strangers instead of locking the door tight against them.

227 **Ingold, Jeanette.** *The Big Burn.*

    Harcourt, 2002, ISBN 978-0-15-216470-6; 2003, pap., ISBN 978-0-15-204924-9. 205p. • Grades 7–9

    ⌒ ACCELERATED READER ⌒ READING COUNTS

A combination of drought, primitive firefighting techniques, and strong winds made 1910 one of the deadliest years in firefighting history. This page-turner is told from the viewpoints of three teens, is based on one of the worst wildfires ever to hit the Northwest. Jarrett loses his job watching the railroad tracks when he attempts to stop a bigger fire. Lisbeth wants to stay forever on the land her sister is homesteading. Seth joins the army hoping he will find the respect that is difficult to attain as a black man in the year 1910, and he ends up fighting fires that may well take his life. As all three teens do some fast maturing, readers learn about the amazing force of wildfires and the bravery of the people who fought to survive that summer.

    Gentle Criteria: In this age of cell phones, helicopters, radar, and other technology, it is easy to forget how primitive firefighting was at the beginning of the twentieth century. Rangers often had to walk blindly into an area choked with smoke, making quick life-or-death judgment calls. All three teens quickly find out what they are made of. This book is both enlightening and thrilling.

228 **Ingold, Jeanette.** *Pictures, 1918.*

    Harcourt, 1998, ISBN 978-0-15-201809-2; Penguin, 2000, pap., ISBN 978-0-14-130695-7. 152p. • Grades 5–9

    ⌒ ACCELERATED READER ⌒ READING COUNTS

This book portrays life in 1918, giving readers a real sense of what was expected of young people growing up in that era. Sixteen-year-old Asia sets her heart on a $55 Autographic camera, thinking it will take much better pictures than her father's Brownie. Asia believes that with a great camera she'll be able to take clearer pictures and remember things better than her mind's-eye camera. Recently she lost some beloved pets in a fire. She saw the shape of the person who started the blaze, but didn't get a clear look. Asia's grandma supports her quest and even lends her the money to buy the camera. Asia wants to apprentice with the local photographer but her parents refuse until her grandma agrees to accompany her each day. Asia's mother is concerned that one day Asia will leave them for a job in a big city.

    Gentle Criteria: This author paints a vivid portrait of what life was like during wartime, mentioning the sacrifices that people made to support the troops overseas. They bought war bonds, held fundraisers, sewed quilts with the local boys' names on them, and worried a lot. Asia's grandmother is a great support, leaving money in her will for Asia and her siblings to go to college, as well as money for Asia to travel to New York to show off her photos.

229   Janke, Katelan. *Survival in the Storm: The Dust Bowl Diary of Grace Edwards.*

Scholastic, 2001, ISBN 978-0-439-21599-2. 189p. Series: Dear America
• Grades 5–9

ACCELERATED READER *READING COUNTS*

Readers learn about Dalhart, Texas, in the year 1935 through the diary of twelve-year-old Grace Edwards. Grace vividly describes how black clouds of dirt descend on her family's farm. They have to put wet towels and blankets around the doors and windows to help trap the dirt. After one horrible sandstorm, the veterinarian must operate on their cow to empty one of its stomachs of dirt. Grace stays in touch with Helen, whose family moved West, and she finds out that people aren't much better off in California. The historical notes section explains that poor farming practices led to the dust bowls.

Gentle Criteria: It is hard to imagine that any family could withstand eight years of such horrible conditions and never lose faith that their circumstances would improve. Grace's family shows the true grit of the American farmer. Grace's mother becomes a nurse when times get bad, and Grace volunteers at the hospital, preparing for her own career.

230   Jocelyn, Marthe. *Mable Riley: A Reliable Record of Humdrum Peril and Romance.*

Candlewick, 2004, ISBN 978-0-7636-2120-9; 2007, pap., ISBN 978-0-7636-3287-8. 279p. • Grades 5–7

ACCELERATED READER *JUNIOR LIBRARY GUILD*

This book is a delightful piece of historical fiction centering on the fight for women's rights. In 1901, fourteen-year-old Mable Riley goes to live with and assist her schoolmistress sister. Mable is determined to bring some adventure into her young life, but she finds her new position as humdrum as her old life at home. That is, until she meets the unusual Mrs. Rattle and joins her Ladies' Reading Circle, which is not really about books at all! Mable quickly becomes a political activist and begins to enlist new members, putting her sister's position as schoolmistress at risk.

Gentle Criteria: This is a novel about the struggle between deciding to do what is right and to simply stay safe. There are warm overtones about Mable's love for her sister and for the forward-thinking women that she meets.

231   Karr, Kathleen. *The Great Turkey Walk.*

Farrar, Straus & Giroux, 1998, ISBN 978-0-374-32773-6; 2000, pap., ISBN 978-0-374-42798-6. 199p. • Grades 5–9

ACCELERATED READER *READING COUNTS*

This is a good old-fashioned tale based on real history. It is the year 1860, and Simon has just finished third grade—for the fourth time. His good-hearted teacher gently tells him that he is now finished with school. But what will our simple Simon do? When he decides to buy a thousand turkeys, herd them from Missouri to Denver, and sell them for five dollars apiece, this seems to be a joke. Ah, but readers beware! Simon may not be smart, but neither is he a fool. A runaway slave, a reformed drunk, a sixteen-year-old girl left alone on the plains, and a father who would have been better off long lost make for lots of chuckles and page turning. Grasshopper plagues and wild Indians do not stop Simon either. When Simon is told he is turkey-brained he considers that to be a step up from being called pea-brained. He is sad when they reach their destination for he fears this is the end of the first real friends he has ever known. He is wonderfully mistaken, and they all begin to plan their next profitable venture together!

Gentle Criteria: Simon runs into some unsavory characters, but his good nature attracts friends, starting with his teacher, who gives him the startup money for his project. When he helps a drunk to get sober, he finds a true friend and excellent worker. In Forrest Gump fashion, Simon finds the good in the world.

232   **Ketchum, Liza.** *Where the Great Hawk Flies.*
Clarion, 2005, ISBN 978-0-618-40085-0. 264p. • Grades 7–9
⌒ ACCELERATED READER ⌒ READING COUNTS

This story is based on real events in the year 1782. Daniel's family is farming in New England and remembers all too clearly the violent raids by Indians and the British during the Revolutionary War. Daniel, his sister, and Indian mother narrowly escaped harm from the Indians who were working with the British; they escaped because a red hawk led them to a cave in which they could hide. Hiram's family has just moved back into the area, next door to Daniel. Hiram was able to escape an Indian's grasp and run away; the red hawk led him to a log in which he was able to hide. Hiram's uncle was not so lucky and was caught and held as a prisoner of war; he finally escaped by burrowing out of his prison. How will this new family live in peace beside Daniel's with his Indian mother? These two families want peace and must find a way to overcome their mistrust.

Gentle Criteria: This is a story about overcoming and seeing prejudice for what it really is—ignorance. The new neighbors immediately mistrust Daniel and his family because they are part Indian, even though they had nothing to do with the tribe that aided the British. Daniel and his family must be patient and not fight ignorance with their own anger and hatred. Readers can easily connect this historical piece with the present day. How do people fresh from a war learn to start over?

233   **Klages, Ellen.** *The Green Glass Sea.*
Viking, 2006, ISBN 978-0-670-06134-1. 321p. • Grades 7–9
⌒ ACCELERATED READER ⌒ READING COUNTS ⌒ JUNIOR LIBRARY GUILD

Some teachers may question why this book is designated a gentle read. The story takes place at Los Alamos, New Mexico, the center in the desert where a group of scientists researched the atom bomb. Almost-eleven-year-old Dewey Kerrigan is staying with her grandmother while her father is out in New Mexico working on a *top secret* project. When her grandmother has a stroke, Dewey is sent to the community where the scientists and their families live. There she meets Suze and her mother. Her father is sent to Washington, D.C., to talk to the government and Dewey moves in with Suze; the two previously antagonistic girls slowly become fast friends. When a terrible accident befalls her father, Dewey finds out just how important good friends are, and all the emotions she has held inside for so long finally come out.

Gentle Criteria: Wisdom, strength, and courage are the three qualities these two girls promise to each other. Dewey has found through experience that no one and no place is forever. She and Suze both know what it is to be an outcast. Juxtaposed against this are the scientists, thrilled to be challenged with the experiment of their lives, and the turmoil they experience when they realize both the good and the bad that it can do. The book ends with the bomb dropping on Hiroshima as they look on the "green glass sea" that the terrible heat created in the desert. The book includes some profanity.

234   LaFaye, A. *Edith Shay.*
Viking, 1998, ISBN 978-0-670-87598-6; Simon & Schuster, 2001, pap., ISBN 978-0-689-84228-3. 183p. • Grades 7–9
⌒ ACCELERATED READER ⌒ READING COUNTS

It is the late 1860s, not long after the Civil War. Katherine Lunden wants nothing more than to leave her family's farm and explore the world. When her aunt needs help on her farm in Michigan, Katherine grabs the chance at a train ticket out of her hometown. When her aunt doesn't show to pick her up at the train station, she decides to go by herself to Chicago. She picks up a bag that has been left behind; it bears the name Edith Shay. Katherine knows that she must find a job quickly, and luck follows Katherine everywhere she goes. She meets good-hearted people who help her in a variety of ways. Even so, she must work terribly hard just to make ends meet. She decides she must return the bag to Edith Shay, and find out who she is. Will she find Edith? Will she be able to survive as a woman on her own and see the world? This story is a good overview of conditions for women at that time. Readers are certain to cheer for Katherine as she makes her way in the world.

Gentle Criteria: This is both a story about a strong young woman who wants to be independent at a time when it was not easy for a woman to do so, and a story about the goodness of strangers. Aeslynn O'Dell, a dressmaker who takes Katherine in, treats her like a daughter. Even in Philadelphia, the stingy Mr. Denison's wife makes sure that Katherine gets the letter of referral that she needs to gain decent employment in the next town. This story supports the fact that goodness and hard work prevail.

235   LaFaye, A. *Worth.*

Simon & Schuster, 2004, ISBN 978-0-689-85730-0; 2006, pap., ISBN 978-1-4169-1624-6. 144p. • Grades 5–7

≈ ACCELERATED READER ≈ READING COUNTS

When eleven-year-old Nate suffers a badly broken leg helping his father bring in the hay, his parents decide to send for an orphan boy to help with Nate's chores. Nate struggles with feeling that he has been replaced. Each boy works his way through his own problems amid the hard world of cattle ranching and farming in nineteenth-century Nebraska. Each boy realizes what true "worth" is in the end.

Gentle Criteria: Strong characters make their way through tough times in this uplifting story.

236   Lalicki, Tom. *Danger in the Dark: A Houdini and Nate Mystery.*

Ill. by Carlyn Cerniglia. Farrar, Straus & Giroux, 2006, ISBN 978-0-374-31680-8. 186p. • Grades 5–9

≈ ACCELERATED READER

Nate Fuller and his mom live with his rich Aunt Alice. His father died of malaria while fighting with Teddy Roosevelt in Cuba, and he and his mom had no means of support, so they went to live with Aunt Alice. She is involved with a spiritualist named Mr. Trane who is connecting her with her dead husband and brother through seances. Nate meets Mrs. Harry Houdini, who invites Nate and his mom to a performance. After the performance, Nate's mom divulges to the Houdinis how worried she is about Aunt Alice and her seances. Mr. Houdini decides to expose Mr. Trane for the fraud that he is, but before he can do so, Mr. Trane kidnaps Nate and demands a ransom. Mr. Trane is determined to get Aunt Alice's money and will stop at nothing to do so. Can Houdini save Nate in time?

Gentle Criteria: This book gives a glimpse into life in the early 1900s in New York City. In real life, Harry Houdini spent a lot of time debunking false spiritualists. Tugging at readers' heartstrings is the fact that Nate still wants to believe that he might be able to communicate with his deceased father even after Houdini tells him the straight facts about spiritualists. And after escaping from his captor, Nate puts himself in danger again to save his aunt from the evil Mr. Trane.

237   Larson, Kirby. *Hattie Big Sky.*

Random House, 2006, ISBN 978-0-385-73313-7. 289p. • Grades 5–7

≈ ACCELERATED READER ≈ JUNIOR LIBRARY GUILD

Sixteen-year-old Hattie is an orphan who has spent most of her life being shuffled from one relative to another. When her Uncle Chester leaves his home-steading claim to her, she moves there by herself and begins to "prove" her claim: 320 acres of fence to put in and crops to grow. Though she has never lived on a farm before, she desperately wants a home of her own, and she is willing to do anything to get it. Juxtaposed against her trials in proving her claim are stories of her friend Charlie who is fighting in World War I, and the prejudice of the community against her German neighbors. She begins each day telling the Lord what she is thankful for. She fears she may be the first homesteader to die of stupidity when she freezes her hands to the water pump. Hailstones the size of golf balls, the 1918 influenza epidemic, crop failure, and babies keep Hattie busy, but in the end she finds something better than a claim: people to love her.

Gentle Criteria: Hattie starts off each day thanking the Lord for having found people to help and love her. She finds out how to make loving connections as she attempts to make her own way, something she rarely experienced when she was being shuffled from one relative to the next. She discovers how to let people help and how to take care of them in return.

238   Lasky, Kathryn. *Christmas After All: The Great Depression Diary of Minnie Swift.*
Scholastic, 2001, ISBN 978-0-439-21943-3. 185p. Series: Dear America
• Grades 5–9
☞ Accelerated Reader ☞ Reading Counts

Author Kathryn Lasky modeled the house and many of the characters in the book after members of her own family. In 1932 the seven-member Swift family takes in a relative who is orphaned. The father has had his work hours reduced. The family moves into three rooms so they don't have to heat the entire house. They keep chickens in the garage to provide eggs and meat. Minnie keeps a diary, and it's through her writing that readers learn what happens to this family. After Minnie's father's workplace closes, he is heard typing late into the night and doesn't join the family for nightly radio listening. Although they can barely make ends meet themselves, the family still goes out to the shanty town to offer food and cookies to the unemployed. When Minnie's dad leaves a note saying he'll be back, the whole family worries that he is gone for good. When he returns on Christmas Eve, readers will want to know whether his mission was successful—and what it was!

Gentle Criteria: In 1932, one out of every three workers was out of a job. This book shows the Swift family's faith that they would come through this ordeal. Minnie's orphaned relative joins the family and provides the real faith that the whole family clings to when the father disappears. The family finds unique and creative ways to make Christmas presents for one another because there is no money to spare. This is an inspiring book that shows the resiliency of the human spirit.

239   Lasky, Kathryn. *Dreams in the Golden Country: The Diary of Zipporah Feldman, a Jewish Immigrant Girl.*
Scholastic, 2003, ISBN 978-0-439-55502-9. 183p. Series: Dear America
• Grades 5–9
☞ Accelerated Reader ☞ Reading Counts

Zipporah Feldman's diary begins as she steps into the "Golden Country." However, it's not quite as golden as Zipporah imagined. Her apartment on the Lower East Side of New York City is small and dark, the boarder is smelly, and her mother and father constantly fight. As a compromise, Zipporah and her sister Miriam rent their mother a sewing machine so she can sew clothes and occupy her time while she is alone at home during the day. In return, Zipporah's father agrees to attend religious services regularly. Her older sister Tovah learns to appreciate the culture in America and organizes a workers' union for women. Zipporah's father also returns to his love of music, earning a spot playing his violin in a prestigious symphony. Zipporah discovers she has a love for acting when her father takes her to the theater for Hanukkah. After attending many of the rehearsals, she becomes part of the stage crew and later gets a role in a play. Improving her English, she is promoted from first grade to eighth grade in the course of a year.

    Gentle Criteria: Zipporah's entire family learns the art of compromise. Zipporah's mother sews, and Zipporah's father attends religious services. Zipporah's father takes another job while playing the violin to make his wife happy. Zipporah's mother wears her traditional wig, still believing it is vain to show her own hair, but adapts in other ways. Forgiveness and acceptance also play an important role in this family. When Zipporah's sister falls in love with a Catholic and runs off to marry him, Zipporah's mother chooses to act as if she is dead. However, when she finally visits home, her mother embraces her with open arms.

240   **Lavender, William.** *Aftershocks.*
        Harcourt, 2006, ISBN 978-0-15-205882-1. 344p. Series: Great Episodes
        • Grades 7–9
        ⌐ ACCELERATED READER

Jessie Wainwright wants nothing more than to become a doctor just like her father. But in the early 1900s most people—including her father—believe the medical field is best left to men. Set alongside the 1906 San Francisco Earthquake and the intolerance and discrimination toward the Chinese population at that time, this story provides dramatic reading. Jessie sees that the discrimination toward the Chinese people is much more blatant than that against women, but both affect her life—especially when her father has an illegitimate child with their Chinese housemaid, and no one in the family will acknowledge the child. When the earthquake strikes, Jessie knows that she must do the right thing for her sister rather than conforming with what society says. In the end Jessie's belief in doing what's right makes the world a better place for her sister, for her mother and father, but most of all, for herself.

    Gentle Criteria: This book is a tale of romance, women's rights, survival, and history, and is about a girl who does the right thing for her sister and herself. She knows that she alone cannot stop discrimination and prejudice, but she does not have to go along with it in her own life. She stands by her sister even though she knows it would be easier not to. She also holds onto her dream of becoming a doctor even though she knows it will be hard and she will not always be accepted. Jessie's belief in doing the right thing makes the world a better place.

241   Lavender, William. *Just Jane: A Daughter of England Caught in the Struggle of the American Revolution.*
Harcourt, 2002, ISBN 978-0-15-202587-8; 2005, pap., ISBN 978-0-15-205472-4. 277p. Series: Great Episodes • Grades 7–9
☞ ACCELERATED READER ☞ READING COUNTS

Fourteen-year-old Jane Prentice, the recently orphaned daughter of an English earl, comes to South Carolina in 1776. Some of her American relatives prefer to remain English subjects, while others are fiercely independent and support the rebels' cause. As the Revolutionary War heats up and creeps closer to her doorstep, Jane is forced to make some choices. Living in a house full of loyalists and falling in love with the major supplier to the rebels, she realizes that war causes heartache for both sides. Many historical characters are brought to life in this engaging book, including George Washington, British general and colonial governor Charles Cornwallis, and Frances Marion, the Swamp Fox. As well as an interesting historical story, this book is also about a young girl learning to make up her own mind and becoming her own woman, not Lady Jane, but Just Jane.

Gentle Criteria: This book is not a graphic depiction of war, but a story about the heartache that war causes and how individuals must decide what is the right thing to do. Both Jane and the man she falls in love with would prefer for there to be no war at all, but they stand firm and help where they think they must.

242   Leeuwen, Jean Van. *Cabin on Trouble Creek.*
Dial, 2004, ISBN 978-0-8037-2548-5. 219p. • Grades 5–9
☞ ACCELERATED READER ☞ READING COUNTS ☞ JUNIOR LIBRARY GUILD

Nine-year-old Daniel and his seven-year-old brother Will have just helped their pa build a crude log house for their family in the Ohio wilderness in 1803. Pa leaves the boys with a six-week supply of food as he heads back to Pennsylvania to fetch his wife and younger children. After six weeks of waiting, Pa and the family still haven't returned. Daniel and Will have filled in the gaps in the cabin and cut enough firewood for the winter. But their cornmeal has been exhausted and they are getting hungry. An Indian named Solomon helps them out. He teaches them how to set a rabbit snare and explains how different plants and barks can be used for their medicinal properties. As winter sets in, the boys become creative, making their own hooks to catch fish and designing a trap to catch a turkey. But when Daniel is wounded by a bear, his leg becomes infected. Have they learned enough to save Daniel? Or will he die from the infection?

Gentle Criteria: Daniel's father goes to Pennsylvania to get the rest of his family and finds his wife deathly ill. He himself succumbs to the illness too, but still starts off for Ohio knowing his sons are there alone. The two combined illnesses delay their arrival by eight months, but they hold out hope that the boys have somehow survived. Solomon is the reason this book is a gentle read. Even though the white man burned his village and killed his people, he still teaches the white boys the skills necessary to survive in the wilderness.

243   Levine, Beth Seidel. *When Christmas Comes Again: The World War I Diary of Simone Spencer.*
Scholastic, 2002, ISBN 978-0-439-43982-4. 172p. Series: Dear America • Grades 5–9
⌒ ACCELERATED READER ⌒ READING COUNTS

Simone Spencer plays a very important role during World War I as a switchboard operator in France. Simone has just graduated from high school in New York and is unsure what to do with her life. She knows she wants to be useful. When her brother Will enlists in the army, she decides she also has to *do* something. Soon after, there is a request for women switchboard operators who are bilingual in English and French—a job that is perfect for Simone. So she leaves home with the same promise as Will: "We will all be together when Christmas comes again." Along the way Simone falls in love with a soldier, only for him to be relocated and later presumed dead. After many months, Simone discovers that he is still alive—although missing a leg.

Gentle Criteria: Simone enlists as a switchboard operator during a time when people were skeptical about women having careers or participating in the military. This book shows strong women who give everything to ensure the success of their military men. Great responsibility rests on these women's shoulders, and they prove the skeptics wrong.

244   Love, D. Anne. *The Puppeteer's Apprentice.*
Margaret K. McElderry Books, 2003, ISBN 978-0-689-84424-9; Simon & Schuster, 2004, pap., ISBN 978-0-689-84425-6. 185p. • Grades 5–8
⌒ ACCELERATED READER ⌒ READING COUNTS

Mouse, an orphan from birth, must gain the courage to make her own way in the world in the Middle Ages. When she escapes from the cook who beats her, she has no place to go. Then she comes across a puppeteer and knows that she wants no other life. But the puppeteer has secrets that cannot be shared, and he takes on Mouse as an apprentice unwillingly. One of the secrets is that he is being followed. When robbers overtake them, Mouse enables them to survive the attack and then goes to find help for the puppeteer. There are some violent moments when a horse is killed, and the thieves are murdered, but this story is about the magic and happiness that Mouse finds in the puppets, and the notion that courage is, as Sir Alfred the puppet so aptly puts it, "nothing more than going ahead even when you feel afraid." Historically accurate, this is an enjoyable tale.

Gentle Criteria: This is an inspiring and touching story of a young girl who must survive on her own during the Middle Ages. Courage, the search for love, good deeds being repaid, and people helping each other are strong themes in this book.

245 **McCaughrean, Geraldine.** *The Pirate's Son.*
Scholastic, 1998, ISBN 978-0-590-20344-9; 1999, pap., ISBN 978-0-590-20348-7. 294p. • Grades 7–9
☞ ACCELERATED READER ☞ READING COUNTS

When Nathan's father dies and leaves him and his sister Maud penniless orphans, it is Tamo, a pirate's son, who stands up for them and takes care of them. Nathan has always been entranced by his book of pirate stories and can hardly believe that he is escaping with a pirate's son. When they make it to the island of Madagascar after a number of adventures, they begin to learn a different set of morals from the ones they were brought up with. The children outwit the pirates more than once and, in the end, they get rid of them without a drop of blood being spilled. Nathan dreamed of becoming a pirate, but he is the one who ends up most like his parson father and he heads home to England. It is mousy Maud who stays to make her home in Madagascar.

Gentle Criteria: Although there are some violent moments with the pirates in this book, it is actually a story about people's hearts leading them where they belong. It also is a wonderful multicultural look at how different people can look at morality in completely different ways. How to celebrate death, and the difference between right and wrong are issues the three children grapple with. Tamo learns that his mother stayed alive waiting for her son to come back and get his father's last treasure, and the Madagascar villagers regularly dig up the bones of their ancestors and talk to them and dance with them. One illuminating moment is when the children realize that sometimes adults are just children in bigger clothes!

246 **McKissack, Pat.** *Nzingha: Warrior Queen of Matamba, Angola, Africa, 1595.*
Scholastic, 2000, ISBN 978-0-439-11210-9. 136p. Series: Royal Diaries • Grades 5–9
☞ ACCELERATED READER ☞ READING COUNTS

This is the diary of Nzingha, a sixteenth-century African princess. Her mother was brought to her tribe as a slave and understood only too well the position of an outsider. Nzingha's early years, her grooming as an African princess, and the rivalries within her own royal family are all documented here.

Gentle Criteria: The historical notes tell us that for forty years Nzingha waged war against the slave traders. She did not profit from the selling of her people; rather, she did her best to protect them. She also breaks stereotypes of princesses as she participates on equal footing with the warriors and the hunters. Long before the United States was even thought of as a country, Nzingha was fighting against the institution of slavery.

247 Madden, Kerry. *Gentle's Holler.*
Penguin, 2005, ISBN 978-0-670-05972-0; 2007, pap., ISBN 978-0-14-240751-6. 237p. • Grades 5–9

Livy Too lives with her seven sisters and two brothers in the mountains. She has a three-year-old sister named Gentle who her family suspects is blind, but they have no money to take her to a doctor to find out. Her father is a banjo player who refuses to work in the mines and continues to hope his talent will be discovered. He works temporary jobs, selling encyclopedias and baby food around the mountain. When he brings home a dog, Livy's mom is furious and says they can't afford another mouth to feed. Then the dog saves Gentle from drowning and is allowed to stay. Livy's grandma visits and pays to take Gentle to a doctor. Livy wins third place in a singing contest and her brother Emmett gets a job. Just when circumstances are improving, her father has an accident and ends up in a coma. Now how will this family survive?

Gentle Criteria: This story features people who are extremely poor but who always remain positive that their circumstances will improve. Livy's parents are raising nine children with very little money, but they love their children and always demonstrate that love.

248 Madden, Kerry. *Louisiana's Song.*
Viking, 2007, ISBN 978-0-670-06153-2. 278p. • Grades 5–9
⁓ Accelerated Reader

In this sequel to *Gentle's Holler* (see above), Daddy has come out of his coma and returns home to live with his family. All the kids are ecstatic and expect everything will return to normal. But Daddy is *not* OK. He doesn't remember many of his children, he hears songs playing in his head, and he can't find the words to describe things anymore. What's worse, he doesn't remember how to play the banjo. Grandma has convinced Mamma to move the whole family to her house in town come December. Now the older children must convince Mamma that they can manage without Daddy's income. Maggie gets a job at the pancake house, Emmett is working on top of Ghost Mountain, Olivia is working on the bookmobile every other day, and Louisiana is sketching portraits for two dollars a piece. Olivia has also just sent a song entitled *Louisiana's Song* to a Nashville publisher. Will the children's efforts be enough for them to stay in Gentle's Holler?

Gentle Criteria: Mamma shows unconditional love for her dependent husband even though she's exhausted from raising ten kids and a newborn baby. All the kids go to work to help make money, so Olivia doesn't understand why Grandma wants them to move. Grandma tells Olivia that Mamma needs to work where she can earn Social Security. But the kids still don't understand; they just want to stay in Gentle's Holler. Grandma continues to support this family even though she's the only one who can see the big picture.

249   Morpurgo, Michael. *The Amazing Story of Adolphus Tips.*
Scholastic, 2005, ISBN 978-0-439-79661-3. 140p. • Grades 5–9
    ACCELERATED READER   READING COUNTS

Boowie has received a diary from his Grandma Lily. In it he reads about Lily's childhood in England during World War II when she first meets African American soldiers Adolphus T. Madison and Harry. Her family has been forced to move away from their farm and move in with her uncle so that the troops could practice for D-Day. Stubborn Lily keeps crawling back over the wired fences to search for her missing cat. Adolphus keeps finding her, scolding her, and telling her he'll find the cat. Lily's family befriends the soldiers and makes them feel at home. During an exercise, however, German submarines sink several ships and Harry is lost in the battle. Adolphus comes to share the news with Lily's family, saying he will continue to fight because once you've experienced freedom, you don't ever want to give it up. Lily falls in love with Adolphus and prays for his safety, even naming her cat after him. A teary ending awaits readers.

Gentle Criteria: Author Michael Morpurgo has a unique ability to portray emotion in his books. Readers will definitely need tissues for the ending. Lily's diary shows the typical —often selfish—but honest thoughts of a twelve-year-old. She does not really miss her father, who is away at war, until she hears his name mentioned. This book is full of selfless acts This is a true feel-good book about a terrible time in history.

250   Murphy, Jim. *My Face to the Wind: The Diary of Sarah Jane Price, A Prairie Teacher.*
Scholastic, 2001, ISBN 978-0-590-43810-0. 179p. Series: Dear America • Grades 5–9
    ACCELERATED READER   READING COUNTS

Jim Murphy uses actual characters and events to make this novel realistic. When fifteen-year-old Sarah Jane's father, the town teacher, dies in Broken Bow, Nebraska, in 1881, Sarah is left all alone and temporarily takes up residence at Ms. Kizer's boarding house. Ms. Kizer tells Sarah that the best thing is for her to be admitted to the Asylum for Girls miles away. Sarah doesn't want to work six days a week in a factory and never see any of the money she has earned. Sarah has watched and helped her father teach all these years, and she is determined to become the new teacher in town. The board barely approves her at half the wages they offered her father, and the school is unsound physically, but she'll have to manage. When a late-March blizzard hits and the roof threatens to come off, will Sarah Jane know what to do to save her fifteen students?

Gentle Criteria: When Sarah believes her father visits her after his death—looking as if he's teaching—she's sure he is telling her that she should teach too. Sarah reasons that if the Bible says that Lazarus rose from the dead, then her father could have returned to guide her as well. Sarah draws on her memories of what her father did in difficult teaching situations and is inspired by those earlier lessons. This is a compelling story that gives readers insight into education in 1881.

251   Murphy, Jim. *West to a Land of Plenty: The Diary of Teresa Angelino Viscardi.*

> Scholastic, 1998, ISBN 978-0-590-73888-0. 204p. Series: Dear America
> • Grades 5–9
> ᔥ Accelerated Reader ᔥ Reading Counts

The Viscardi family has joined many other families who are taking a train west and then venturing by wagon train to the new community of Opportunity, Idaho. Mr. Keil is based on a real man who actually transported the body of his dead son in a leaded casket filled with alcohol so that he could bury him back home. When Antoinnetta catches Teresa with an almanac, she blackmails Teresa into letting her write in the diary as well. We learn through their writings how Papa Viscardi felt that going west was the only way to make a better life for his children—they would be leaving the prejudice of the East behind. Readers get a realistic account of just how difficult the trip was through descriptions of the people who die along the way. Readers also learn of grown men acting like donkeys when they hear of discoveries of silver; many men left the wagon train in search of silver riches only to return feeling like fools. There's an interesting epilogue that tells what happened to each of the main characters, as well as representative drawings of the period.

Gentle Criteria: What could be gentler than reading the perspective of two children who describe what they see and experience through letters sent to their former teacher and friends? The author also chooses to prevent Teresa from shooting men who are going to take their mule, although Teresa does fire the gun three times to show she means business. The parents of these families love their children very much to be willing to endure the hardships they encounter on this journey.

252   Napoli, Donna Jo. *Daughter of Venice.*

> Random House, 2002, ISBN 978-0-385-90036-2; 2003, pap., ISBN
> 978-0-440-22928-5. 274p. • Grades 7–9
> ᔥ Accelerated Reader ᔥ Reading Counts

In the year 1592, Donata is a member of a noble family. One son and one daughter will marry. The rest of the sons will be educated to help support the family, and the rest of the daughters will go to the convent or become maiden aunts to take care of other family members' children. None of this is acceptable to Donata, who is extremely intelligent. She convinces her father to allow her to sit in on her brothers' tutoring sessions, and she sneaks away from the house dressed in boys' clothes to explore the city and experience the freedom of thought and movement that her brothers enjoy. This is not only a wonderful piece of historical fiction about Venice in the 1500s, but also a passionate book about women working for their freedom. Based on a real person who lived in Venice in 1678 and obtained a doctorate in philosophy, this is an inspiring read indeed.

Gentle Criteria: A girl from a privileged family sees the injustices in the world around her, not just for herself but also for those who are less fortunate. When she makes friends with a Jew who must by law live in the ghetto, she starts to see beyond her life. When she runs errands to make money to buy food, like any poor boy living at that time, she realizes how much difference it makes when people are kind. These experiences and some education transform her life from a solitary existence in a noble house to a vision of what the world could become.

253   Naylor, Phyllis Reynolds. *Blizzard's Wake.*
Atheneum, 2002, ISBN 978-0-689-85220-6; Simon & Schuster, 2004, pap., ISBN 978-0-689-85221-3. 212p. • Grades 5–9
⌐ ACCELERATED READER ⌐ READING COUNTS ⌐ JUNIOR LIBRARY GUILD

Kate's mother was killed by a drunk driver, and Kate daydreams about punishing him when he gets out of prison. She imagines driving down the road and seeing him walking, and then she just veers off the road and runs him down to repay him for taking her mother's life. Kate is trapped by her mother's death, and she can't move forward with her life. Then a late-March storm hits, and Kate's dad and brother are trapped in the car a hundred feet from their barn—they can't see a foot in front of them. Coincidentally, Zeke, the man who caused her mother's death, has been released from prison early for good behavior. He is caught in the same storm and ends up finding Kate's dad and brother's in their car. Her father saves Zeke's life, and Kate ends up saving all their lives by stringing the clothesline from the barn to the car so they can find their way inside. Now Kate is faced with Zeke. Zeke seriously cuts himself while chopping wood, and Kate must administer the ether while her father operates. Will she purposely overdose him?

Gentle Criteria: This story is based on a real blizzard in March 1941. Kate is trying to figure out how her brother and dad have moved on with their lives while she is still so upset about the loss of her mother. The book points out how precious life is, and why we must understand that the past can't be changed, so we must get on with the process of living. Kate finally forgives herself for the cruel words she said to her mom on that fateful day, and she is able to forgive Zeke.

254   Nuzum, K. A. *A Small White Scar.*

Joanna Cotler Books, 2006, ISBN 978-0-06-075640-6. 180p. •
Grades 7–9

⤝ Accelerated Reader ⤝ Reading Counts

Fifteen-year-old Will has always been expected to look after his twin brother
Denny, who has Down syndrome. When Will makes up his mind to take off on
his own to compete in rodeos, Denny follows him—much to Will's dismay.
After a near-drowning in a flash flood and a bite from a rattlesnake, Will resigns
himself to the fact that he will never escape his full-time job of looking after
Denny. But after an episode at the doctor, Will realizes that Denny has taught
him more about being a man than he ever knew. In the end, doing the right
thing turns out to be the best thing: Denny finds a new home where he can feel
useful, and Will returns to the life that he loves. The rodeo scenes are exciting,
and life on a ranch is vividly portrayed.

   Gentle Criteria: When Will is able to do the right thing by both Denny
and the coyote he has been tracking for weeks, he realizes what being a man
really means. Their father loves his sons deeply and deliberately made the decision when the twins were just babies not to institutionalize Denny. It is the family's love for one another that in the end saves them all.

255   Park, Linda Sue. *A Single Shard.*

Houghton Mifflin, 2001, ISBN 978-0-395-97827-6; Random House,
2003, pap., ISBN 978-0-440-41851-1. 152p. • Grades

⤝ Accelerated Reader ⤝ Reading Counts

Tree-ear is an orphan who lives under a bridge with Crane-man in twelfth-cen-
tury Korea. He forages for food in the trash every day. After spying on Min, a
master potter, he gets the courage to ask for a job, hoping Min will teach him
the trade of pottery making. Min says he cannot pay him but can feed him in
return for his services. Tree-ear saves half of each lunch to share with Crane-
man at night, but Min's wife soon notices and refills his bowl before he leaves
each night. Min is then given the opportunity to show a piece to the Royal
Emissary and perhaps win a commission. Min is too old to make the journey to
Songdo, so Tree-ear takes it in his place. Min's whole future rests on Tree-ear's
success. This is a story of young Tree-ear's determination to become what he
desires in spite of the obstacles presented.

   Gentle Criteria: Tree-ear is an amazing example of a person whose glass
is always half full. He takes whatever life gives him and continues to dream of
becoming a potter. He has become an honorable man through listening carefully
to Crane-man, who says he would never steal as he would be no better than a
dog. Even after Min tells Tree-ear he'll never teach him the skill of pottery, Tree-
ear still offers to make this dangerous journey to Songdo for Min and his wife.

🐞   Newbery Medal, 2002

256   Paulsen, Gary. *Alida's Song.*

Delacorte, 1999, ISBN 978-0-385-32586-8; Random House, 2001, pap., ISBN 978-0-440-41474-2. 88p. • Grades 5–8

⌒ ACCELERATED READER ⌒ READING COUNTS

This book is based on one of Gary Paulsen's summers as he was growing up. Gary's grandmother, knowing that Gary has had another hard year at school and with his alcoholic parents, has Gary come to work on the farm where she is the cook. Gary describes it as the best summer of his life, with hard work but good companionship, and even Saturday night dances after his Grandmother Alida teaches him how to dance. This summer helps solidify the good in Gary, builds his self-confidence, and keeps him from following in his parents' footsteps.

Gentle Criteria: Besides the pleasant storyline, readers will be deeply touched at the end when Gary reads a box of letters from his now-deceased grandmother. While reading the letters he realizes that Olaf and Gunner couldn't spare the eighteen dollars he was paid every week for working the farm. His grandma gave Olaf her own money to pay Gary so he would feel like a hard-working, earning man. This book demonstrates the lengths a family member will go to for a relative in trouble.

257   Paulsen, Gary. *The Legend of Bass Reeves: Being the True and Fictional Account of the Most Valiant Marshal in the West.*

Random House, 2006, ISBN 978-0-385-90898-6. 137p. • Grades 7–9

⌒ ACCELERATED READER ⌒ READING COUNTS ⌒ JUNIOR LIBRARY GUILD

This is a fictionalized account of an amazing but little-known marshal of the Old West, Bass Reeves. While many of the well-known names of the day—such as Billy the Kid, Wild Bill Hickock, and Wyatt Earp—were in reality little more than street thugs, Bass Reeves was an African American lawman who always went by the letter of the law, rarely fired first, and brought thousands of outlaws to justice. Born a slave and having suffered from prejudice and bigotry all his life, he nevertheless defended the law that had kept him subservient for so long. Even at the age of eighty-one he was hired as a marshal because of his reputation for fairness and excellence. He was honest and honorable. When his own son killed his wife, he arrested him and sent him to prison. In this book, Gary Paulsen tells the story of Reeves' amazing life as a boy and as a lawman.

Gentle Criteria: This book is a gentle read because of the great character of its subject. Honorable, fair, always willing to give the outlaw a chance to surrender before he started firing, Bass Reeves was an amazing individual—even before readers consider the fact that he was born a slave. There are some grisly details of the attacks that Bass witnessed as a boy and an adult, but this book is worth including because of the great character of this man.

258 Paulsen, Gary. *The Quilt: A Companion to Alida's Song.*
Wendy Lamb Books, 2004, ISBN 978-0-385-90886-3; Random House,
2005, pap., ISBN 978-0-440-22936-0. 83p. • Grades 5–8
⌒ ACCELERATED READER ⌒ READING COUNTS

Grandmother Alida proves once again what a powerful force she is in the young
Gary Paulsen's life. When a relative, Kristina, who is with child needs help running the farm, Grandmother Alida and young Gary arrive to help. It is Gary's
first experience on a farm and everything is an adventure. When Kristina goes
into labor, women from all over descend upon the farm to help deliver her
child. Gary is shocked to hear the sounds that are coming from his cousin. Gary
is witness to the women's quilt-making as they add family members who have
passed on. Gary asks to hear the stories of these ancestors. Shortly after the birth
of Kristina's baby boy, named after his father, a soldier and preacher arrive at
their door. It is Grandmother Alida who holds the family together when they
deliver their news.

    Gentle Criteria: Real life isn't always a fairy tale, and this book illustrates
that the matriarch, Grandmother Alida, is all too aware that life must go on no
matter what happens. When Kristina's husband, Olaf, is killed, Grandmother Alida
thanks the messengers for doing their job and tells them they can now go so she
can do hers. Her job is to keep the family moving forward—surviving the bad
times and enjoying the good. This book is full of courageous, determined women.

259 Paulsen, Gary. *Tucket's Gold.*
Random House, 1999, ISBN 978-0-385-32501-1; 2001, pap., ISBN
978-0-440-41376-9. 97p. Series: Tucket Adventures • Grades 5–8
⌒ ACCELERATED READER ⌒ READING COUNTS ⌒ JUNIOR LIBRARY
GUILD

This is the fourth installment in the series. When Francis, Lottie, and Billy, along
with the one-armed mountain man Grimes, are being tracked by vicious
Comancheros, Grimes takes the packhorses and leads them off in a different
direction, to draw the Comancheros away from the young ones. Fourteen-year-
old Francis, ten-year-old Lottie, and her seven-year-old brother Billy must cross
a desert to make it back to the Oregon Trail so Francis can find his family.
Along the way they stumble across a dead Spaniard's bones—and his gold and
silver. Continuing their journey, Francis is bitten by a rattlesnake and would
have died had it not been for the Indians who found and saved him. Francis
considers remaining with the Indians permanently but has an overwhelming
desire to find his family. As they set out again, Lottie and Francis are captured by
outlaws Courtweiler and Dibs. They are about to be killed when little Billy uses
his bow and arrows to save them. They now have their gold, silver, and horses
back and can return to the search for Francis' parents.

    Gentle Criteria: Francis continues to make Lottie and her little brother
Billy part of his extended family after their parents die from cholera. This story
demonstrates that people don't have to be related to be part of a family.

260   Peck, Richard. *Fair Weather.*

Dial, 2001, ISBN 978-0-8037-2516-4; Penguin, 2003, pap., ISBN 978-0-14-250034-7. 139p. • Grades 5–7

☞ ACCELERATED READER ☞ READING COUNTS

Rosie's family receives an invitation from Aunt Euterpe to come to Chicago and see the 1893 World's Columbian Exposition. This is a warm story about a family from the country going to the big city to see the sights. It is also a wonderful period piece. They meet Lillian Russell, Buffalo Bill Cody, and generally get introduced to members of Chicago society. Snapping turtles in the kitchen, bullfrogs in the sheets (thanks to Rosie's little brother Buster), and a sly plan by her sister Lottie to meet up with her beau keep things hopping during this entertaining visit.

Gentle Criteria: Besides being a wonderful historical account, this is a warm story of a family that sticks together and helps a lonely woman find her way.

261   Peck, Richard. *Here Lies the Librarian.*

Penguin, 2006, ISBN 978-0-8037-3080-9. 160p. • Grades 5–9

☞ ACCELERATED READER ☞ READING COUNTS

This is another fine piece of historical fiction by Richard Peck. In 1914, fourteen-year-old Eleanor "Pewee" McGrath, a tomboy and budding motor mechanic, meets up with four young ladies who have library science degrees and will replace the town librarian, who has died. The four decide to share the job four ways, asking their fathers to contribute to the improvement of the town library with items such as shelves, books, lights, and a "photostat" machine. The newspaper proclaims that there is now "a bevy of book beauties" intent on improving the library. In between learning to drive a car, saving dogs, and learning to wear a dress, Eleanor finds herself persuaded to get out of her overalls and into the library, shelving books and holding social teas.

Gentle Criteria: Young Eleanor learns important lessons from these four beautiful and self-sufficient librarians: No one can make you into anything; that's *your* job, and, they don't *let* you be something—you must give yourself permission to be that something. This is an entertaining book about believing in oneself.

262   Peck, Richard. *A Long Way from Chicago.*

Dial, 1998, ISBN 978-0-8037-2290-3; Penguin, 2004, pap., ISBN 978-0-14-240110-1. 148p. • Grades 5–7

☞ ACCELERATED READER ☞ READING COUNTS

Two city children make their way each summer for seven years to their grandma's house in the country outside Chicago. Besides being a wonderful portrayal of the Depression era in the United States, this is a story of a rough-around-the-edges old woman. Overturned privies, the first automobile, Prohibition, and more make for a heart-warming and entertaining piece of historical fiction.

Gentle Criteria: Readers will both laugh and cry at the ups and down of town and country life during the Great Depression. The people are real, and no one is perfect, but the children begin to understand the deep feelings and warmth found in their grandmother's small town.

🐝 NEWBERY HONOR BOOK, 1999

263   Peck, Richard. *On the Wings of Heroes.*

Dial, 2007, ISBN 978-0-8037-3081-6. 148p. • Grades 5–9

Davy Bowman has two heroes: his father and his older brother. His father, who fought in World War I, is the biggest kid on the block, playing pranks on the neighborhood kids and joining in their games. His older brother seems to be able to do anything, and to be a success at it. But when Davy's brother joins up to fight in World War II, the life seems to go out of his father. Davy's dad finally tells him that the worst part of the war was seeing what people were capable of doing to each other.

Gentle Criteria: Richard Peck has a rare way of enabling readers to relive the innocence and fun of childhoods spent playing outdoors. The adults in Davy's life have his best interest at heart, even when he doesn't understand it. Few people do historical fiction as delightfully as Richard Peck. This book can be a great read-aloud or a study of historical America.

264   Peck, Richard. *The River Between Us.*

Dial, 2003, ISBN 978-0-8037-2735-9; Penguin, 2005, pap., ISBN 978-0-14-240310-5. 164p. • Grades 6–8

☞ ACCELERATED READER ☞ READING COUNTS

With the Civil War looming, a steamboat from New Orleans calls at Tilly's town and deposits two strange women: one light, one dark, presumed to be her servant. Tilly's family takes them in as boarders, a move that changes their family structure forever. Many-layered, this book is a snapshot of the Civil War, but it is also about the prejudice of the times and the lengths that people went to protect their loved ones. It is especially a look at the city of New Orleans and how the black and white societies lived side by side. Many years later, grandchildren visit the city and discover family secrets they never imagined.

Gentle Criteria: Although this book has its share of prejudice and horrors of war (doctors throw amputated arms in the river as they fight to save men's lives), it is essentially a story of love and family relationships.

265   Peck, Richard. *The Teacher's Funeral: A Comedy in Three Parts.*

Dial, 2004, ISBN 978-0-8037-2736-6; Penguin, 2006, pap., ISBN 978-0-14-240507-9. 190p. • Grades 5–7

☞ ACCELERATED READER

This is a laugh-out-loud story set in rural Indiana in the first years of the 20th century. When the teacher dies not long before school is to start, fifteen-year-old Russell Culver has high hopes this will mean the end of the small country school. No such luck. His sister Tansy is hired as the replacement teacher, and he knows all hope is lost. Full of good old-fashioned country humor, this book will amuse readers of all ages.

Gentle Criteria: Peck's droll humor and wry comments about country life make readers love all the characters in this book, even the unsavory ones. As could only happen in a small town, people understand each other and find a way to live together. One of the best parts is the final chapter when the author looks back and lets readers in on who ended up with whom. What fun!

266 Peck, Richard. *A Year Down Yonder.*
Penguin, 2000, ISBN 978-0-8037-2518-8; Puffin, 2002, pap., ISBN 978-0-14-230070-1. 130p. • Grades 5–7
⌒ ACCELERATED READER ⌒ READING COUNTS

In this sequel to *A Long Way from Chicago* (see above), Mary Alice returns in 1937 to her grandmother's house, where she and her brother spent the last seven summers. Now she is to spend the whole year there attending high school because her parents cannot afford for her to stay with them. Although it is very different from Chicago, Mary Alice grows to love the small town *and* her grandmother's strange ways. Assisting an elderly neighbor, she realizes that their homebound son, blinded and disabled in the Great War, could have been her father. Halloween in this small town is not trick-or-treat, but vittles and vengeance, as four boys find out when they try to tip over her grandmother's privy. Mary Alice realizes that her grandmother's earnings from trapping all winter went to bring her brother home for a visit on leave from the war. She learns from her grandmother how to keep her business private while quietly helping others.

Gentle Criteria: This rough grandmother's way of keeping order and taking care of those she loves will bring both laughter and tears. There is a lot of love and neighborliness in this place far from Chicago.
♣ NEWBERY MEDAL, 2001

267 Ray, Delia. *Ghost Girl: A Blue Ridge Mountain Story.*
Clarion, 2003, ISBN 978-0-618-33377-6. 216p. • Grades 5–9
⌒ ACCELERATED READER ⌒ READING COUNTS

This is a wonderful story of forgiveness. April's younger brother Riley died in a fire while under her care, and April knows that her mother will never forgive her because Riley was her favorite. President Hoover vacations in the Blue Ridge Mountains near them and discovers that the children have no school. He and Mrs. Hoover make it possible for a school to be built and a teacher, Miss Vest, hired. Even though April's mother is against it, her Aunt Birdy and the schoolteacher convince her to let April attend the new school as long as she gets her chores done. But there are more secrets behind her brother's death than April's mother knows. The truth finally comes out and it looks as if things will never be the same for April's family again. When Aunt Birdy is on her deathbed, forgiveness is found, but not without a price. This story is based on a school that President and Mrs. Hoover built near their vacation cabin and on the real Miss Vest's letters.

Gentle Criteria: April and her mother eventually find peace. The people who live on the mountain are not portrayed as poor and ignorant. Readers will want to visit President Hoover's old vacation spot and the national park in the Shenandoah Mountains.

268   Ray, Delia. *Singing Hands.*

Clarion, 2006, ISBN 978-0-618-65762-9. 248p. • Grades 5–9

⌒ ACCELERATED READER ⌒ READING COUNTS

The year is 1948, and Gussie Davis, the hearing daughter of deaf parents, is bored. To pass the time she keeps herself occupied by humming during the deaf church service—*Happy Birthday* at Christmas for the baby Jesus—and by dressing up as an escaped convict to scare her older sister. When her various misdemeanors come to light, she loses her coveted weeklong trip to her aunt's house. Instead, she completes spelling lists for one of the boarders, a retired teacher, and accompanies her father on a visit to the deaf college. As she works her way through her punishment, she discovers firsthand what the words on the spelling lists mean: integrity, knavery, imprudence, impropriety, mortification, perfidy, ignominy, and acrimony. Readers will laugh out loud at some of the antics; for example, when the underwear she stuffed into the escaped convict's outfit falls out in front of her older sister's boyfriend.

Gentle Criteria: Real examples of character abound in this entertaining story—both good and bad. Gussie makes herself do what's right even when every bone in her body protests. As her mother tells her, sometimes you just have to do what's right and hope you will be surprised with the results.

269   Rinaldi, Ann. *The Journal of Jasper Jonathan Pierce: A Pilgrim Boy, Plymouth, 1620.*

Scholastic, 2003, ISBN 978-0-439-55511-1. 155p. Series: My Name Is America • Grades 5–9

⌒ ACCELERATED READER ⌒ READING COUNTS

Author Ann Rinaldi does a wonderful job of mixing real historical characters with fictional characters. The story covers the *Mayflower*'s landing in Plymouth in the year 1620 and describes the actions the Pilgrims took to survive that first year. Even with their faith and effort, half of the 102 original settlers died. When the ship *Fortune* arrived in December 1621, carrying thirty-five more pilgrims, the original group had completely run out of provisions. Fortunately for the settlers they were befriended by Squanto, who had been captured in 1605 and taken to England where he learned English. He made his way back to America with Captain John Smith in 1614. Squanto teaches the newcomers to plant crops using fish as fertilizer, something that in all likelihood kept them from starving that first year. Readers learn all about the Pilgrims' adventures through the journal of Jasper Jonathan Pierce, a record he is keeping to show to the brother he left behind in England.

Gentle Criteria: The author emphasizes that the Pilgrims felt they had a higher purpose. They believed that they had to endure these hardships not only for themselves but also for the future good of mankind. They were willing to make huge sacrifices so that their families would have the freedom to worship as they wanted. Six future presidents would descend from that *Mayflower* passenger list.

270   Rocklin, Joanne. *Strudel Stories.*
Delacorte, 1997, ISBN 978-0-385-32602-5; Random House, 2000, pap., ISBN 978-0-440-41509-1. 131p. • Grades 5–9
☞ ACCELERATED READER ☞ READING COUNTS

This story features several generations of Jewish families making strudel. As they cook they tell stories, because everyone knows that strudel will not taste as good without adding the stories. One tale is about Eli's name being changed to Yakov, so the angel of death gets confused and can't find him. When Eli awakens from his near-death experience, he looks at his momma and starts singing the song Yakov used to sing—and she faints! In another strudel story, Bertha recounts her family's journey to the United States. When they arrive at Ellis Island, she is so scared that she can't make her tongue work. The examining doctor considers her feeble-minded and puts a chalk X on her coat lapel; the next station will determine whether to ship her back. Bertha gets angry and yells her name, but it's too late; so instead, she turns her coat inside out and gets to stay with her family. The common theme in all of these stories is the humanity of the people and, of course, the strudel.

Gentle Criteria: The love inherent in the making of the strudel runs through these stories. When Momma is depressed and can barely function, telling stories and making strudel helps. When young Abe is misbehaving, Sarah makes him help her with the strudel. They talk and Abe cleans up his act. This is just one of many examples of the strudel effect.

271   Ryan, Pam Muñoz. *Esperanza Rising.*
Scholastic, 2000, ISBN 978-0-439-12041-8; 2002, pap., ISBN 978-0-439-12042-5. 262p. • Grades 5–9
☞ ACCELERATED READER ☞ READING COUNTS ☞ JUNIOR LIBRARY GUILD

There is an old Mexican proverb that says that the rich person is richer when he becomes poor than the poor person is when he becomes rich. Esperanza—Esperanza means "hope" in Spanish—is the daughter of a wealthy Mexican rancher and has never wanted for anything. Her father is killed, and her uncles want to take over his ranch. Not willing to live under the uncles' terms, Esperanza and her mother leave—penniless—with their servants to go to America, where they earn their living as farm laborers. Esperanza, who has never even associated with laborers, must now become one. She does not know how to cook, sweep with a broom, change a diaper, or—for that matter—wash herself in a bathtub. When her mother contracts Valley Fever after a violent dust storm, Esperanza knows it is time to be the strong one and support herself and her mother. She considers what her aunt told her when teaching her to crochet: Never be afraid to start over.

Gentle Criteria: This story, set in the 1920s and 1930s in Mexico and America, is based on the author's grandmother. Although full of hard times, this novel is about hope. Esperanza learns at a young age that income has very little to do with happiness or goodness.

🐝   Pura Belpré Award (Narrative), 2002

272   St. Anthony, Jane. *The Summer Sherman Loved Me.*

Farrar, Straus & Giroux, 2006, ISBN 978-0-374-37289-7. 136p. •
Grades 5–7

Twelve-year-old Margaret must find a way to deal with her changing relationship with her mother, her childhood friend who now wants to be her boyfriend, and her own mixed-up feelings about whether she wants to be a kid or an adult. When Sherman whispers loudly through the porch screen that he loves her, she knows everything is about to change. This is a sweet but realistic story about making the transition from child to adult. Among the characters in this 1960s neighborhood are a delightful set of twins, a houseful of wild boys, a sweet son who takes care of his elderly mother and his wonderful roses, and a smart-mouthed best friend who tells it like it is.

Gentle Criteria: There is nothing more to this early romance than two gentle kisses. The parents in the story are not perfect, but they love their children with a passion, as evidenced when there is an accident or when a child goes missing.

273   Schmidt, Gary D. *The Wednesday Wars.*

Clarion, 2007, ISBN 978-0-618-72483-3. 264p. • Grades 5–9

Holling swears that his seventh-grade teacher, Mrs. Baker, hates him. She sends him to the office, suggesting that he retake sixth-grade math on Wednesday afternoons while everyone else is at religious education. The principal instructs Mrs. Baker to work with him every Wednesday afternoon instead. while the other kids are gone. On these Wednesdays, he cleans chalkboards and then the rat cages—until they escape—and then he is finally instructed to read Shakespeare. When he appeals to his father for help, he receives none. Eventually, Holling realizes what a treasure Mrs. Baker is, and that it's actually his own dad who is the selfish jerk. Mrs. Baker drives him to the opening-day baseball game that his father forgot. Mrs. Baker, an Olympic medalist, teaches him how to run properly. And Mrs. Baker teaches him through Shakespeare that one must learn all there is to learn, and be honest, good, and kind to others.

Gentle Criteria: This story is truly a historical masterpiece that brings characters from the 1960s into the story—Mickey Mantle, Robert Kennedy, Martin Luther King, Jr., and the Vietnam War all have an impact. When Holling's sister leaves for California with a hippie to find herself, it is Holling who cashes in his savings and sends the money to her via Western Union so she can get home. Holling, because of the guidance offered by Mrs. Baker, is bound to become a much better man than his father, and he proves in the story that he already is.

274   Selznick, Brian. *The Invention of Hugo Cabret.*

Ill. by author. Scholastic, 2007, ISBN 978-0-439-81378-5. 533p. •
Grades 5–7

◠ Accelerated Reader ◠ Junior Library Guild

It is 1931. Hugo Cabret is living alone behind the clockworks in a Paris train station. His father, a clockmaker, discovered an automaton hidden away during his job working at a museum. He and Hugo became obsessed with the automaton, a robot-like creation that can perform some human functions, such as writing. One night, Hugo's father stays after work to tinker with it and is accidentally locked in the museum. When fire breaks out Hugo's father dies. Hugo is taken to live with his uncle at the clockworks. When his uncle doesn't return one day, twelve-year-old Hugo takes it upon himself to keep the clocks running and to try to survive. Then he discovers the remains of the automaton in the ashes of the fire and is convinced that it will contain a message from his father if only he can get it to work. And then the real mystery begins, with a man who runs a toy store, the young girl who lives with him, and a heart-shaped key she wears around her neck. Based on the life of cinematographer Georges Melies, this book will touch readers' hearts as Hugo and Isabelle discover who the real Melies is.

Gentle Criteria: Herein there is a boy who loved his father, a toymaker who has given up hope, a mystery to be solved, friends to be made, and a glimpse of the beginning of the twentieth century in Paris. As Hugo and Isabelle add trust to their friendship, more of the mystery is solved. The old toymaker who has given up on his career is brought back to life just as the automaton is. Hugo figures the entire world is one big machine. Machines need a reason to run, and so Hugo must be there for a reason too. With everybody's help, Hugo and Isabelle mend not only the automaton but also the old man.

 Caldecott Medal, 2008

275 Smith, Roland. *The Captain's Dog: My Journey with the Lewis and Clark Tribe.*

Harcourt, 1999, ISBN 978-0-15-201989-1; 2000, pap., ISBN 978-0-15-202696-7. 287p. • Grades 7–9

⌐ ACCELERATED READER ⌐ READING COUNTS

Two men who were on the expedition with Lewis and Clark to find the famed Northwest Passage come across Meriwether Lewis's lost dog, Seaman. With the dog is a red journal: Lewis's personal diary. As they read aloud and translate the journal for the Indian taking care of the dog, the dog reminisces and gives his perspective of what happened along the way. Not until the end of this heartwarming story do we find out how the journal survived and how the dog ended up where he is. Watching Sacajawea yell at her husband, fighting off wolves and grizzly bears, smelling a cat's scent and discovering the cat is in fact a mountain lion, and biting a stampeding buffalo's ear to distract it from the men sitting in camp all make for exciting reading. Students who have learned about Lewis and Clark in class will find this an entertaining version of what really happened. A map of the expedition and an informative note from the author are included.

Gentle Criteria: A loyal dog is about as heartwarming as you can get. This story also illustrates what truly good people Lewis and Clark were, as were the Indians and other people who helped them on their amazing journey.

276 Staples, Suzanne Fisher. *Under the Persimmon Tree.*

Farrar, Straus & Giroux, 2005, ISBN 978-0-374-38025-0. 275p. • Grades 7–9

⌐ ACCELERATED READER ⌐ READING COUNTS ⌐ JUNIOR LIBRARY GUILD

Shortly after September 11, 2001, Najmah's father and brother are taken by the Taliban in Afghanistan and forced to fight for them. When the Americans bomb Afghanistan, Najmah sees her mother and new brother killed. At the same time in Peshawar, Nusrat, an American, is waiting hopefully for her doctor husband to return from a clinic in the north of the country. To pass the time, Nusrat teaches the refugee children. Told in alternating chapters, this story shows how Najmah and Nusrat eventually find each other amidst hope and despair, and they help each other through tough times. Although the ending leaves readers wondering what the future holds, readers can be assured these two will always strive to make the country they love the best it can be.

Gentle Criteria: Although this is a tough book to read at times, there is such a strong thread of hope, love, loyalty, and strength that it needs to be included here. When Najmah tells Nusrat what has happened to her, it takes her breath away that such a young child should have experienced such horrific things. Najmah understands that she must learn to trust someone or she will never survive. Nusrat's husband returned to Afghanistan out of love for his family and country, and Nusrat has come to feel the same way. When Najmah chooses to stay in the country she loves, Nusrat is amazed, knowing the hardships Najmah has chosen. Readers in grades 7 to 9 who are ready for a more mature read will find their hearts touched by this inspiring story.

277   Stolz, Joelle. *The Shadows of Ghadames.*
Random House, 2004, ISBN 978-0-385-90131-4; 2006, pap., ISBN 978-0-440-41949-5. 119p. • Grades 7–9
☞ Accelerated Reader ☞ Reading Counts ☞ Junior Library Guild

At the end of the nineteenth century in southern Libya, eleven-year-old Malika's father is away on business, leaving her with his two wives. They hear a disturbance in the middle of the night. Going out to investigate, they discover a stranger, seriously hurt. They drag him inside even though it is forbidden to have another man in the house. They hide him and take care of him. While he recuperates, the man teaches Malika to read. He tells Malika that the word of God is for everyone to read—not just men—and that ignorance is a darkness. Malika discovers that there are other worlds outside the roof of her house—and the stranger discovers that the restricted world of women is not as ignorant as he believed. When he has to dress as a woman in order to escape, he is further humbled. Readers will be left hoping that the stranger will meet up with Malika again.

Gentle Criteria: This is another positive book that portrays a different culture, featuring strong messages about respecting differences and providing equality for both men and women. Malika's father tells her that only weak men fear educated women. He chooses not to own slaves because he thinks it is wrong, even though it would help him develop his lands and prosper.
🌺   Mildred L. Batchelder Award, 2005

278   Sturtevant, Katherine. *At the Sign of the Star.*
Farrar, Straus & Giroux, 2000, ISBN 978-0-374-30449-2; 2002, pap., ISBN 978-0-374-40458-1. 140p. • Grades 7–9
☞ Accelerated Reader ☞ Reading Counts ☞ Junior Library Guild

This is an engaging piece of historical fiction set in London in the 1600s, when women had few rights. Meg is a young girl whose mother died while giving birth to a child who also died. Her father is a bookseller and publisher with contacts with all the best-known figures in London's literary scene. Meg has grown up reading anything she likes in her father's store and helping him with his business. But everything changes when he decides to take a new wife. Her inheritance is now threatened, and she must be trained either to be someone's wife or to go into service in another household. Meg is horrified. When her stepmother gives birth to a son—and heir—Meg realizes she will have to be clever and find a way to make her own way in the world. She discovers a new woman playwright among the literary texts, and finds that she herself has a talent for writing. Told by a local astrologer to steer her own boat into the wind, Meg finds a way both to love her baby brother and to take charge of her own life.

Gentle Criteria: This is a positive story about a young woman striving to take control of her own life at a time when women had few legal rights. Meg loves her new brother in spite of herself, and she finds ways to work around her lost inheritance. When her stepmother is determined to breastfeed despite her father's opposition, Meg collects educated texts in favor of it that she knows will make a positive impression on him. This is a book about being educated and thinking for oneself. A few bawdy passages are part of the time she is living in, such as the crowd helping to undress the bride and groom at the marriage bed, and superstitions concerning dreaming of lovers and having babies that look like them.

279   **Tingle, Rebecca.** *The Edge on the Sword.*
Putnam, 2001, ISBN 978-0-399-23580-1; Penguin, 2003, pap., ISBN 978-0-14-250058-3. 277p. • Grades 7–9
⌒ Accelerated Reader ⌒ Reading Counts

Aethelflaed of West Saxony, daughter of King Alfred in the late 800s, is promised in marriage to Ethelred of Mercia in the hopes of strengthening the ties between the two countries. On the day that she is betrothed to Ethelred, she acquires a bodyguard named Red who shadows her every move to keep her safe for her future husband. She is angry at being shadowed, and on the day that she finally outwits Red, she is kidnapped. He rescues her but tells her father that now he will teach her to defend herself. He brings her a coat of mail and teaches her to fight. When he is slain taking her to her wedding, she finds herself leading the men who are supposed to be protecting her. Not without some blood and gore—there is a scene where a slain leader's head is in the middle of the enemy camp—this is a stirring story of a strong young woman and the noble fight she leads to protect her people.

Gentle Criteria: This is a piece of historical fiction based on the life of a young girl. Red the bodyguard wears his old slave rings as a reminder that he was not able to save his family when his king betrayed him. Readers will be brought to tears at the end of the story when Ethelred locates his bride as he promised he would, but Red does not make it back to camp. Aethelflaed goes to a strange country to wed a man she does not know, but she does it to keep two countries safe. She is no fragile woman but a force to contend with, and she is well-respected for it.

280   Vega, Diego, and Jan Adkins (reteller). *Young Zorro: The Iron Brand.*

HarperCollins, 2006, ISBN 978-0-06-083946-8. 233p. • Grades 5–7

☞ ACCELERATED READER

This book is about Zorro as a child. Diego is the son of Don Diego de la Vega, and he has a milk brother, Bernardo, who was nursed by Diego's mother and is being raised by Diego's family because his mother was murdered when he was a baby. Bernardo and Diego discover the disappearance of more than forty skilled tradesmen from town and two hundred head of cattle. On a cattle drive, they put out a small brush fire and find a branding iron that is a clue to the missing cattle and tradesmen. They solve the mystery with the help of Trinidad, an orphaned girl who is as comfortable in a boat as they are on horses. This is an entertaining adventure that gives some background to this legendary character and the Old West.

Gentle Criteria: Don de la Vega shares his philosophy freely with his sons Diego and Bernardo. They hang on his every word, and readers can envision them absorbing some of the injustices that take place in this story, applying them to Zorro's adult code of conduct. Diego also experiences the goodness of El Chollo, who steals from the rich and gives to the poor. These are people who shape the code of conduct that Zorro exemplifies.

281   Wait, Lea. *Stopping to Home.*

Margaret K. McElderry Books, 2001, ISBN 978-0-689-83832-3; Simon & Schuster, 2003, pap., ISBN 978-0-689-83849-1. 152p. • Grades 5–7

☞ ACCELERATED READER ☞ READING COUNTS

It is the year 1806 in Wiscasset, Maine, and eleven-year-old Abby's mother has just died from smallpox. Her father has been away at sea for months, and she does not know if he will return. The kindly doctor who looks after Abby's family asks a young matron to take her and her brother in; the matron's husband is also sick with smallpox. Abby will be able to help because she and her brother have already had the disease and are now immune to it. When the husband, a wealthy sea captain, dies, Abby holds her breath. Will the young woman decide to go back to her family, leaving them homeless again? But the new widow is an independent young woman who has no intention of looking for another husband or being dependent on her family. The only question is how will she make a living once the funds are gone? Abby and her brother not only help to solve this problem, but they also find a new home and plenty of love to go around.

Gentle Criteria: Without the good folks in this story, Abby and her brother would have ended up in an orphanage—or worse. The story behind Abby's mother's wooden eider duck is a recurring theme: When the male ducks leave their families and go to sea, the female ducks and their young stay so close together that they are called a "raft" of eiders. If anything happens to one of the mothers, the remaining females raise the young as their own. The young widow

Lydia, and Abby and all of their friends all manage to do the very same thing and create a warm home of their own.

282   **Weil, Sylvie.** *My Guardian Angel.*
Arthur A. Levine, 2001, ISBN 978-0-439-57681-9; Scholastic, 2007, pap., ISBN 978-0-439-57682-6. 202p. • Grades 5–9
✎ ACCELERATED READER ✎ READING COUNTS

This is a wonderful story about compassion and tolerance, based on real people. In 1096, Elvina, a twelve-year-old Jewish girl, helps a wounded Crusader who would much rather be learning than fighting. He has tried to run away from the fighting but now he is wounded. She knows it is right to help people in trouble, but she also knows that the Crusaders have been rampaging through the countryside, hurting many of the Jewish faith. When she decides to hide the Crusader, she knows that she is going against the wishes of everyone in her small village. But how can she hurt someone who merely wants to learn, just as she does? In return for her kindness to the Crusader, her two brothers are returned to the family, but her family does not forgive her for her transgression against the whole village. It is when her father's life is spared by the Crusaders that he acknowledges her great gift to him and to the village. Historical notes are provided at the end.

    Gentle Criteria: Without Elvina's compassion and kindness, her brothers, her father, and probably the entire village would not have survived. The villagers could have battled the Crusaders but decided that it was best to help them. Elvina's tolerance and diplomacy make the difference between heightening friction and finding common ground with strangers. What a role model! Conflict resolution at all levels could be discussed in conjunction with this novel, which is both informative and uplifting.

283   **Whelan, Gloria.** *Listening for Lions.*
HarperCollins, 2005, ISBN 978-0-06-058175-6; 2006, pap., ISBN 978-0-06-058176-3. 194p. • Grades 7–9
✎ ACCELERATED READER ✎ READING COUNTS ✎ JUNIOR LIBRARY GUILD

Thirteen-year-old Rachel is orphaned when her missionary parents die in East Africa during an influenza epidemic. Rachel is immediately snatched up by the Pritchards, whose daughter Valerie also perished from the flu. The Pritchards intended to send Valerie to England to meet her wealthy grandfather and get back in his good graces. They now convince Rachel—who has nowhere else to go—to pretend to be Valerie. Rachel sets off on the journey to England, intending to inform the grandfather of the truth as soon as she arrives. But when she meets the man she is convinced that the truth will be too much for him. As time passes, she endears herself to him, watching the birds on his grounds and telling him stories of the Africa that she loves. But the truth is revealed when the

Pritchards arrive. Instead of being punished as she expects, Rachel discovers that he loves her no matter who she really is.

Gentle Criteria: This is a strong story of love for the people Rachel cares about and for the land she grew up in. Rachel is a good soul who finds a kindred spirit in the grandfather whom she sets out to fool. She ends up loving him as much as any real grandfather. Her wish to become a woman doctor and help needy African people is commendable and heartfelt.

284   Whitesel, Cheryl Aylward. *Blue Fingers: A Ninja's Tale.*
Clarion, 2004, ISBN 978-0-618-38139-5. 252p. • Grades 5–7
☞ Accelerated Reader ☞ Junior Library Guild

Based on historical fact, this is the story of Koji, who was born in the year 1545 in Japan. As a twin he is considered unlucky. Through a surprising turn of events, he is kidnapped by a ninja clan. The only way to escape is to die. He is trained unwillingly to be a ninja. Only when he discovers that the samurai have burned his family's village does he become a true part of the clan. In their adventures against the samurai, Koji discovers what true loyalty is.

Gentle Criteria: Although full of hardship and fighting, this is really a story of loyalty, endurance, and yearning for family. In the end Koji finds happiness. It's a great adventure story with enduring themes.

285   Winthrop, Elizabeth. *Counting on Grace.*
Wendy Lamb Books, 2006, ISBN 978-0-385-90878-8; Random House, 2007, pap., ISBN 978-0-553-48783-1. 232p. • Grades 5–9
☞ Accelerated Reader ☞ Reading Counts ☞ Junior Library Guild

Strong-willed Grace is able to start working in the mill at age twelve (instead of the regulation fourteen) because her mother uses a birth certificate from a baby who died fourteen years ago to get her in. Her family needs the money. Arthur, who is forced to leave school to work in the mill, purposefully puts his hand into a machine and loses two fingers, thinking he won't have to work there anymore and can return to school. Unfortunately, the mill evicts both him and his mother, and he is forced to seek handouts from relatives. The teacher teams up with Grace and Arthur, and they write a letter to try to correct the illegal use of children in the mill, resulting in the teacher being fired. Grace gets hired as the temporary teacher in her absence.

Gentle Criteria: The subject of this story is child labor, but with an emphasis on the good people who tried to put a stop to it. The characters are enjoyable, and the author takes a disturbing subject and brings it to life. She points out how families were dependent on their children to work as soon as they could to help make ends meet. Grace's limited education helps her to realize that the storekeeper is adding charges to their bill, so her education proves worthwhile. The teacher is willing to risk her job to change Grace's life. The dangers of the mill are exposed and readers get a clear view of what it was like to live in these times. This book should be recommended to mature readers because of its subject matter.

286 Woodworth, Chris. *Georgie's Moon.*
Farrar, Straus & Giroux, 2006, ISBN 978-0-374-33306-5. 167p. •
Grades 5–9
⌐ ACCELERATED READER

When twelve-year-old Georgie moves to yet another town because her dad is fighting in the Vietnam War, she has a giant chip on her shoulder. She's irritated with the kids her mom is babysitting. She is mad at the kids in school who are against the war. She is upset that her mom won't let her look for her dad on the news every night. When her mom makes her visit the school counselor, she even breaks a ship in a bottle that the counselor's father made for her—just to send the counselor the message to *back off* and leave her alone. Georgie's one friend, Lisa, has also made her mad because Lisa never told Georgie that her brother ran away to Canada rather than joining the service. Finally, Georgie's dad's army buddy arrives to deliver a letter to Georgie. It is a letter that her dad wrote to give to her if he died, and Georgie must now face what she has been denying all along: Her father is dead. After reading the emotional letter, Georgie knows she now has new standing orders: To take care of her mom and to remember that her father always loved her.

Gentle Criteria: This is an excellent book that conveys the message that young people often misbehave because they don't know how to deal with emotional issues that are taking place at home. Readers will be shocked when Georgie's mom sells the television to prevent her from searching for her father every night on the news. Then readers understand that her mother sold the TV to force Georgie to accept her father's death. This book proves how a patient counselor, parent, and friend can help.

Mystery and Detective Stories

287 Anderson, Janet S. *The Last Treasure.*

Dutton, 2003, ISBN 978-0-525-46919-3; Penguin, 2004, pap., ISBN 978-0-14-240217-7. 257p. • Grades 5–7

☞ ACCELERATED READER ☞ READING COUNTS

On his thirteenth birthday, Ellsworth receives a card containing three hundred dollars for a bus ticket to meet the family his father never talks about. Here is his chance to meet them. He discovers even more mysteries when he arrives there! Long ago the family patriarch built ten houses on a square, and then cleverly hid three treasures among the houses. Two of the treasures have been found, each in a time of great need. Once again, the family is in need, and it is up to Ellsworth and his cousin to find the third treasure. They will have to get the whole family to work together to succeed. Will they be able to do it?

Gentle Criteria: This is a multilayered mystery. There is the underlying question of why Ellsworth's father has cut off all ties with his family, and there is Ellsworth's own need for a family and a place where he belongs. Most of all, this story is about family, and how no one but family knows all the stories that make up a family's past. Even with their differences, they all love each other. There is a sense of continuity, of generations of people who belong to each other. But most of all, the story helps everyone discover what the real treasure is: themselves.

288   Balliet, Blue. *Chasing Vermeer.*
Ill. by Brett Helquist. Scholastic, 2004, ISBN 978-0-439-37294-7; 2005, pap., ISBN 978-0-439-37297-8. 254p. • Grades 5–7
☞ ACCELERATED READER ☞ READING COUNTS

Three people receive mysterious letters telling them to embark on a quest to find the truth behind a Vermeer painting. Eleven-year-olds Petra and Calder combine their talents and ingenuity to uncover an international art scandal. This is a well-plotted mystery reminiscent of *The Westing Game* and *From the Mixed-Up Files of Mrs. Basil E. Frankweiler*. Great illustrations and a set of pentominoes (a mathematical tool consisting of twelve pieces) provide clues—which are neither obvious nor simple—throughout the book.

Gentle Criteria: There are lots of possibilities for math and language arts teachers and book clubs with this book. A delightful companion Web site is also available.

289   Balliet, Blue. *The Wright 3.*
Scholastic, 2006, ISBN 978-0-439-69367-7. 318p. • Grades 5–7
☞ ACCELERATED READER ☞ READING COUNTS

Petra, Calder, and Tommy are back in this sequel to *Chasing Vermeer* (see above). The famous Robie House in Chicago, built by Frank Lloyd Wright, is in danger of being demolished, and the three sixth graders and their classmates take it upon themselves to save the house. Along the way they uncover information that leads them to believe someone is sabotaging their efforts. This is a great read that includes fascinating details about Wright's art.

Gentle Criteria: There are a lot of teachable moments in this entertaining book full of information about art and well-known landmarks in Chicago. Positive examples of teamwork and friendship abound, and positive adult models include the teacher, parents, and other adults interested in saving what is an important piece of art.

290   Broach, Elise. *Shakespeare's Secret.*
Henry Holt, 2005, ISBN 978-0-8050-7387-4. 250p. • Grades 5–7
☞ ACCELERATED READER ☞ READING COUNTS ☞ JUNIOR LIBRARY GUILD

Hero and Danny discover a long-lost heirloom and become mixed up with the crazy old lady next door. This mystery includes historical references to whether De Vere was the real Shakespeare and where the necklace belonging to Ann Boleyn is really located.

Gentle Criteria: This book is a great instrument for introducing students to both Shakespeare and good mystery writing. As in *Chasing Vermeer*, capable young people follow the clues and solve the mystery. Basing the story on historical fact makes it even more interesting and useful.

291   Brockmeier, Kevin. *Grooves: A Kind of Mystery.*
HarperCollins, 2006, ISBN 978-0-06-073692-7. 199p. • Grades 5–7
⌇ Accelerated Reader ⌇ Reading Counts

Seventh-grader Dwayne Ruggles discovers that the grooves in the potato chips and jeans from Howard Thigpen's factories are encoded with secret messages. Somebody desperately needs help! A Spark Transplantation Machine, Ghostbuster records, rhinestone jackets, a teacher who lives above a comic book store, and the ability to act like a chicken all serve Dwayne well as he tries to save the factory workers and keep his friends from harm. A super-tall friend named Kevin and an oddball girl named Emily do their part to make things come out right. This book will make readers want to investigate fingerprints and how sounds are recorded.

   Gentle Criteria: This fun classroom read is an unusual mystery with a science fiction twist. It includes lots of scientific facts and clever kids. Friendship plays a part as does a grandfather who encourages Dwayne to think for himself. Readers will not put this book down!

292   Clements, Andrew. *Room One: A Mystery or Two.*
Ill. by Chris Blair. Simon & Schuster, 2006, ISBN 978-0-689-86686-9. 162p. • Grades 5–6
⌇ Accelerated Reader ⌇ Reading Counts ⌇ Junior Library Guild

Ted lives on a farm outside a small town in Nebraska and attends a one-room schoolhouse with eight other students. As he delivers newspapers one morning, he glimpses a face in the window of an abandoned house—and sees an opportunity to solve a mystery. He discovers that a mother and two children are living there; their father was killed in Iraq. Their mother is having a difficult time coping while trying to get away from another man who won't leave her alone. Ted sneaks food to the family, but his teacher sees him and is suspicious. To continue helping this family Ted must share his secret. The whole town turns out to help this family in need and in the process they also help themselves. Ted not only helps this mother cope with her problems but also demonstrates what a great place his small town is.

   Gentle Criteria: This short book is a touching read. Its message is loud and clear: people need each other to survive. The mother in the story thinks she is all alone but soon learns there is an entire town willing to help her. This story illustrates that sometimes you have to take a risk and tell people that you need help.

293   Colfer, Eoin. *Half-Moon Investigations.*
Hyperion, 2006, ISBN 978-0-7868-4957-4. 290p. • Grades 5–7
⌇ Accelerated Reader

Twelve-year-old Fletcher Moon, nicknamed Half-Moon because of his height, is the world's youngest detective. Little does he know that he will soon become a prime suspect when a classmate hires him for a case. As Fletcher starts to uncover clues to who really stole rock-singer Shona Biederbeck's lock of hair (originally purchased on eBay by his classmate), he discovers a larger plot, ultimately involving the winner of the school talent show. There are wonderfully amusing moments in this book. When Red Sharkey hides Fletcher in his house, his well-to-do siblings move Fletcher's entire bedroom out of his parent's house along with his father's credit card. Red, the town good-for-nothing, owns a library card—and is found reading *Black Beauty*!

Gentle Criteria: This author has captured the essence of middle-school mentality and thrown in lots of humor. The story here is that the people you least expect to have good intentions usually turn out to be the good guys, as is often true in real life. There will undoubtedly be more books about the exploits of this budding young detective.

294   Jennings, Richard W. *Mystery in Mt. Mole.*

Houghton Mifflin, 2003, ISBN 978-0-618-28478-8. 144p. • Grades 6–8

☞ ACCELERATED READER

Shortly after a tornado hits the town where Andrew J. Forrest lives, grasshoppers appear everywhere, strange rumblings occur, and Assistant Principal Farley, the least-liked person in town, disappears. When his school is closed indefinitely, Andrew takes it upon himself to find out what really happened to Mr. Farley. Little does he expect the secrets he will uncover about the town, the people who live there, and most of all, the town's famous landmark, Mt. Mole. Nothing is as it seems, and Andrew has been living with the truth right under his nose! Readers will be intrigued by the town's characters and Andrew's views on small-town life. All ends well, but there is still one last mystery to keep readers wanting more.

Gentle Criteria: This is a story about simple small-town life, filled with quirky characters and mystery. Andrew gets a real, grown-up kiss, discovers that some of the people he didn't like are not so bad after all, and recognizes his own strength of character.

295   Klise, Kate. *Regarding the Bathrooms: A Privy to the Past.*

Ill. by M. Sarah Klise. Harcourt, 2006, ISBN 978-0-15-205164-8. 145p. • Grades 5–8

☞ ACCELERATED READER

This is Book Four in the *Regarding* series (see the previous volumes below). Principal Walter Russ has contacted Florence Waters again, hoping she will write his conference speech and fix up his bathroom. The students are taking summer school and have decided to be interns in businesses around town rather than studying. Some are being detectives, others are working for the newspaper.

All these jobs will come in handy when convicts Sally Mander and Dee Eel escape from jail. And the police are going to arrest Florence Waters in the case of stolen artifacts that are being sold on the Internet. They say she's been traveling the world and hiding her goods in Geyser Creek. Will the children be able to use the skills they learned during their internships to save Florence Waters from jail—and find the missing prisoners?

Gentle Criteria: Sometimes you just need to read a book that will make you chuckle. This witty volume is full of clever wordplay. The proctologist's name is Dr. Gladys Ownleepoup. An eruption helps to reveal the origin of the town's volcanic mountain's name: Jawlseedat. The first thing out of someone's mouth after the bang is, "Did ya all see that?" This is a clever, entertaining book with lots of humorous, engaging drawings.

296   **Klise, Kate.** *Regarding the Fountain: A Tale, in Letters, of Liars and Leaks.*
Ill. by M. Sarah Klise. Avon, 1998, ISBN 978-0-380-97538-9; Harper-Collins, 1999, pap., ISBN 978-0-380-79347-1. 138p. • Grades 5–8
⬿ ACCELERATED READER ⬿ READING COUNTS

This is Book One in the Regarding series. Dry Creek Middle School's water fountain has sprung a leak. Curiously, two businesspeople—Dee Eel and Sally Mander—do not want it to be repaired. They built the middle school thirty years before, and the town hasn't had water since. Everyone has to buy water from Dee Eel and go swimming at Sally Mander's pool. When an artistic designer, Florence Waters, offers to replace the water fountain, Dee Eel and Sally Mander try to stop her. Students armed with cameras and recording equipment are encouraged by their teacher and Florence to investigate further. What they turn up will bring life back to the town and land a couple of criminals behind bars.

Gentle Criteria: This book uses a unique approach in sharing its story. It is a chronological compilation of letters, memos, faxes, and so forth. Clever names such as Barry Cuda for the town's lawyer and Anne Chovey for the judge add to its charm. This book may inspire young writers to create similar stories. The entertaining storyline will delight even younger students.

297   **Klise, Kate.** *Regarding the Sink: Where Oh Where Did Waters Go?*
Ill. by M. Sarah Klise. Gulliver, 2004, ISBN 978-0-15-205019-1; Harcourt, 2006, pap., ISBN 978-0-15-205544-8. 133p. • Grades 5–8
⬿ READING COUNTS

This is Book Two in the Regarding series. Geyser Creek Middle School (formerly Dry Creek Middle School) is in need of a new sink and wants to hire Florence Waters to design a sink comparable to the wonderful fountain she created previously. Unfortunately, Florence is missing and the sixth-grade students will have to use their detective abilities to find her. Meanwhile, Senator Sue Ergass is making all schools serve beans for lunch. She's also asking everyone to send beans to China so the Chinese will stop eating the endangered Sinking Blinking Spotted Suckerfish. Senator Ergass has recently received a $100 million contribution from GASP. When the school sink blows up and the kids notice paint stains under Senator Ergass's gloves, they know there is something fishy going on. The air is becoming so foul it's hard to breathe. Cows are not producing as much milk, and the Chinese aren't eating the beans. Will the sixth-grade students solve the mystery and find their lost friend?

Gentle Criteria: This book is written in such a unique style with lots of letters, postcards, memos, newspaper ads, and similar communications that will attract even a reluctant reader with their wit and unique illustrations. The cranky principal is the last person one would expect to silently bid $100,000 for a letter from Florence. His generosity not only provides the funds the students need to fly to China to search for Florence, but also shows what a sentimental person he is. He bids on the letter because it contains positive words that were never spoken to him before.

298   Klise, Kate. *Regarding the Trees: A Splintered Saga Rooted in Secrets.*
Ill. by M. Sarah Klise. Harcourt, 2005, ISBN 978-0-15-205163-1; 2007, pap., ISBN 978-0-15-206090-9. 148p. • Grades 5–8
⌒ ACCELERATED READER ⌒ READING COUNTS

This is Book Three in the Regarding series. If you like trees and sappy dialogue—no pun intended—this book will amuse you no end with characters like Leif Blite, Angel Fisch, and Justin Case (a judge). This story is about a principal who is going to be evaluated and believes he needs to trim and cut down trees to improve his evaluation. The artist named Florence who installed a fountain and sink at the school is often consulted on such matters, but the principal's mention of a "proposal" is misunderstood. Meanwhile a crisis arises on the food front, with chefs Angel Fisch and Angelo locked in rivalry. This creates a split in the community; all the males side with Angelo and all the females with Angel. Leif Blite is on his way to evaluate the principal. Will the principal get everything in shape in time to save his job? Will the town stop feuding over whose food is best? Will the tree lovers save the trees?

Gentle Criteria: Lots of clever wit and humor are contained in this collection of letters and memos that keep readers abreast of what's happening in the small town. During the feud the men want to rename the town "Guys R Creek," while the women want to call it "Guys (It's) Her Creek." This story shows how a little love and caring can cure just about anything.

299 **Springer, Nancy.** *The Case of the Missing Marquess: An Enola Holmes Mystery.*
Philomel, 2006, ISBN 978-0-399-24304-2. 216p. • Grades 7–9
☞ ACCELERATED READER ☞ READING COUNTS

Enola Holmes, the younger sister of the renowned detectives Sherlock and Mycroft Holmes, awakens on her fourteenth birthday to discover that her mother has mysteriously disappeared. Among the birthday presents that her mother left her is a book of ciphers, something Enola hates to do. When her two older brothers arrive, it is clear that they—not her mother—were left in charge of her father's estate. She finds that her mother has defied convention by not managing either Enola or the estate the way society expects. Enola promptly runs away to try to find her mother and to escape the dreaded boarding school where she will finally be made to act like a lady. Along the way she uncovers a kidnapping (of the marquess in the title), escapes murderous villains, and eludes her perceptive older brother Sherlock.

Gentle Criteria: Enola, her mother, and even the spoiled Marquess of Basilwether find positive ways to escape the authoritarian times that they live in. Enola is clever and resourceful and she and her mother are excellent, positive female protagonists. Readers will be entranced by them and will want to emulate their confidence in their abilities.

Fantasy

300   Almond, David. *Skellig.*

Delacorte, 1998, ISBN 978-0-385-90101-7; Chivers, 1999, pap., ISBN 978-0-7540-6066-6. 182p. • Grades 5–8

☞ READING COUNTS

Ten-year-old Michael's life is in an upheaval. His parents have bought a new house to fix up, and the new baby comes earlier than expected and is hospitalized. Trying to adjust both to a new neighborhood and the long days that his parents spend at the hospital, Michael investigates the dilapidated garage next to his house and discovers a strange creature. Is it a man, a giant owl, an angel, or a little bit of all three? And can this magical being somehow make his baby sister well? Michael and his friend Mina help the strange creature recover his strength and in return are rewarded.

Gentle Criteria: Enduring themes of love and family run through this book. Two children help a disguised angel and are rewarded immeasurably—not in gold, but in the things that really matter—family and good health.

301   Anderson, Janet S. *Going Through the Gate.*

Dutton, 1997, ISBN 978-0-525-45836-4; Penguin, 2000, pap., ISBN 978-0-14-130698-8. 134p. • Grades 5–7

☞ ACCELERATED READER ☞ READING COUNTS

Five sixth-grade students are ready to graduate from the last one-room schoolhouse in the county, but there is something mysterious about the sixth-grade graduation. Twenty-five years ago one person in their small town lost an eye, and no one will talk about what happens during graduation. Each of the five students has spent this year getting to know a wild creature and imagining what it would be like to be that creature. Magically on their graduation day they will all go through the gate and become that creature for a short time. They must remember, however, that some of them have chosen to be prey and some have chosen to be predators. Miss Clough, their teacher, is getting old, and things don't go entirely as they should, but the children manage to set things right, and through their love for each other bring back the one student who almost didn't make it. This is a story about caring for God's creatures and having empathy for all people in the world.

Gentle Criteria: This is a short story about taking care of all of God's creatures. Each of the students has a problem in his life, and becoming another creature helps to put that in perspective. It is the student who almost doesn't make it back, however, that shocks them all into realizing that they must care for each other.

302   Avi. *The Book Without Words: A Fable of Medieval Magic.*
Hyperion, 2005, ISBN 978-0-7868-0829-8; Disney, 2006, pap., ISBN 978-0-7868-1659-0. 203p. • Grades 5–7
⌒ Accelerated Reader ⌒ Reading Counts

Written as a fable and based in medieval England, this is the story of a magical book without words that only those with a strong desire—and green eyes—can read. Master Thorston wishes to live forever, and with his magical book—and the sacrifice of a couple of other lives—he may be able to do it. But as his servant girl Sybil so cleverly points out, what good is it to live forever if you never live a life? Sybil and those she befriends have the courage and goodness to see what really matters and are able to put the book in the right hands in the end, but not without much trial and tribulation. As the old proverb at the beginning of the book says, "A life unlived is like a book without words."

Gentle Criteria: Sybil and those she befriends have never known a loving hand but are able to respond in kind once they experience one. Written in fable form, this is a story of magic, evil, and goodness that wins in the end.

303   Barry, Dave, and Ridley Pearson. *Peter and the Shadow Thieves.*
Ill. by Greg Call. Hyperion, 2006, ISBN 978-0-7868-3787-8. 556p. •
Grades 5–8
⌒ Accelerated Reader

In this sequel to *Peter and the Starcatchers* (see below), Molly is in danger when Lord Ombra comes to the island looking for the stardust and finds that Molly and her father have taken it to London. Peter flies to London with Tinker Bell to warn Molly. With scary Lord Ombra—a thief who steals people's shadows along with their souls—right behind them, Peter, Molly, and Molly's friend George Darling race to find her father and the stardust before Lord Ombra does. There are scary and amusing moments throughout the book.

Gentle Criteria: There are some terrible moments when Lord Ombra drains the souls from people who stand in his way, but this is still a story about good overcoming evil. Molly's father says that even when their families are in danger, the Starcatchers must protect the starstuff above all else. But when it comes to choosing between his wife and child and the stardust, he makes a desperate move to save his family first. Love conquers all, and good people must do all they can to protect the world from evil.

304   **Barry, Dave, and Ridley Pearson.** *Peter and the Starcatchers.*
Ill. by Greg Call. Hyperion, 2004, ISBN 978-0-7868-5445-5; Disney, 2006, pap., ISBN 978-0-7868-4907-9. 451p. • Grades 5–8
✑ Accelerated Reader ✑ Reading Counts

This book is a prequel to *Peter Pan*. Peter is one of five orphans put on the *Never Land*, a ship that will carry them to be slaves for King Zorboff. Peter sees a man who is transformed when he touches a chest that is being loaded onto the ship. Peter makes friends with Molly, who can talk to the porpoises, and discovers that Molly and her father are Starcatchers. The Starcatchers are trying to gather magical dust before the Others get to it and use it for evil. The dust is an amazing thing: It can make people fly, transform fish into mermaids, stop aging, and heal terrible wounds. The dust can also, however, enable evil and can kill if given in overdoses. Fans of the original *Peter Pan*, either the movie or the book, will be curious to find out how mermaids came to be; why Peter's island is named NeverLand; how the large crocodile got loose to wander the island; who (or what) Peter's fairy really is; why Peter can fly; and most of all, why Peter never grows older.

Gentle Criteria: This is a good old-fashioned adventure with Peter and Molly as leaders who aim to keep their friends and family safe. One of the best parts of this great book is that it will persuade readers to pick up the original *Peter Pan* and reread it.

305   **Beck, Ian.** *The Secret History of Tom Trueheart.*
HarperCollins, 2007, ISBN 978-0-06-115211-5. 343p. • Grades 5–8

Tom Trueheart lives with six brothers who all get to go out on adventures. The Trueheart family works for the Story Bureau, which writes the beginnings of stories, fables, and fairy tales. One of the six Trueheart brothers takes the role of the hero, finishes the story, and reports the end to the Story Bureau. Then the story is written up and sold for readers to enjoy. Unfortunately, one of the story writers has become disgruntled. He kidnaps the brothers so the stories will never be finished. In the absence of Tom's brothers, the bureau has no choice but to send Tom on his first adventure. Tom must find his brothers, rescue them, and make sure they complete their stories. He must also be on the lookout for the villainous writer. Will he be able to complete the stories of Jack and the Beanstalk, the Frog Prince, Rapunzel, and Sleeping Beauty, or is storytime lost?

Gentle Criteria: Showing great bravery and courage, Tom is happy to oblige the Story Bureau because he loves his family. Tom shows how clever and resourceful he is when he talks Rapunzel out of cutting her hair. And Tom has the foresight to keep one of the magic beans in case he needs it later.

306 **Beckhorn, Susan Williams.** *The Kingfisher's Gift.*
Philomel, 2002, ISBN 978-0-399-23712-6. 182p. • Grades 7–9
⌁ ACCELERATED READER ⌁ JUNIOR LIBRARY GUILD

Franny's fairies are on a quest to find the kingfisher's feather that will enable their little girl to fly. They get their chance to find it when Franny is sent to her grandmother's place for the summer, where the feather was lost. This book will take readers by surprise. What appears at first to be a fantasy about a little girl and the fairies she loves is actually about several people and the sorrows and wishes that they hold close to their hearts. There is Ida the maid who gave away a baby that no one knows about; Grandmother Morrow who did the same thing secretly many years ago; Henry the chauffeur who misses his dead wife and the children they never had; Franny who grieves equally for her father who just died and the fairy stories he wrote that her mother burned in her grief; and Franny's mother, who desperately misses her husband. Franny's fairies bring badly needed healing to this group of people. Although the magical feather is located, nothing turns out as expected.

Gentle Criteria: There are two strong themes in this sweet story. Children are given to us for joy and love, and we must look toward the happiness and beauty in life even in the middle of sorrow, for that is what will sustain us. This is a wonderful story of grandparents, parents, children, and the people who are gone but still loved.

307 **Bell, Hilari.** *Shield of Stars.*
Simon & Schuster, 2007, ISBN 978-1-4169-0594-3. 267p. Series:
Shield, Sword, and Crown • Grades 7–9
⌁ ACCELERATED READER ⌁ JUNIOR LIBRARY GUILD

In this first volume in the series, Weasel is a former pickpocket who has been taken under the wing of Justice Hollis. When Hollis is arrested for treason, Weasel sets out to rescue him, putting himself in the middle of many dangerous adventures. When he is caught—after being set up by bandits he offers to help—he ends up in a castle room with Arisa, a girl arrested for helping to smuggle goods. This clever pair manages to escape, and the two begin to search for the Falcon, who turns out to be Arisa's mother. Weasel has been told that the Falcon is the only person with the power to help him. When they accidentally come across a strange and very old shield, they pretend it is the one that has been missing for centuries and decide to barter it for Justice Hollis's life. Could it be the real thing? Weasel has strange feelings about it and many more questions about his own past.

Gentle Criteria: While this book can be edgy at times—Arisa breaks a man's fingers when he tries to grab her breast, and the Falcon threatens to slit a throat as they rescue Hollis—it is really about two young people who are ultimately true at heart. Weasel tries to do the right thing with the least amount of damage and shows promise of becoming a good future leader.

308 Berkeley, Jon. *The Palace of Laughter.*

> HarperCollins, 2006, ISBN 978-0-06-075508-9. 427p. Series: Wednesday Tales • Grades 5–9

This is the first installment in the Wednesday Tales series. Miles Wednesday, having escaped from an orphanage, lives on his own in a huge barrel outside Larde. His only companion is Tangerine, a stuffed toy bear. When the evil Circus Oscuro comes to town, Miles finds Little, a song angel, being held prisoner. Little had followed a storm angel, Silverpoint, to earth and both angels were captured by the Great Cortado. Miles frees Little and she in turn brings Tangerine to life. Miles and Little, with the help of a tiger, travel to Cortado's Palace of Laughter—where he steals people's ability to laugh—in hopes of freeing Silverpoint and Tangerine.

> **Gentle Criteria:** Miles knows that Little will return to her home in the sky when she frees Silverpoint. But wise words from the tiger convince him that it's better to have a friend for ten days than to have a locked heart for a hundred years.

309 Billingsley, Franny. *Well Wished.*

> Simon & Schuster, 1997, ISBN 978-0-689-81210-1; 2000, pap., ISBN 978-0-689-83255-0. 170p. • Grades 5–7
>
> ⌐ Accelerated Reader ⌐ Reading Counts

The village of Bishop Mayne has a magical wishing well, and each resident gets one wish in a lifetime. However, the well often turns a wish around, making its owner regret he made it. When Catty talks her friend Nuria into wishing that Catty can walk again, Nuria wishes that Catty has a body just like hers. The well switches their bodies, so that now Nuria is stuck inside Catty's body with its lifeless legs. The wish cannot be undone unless both agree, which Catty will not do. Only a mind as clever as Nuria's can figure out how to cancel the spell. This is an entertaining fantasy with the sharpest mind winning!

> **Gentle Criteria:** Both girls' parents immediately know that something has changed even though they cannot see the difference. Both girls find out that what they had was more precious to them than anything they could wish for. And in the end, a quick mind outwits a magical well!

310 Calhoun, Dia. *The Phoenix Dance.*

> Farrar, Straus & Giroux, 2005, ISBN 978-0-374-35910-2. 273p. • Grades 5–9
>
> ⌐ Accelerated Reader

Phoenix is of apprentice age and wants to make shoes for the royal family. Her aunts allow her to do so, but her boss soon loses his title as Royal Shoemaker when the princesses wear out their shoes night after night. Phoenix suffers from an illness called the Two Kingdoms. She goes back and forth between the Kingdom of Brilliance, where she has enough energy to draw twenty shoe designs, to the Kingdom of Darkness, where she is depressed for weeks and unable to work. Phoenix acquires a cloak that makes her invisible and sets out to help the shoemaker and the princesses. Phoenix discovers that the princesses dance every night because of a spell cast upon them. Phoenix also learns that she can cure her illness but must choose whether to cure her illness or save the princesses.

Gentle Criteria: What a wonderful book this is to help explain bipolar disorder—the illness of two kingdoms—to young people. When Phoenix is forced to choose between curing her disease and saving the princesses, she chooses to save their lives. Phoenix points out that her weight gain and the other side effects of her medication are the price she must pay to remain functional. She chooses to live a functional life rather than the highs and lows of the two kingdoms.

311   Chabon, Michael. *Summerland*.
Disney, 2003, ISBN 978-0-7868-2662-9; 2004, pap., ISBN 978-0-7868-1615-6. 500p. • Grades 7–9
⌒ Accelerated Reader ⌒ Reading Counts

Ethan Feld, who lives on Clam Island, Washington, is recruited to save the world through a baseball game with trolls, giants, and a sasquatch. Summerland is a magical part of the island. It exists on a gall, a place where our world and the next world are somehow grafted together; this means that good and bad can intersect, sometimes causing great destruction. An evil being called Coyote plans to poison the great tree of life, thereby causing all worlds to end, and he aims to do so by using Ethan's father's scientific formula. Science fiction, Indian lore, and folklore are all combined in this story about a group of baseball players who must save the world.

Gentle Criteria: This story has all the classic marks of good winning over evil. Coyote (known also as Shaitan or Satan) tries to trick the players into giving him what he needs to poison the tree of life. There are many elements for book clubs to use for discussion—good versus evil; fairy tales; Indian folklore; and, of course, baseball. The overall story is a reflection of what has been lost in the modern quest to build bigger and better things, instead of sitting back and enjoying the slower things in life, such as the game of baseball.

312   Codell, Esme Raji. *Diary of a Fairy Godmother*.
Ill. by Drazen Kozjan. Hyperion, 2005, ISBN 978-0-7868-0965-3; Disney, 2006, pap., ISBN 978-0-7868-0966-0. 170p. • Grades 5–8
⌒ Accelerated Reader

Hunky Dory is the best witch in the class, and her witch mother says she'll be the wickedest witch wherever the four winds blow. Hunky Dory, however, wants to become a fairy godmother and grant wishes of goodwill rather than cast evil spells. When she tells her teacher and mother this news, she is thrown out of school and out of her cave. Hunky Dory isn't upset; she just goes about beginning her new career. She grants a wish that brings her a shack to live in. She creates a wishing well in which people can drop a gold coin in exchange for a wish. She soon learns that she should wear a hat when she's in the well as those coins hurt. She finds out that when she was born her aunt bestowed the gift of conflict on her, which explains why Hunky Dory would always turn frogs back into princes. This story does a delightful job of weaving in known fairy tales.

Gentle Criteria: Besides the humor of realizing that Hunky Dory had a part in several fairy tales—such as Rumpelstiltskin, Goldilocks, Red Riding Hood, and Cinderella—this story contains a lot of shared wisdom. Lemon, a former fairy godmother, imparts the most impressive statement of the book when she tells Hunky Dory that, "Anything worth wishing for is worth going out and getting for yourself." This is an enjoyable story with tidbits of wisdom interspersed.

313 Collins, Suzanne. *Gregor and the Code of Claw.*
Scholastic, 2007, ISBN 978-0-439-79143-4. 412p. Series: Underland
Chronicles • Grades 5–9
☞ Accelerated Reader

The war with the rats continues in this fifth volume in the Underland Chronicles. When Gregor finally sees the prophecy of Time, he reads that the warrior will die. In all the other prophesies, Gregor was the warrior; now Gregor must mentally prepare himself to die. He could run back to his life in New York, but he's too loyal. He wants to protect Regalia, and his new friends in this home beneath the earth. When Gregor ignores an order to stay in Regalia, Solovet has him imprisoned in a dark cell. This is a blessing in disguise because Gregor learns to perfect his echolocation technique so that he can now see in the dark. When a prophecy says a princess will unravel the secret code the rats are using, everyone assumes it is his sister Boots. But when Lizzy arrives on the scene, she is also considered a princess. Ripred takes Gregor aside and tells him he doesn't believe the founder's prophecies, and that people read into them what they want to believe. This insight gives Gregor hope that he may survive the battle with Bane after all.

Gentle Criteria: When he returns to New York Gregor realizes that the same horrific scenes are unfolding nightly on the TV news from around the world. Finally, at least, there has been a settlement of the war down under, and hopefully they have learned enough to allow peace to reign.

314 Collins, Suzanne. *Gregor and the Curse of the Warmbloods.*
Scholastic, 2005, ISBN 978-0-439-65623-8; 2006, pap., ISBN 978-0-
439-65624-5. 358p. Series: Underland Chronicles • Grades 5–7
☞ Accelerated Reader ☞ Reading Counts

In this third volume in the series, Gregor's mom refuses to let him go to the Underland to help with the plague affecting all warmbloods, and the giant rats send Overland rats into the walls to persuade her to change her mind. This time Gregor's mother goes to the Underland with Gregor and his sister, but she is stricken by the plague. Gregor, his sister, rats, bats, and a roach go on a quest to find a cure. Readers will cheer them on as they face adversities and figure out the prophecy of the curse of the warmbloods.

Gentle Criteria: Courage and the ability to work with many different kinds of people and creatures enable Gregor and his friends to succeed. The creatures overcome their prejudices and bring about a positive ending. Booktalkers and teachers can use this series as an instrument to talk about prejudices and stereotypes.

315   Collins, Suzanne. *Gregor and the Marks of Secret.*
Scholastic, 2006, ISBN 978-0-439-79145-8. 343p. Series: Underland Chronicles • Grades 5–7
☞ ACCELERATED READER ☞ READING COUNTS

This is the fourth book in the Underland Chronicles. Luxa, queen to be of Regalia, is separated from her group but saved by the mice known as the nibblers. She tells them that if they ever need her help, they should simply send her crown to her via one of her scouts, and she'll come to their rescue. At the beginning of this tale, her crown arrives and she and Gregor set off to locate the nibblers.

Gentle Criteria: Once again, the creatures overcome their prejudices and stereotypes to succeed where others might fail. Giant bats, cockroaches, humans, and a giant rat named Ripred put aside their differences to work together for a common cause. Creatures who would be expected to be common enemies are now allies. Gregor is appalled to learn that the other animals of the kingdom call humans killers, and hopes to change this notion by making peace among all creatures.

316   Collins, Suzanne. *Gregor and the Prophecy of Bane.*
Scholastic, 2004, ISBN 978-0-439-65075-5; 2005, pap., ISBN 978-0-439-65076-2. 312p. Series: Underland Chronicles • Grades 5–7
☞ ACCELERATED READER ☞ READING COUNTS

This book is the sequel to *Gregor the Overlander.* When giant cockroaches kidnap Boots during a sledding outing, Gregor must leave his ailing father and return to the Underland to retrieve Boots. There he realizes that the roaches were sent to capture Boots to protect her from the giant rats who were trying to fulfill the prophecy of Bane. Now Gregor must embark on another journey in which he will face the giant white rat to save the Underland's city of Regalia once again. During this trek his party of bats, roaches, a smelling seer rat, and Underlanders encounters flesh-eating insects, sea serpents, and vicious rats. Gregor also finds out that he has a certain gift.

Gentle Criteria: This book demonstrates how people can overcome their differences to contribute to a common cause.

317   Collins, Suzanne. *Gregor the Overlander.*

Scholastic, 2003, ISBN 978-0-439-43536-9; 2004, pap., ISBN 978-0-439-67813-1. 311p. Series: Underland Chronicles • Grades 5–7

⚬ ACCELERATED READER ⚬ READING COUNTS

This is the first book in the Underland Chronicles. Gregor lives in an apartment building in New York with his mother, grandmother, and two sisters. His father disappeared two years ago. One day he follows his two-year-old sister Boots through a grate in the laundry room and they find themselves in an underworld with giant cockroaches, bats, spiders, and humans who are at war with the six-foot-tall rats. He also finds out that his father may still be alive, and that it has been prophesied that a son of the sun will lead the Underlanders to salvage their future by going on a quest to save his father.

> **Gentle Criteria:** Courage is abundant in this story. Gregor's sister befriends the roaches that everyone else despises, and they end up saving everyone's lives. Gregor's quest will improve his life in ways he does not suspect. Besides the death of a likable roach and a couple of spiders on the good side, and a lot of rats on the bad side, violence is part of the war story line, but is not overly graphic.

318   Conford, Ellen. *The Frog Princess of Pelham.*

Little, Brown, 1997, ISBN 978-0-316-15246-4. 106p. • Grades 5–9

⚬ ACCELERATED READER ⚬ READING COUNTS

Chandler, an orphan since the age of nine, will inherit millions in three years. In the meantime her cousin is in charge of her life, handling all financial affairs. Midwinter break is coming up, and her cousin has decided to enroll her in a survival camp in Idaho while he and his girlfriend go to Switzerland. But the day before she is to leave, Danny, whom she has a crush on, kisses her and *she turns into a frog*! Neither of them can believe what has happened; Danny only kissed her because his friend Mason bet him a dollar he wouldn't do it. Now Chandler is stuck and neither of them has any idea what to do. She gets really scared when the thought of juicy slugs doesn't bother her anymore. In desperation they go on a local talk show. Once the news is out the CIA comes knocking on the door. Will Chandler and Danny figure out what to do before the CIA takes her into custody and her cousin returns from Switzerland?

> **Gentle Criteria:** This is a clever twist on an old fairy tale. In the end, just like any good fairy tale, only a good deed will bring the desired result. When Chandler sacrifices herself to protect Danny, she changes back into a girl. Chandler learns that she is capable of making more friends—Danny is definitely one of them—and that the ones she has really do care about her, not just her money. Chandler and Danny both do some growing up and make the world a better place.

319   Constable, Kate. *The Singer of All Songs.*

Arthur A. Levine, 2002, ISBN 978-0-439-55478-7; Scholastic, 2005, pap., ISBN 978-0-439-55479-4. 297p. Series: Chanters of Tremaris • Grades 7–9

☞ ACCELERATED READER ☞ READING COUNTS ☞ JUNIOR LIBRARY GUILD

The first installment in a trilogy. Calwyn, a young priestess of ice magic, has never been outside the walls that keep the stronghold realm of Antaris safe. When she finds Darrow, injured and inside the walls, no one can imagine how he managed to cross the magic barrier. He tells her that a sorcerer is after him. When the sorcerer, Samis, also breaches Antaris's wall, Calwyn helps Darrow flee to safety and decides to join him. She discovers that there is a whole world out there, not all of which looks favorably on magic or chanters such as she. She and Darrow pursue their quest to overcome Samis and save their broken world of Tremaris. In order to do this, they must keep Samis from mastering the nine powers. Along the way they meet other chanters, outwit pirates, and discover ancient objects that can help them. Calwyn discovers she is also capable of mastering more than one of the powers, and she will have readers wondering if she or Samis will end up "The Singer of All Songs."

  Gentle Criteria: This story contains two strong themes. One is that those who see an evil thing unfold and don't do anything to stop it are just as bad as those who do the evil. The other is that life is a dance—not a battle. Calwyn imagines all the peoples of the world of Tremaris uniting and sharing their wisdom to create a better world, and she decides to fight for this dream.

320   Constable, Kate. *The Tenth Power.*

Arthur A. Levine, 2006, ISBN 978-0-439-55482-4; Scholastic, 2007, pap., ISBN 978-0-439-55483-1. 306p. Series: Chanters of Tremaris • Grades 7–9

☞ ACCELERATED READER

In this final volume in the trilogy, Calwyn returns to the ice enclave hoping to be taken care of after she has lost her chanting powers. Instead she finds out about a mysterious Tenth Power that could possibly save the world and heal all of them including her beloved Darrow. We find out more about all the characters in the trilogy, including Calwyn's family history and where Samis is headed. Calwyn's quest to find the other half of the wheel and to unite the lands once again will keep readers turning the pages.

  Gentle Criteria: This book is a borderline gentle read, but it needs to be included because of its theme of unity—we won't survive if we do not work together. Calwyn's world is ready to splinter and fall apart because the factions have forgotten that they are all part of each other. Readers will be intrigued with the Samis storyline as he flies away in the spaceship that brought the chanters there in the first place. There is fighting, bloodshed, and some kissing as Calwyn becomes a woman. This book is mostly about goodness and the future of a world where people *must* learn to live and work together.

321   Constable, Kate. *The Waterless Sea.*

> Arthur A. Levine, 2003, ISBN 978-0-439-55480-0; Scholastic, 2006, pap., ISBN 978-0-439-55481-7. 314p. Series: Chanters of Tremaris • Grades 7–9
>
> ☞ ACCELERATED READER ☞ READING COUNTS ☞ JUNIOR LIBRARY GUILD

This is the second book in the Chanters of Tremaris trilogy. This story opens with Calwyn and her friends taking over the pirate ships and rescuing the wind-workers and other hostages. When they meet and rescue Heben, he tells them of his quest to save his twin siblings from the Palace of Cobwebs. They all travel there, disguise themselves as members of the court, and attempt to rescue the children. Readers will learn more about Darrow's past and his connection to the Palace of Cobwebs and the Black Palace. When Darrow joins them, they are able to overthrow the sorcerers and begin to rebuild Tremaris as a republic rather than an empire. Calwyn is able, through great effort, to begin to heal the land itself and create goodwill among the people, but in the process she loses her ability to chant. At the end of the book readers are left with more questions: Is Samis really still alive? Can Calwyn's chanting ability be restored? They will be anxious to read the next book.

> **Gentle Criteria:** This book is full of courage as Darrow, Calwyn, and the others do the right thing, which is not always the easy thing. When they overtake the pirate ships, they do not punish the pirates as the captives want them to. Calwyn tells them that retaliating would make them no better than the pirates. Their whole purpose in being is to enable all the peoples of Tremaris to live freely and happily, a truly noble goal.

322   Coombs, Kate. *The Runaway Princess.*

> Farrar, Straus & Giroux, 2006, ISBN 978-0-374-35546-3. 279p. • Grades 5–9
>
> ☞ ACCELERATED READER

An amiable baby dragon, a young wizard who just wants hot chocolate and a sleepover, and a princess who knows she was meant for more than twirling her tresses and swooning, make for a very amusing twist on the traditional fairy tale. Meg's father, the king, decides to hold a contest. The lucky prince who rids the land of the robbers, the witch, and the dragon will get half the kingdom and the princess's hand in marriage. What a surprise when it is the princess who wins the contest—although not in the way readers will expect. Along the way Meg learns a lot about the kingdom she will rule one day, and that people are not always what they seem.

Gentle Criteria: This is a tongue-in-cheek look at all things princely. Meg longs for an adventure, but once she is in the middle of one, she realizes that she is just miserable, cold, wet, and scratchy. When she meets the witch, the dragon, and the robber band, she realizes that they are really people in need of help. She begins to think in terms of how she can help them once she is the monarch. A humorous look at long-held stereotypes.

323   Cooper, Susan. *The Boggart and the Monster.*
Margaret K. McElderry Books, 1997, ISBN 978-0-689-81330-6; Simon & Schuster, 2004, pap., ISBN 978-0-689-86931-0. 185p. • Grades 5–7
☞ Accelerated Reader ☞ Reading Counts

A companion volume to *The Boggart* (1993). The boggart is a mischievous spirit who lives in Castle Keep with the lawyer who purchased the castle from Jessup and Emily's family. It accidentally stows along with them on a camping trip when they come to visit. The boggart discovers that the Loch Ness monster Nessie is actually another boggart he knew in the ancient days. Nessie is now unable to shape-shift and change form to get out of the loch. As the boggart and the children encourage Nessie to change form and leave the loch, scientists are close to obtaining proof that the monster actually exists. There are many amusing moments in this suspenseful fantasy. At one point the children wrap their friend's father up like a mummy in a sleeping bag in order to keep him from taking pictures of the monster. The boggarts are also immensely amusing themselves.

Gentle Criteria: This story is packed with the antics of amusing, mischievous spirits and good-natured adults. It is their friendship with the selkies, the magical seal folk who can go back and forth from human to seal form, that enables the children to save Nessie from centuries of being stuck in the loch.

324   Cooper, Susan. *King of Shadows.*
Margaret K. McElderry Books, 1999, ISBN 978-0-689-82817-1; Simon & Schuster, 2001, pap., ISBN 978-0-689-84445-4. 186p. • Grades 5–8
☞ Accelerated Reader ☞ Reading Counts

Lucky Nat Field is chosen to be part of an all-boy troupe performing *A Midsummer Night's Dream* in the newly renovated Globe Theatre in London. But one night Nat becomes seriously ill, and when he wakes, it is the year 1599. He has mysteriously switched places with a boy from the past. While Nat is with Shakespeare, the boy from the sixteenth century is in a London hospital with bubonic plague. This time-travel fantasy gives the reader detailed information about how people lived in Shakespeare's London: ten-year-old children worked in the theatre, and women were not allowed on the stage. Nat wishes fervently that he could give William Shakespeare a ballpoint pen, and he realizes how sewers and toilet paper have improved the modern world. The best line in this story, however, is when Shakespeare helps Nat come to terms with both of his parents' deaths by writing a poem that says love is an "ever-fixed mark" that never changes.

Gentle Criteria: Although this story includes the deaths of Nat's mother from cancer and his father from suicide, it is about Nat coming to terms with his grief. He realizes he is still able to hold on to his love for them no matter what happens. This is also an entertaining and enlightening book about William Shakespeare and the times in which he lived. Teachers looking for a good read about this time period will find this book to be an excellent choice.

325   Corder, Zizou. *The Chase.*

Ill. by Fred Van Dreelen. Dial, 2004, ISBN 978-0-8037-2984-1; Penguin, 2005, pap., ISBN 978-0-14-240454-6. 262p. Series: Lionboy • Grades 5–8

☞ ACCELERATED READER ☞ READING COUNTS

In this sequel to *Lionboy* (see below), Charlie finds himself in the King of Bulgaria's palace in Venice. He must still find his parents and help the lions return to their native home. As Charlie talks with more cats, he learns that the drug companies have created cats that cause asthma. His scientist mother's cure for asthma threatens their profits. Charlie succeeds in rescuing his parents and returning the lions to their native land, with many adventures along the way: Rafi, who is working for the bad guys, ends up in a mental ward; Charlie's parents must escape through the smelliest of garbage chutes; and the people overthrow the Doge of Venice when they believe that Charlie and one of the lions are Saint Mark and his guardian lion returning to save them.

Gentle Criteria: This book, filled with gentle themes of love and respect, is also packed with amusing and suspenseful adventures. Charlie understands that no creature should be held captive, and his deep love for his parents is what saves them.

326   Corder, Zizou. *Lionboy.*

Dial, 2003, ISBN 978-0-8037-2982-7; Penguin, 2004, pap., ISBN 978-0-14-240226-9. 275p. Series: Lionboy • Grades 5–8

☞ ACCELERATED READER ☞ READING COUNTS

This is the first volume in the Lionboy series. When Charlie is a baby, his blood is mingled with a baby leopard's that his father helped to raise. From this point on Charlie is able to talk to and understand all kinds of cats. Charlie returns home from school one day to find that his scientist parents have both disappeared. The cats let Charlie know that his parents were kidnapped and there is no time to waste. Charlie escapes and ends up working with the lions on a circus boat bound for Paris. No one knows, of course, that Charlie can talk to the lions. As the circus ship gets closer to Paris, Charlie realizes that the lions have been captured and forced to perform. Charlie and the lions help each other escape in Venice where they board the Orient Express, meet the king of Bulgaria, and find temporary safety. This captivating story will have readers wanting to quickly find the second book in this series, *The Chase* (see above).

Gentle Criteria: Important themes abound in this book, including prejudice, ecology, love for family, and honor. When Charlie, who is biracial, is told that people from London are white, he retorts that they are of many races. This book is set in a near future in which cars have been outlawed because of pollution and asthma is a serious health issue. The most important theme is the respect that Charlie has for the animals. He knows they should be running free in their native land.

327 **Corder, Zizou.** *The Truth.*
Dial, 2005, ISBN 978-0-8037-2985-8; Penguin, 2004, pap., ISBN 978-0-14-240705-9. 232p. Series: Lionboy • Grades 5–8
☞ Accelerated Reader

This is the third and final volume in the Lionboy series. Just as Charlie thinks that he and his parents are safe, the Corporacy kidnaps Charlie for his desirable cat-speaking abilities. The Corporacy knows that Charlie's parents will try to rescue him; it will then have all three of them. However, Charlie's parents and animal friends have more talents than the Corporacy bargained for! The King of Bulgaria rides his lion bareback to save Charlie; Sergei the mangy cat manages to help him wherever he is held; Charlie's cat-speaking blood keeps him from being brainwashed; the ne'er-do-well Rafi turns out to be Charlie's cousin; a surprise visit from the leopard that originally caused Charlie to have cat-speak helps in the rescue; and Ninu the chameleon learns computer language to free the rest of the island.

Gentle Criteria: Although there is an underlying tone of Big Brother here, the strong thread that runs through this trilogy is that people must help each other. Charlie's father knows he is capable of saving Charlie and himself, but it is Charlie who insists that all the animals and people on the island must be saved. If we only take care of ourselves, the world has no chance of becoming a better place. The people and animals that Charlie helps return the favor by helping Charlie and his family escape to safety.

328 **Curry, Jane Louise.** *The Black Canary.*
Margaret K. McElderry Books, 2005, ISBN 978-0-689-86478-0. 279p. •
Grades 7–9
☞ Accelerated Reader ☞ Reading Counts

Biracial twelve-year-old James, whose parents are both world-class musicians, is determined *not* to be musical. When his family has the rare chance to spend a real family vacation in London, James is pleasantly surprised. But then his mother is asked to fill in for a sick musician and do a tour of Europe while he and his father stay in London. No way is James going to have a good time. Then he discovers a time portal in his uncle's London flat and gets stuck in 1600 London. He is kidnapped for his voice and discovers his real talent. Will he make his way back through the portal, or will he decide to stay and sing for the queen? Will he let his enjoyment of the times blur his memories and his need to go home? Readers will enjoy this representation of London in the early 1600s, particularly of the lives of musicians and actors.

Gentle Criteria: James has denied himself the pleasure of his musical talents because of his frustration with his parents. He longed for an everyday family life but his time travel reveals the riches his parents have exposed him to, and how much he really does love them.

329   De Mari, Silvana. *The Last Dragon.*

Disney, 2006, ISBN 978-0-7868-3636-9. 361p. • Grades 5–9

☞ ACCELERATED READER ☞ READING COUNTS

Relentless rains have come and drowned the camp, and Yorsh alone has survived, the last living elf. Yorsh joins up with humans Sajra and Monser, who try to care for him. But when Yorsh revives a rabbit that Monser killed for supper, Monser and Sajra wonder if they're doing the right thing caring for a creature that doesn't believe in eating anything that thinks. They discover a prophecy that says the rain and wickedness won't stop until the last elf meets the last dragon. They find the dragon and Yorsh cares for her during the last years of her life; as the end comes near, she lays an egg and then flies off to die. Yorsh raises the baby dragon Erbrow, and teaches it how to fly. Then Yorsh and Erbrow try to fulfill the prophecy.

Gentle Criteria: The main character Yorsh cares for all living creatures. Three times he brings a creature back from the dead. He also heals a girl who has a missing finger. Each healing causes him great weakness, but he is happy to sacrifice himself for all living things. He also forfeits his own happiness to care for the old dragon. When Erbrow becomes an adult, his egotistical side appears, making him a difficult dragon to live with. In the end, however, Erbrow makes the ultimate sacrifice for Yorsh's friends.

330   Deriso, Christine Hurley. *Do-over.*

Delacorte, 2006, ISBN 978-0-385-73333-5. 183p. • Grades 5–9

☞ ACCELERATED READER

Just at the end of Elsa's sixth-grade year, her mom dies suddenly of a brain aneurysm. Then her father tells her they are moving to a better job for him and to be closer to her grandmother. Elsa is glad; she is tired of being the poor little girl whose mother died. All she wants is to be normal, but she finds it harder to fit in at the new school than she hoped. She makes friends with the school geek, Martin, but she is shunned by the popular Darcy. One night her mother appears to her and gives her a magic locket. Elsa now has the ability to rewind time ten seconds and "do over" what just happened. Elsa progresses from using this gift to her advantage with her homework to using it to get revenge on people who are mean to her. She finally realizes that she is capable of making it without the locket. There are many adventures on her journey—from putting window cleaner and toothpaste in her enemy's hair to saving a little boy from skinning his knee.

Gentle Criteria: There are many lessons to be learned here. When her mother gives her the magic locket, she tells Elsa to be true to herself. Elsa's grandmother tells her that the women in their family never mask their intelligence. Elsa realizes that people who seem to be mean are often just confused and insecure; for example, Darcy says her father is a big Hollywood producer but he's actually in prison.

331   DiCamillo, Kate. *The Miraculous Journey of Edward Tulane.*
Candlewick, 2006, ISBN 978-0-7636-2589-4. 198p. • Grades 5–6
◆ ACCELERATED READER ◆ READING COUNTS ◆ JUNIOR LIBRARY GUILD

Reminiscent of *The Velveteen Rabbit*, this book will appeal to all ages. Edward Tulane is a china rabbit that is greatly treasured by his owner. Edward, however, does not really love anyone but himself. When two mischievous boys steal him from his owner, he begins a long and complicated journey. Various owners teach him about love and loyalty, and Edward gradually changes for the better.

Gentle Criteria: This is a powerful story about the potential for love to change even the most self-centered individuals.

332   Divakaruni, Chitra Banerjee. *The Conch Bearer.*
Millbrook, 2003, ISBN 978-0-7613-2793-6; Simon & Schuster, 2005, pap., ISBN 978-0-689-87242-6. 265p. • Grades 5–8
◆ ACCELERATED READER ◆ READING COUNTS

Anand, his mother, and his mute sister have lived in a shack in India ever since his father disappeared. Anand stops attending school to work at a tea shop while his mother works as a cook. His sister hasn't spoken since she witnessed a murder. Anand prays for help to end this dire situation, and Abhaydatta, an old "healer," appears. He tells Anand that he needs his assistance in transporting a conch shell back to the brotherhood located in the Himalayas. Anand's mother agrees to let him go after the healer proves he is genuine by healing Anand's sister. During the journey they are chased by an evil ex-healer named Surabhanu. Anand and Nisha, a street child who has joined Anand on his journey, face a number of challenges before undergoing one final test. Anand must say which of the three virtues is most important: honesty, loyalty, or compassion.

Gentle Criteria: Anand shows his compassion by his willingness to hand over the mystical conch shell and passes the final test. He must then choose whether to join the brotherhood—where he will learn to be a healer—or return to his family. A viewing window shows him that his father has returned and that his family is cared for once again. So he asks that his family's memory of him be removed so that he can help the whole world.

333   Donaldson, Julia. *The Giants and the Joneses.*
Ill. by Greg Swearingen. Henry Holt, 2005, ISBN 978-0-8050-7805-3.
215p. • Grades 5–8
  〜 ACCELERATED READER

Colette, Stephen, and toddler Poppy are siblings. They are outside playing when a giant girl named Jumbeelia climbs down from the beanstalk she has grown. She happens upon the siblings and takes them, a riding mower, and a sheep back up the beanstalk with her. Jumbeelia places them in her doll house and feeds them with one *huge* french fry. Jumbeelia's mean brother finds them and plays with them in a much rougher manner. When Poppy is injured by Jumbeelia's cat, Jumbeelia and her grandma place Poppy in a birdcage to mend her wounds. Poppy learns the giants' language and explains to Jumbeelia that they miss their parents and want to go home.

  Gentle Criteria: This book really makes readers consider how they relate to the rest of the world. Colette collects all sorts of things but they are all inanimate; she comes to realize what a responsibility it is to collect living things. When Jumbeelia gets a new cat, she loses interest in the little humans and even forgets to feed them. Jumbeelia doesn't understand the stress her pet humans are under until Poppy learns her language and explains it to her.

334   Dunmore, Helen. *Ingo.*
HarperCollins, 2005, ISBN 978-0-06-081853-1. 328p. • Grades 5–9

Sapphire (otherwise known as Sapphy), her brother Conor, and their parents live by the ocean. Sapphy's father, Mathew Trewhella, has the same name as the man who used to sing so beautifully that he could calm the seas. Mathew, according to ancient Granny Carne, was part Mer and disappeared back to his sea family. Lately Sapphy's father has become restless and is singing just as beautifully as the first Mathew Trewhella. One night he disappears. A year later, Conor and Sapphy hear voices calling them to the sea. They meet Mer people who take them underwater to Ingo. Their Mer blood allows Conor and Sapphy to breathe underwater. When they return home after this first outing, Conor is sure that it's not safe to continue going to the sea—it makes them want to forget about the earth altogether. Their mother is moving forward with her life with a new man, but Conor and Sapphy are convinced their father is still alive.

  Gentle Criteria: This book shows the two separate worlds of Ingo and Air, and how Conor and Sapphy can pass between them. Conor and Sapphy never give up hope of finding their father, but they also allow their mother to get on with her life.

335   Farmer, Nancy. *Sea of Trolls.*

Simon & Schuster, 2004, ISBN 978-0-689-86744-6; 2005, pap., ISBN 978-0-689-86746-0. 459p. • Grades 5–7

☞ ACCELERATED READER ☞ READING COUNTS

Nancy Farmer has written another wonderful fantasy interwoven with historical facts about the Middle Ages. Jack and his little sister Lucy are captured by Vikings. Readers are quickly moved from historical fact to fantasy as Jack goes on a quest to the land of the trolls to reverse a spell for the queen and save his sister. Notes at the end of the book inform readers of the true historical events that led to legends like *Beowulf.*

Gentle Criteria: This is another tale of understanding. Although appalled by the Vikings' thirst for blood, Jack grows to understand and even like them as he travels with them. Humorous moments throughout the quest lead readers to do the same.

336   Ferris, Jean. *Once Upon a Marigold: Part Comedy, Part Love Story, Part Everything-but-the-Kitchen-Sink.*

Harcourt, 2002, ISBN 978-0-15-216791-2; 2004, pap., ISBN 978-0-15-205084-9. 266p. • Grades 5–7

☞ ACCELERATED READER ☞ READING COUNTS ☞ JUNIOR LIBRARY GUILD

Edric the troll comes across a boy who has run away from home. Edric takes the boy home with him and raises him as his son. Eleven years later, the boy, Christian, is ready to make a life of his own. Using a telescope that he invented, he spies on the Princess Marigold and falls in love with her. He goes to work in the castle and discovers that the queen is plotting to get rid of Marigold. When he tries to warn her, he and his friends are thrown into the dungeon. Added to this mix are an incompetent tooth fairy that Edric is trying to put out of business, a guard who has trouble keeping his pants up, Christian's talent to invent useful items, and Marigold's ability to understand people's thoughts when she touches them. In the end Christian's true origins are revealed and they all live happily ever after.

Gentle Criteria: Loyalty, love, companionship—the makings of a truly gentle story.

337   Fletcher, Susan. *Alphabet of Dreams.*

Simon & Schuster, 2006, ISBN 978-0-689-85042-4. 294p. • Grades 7–9

☞ ACCELERATED READER ☞ READING COUNTS ☞ JUNIOR LIBRARY GUILD

What a hopeful book! Not long before the birth of Christ, Mitra and her younger brother Babak, who has the ability to foresee the future, are exiles from Persia. Mitra and Babak come to the notice of a magus named Melchior. He welcomes them into his caravan, which is following the signs in the stars. They are joined by two other magi. Babak has frightening dreams that wear him down physically and emotionally. During the journey, Mitra realizes that good people and hope are everywhere, and that a king can be born in a tiny hovel.

Gentle Criteria: This is a more mature read. Mitra goes through the process of changing from a girl into a young woman. The story also highlights the political position of the magi. The best part is at the end, when Babak begins to heal from his terrible prophetic dreams after sleeping with a tiny piece of the baby's blanket.

338   **Funke, Cornelia.** *Dragon Rider.*

Scholastic, 2004, ISBN 978-0-439-68513-9. 523p. • Grades 5–8
⌐ ACCELERATED READER ⌐ READING COUNTS

Humans are headed toward the hidden valley where the dragons reside. Firedrake, a dragon, and his brownie companion set off to get a map from Rat's cousin so they can find the Rim of Heaven—a place so remote that no human will ever find it. While meeting Rat's cousin, they come across a homeless boy, Ben, who joins them on their quest. When they bump into a set of dwarfs, they are infiltrated by a spy named Twigleg who is a homunculus, a man-made creature who is bound to his master. Although Twigleg keeps reporting to his master, the dreaded dragon killer Nettlebrand, his wide knowledge base also assists the party in surviving fairies and other creatures along the way. Fortunately, Twigleg becomes a double agent after learning to care for Ben, who has been the first being ever to treat him with kindness. Another cousin of Rat joins them in the Himalayas and they set out to rid the world of the horrible Nettlebrand once and for all. If they can succeed, all the other dragons will come out of hiding and inhabit the Rim of Heaven once again.

Gentle Criteria: In the beginning, brownies and dragons don't trust humans, but by the end species that have nothing in common work together to rid the world of an evil creature that was created for the sole purpose of destroying dragons. Readers will be surprised to find what gentle creatures dragons are. They don't eat people; they actually don't eat at all—they nourish themselves on moonbeams. Their breath can also cure the sick. This story is a delightful portrayal of dragons, and an introduction for young readers to many kinds of magical creatures.

339   **Funke, Cornelia.** *Inkheart.*

Scholastic, 2003, ISBN 978-0-439-53164-1; 2005, pap., ISBN 978-0-439-70910-1. 534p. • Grades 6–8
⌐ ACCELERATED READER ⌐ READING COUNTS

Book lovers will enjoy this story. When Meggie's father reads aloud, the characters come alive—not always for the better. When an evil ruler named Capricorn emerges from a book into the middle of their living room, they must find a way to stop him. Characters both good and bad fill the pages of this book, and readers will not be able to put it down until they learn the ending.

Gentle Criteria: This is a good old-fashioned read, with good and evil characters. Each chapter begins with a quote from a well-known book or piece of literature. Avid readers will be rewarded when they recognize these quotes.

340   Gerson, Mary-Joan, reteller. *Fiesta Femenina: Celebrating Women in Mexican Folktales.*
Ill. by Maya Christina Gonzales. Barefoot Books, 2001, ISBN 978-1-84148-365-8. 64p. • Grades 5–9
☞ ACCELERATED READER

Herein is a collection of eight Mexican folktales, each celebrating a different heroine and focusing on the importance of women in Mexican culture. "Rosha and the Sun" tells the story of a brave girl who rescues the Sun and explains why Mexican girls have lights in their eyes and moles live underground. "The Hungry Goddess" relates the creation of the Earth. "Why the Moon Is Free" is an amusing tale of a man (the Sun) who is unable to please the woman he is in love with (the Moon). "Blancaflor" tells how the Devil's daughter and the boy she loves manage to outwit the Devil and share their life together. All these delightful stories emphasize women's strength, intelligence, and humor. An introduction, pronunciation guide, and source notes are included.

Gentle Criteria: Criteria: This book provides both a positive portrayal of Mexican culture and a wonderful way of looking at the female role. Full of love and cleverness, these tales will be enjoyed by all.

341   Hale, Shannon. *Enna Burning.*
Bloomsbury, 2004, ISBN 978-1-58234-889-6; 2006, pap., ISBN 978-1-58234-906-0. 317p. Series: Books of Bayern • Grades 6–9
☞ ACCELERATED READER

In this second volume in the series, Enna's brother Leifer brings home a mysterious piece of vellum that reveals how to control fire. Although Enna has doubts about the power and what it is doing to her brother, when her country goes to war she chooses to use the power herself. Will the power destroy her as it did her brother, or will it save her country, or both?

Gentle Criteria: The horror of war is strongly portrayed, but in the end truth and justice prevail, and Enna struggles to do the right thing. Strong female characters want only the best for their country and their loved ones, and love does win out in the end.

342   Hale, Shannon. *The Goose Girl.*
Bloomsbury, 2003, ISBN 978-1-58234-843-8; 2005, pap., ISBN 978-1-58234-990-9. 383p. Series: Books of Bayern • Grades 6–9
☞ ACCELERATED READER ☞ READING COUNTS

This first volume in the Books of Bayern series retells the Grimm fairy tale "The Goose Girl." Princess Anidori's stepmother the queen sends her off to the neighboring kingdom to marry the prince. On the way the princess is betrayed by her lady-in-waiting, and must disguise herself as a simple goose girl in hopes of escaping when the time is right. Her magical ability to talk with the birds and the wind helps her along the way. There is a clever twist at the end when the prince she hides from turns out to be the one true love she has been hoping for.

Gentle Criteria: Those using this book will want to be aware of the harshness of the battles. Ungolad's bloody body is removed from the throne after he tries unsuccessfully to usurp the king, and dead bodies are hung on walls as a warning. Even with the gruesomeness of some of the fighting, this is the story of a strong and courageous young woman who receives justice and wants to show the people a better way.

343   Hale, Shannon. *Princess Academy.*
Bloomsbury, 2005, ISBN 978-1-58234-993-0. 314p. • Grades 5–7
☞ ACCELERATED READER ☞ READING COUNTS

Miri has always felt useless. Her father will not allow her to work in the quarry that sustains the village. When the prince announces he will choose his bride from among the village girls, Miri and the others are sent to an academy to be trained in the ways of the court. Miri discovers she is not as alone as she thought and that she is smarter and more talented. This is a story of a girl who realizes how much she is capable of and who finds ways to put these abilities to good use. After many exciting events, a bride is chosen—not necessarily the one the reader was expecting.

Gentle Criteria: Miri learns that her father's strong love for her is the reason he won't allow her to work in the quarry. It is not that he thinks she is weak and good for nothing. The principles of diplomacy and commerce that the girls learn actually have a lot to say about being loyal and true to your friends and community. Miri discovers that it is more important to her for the village to succeed than for her to succeed alone and without them.

☙   NEWBERY HONOR BOOK, 2006

344   Hale, Shannon. *River Secrets.*
Bloomsbury, 2006, ISBN 978-1-58234-901-5. 290p. Series: Books of Bayern • Grades 6–9
☞ ACCELERATED READER ☞ READING COUNTS

This is the third book in the series. War has been declared over, and now the Bayern contingent must go to Tiran to be ambassadors of peace and collaboration. Enna has learned to control her fire-burning, and she vows to use her energy to produce positive change. Razo, mediocre foot soldier at best, is unsure why he has been chosen to go. When burned bodies start showing up, Razo fears the worst. Spies and intrigue fill this book, while the Bayern contingency strives desperately to find out who is causing this before war erupts again.

Gentle Criteria: This book is full of tender emotions—Razo's first kiss, Finn learning to play the harp and singing to Enna while he proposes—as well as intrigue and danger. This book is about good and honorable people doing the right thing. Razo learns a lot about himself and what he finds lacking in his life.

345   Hart, J. V. *Capt. Hook: The Adventures of a Notorious Youth.*
Ill. by Brett Helquist. HarperCollins, 2005, ISBN 978-0-06-000221-3.
337p. • Grades 5–9
⁀ ACCELERATED READER

This book shows readers the young man who will become Captain Hook. The story follows James Matthew, beginning with his aunt dropping him off at Eton School for Boys. House captain Arthur Darling is quick to point out that James is the bastard son of Lord B. James befriends Jolly Roger and soon becomes the leader of the underclassmen against the oppressive seniors, guiding the underclassmen to an unusual victory in the Wall game. James's methods may seem crude but he is always the lesser of two evils. He meets a princess, falls in love, and sails on a slave ship owned by his father. He leads a mutiny to take over the ship and free the slaves. Readers are shown glimpses of his preoccupation with finding Neverland, where one never grows old and where he plans to make his princess his queen.

Gentle Criteria: This book shows that Captain Hook was not always a cruel pirate. He actually appears to be a goodhearted lad who has few loves in his life—his aunt, Jolly Roger, Electra the spider, and the princess. He has seen his father only a few times. Seeing this unexpectedly gentle side of a character we have come to despise will leave readers wondering what turned Captain Hook to the dark side.

346   Haydon, Elizabeth. *The Floating Island.*
Ill. by Brett Helquist. Tom Dougherty Associates, 2006, ISBN 978-0-7653-0867-2. 368p. Series: The Lost Journals of Ven Polypheme • Grades 5–8
⁀ ACCELERATED READER

Ven Polypheme is a Nain whose family has abandoned its underground roots to live among humans and build ships. Ven has a hunger for adventure. When he takes a ship out for its final inspection, it is attacked by Fire Pirates. Pirate ships take no prisoners and Ven uses chemicals to protect the crew, in the process setting both ships on fire. He awakens on a floating piece of debris and is kept alive by a mermaid. An albatross has guided the mermaid to him, as well as a ship that will rescue him. Since Ven is from an ancient people, the captain of the rescue ship uses Ven to summon the mysterious Floating Island. Once on the island, Ven can whisper into the huge conch shell to tell his family he is fine. When he is back on land, however, Ven is arrested on charges of sinking the ship and stealing another passenger's ring. These are trumped-up charges by a man who wants Ven to summon the island for his own evil purposes.

Gentle Criteria: When his friend Ida becomes hurt in the process of helping get rid of an evil spirit, Ven does not hesitate to risk his life to save Ida by calling forth the Floating Island again. Ven's ability to tell the truth gets him out of prison and lands him a job as a reporter for the king. The king is so impressed with Ven that he asks him to explore the world, writing down the stories and magic he encounters. Strong friendships and steadfast morals help Ven accomplish his goals.

347   Helgerson, Joseph. *Horns and Wrinkles.*

Houghton Mifflin, 2006, ISBN 978-0-618-61679-4. 357p. • Grades 5–7

Duke is hanging his cousin Claire over the side of a bridge when an old lady in a rowboat blows some dust toward them that enables Claire to descend like a feather. A horn then grows over Duke's nose, and he screams that the old lady did it. The old lady is the Blue-Winged Fairy, and she tells Claire that a River Troll cast a spell on Duke for being a bully. She also says the horn will disappear as soon as Duke does an unselfish act. Claire continues to try to help her cousin, but he insists on being defiant until he finally becomes a rhinoceros. His behavior also causes almost all of his relatives to be turned to stone. Claire asks the Blue-Winged Fairy to help her reverse the spell and finally get Duke to do something unselfish.

Gentle Criteria: Claire continually assists her cousin Duke even though he is ungrateful and mean. She just knows there is some good in him somewhere.

348   Henderson, Kathy, reteller. *Lugalbanda: The Boy Who Got Caught Up in a War.*

Ill. by Jane Ray. Candlewick, 2006, ISBN 978-0-7636-2782-9. 72p. • All ages

☞ ACCELERATED READER ☞ READING COUNTS ☞ JUNIOR LIBRARY GUILD

This story about a young boy in ancient Iraq who saves his country from war is older than the Bible, the Koran, and the Torah. Originally discovered in clay tablet form in the nineteenth century, it was not translated into English until the 1970s. Traveling with his father the king and his warrior brothers to take over a country, Lugalbanda falls ill and is left behind. When the sun god decides to let him live, he continues on, looking for his family. As he passes through mountains, he comes across the nest of the Anzu bird, the monster of the skies. Rather than fight it or hurt the baby bird, he decides to honor it and see if it will help him find his family. In return he is granted gifts that will enable him to live a fruitful life. Once he finds his family, he is able to tell them how to survive the war. They must now learn to live in peace. Historical notes are included.

Gentle Criteria: This is a story about doing good deeds and learning to live well. Lugalbanda's father must learn that the way to get what he wants for his country is not to take it from others. Cooperation will have better results. Lugalbanda demonstrates this when he does the monster bird a favor in the hope that one will be returned to him.

349   Hill, Pamela Smith. *The Last Grail Keeper.*
Holiday House, 2001, ISBN 978-0-8234-1574-8. 227p. • Grades 5–9
☞ ACCELERATED READER

Sixteen-year-old Felicity has joined her mother who is working on translating findings from archaeological digs. When there are whispers that King Arthur's Holy Grail has been discovered, Felicity faints, goes into a trance, and sees the Holy Grail's discovery in her mind's eye. She has more visions and then is visited by what appears to be the ghost of Morgan Le Fey, or the Lady in the Lake. Le Fey has actually time-traveled, having been taught to do so by Merlin. Le Fey explains to Felicity that she is the last in a long generation of Grail Keepers; moreover, the Holy Grail has been discovered and Felicity must retrieve it before the evil Mordred gets his hands on it. Le Fey explains to Felicity that if Mordred destroys the Holy Grail, she will cease to exist, and her mother will have an alternate history in which she marries Mordred and has a boy instead of Felicity. Le Fay gives her a necklace that will disguise her from Mordred, but Felicity is unwilling to wear it. When the necklace falls into the hands of Mordred, is that the end of Felicity and the Holy Grail?

Gentle Criteria: The reader can understand Felicity's refusal to embrace the idea that she is related to earlier Keepers of the Holy Grail. How many of us would believe such visions? When threatened by Mordred, Felicity tells King Arthur to save the Holy Grail so that all mankind will benefit from its presence.

350   Hoeye, Michael. *Time Stops for No Mouse.*
Putnam, 1999, ISBN 978-0-399-23878-9; Penguin, 2003, pap., ISBN 978-0-698-11991-8. 250p. • Grades 5–9
☞ ACCELERATED READER ☞ READING COUNTS

When a mouse brings a watch to his shop and fails to return to claim it, Hermux Tantamoq, fellow mouse and watch repairer extraordinaire, suspects foul play. He ends up in the middle of a quest for the elixir of eternal youth, complete with journals of jungle expeditions and rare plants that mysteriously make him feel much younger when he nibbles on them. Dastardly scientists and money-hungry cosmetic moguls make for an exciting but tongue-in-cheek look at the beauty industry and the quest to make oneself look younger. This is a great mystery with clues sprinkled liberally throughout. Clever readers will have fun figuring out who the bad guy really is while they read about the trials and tribulations of customers attempting to become more beautiful and youthful.

Gentle Criteria: At the end of each day Hermux writes in his journal all of the things he is thankful for. There are many subtle statements in this clever book about stereotypes (not *all* rats are sneaky, for example). Best of all, is the wonderful thing Hermux chooses to do with the powerful elixir.

351   Hoffman, Alice. *Aquamarine.*
    Scholastic, 2001, ISBN 978-0-439-09863-2; 2002, pap., ISBN 978-0-439-09864-9. 105p. • Grades 5–9
    ⌐ Accelerated Reader ⌐ Reading Counts

This is a touching story of friendship, love, and growing up. For as long as they can remember, Claire and Hailey have spent every summer at the Capri Beach Club. Claire's parents both died in an accident, and Claire lives with her grandparents. Hailey's mother is divorced and busy supporting the two of them. But life is quickly changing for both girls. Claire's grandparents are moving to Florida and taking her with them. The Capri Beach Club is to close at the end of the summer; it will be turned into a bird sanctuary. Although the club is becoming dilapidated, the girls do not care. Raymond, the hunk who works at the snack bar, is equally sentimental about the place where he has worked for all the summers of his school years. When a bad storm washes a mermaid into the murky swimming pool, the mermaid falls in love with Raymond. The two girls plot to get Raymond and the mermaid together.

Gentle Criteria: This is a bittersweet story about a special time in these two girls' lives. Never again will they have such carefree summers and spend every moment together. Raymond has the same kind of emotions about leaving for college. And the spoiled mermaid loves someone for the very first time. This story is about friendship and the power of love and memories to last forever.

352   Ibbotson, Eva. *The Beasts of Clawstone Castle.*
    Ill. by Kevin Hawkes. Dutton, 2006, ISBN 978-0-525-47719-8. 243p. • Grades 5–8
    ⌐ Accelerated Reader ⌐ Reading Counts ⌐ Junior Library Guild

Madlyn and Rollo have been sent to stay with relatives for the summer. Upon arrival, they find out that Clawstone Castle is barely making ends meet. When they ask Great-Aunt Emily and Great-Uncle George why they don't just sell the castle, they learn about their beloved purebred white cows. Madlyn and Rollo decide a haunted castle would attract more tourists and interview some ghosts. Tourism does increase, but the owners of the nearby Trembellow Towers are infuriated—they want to close down the castle and turn it into condos. They hire imposter health inspectors to declare the white cows diseased. When one of the ghosts goes to pay her respects to the cows, she finds them gone. An oil king hired by Trembellow Towers has taken them to an island to try to turn them into unicorns. With the help of the ghosts, Madlyn and Rollo set out to rescue the missing cows. In the end, a distant relative saves the day when he discovers an item of great value in the castle and prevents it from closing.

Gentle Criteria: Readers might expect a ghost story to be frightening, but when the kids are the ones interviewing the ghosts it turns comical. This story shows caring on the part of family and ghosts.

353   Jennings, Richard W. *Orwell's Luck.*
Houghton Mifflin, 2000, ISBN 978-0-618-03628-8; 2006, pap., ISBN 978-0-618-69335-1. 146p. • Grades 6–8
ACCELERATED READER   READING COUNTS

A young girl discovers an injured rabbit in her driveway when she goes to get the paper to read her daily horoscope. She takes the rabbit in and tries to help him the best she can. When she finds mysterious messages in her daily horoscope that do not appear in anyone else's paper, she wonders whether the rabbit has magic abilities. Winning lottery numbers and advance warnings of pop quizzes in school are there for the taking, but she does not recognize them until it is too late. As her grandmother tells her, things always happen for a good reason, but sometimes we don't know what it is until later. Love and magic help this girl to look at the things that happen in her life—both good and bad—in a new way.

Gentle Criteria: This is a warm story about the magic of love and having people in your life who support you. The people in this family support each other through job loss, a new baby, and an injured animal. When the rabbit sends magic messages, it is to help the young girl understand that whatever happens to her, life is good.

354   Jennings, Richard W. *Scribble.*
Houghton Mifflin, 2004, ISBN 978-0-618-43367-4. 149p. • Grades 5–9
ACCELERATED READER

Lawson is grieving over the death of his friend Jip (Jennifer I. Palmer) and recalls conversations with her. Lawson was with Jip when she adopted the dog called Scribble. When Scribble bit her on the lip, she gave the feisty dog to Lawson. Since her death, Scribble has been sensitive to the ghosts that Lawson himself has started to see and talk to. The reader must decide whether these conversations with ghosts are real or just his way of grieving. The ghost of Nat King Cole tells Lawson to find the strong box in Jip's house. Inside the box is the gift that Lawson desires the most: a video of Jip.

Gentle Criteria: This book gives readers insight into what it is like to lose a loved one, from Lawson's parents bickering over whether Lawson should go to J. I. P.'s funeral to Lawson's feelings of guilt about talking to another girl.

This book portrays the important part that Scribble the dog has in helping Lawson to cope.

355 Keehn, Sally M. *Gnat Stokes and the Foggy Bottom Swamp Queen.*

Philomel, 2005, ISBN 978-0-399-24287-8. 152p. • Grades 5–9
⌐ ACCELERATED READER ⌐ READING COUNTS

Twelve-year-old Gnat Stokes was left on her father's doorstep. Gnat has just made a mess of things by accidentally burning down the town's mill. She's now determined to make up for this mistake by finding Goodlow Pryce, who went missing seven years ago. The story involves an evil swamp queen, a variety of swamp beings, and some magical powers. Gnat realizes that she is the daughter of the swamp queen. She will have to face down her own mother to save Goodlow from being sacrificed to the devil, and to change her mother into a mortal again.

Gentle Criteria: This story is an Appalachian version of the Scottish ballad "Tam Lin." It's heartwarming that Gnat is determined to make the townspeople like her again, and she is honorable in wanting to bring back a lost boy. Gnat shows what a big heart she has by willingly putting herself in danger by entering the enchanted swamplands to find Goodlow. She then shows she has an even bigger heart by giving Goodlow to Penelope, even though she has also fallen in love with him.

356 Kerr, P. B. *The Akhenaten Adventure.*

Scholastic, 2004, ISBN 978-0-439-67019-7; 2005, pap., ISBN 978-0-439-77135-1. 355p. Series: Children of the Lamp • Grades 5–8
⌐ ACCELERATED READER ⌐ READING COUNTS

This is the first volume in the series. When twins Philippa and John undergo anesthesia to have their wisdom teeth removed, they have a dream in which their Uncle Nimrod summons them to Paris. Their parents agree to send them away for the summer. Uncle Nimrod explains that now that their wisdom teeth have been removed they can start using their djinn, or magical genie, powers. He trains them to grant wishes only sparingly, and they realize the potential consequences when Nimrod is captured by Iblis, an evil djinn. Now they must use their intellect and newfound powers to save Uncle Nimrod.

Gentle Criteria: This entertaining read would be rated PG if it were a movie. One person is murdered but readers are not witnesses to the act. When they need a car, the twelve-year-old twins dream up a pink sports car with sand-ready tires—a combined interpretation of what is cool.

357 Kerr, P. B. *The Blue Djinn of Babylon.*

Scholastic, 2006, ISBN 978-0-439-86518-0; pap., ISBN 978-0-439-67022-7. 371p. Series: Children of the Lamp • Grades 5–8
⌐ ACCELERATED READER ⌐ READING COUNTS

In this second book in the series, Philippa is taking part in an Astaragali tournament, when a servant of the Blue Djinn of Babylon tells Uncle Nimrod that he has stolen the Solomon Grimoire. In the wrong hands, the Solomon Grimoire could be used to bind all of the djinn to do one's bidding. He tells Uncle Nimrod that he would only feel safe giving it to the twins on a train, where he won't be threatened by Nimrod's magic. While on the train, Philippa is kidnapped and taken to the hanging Palace of Babylon, where if she breathes the air long enough and drinks and eats enough she will become cold-hearted, which would make her an excellent replacement for the Blue Djinn. The Blue Djinn is neither on the side of good or evil but dispenses judgments when they need to be made, and rules over all genies. John must now traverse the desert in search of Philippa—without using any magic that might alert the Blue Djinn to his arrival.

Gentle Criteria: Not only is John willing to risk many dangers to save his sister, but his uncles are willing to risk all as well. Mothers always sense when their children are in danger, and the twins' mother arrives just in time to turn a would-be assassin into a kitty cat. Time after time these family members are there for each other.

358   Kerr, P. B. *The Cobra King of Kathmandu.*

Scholastic, 2007, ISBN 978-0-439-67023-4. 373p. Series: Children of the Lamp • Grades 5–9

This is the third book in the Children of the Lamp series. The leader of the Cult of the 9 Cobras has sent men to try to steal twins John and Philippa's wisdom teeth so he can bind them to do his bidding. Uncle Nimrod and Rakshasis go to India to try to determine who the thieves are, but they are captured and put on ice so that they can't use the powers they posses as djinn. John and Philippa, with the help of an angel, create two elsewheres who are their doubles and will take their places so their parents won't realize they have left New York for India. New adventures await them as they take Nimrod's butler with them to try to find the Cobra Talisman that was made with Rakshasis's teeth, binding him to whoever possesses it. They make their way to the Cobra King's lair where he captures the young djinn and plans to use their blood to make himself a djinn so he can rule the world.

Gentle Criteria: As in the Harry Potter books, the main characters in this series never die. Minor characters do die, which helps to make the dangers that these children face more believable. When the twins and Dybbuk arrive at the enlightened guru compound, they are given the job of manning computer help lines. Their jobs are to tell the computer owners who call all the wrong information so that they will get frustrated and break up their computers. What an amusing part of the story! How the kids rescue the adults is also intriguing.

359   Kessler, Liz. *Emily Windsnap and the Castle in the Mist.*
Ill. by Natacha Ledwidge. Candlewick, 2007, ISBN 978-0-7636-3330-1.
204p. Series: Emily Windsnap • Grades 5–8

In this third volume in the series, Emily has convinced Neptune to allow her parents to live at Allpoints Island, where mer people and humans coexist in peace. When Emily comes across a diamond ring that Neptune threw away years ago, Neptune is so angry that he creates a storm. Emily and her friends Millie and Shona find themselves hundreds of miles from the island in a sinking ship. Neptune and his human love, it seems, exchanged rings to signify their everlasting love. She loved Neptune so much that she swam out to meet him, but drowned. Neptune then threw the rings into the sea and has been angry ever since. He keeps her children locked up in a castle in the mist. Emily has also been cursed, and at the summer equinox will transform into either all human or all mermaid. The only way Emily can break the curse is to find the pearl ring and reunite it with the diamond one, at which point all of mankind will get along again.

   Gentle Criteria: Emily seems doomed always to be the instigator of trouble. When Emily meets Aaron, who is imprisoned in the castle in the mist, she feels an instant connection and is compelled to find the pearl ring and end the curse. Emily also has other reasons to succeed. She doesn't want to have to choose between becoming human or mermaid, and she doesn't want Neptune to force her parents to stop seeing one another. Her strong friendship with both land and sea friends Millie and Shona help her once again save the day.

360   Kessler, Liz. *Emily Windsnap and the Monster from the Deep.*
Candlewick, 2006, ISBN 978-0-7636-2504-7; 2007, pap., ISBN 978-0-
7636-3301-1. 219p. Series: Emily Windsnap • Grades 5–8
   ∼ Accelerated Reader ∼ Reading Counts

In the first volume in the series, Emily convinced King Neptune to allow her family to stay together even though her mother is not a mermaid. They are now learning to live together. Emily had a hard time fitting in at her old school and is anxious to prove to her new classmates how brave and daring she can be. When a couple of girls show her a forbidden part of the ocean, she figures she'll show off and make new friends. What she and her friend Shona do instead is wake up the monster Kraken, who sleeps for one hundred years at a time and is in Neptune's control. Emily wakes him eight years early, so he's in a foul mood and begins taking it out on passing ships. Neptune demands to know who else woke Kraken. Emily is torn between telling on her best friend and saving the lives of innocent people on a ship that has wandered into Kraken's waters. When Emily hears that only she and Shona can control the beast, she relents and stops the destruction.

   Gentle Criteria: Emily once again forces King Neptune to change his ways by convincing him that allowing Kraken to sink ships for his own personal gain does not outweigh the cost of innocent life. King Neptune shares the poem that will save Emily from the clutches of Kraken. "When Old Hatred's rift is mended, Thus the Kraken's power is ended." Will Mandy, her former enemy, be able to mend fences in time to save Emily, who used to be her friend?

361   Kessler, Liz. *The Tail of Emily Windsnap.*
Candlewick, 2003, ISBN 978-0-7636-2483-5; 2006, pap., ISBN 978-0-7636-2811-6. 209p. Series: Emily Windsnap • Grades 5–8
☞ ACCELERATED READER ☞ READING COUNTS

This is the first volume in the Emily Windsnap series. Twelve-year-old Emily Windsnap lives with her mother on a houseboat. Her mother doesn't remember anything about her father and is terrified of the water. When Emily signs up for swim lessons, she impresses the instructor with her amazing ability—but she's only in the water a few minutes before she has a weird sensation in her legs. Later that night she is drawn toward the water again and this time discovers that her legs have transformed into a mermaid's tail. Emily begins sneaking out at night to swim and meets Shona, another mermaid. They become best friends, and Shona realizes that Emily has the same last name as a merman she learned about in school. Emily becomes aware that her father didn't abandon her but was put in Neptune's prison for loving a mortal. Her mother's memory of him is being blocked. Emily is now determined to find her father and rescue him.

Gentle Criteria: The theme of the book, as Emily so eloquently states when addressing Neptune during her trial, is: "You can't outlaw love." Emily doesn't understand why her mother has never told her anything about her father until she realizes that her 3:00 P.M. tea partner, Mr. Beeston, has been slipping her drugs that keep her from remembering. This fact, combined with her discovery that she is half mermaid, is the driving force behind her wish to restore the love her parents shared for one another.

362   Kindl, Patrice. *Goose Chase.*
Houghton Mifflin, 2001, ISBN 978-0-618-03377-5; Penguin, 2002, pap., ISBN 978-0-14-230208-8. 214p. • Grades 7–9
☞ ACCELERATED READER ☞ READING COUNTS ☞ JUNIOR LIBRARY GUILD

This book is a clever fantasy with twists on several fairy tales. Goose Girl is trapped in a tower faced with a terrible choice: to marry the king or the spineless prince. Her loving geese help her escape, which begins the adventures. In the end she discovers who she really is—a princess all on her own—someone who is able to make her own decisions.

Gentle Criteria: Readers will love the allusions to well-loved fairy tales. The best part of this old-fashioned story, however, is the princess who stands on her own two feet.

363   Kladstrup, Kristin. *The Book of Story Beginnings.*
Candlewick, 2006, ISBN 978-0-7636-2609-9. 360p. • Grades 5–7
⌐ ACCELERATED READER ⌐ READING COUNTS ⌐ JUNIOR LIBRARY
GUILD

This book contains a unique and delightful fantasy! When her father loses his job, and her aunt Lavonne leaves the family house to him, Lucy finds herself moving to Iowa. The strange disappearance of her great-uncle Oscar in 1914—he supposedly rowed away on an ocean outside their house one night—and her discovery of his mysterious Book of Story Beginnings leads to an adventure that Lucy could never have dreamed up even in her wildest imaginings. A ship of orphans, a king who loves cats, a queen who loves birds, and a father who turns into a magician are the story beginnings that Lucy and her great-uncle Oscar must deal with when he reappears, the same age he was on the day he disappeared. Can these two survive the middle and manage to make the stories have happy endings? How will Oscar get back to the past and how will Lucy get her father, whom she has endangered, back to Iowa? What fun a classroom teacher can have using this book for writing projects.

    Gentle Criteria: This book of clever story beginnings and their basis in real life remind readers that everything they dream and do has an effect on others. Oscar and Lucy find out that the happiest endings are the ones that feel like beginnings.

364   Leavitt, Martine. *Keturah and Lord Death.*
Boyds Mills, 2006, ISBN 978-1-932425-29-1. 216p. • Grades 5–9
⌐ ACCELERATED READER ⌐ READING COUNTS ⌐ JUNIOR LIBRARY
GUILD

Keturah has known Lord Death all her life—from the moment her mother died while giving birth to her. Keturah follows a large buck into the woods and becomes lost. After three days, Lord Death comes to collect her. But Keturah is not ready—she wants to find a true love, have a child, and live in a modest home. Lord Death tells her that if she can find true love in one day, he will spare her life. When she fails to find a true love the next day, Keturah offers to tell Lord Death a story in exchange for yet another day, delaying the ending of the story until the next day. Lord Death obliges, and Keturah visits the Soor Lily, who gives her an eye that will stop moving when she encounters true love. Keturah continues the story each night and postpones the ending again until the next day, trying to buy time to find true love. Finally, Lord Death has had enough procrastination and tells her to seek no more delays. Will Keturah find her true love before the day is out? Readers will be touched and surprised by the ending.

    Gentle Criteria: Although the title of this book suggests it is about death, it is actually about love. Keturah has always been familiar with death. Not until Lord Death gives her a reprieve from death does Keturah finally stop and see how beautiful the world is. The beauty of the sun, the joy of watching children play, the wonderful scent of flowers, and the pleasure of having friendships are just a few of the things that can be taken for granted. Seeing how Keturah finally accepts her fate and finds love in an unexpected place is the author's way of sharing the love she had for her sister who died from cystic fibrosis at the age of eleven.

365   Levine, Gail Carson. *Cinderellis and the Glass Hill.*
Ill. by Mark Elliott. HarperCollins, 2000, ISBN 978-0-06-028337-7; 2004, pap., ISBN 978-0-06-056043-0. 104p. Series: The Princess Tales • Grades 5–7
☞ ACCELERATED READER ☞ READING COUNTS

This volume in the Princess Tales series is modeled on the "Cinderella" fairy tale. Ellis was showing his two uncaring brothers his latest invention—powder that made a cup fly up the chimney—when ash fell on him and they began calling him Cinderellis. Nothing he does pleases his brothers, but he continues to create inventions for his own enjoyment. Ellis catches three enchanted horses that eat up their wheat fields every year. When the king announces he will give the hand of his daughter, Princess Marigold, in marriage to anyone who can ride a horse up the glass pyramid and retrieve three golden apples, Ellis is determined to show he can do so. But Ellis doesn't want to marry the princess; he has fallen for a royal maid he met while examining the pyramid. What Ellis doesn't know is that the royal maid is the princess in disguise, and she is also in love with Ellis. When Ellis uses his sticky powder to climb up to get the apples, the princess pours olive oil to make him slip, not knowing it is Ellis behind the mask.

    Gentle Criteria: Ellis and Marigold are in the same place in their lives; they want to make friends. Until they do, Ellis is friends with horses while Marigold befriends a cat. When Ellis and Marigold talk, they know right away that they love each other. But Marigold must leave before her father sees her disguised as a maid. When Marigold accompanies her father to find the man with the golden apples, she's pleased to learn the man is Ellis.

366   Levine, Gail Carson. *Ella Enchanted.*
HarperCollins, 1997, ISBN 978-0-06-027511-2; 1998, pap., ISBN 978-0-06-440705-2. 232p. • Grades 5–8
☞ ACCELERATED READER ☞ READING COUNTS

This story is based on the tale of "Cinderella." At birth, Ella has the gift of obedience bestowed upon her by the fairy Lucinda, but it is a curse in disguise. Whatever anyone commands her to do, she must do. When her father remarries, she is at the mercy of her stepmother and stepsisters. She becomes little more than a scullery maid. So Ella goes on a quest to find Lucinda and convince her to take back the gift. But when she finds Lucinda, the fairy can't retract the gift because she has taken an oath never to practice magic because of the harm she has done. In the meantime, she falls in love with the prince but must refuse his command to marry him because she knows it could mean his death. This selfless action breaks the spell.

Gentle Criteria: True unselfish love is what enables Ella to break the spell of obedience. She knows she would rather die than hurt the prince, and her courage sets her free.

⚘ NEWBERY HONOR BOOK, 1998

367 **Levine, Gail Carson.** *Fairest.*

HarperCollins, 2006, ISBN 978-0-06-073409-1. 326p. • Grades 7–9
⌐ ACCELERATED READER ⌐ READING COUNTS ⌐ JUNIOR LIBRARY GUILD

In this book by the author of *Ella Enchanted*, Lucinda the fairy once again gives a well-intentioned but disastrous gift, this time in the form of a magic mirror for King Oscaro and Queen Ivi's wedding. Aza, born in a land where beauty and singing are highly prized, has the most beautiful voice of all—but she is *ugly*. In a chance set of circumstances, she is befriended by the desperate Queen Ivi and used by both the queen and the mirror for ill-gotten gains. Hidden by the gnomes and loved by the prince, Aza begins to understand that beauty is truly in the eyes of the beholder.

Gentle Criteria: Aza is a strong character who is able to fight the temptation to use the mirror for her own gain. She will always do what is necessary to protect and care for the people she loves. When the prince tells her that he is disappointed when she becomes merely pretty, she understands that real beauty runs deeper than cosmetic appearance. She becomes what the people who truly love her already saw her to be.

368 **Levine, Gail Carson.** *Princess Sonora and the Long Sleep.*

Ill. by Mark Elliott. HarperCollins, 1999, ISBN 978-0-06-028065-9.
105p. Series: The Princess Tales • Grades 5–7
⌐ ACCELERATED READER ⌐ READING COUNTS

This Princess Tales story is another clever version of the well-known "Sleeping Beauty" fairy tale. Princess Sonora is given many wonderful gifts before the spiteful fairy Belladonna says she will prick her finger and die. One of the gifts is to be ten times smarter than anyone else. Princess Sonora vows that she will prick her finger on the spindle when she chooses—not because a fairy predicted that she will. Will she get her way? Readers will love her determination but will be aghast when things do not go as planned. Into the story comes a young prince who wants nothing more than the answers to his questions—making for a delightful turn of events.

Gentle Criteria: Once again, Levine has created a princess who wants more out of life than to sit on a throne and look pretty. Intelligence and goodness win out in this unique fairy tale.

369   Levine, Gail Carson. *The Princess Test.*
Ill. by Mark Elliott. HarperCollins, 1999, ISBN 978-0-06-028063-5.
91p. Series: The Princess Tales • Grades 5–7
⌁ ACCELERATED READER ⌁ READING COUNTS

This is the first book in the Princess Tales series. Modeled after "The Princess and the Pea," this is the story of Lorelei, a very picky young maiden. As a baby, all she did was cry—her diaper was too rough, her crib was too hard, and on and on. But once she starts talking, she stops crying and simply explains what the problem is. Now she is older, but every time she tries to do work around the house—except for her very beautiful embroidery—she either gets hurt or wreaks such havoc that it is not worth having her do the task. When her mother dies, her blacksmith father realizes he must find someone to take care of her when he is away. The maid he employs soon wearies of Lorelei's accidents and manages to lose her in the forest one day. Lorelei then wanders into the castle and straight into a test being given to young ladies who wish to marry the prince. Parsley in the bouquets, a pea under the mattress, a dry noodle in the salad—picky Lorelei spots them all—and she is the one the prince really wants anyway. This is such a clever and amusing story!

    Gentle Criteria: True love wins out in this entertaining retelling. The prince doesn't care whether Lorelei was born a princess. He is simply desperate for her to pass the test so he can marry her. Lorelei is far more concerned about her supposedly lost serving maid and the villager's sick child than her own problems, even though she is so particular. Readers will want to read the rest of this clever series.

370   Levine, Gail Carson. *The Two Princesses of Bamarre.*
HarperCollins, 2001, ISBN 978-0-06-029316-1; 2003, pap., ISBN 978-0-06-440966-7. 241p. • Grades 5–7
⌁ ACCELERATED READER ⌁ READING COUNTS ⌁ JUNIOR LIBRARY GUILD

There are two princesses of Bamarre: Addie has always been the shy, timid one, and Meryl the bold, adventurous one. Someday, Meryl says, she will go out and save the kingdom, but Addie wants her to stay home and keep Addie safe. When Meryl becomes sick with the Gray Death, Addie must go out into the world in search of a cure, fulfilling the prophecy in the epic poem. It says that when the timid go forth with the strong, a hero will appear and Drualt will return to save them. A magical tablecloth that provides food on which the flying gryphons gorge themselves to death, boots that can travel seven leagues for each step, and a spyglass enable Addie to travel quickly. Finally Addie must tackle the dragon. It was the dragon's mother's last belch of fire that caused the Gray Death to fall upon the humans. Addie and Meryl are able to rid the kingdom of the pestilence—but not without some unexpected events.

Gentle Criteria: According to the prophecy, the cure for the Gray Death will be found when cowards find courage and rain falls over all of Bamarre. Addie's deep love for her sister gives her the courage to go out into the world and find the cure. She and the dragon exchange sayings, among them "Food for thought requires a mind with teeth." Addie must stop being a timid little mouse and take responsibility for herself. Doing so requires a clear head and a strong heart.

371   Levine, Gail Carson. *The Wish.*
HarperCollins, 2000, ISBN 978-0-06-027901-1. 197p. • Grades 7–9
ᕋ Accelerated Reader ᕋ Reading Counts

Eighth-grader Wilma offers an old woman her seat on the bus. When the old woman grants her a wish, Wilma knows exactly what she wants—to be the most popular person in her school—but she forgets that she will graduate from this school in only three weeks! Those three weeks start out golden; everybody in school suddenly wants to be her best friend. Wilma is no longer one of the lonely outsiders no one wants to know. As time passes, however, she wishes that people liked her for herself and not because they are bewitched. She tries to become a real friend instead of saying only what she thinks will get her into the right crowd. Jared ends up being the boy she chooses over all others because he liked her before the spell was cast. Eventually she befriends the loners and makes them part of the crowd. Wilma finally finds self-assurance. In the end, she learns how to be a real friend that people want to keep.

Gentle Criteria: Popularity is the dominant theme here. Wilma turns it into a journey of discovery about what a real friend is. If you want friends you have to be a friend, and Wilma learns how to do that. In the end she shares the truth with her friends.

372   Lowry, Lois. *Gossamer.*
Houghton Mifflin, 2006, ISBN 978-0-618-68550-9. 140p. • Grades 5–7
ᕋ Accelerated Reader ᕋ Reading Counts ᕋ Junior Library Guild

Littlest One, in training to be a dreamgiver, attempts to help a troubled foster child deal with his fears and fight off the Sinisteeds who give nightmares. This story is a gentle tale about how dreamgivers can touch the things that give us comfort, such as a well-loved picture or a baby's blanket, and then give us dreams to soothe the troubles that we had during the day.

Gentle Criteria: This book is a quiet statement of how a multitude of little things sustain and comfort us throughout our lives, and why the things that we love—and that love us back—give us the courage to face the hardships in our lives.

373   Lubar, David. *Wizards of the Game.*
Philomel, 2003, ISBN 978-0-399-23706-5; Penguin, 2004, pap., ISBN
978-0-14-240215-3. 166p. • Grades 7–9
  ☞ ACCELERATED READER

Mercer, Ed, and Michelle are elected to come up with a fund-raising idea for
their junior high class. Mercer loves to play fantasy games and suggests they have
a tournament and raise money to donate to a food shelter. Ed is quite spiritual
and objects to the idea, writing a letter to the local newspaper informing the
community of how they are playing "demonic games in the school." His letter
upsets the community, resulting in picketing at the school and a heated debate at
the school board meeting. Mercer's fundraising idea is forbidden. When he's at
the shelter, however, he meets four strangers from a foreign land who call him
Magus and ask for his help. He discovers that what he's been role-playing is
actually real. These four wizards—with limited powers in this world—need his
help to return to their world. When they show him their powers, he consults
with other game players who think they know enough magic to help the wizards get back to their world. Unfortunately, when a portal is opened—instead of
the wizards going in—a monster comes out!

  Gentle Criteria: This story is a good example of freedom of speech. Mercer and Ed have the freedom to voice their beliefs, and even though Ed gets the
game stopped, he changes his mind and gives the game a try to help the wizards.
His second newspaper article gets the game reinstated at school. Seeing how Mercer, Ed, and Michelle recognize the Food Kitchen as a noble cause is uplifting.

374   McCaughrean, Geraldine. *Peter Pan in Scarlet.*
Ill. by Scott M. Fisher. Simon & Schuster, 2006, ISBN 978-1-4169-
1808-0. 309p. • Grades 5–7
  ☞ ACCELERATED READER

This book is the only sequel to *Peter Pan* authorized by the Great Ormond Street
Hospital for Children in London, the organization to which J. M. Barrie left all
rights to the original book. In 2004, this organization held a contest to see who
would win the right to write a sequel. This author has done a wonderful job with
the fantasy, capturing Peter Pan's refusal to grow up and featuring the characters
who love him. As the story opens, nightmares have started to leak out of Neverland and reach Wendy and the Lost Boys, long after they have grown up. Convinced that Peter must be in trouble, they return to help him—of course, they
must first become children again. They find a fairy (born when a baby laughs for
the first time), put on their children's clothes, fight Hook once again, and end up
having many delightful adventures. Michael is the only one of the boys who does
not make it back on this second adventure—he was "lost" in the Great War.

  Gentle Criteria: Underlying this wonderful fantasy is the point that all
grownups are children at heart. Wendy kisses Hook goodnight for the first time

in his life, enabling him to sleep and to heal. Children's sense of imagination and fun is amply illustrated in this delightful read.

375   McNamee, Eoin. *The Navigator.*

Ill. by Jon Goodell. Wendy Lamb Books, 2006, ISBN 978-0-375-93910-5. 342p. • Grades 5–9

∾ ACCELERATED READER

Owen is a loner living with a mother who grows less coherent every day. He's playing down at the river—even though he's scared of water—when he sees a very small man who is dressed like a soldier. The man tells Owen to follow him, and he soon finds himself in the midst of a large group of small people calling themselves the Wakeful and claiming that he is the Navigator. The Wakeful remain asleep until they are called upon to fight the Harsh. Owen finds all this hard to believe until the Harsh start shooting rays of lethal ice at them. Fortunately, the Harsh can't cross running rivers. Owen was told his father committed suicide, and some of the Wakeful believe that he stole the Mortmain. The Harsh are turning back time, causing all living things on unprotected land to disappear. If Owen is going to save the world, he must find the Mortmain and must deliver it to Puissance before time reverses too far and before an unknown spy and the enemy stop him.

Gentle Criteria: This book has plenty of action and adventure without violence. A memory machine shows Owen where the Mortmain was lost and that his father actually saved him from the sinking car, explaining his fear of water. Owen is determined to restore his family's reputation by crossing the river into Harsh territory to look for the missing Mortmain. This is a gratifying story in which Owen places himself in danger in hopes of saving the world and returning to his mother.

376   Martin, Ann M., and Laura Godwin. *The Doll People.*

Hyperion, 2000, ISBN 978-0-7868-2372-7; Disney, 2003, pap., ISBN 978-0-7868-1240-0. 256p. • Grades 5–7

∾ ACCELERATED READER ∾ READING COUNTS

This story is a delightfully old-fashioned fantasy about a family of dolls. Annabelle and the rest of her doll family have lived in their dollhouse for several generations. Annabelle begins to read the journal of her Aunt Sarah, a brave doll who dared to venture outside the dollhouse and mysteriously disappeared. When the Funmarts move in with their newer, plastic dollhouse and accessories, the fun *really* begins.

Gentle Criteria: While this is a story of two different generations learning to get along, it is also a light fantasy based on every girl's secret wish—that her dolls will come alive!

377   Martin, Ann M., and Laura Godwin. *The Meanest Doll in the World.*

Hyperion, 2003, ISBN 978-0-7868-0878-6; Disney, 2005, pap., ISBN 978-0-7868-5297-0. 260p. • Grades 5–7

🡒 ACCELERATED READER 🡒 READING COUNTS

Dolls Annabelle and Tiffany continue the friendship that started in *The Doll People* (see above). They have several adventures—hiding in a school backpack, mistakenly being taken to school, and getting carried to another person's house. But their most difficult challenge of all is trying to control Princess Mimi, a dreadful doll who threatens all of them.

    Gentle Criteria: Fans of *The Doll People* will enjoy the continuation of this old-fashioned adventure featuring dolls that come to life.

378   Martin, Rafe. *Birdwing.*

Arthur A. Levine, 2005, ISBN 978-0-439-21167-3; Scholastic, 2007, pap., ISBN 978-0-439-21168-0. 358p. • Grades 5–7

🡒 ACCELERATED READER 🡒 READING COUNTS

This is a variation of the Grimm brothers' story about the six swans. It tells the tale of Ardwin, or Birdwing, the brother whose shirt did not totally cover him so that when he and his brothers were finally transformed back into humans, he was left with one wing instead of two human arms. His three brothers go on to lead normal, human lives, but Birdwing is a freak to both birds and humans. Throughout his fairy-tale-like quest, he finds acceptance both within himself and from the people who truly love him. This book is filled with great adventure and mystic capabilities, including wizards, the ability to understand animals, the meaning of true love, witches who transform into animals, magical spells, and much more.

    Gentle Criteria: This is a story of love and acceptance. The underlying theme of how those with disabilities are perceived is a strong and positive one. When Birdwing finally accepts himself and learns to love his differences, he finds true happiness.

379   Martin, Rafe. *The World Before This One: A Novel Told in Legend.*

Arthur A. Levine, 2002, ISBN 978-0-590-37976-2; Scholastic, 2005, pap., ISBN 978-0-590-37980-9. 195p. • Grades 5–7

🡒 READING COUNTS

Based on several Seneca Indian legends, this story follows Crow and his grandmother, who have been cast out from their village. After scraping by to survive, Crow is finally old enough to hunt. One day while searching for food, he comes upon a talking boulder that tells him stories of the world before this one. Crow and his entire village relearn tales that show love, forgiveness, and how to live as one with the earth. Beautiful cut-paper sculptures illustrate the power and depth of the legends told in this story.

Gentle Criteria: This is a book of Indian folklore with strong messages about living ecologically and in peace.

380 **Morris, Gerald.** *The Lioness and Her Knight.*

Houghton Mifflin, 2005, ISBN 978-0-618-50772-6. 343p. Series: The Squire's Tales • Grades 7–9

⌐ ACCELERATED READER ⌐ READING COUNTS ⌐ JUNIOR LIBRARY GUILD

This first installment in the Squire's Tales series was named one of the Top Ten Youth Romances of 2006 by *Booklist*. Luneta's mother is at has wit's end with her, so Luneta is sent to spend time with Laudine, a family friend. She is accompanied by her cousin Sir Ywain, who is dying for adventure. They pick up their friend Rhience, who has been made to play a fool for a year for bothering the storm stone. When Sir Ywain accidentally sets off the storm stone, he is attacked by Laudine's husband, whose task it is to protect the stone. Sir Ywain mortally wounds him in self-defense and falls in love with Laudine. Luneta, who is always playing the matchmaker, arranges for them to marry in six months, but Sir Ywain is now off hunting game and forgets about the time. When Luneta informs him that Laudine no longer wants him, he runs off into the woods naked and insane. Luneta is then trained to be an enchantress by her aunt Morgan Le Fay. Luneta then restores Sir Ywain to his former self, and they continue to rescue people in distress. Luneta determines a way to reunite Laudine and Sir Ywain, finding that she too is falling in love.

Gentle Criteria: There is some death in this book, but it happens to the evil and mean people. Everyone assumes that the lioness in the title is of the four-legged kind, but actually the lioness is Luneta. Readers might think this is a love story between Sir Ywain and Laudine, but it is really about a much deeper love—the bond that develops between Luneta and Rhience. The central characters of the book adhere to a strong code of ethics. What else would one expect from relatives of King Arthur?

381 **Morris, Gerald.** *The Quest of the Fair Unknown.*

Houghton Mifflin, 2006, ISBN 978-0-618-63152-0. 264p. Series: The Squire's Tales • Grades 5–9

⌐ ACCELERATED READER ⌐ READING COUNTS ⌐ JUNIOR LIBRARY GUILD

This second book in the Squire's Tales series is an adventure in which Beufis, who has never met another person in his life, sets out to find his father. His dying mother tells him that he is the son of one of the knights of King Arthur's Round Table. When he shares his story with knights he meets, they ask him what his mother's name was; he replies, "Mother." So you can imagine that finding his father might be quite difficult. On his journey to the king's court, he encounters would-be bandits but has no difficulty defending himself. He befriends young Galahad and joins him on a journey to find the Holy Grail. He encounters more evil people, a beautiful girl who wants to join him on his adventure, and even a dragon who was once a princess. Readers will enjoy watching Beufis learn and grow to manhood.

Gentle Criteria: No one dies in the knights' fights here. When Carl of Carlisle tricks one of the knights into doing the honor of chopping off his head, the action actually removes the curse that was on him and returns him to normal. This is an enjoyable read with lots of excitement.

382   Mull, Brandon. *Fablehaven.*

Ill. by Brandon Dorman. Shadow Mountain, 2006, ISBN 978-1-59038-581-4; Simon & Schuster, 2007, pap., ISBN 978-1-4169-4720-2. 359p. Series: Fablehaven • Grades 5–8

This is the first book in the Fablehaven series. Kendra and Seth are sent to stay with their grandparents while their parents go on a seventeen-day cruise. What Kendra and Seth don't understand is why Grandpa won't let them go into the barn or the woods. Kendra finds a secret journal that tells them to drink the milk. When they drink the milk that one of the workers left out for the bugs, they suddenly see fairies flying around. Grandpa then shares with them the truth about Fablehaven. It is a refuge for mythical creatures, saving them from extinction. Special pacts keep the dangerous creatures from injuring the others. However, Seth lets the dangerous ones into the house during the summer solstice, with unfortunate results. It is up to Kendra to save the day. This story is full of adventure.

Gentle Criteria: Even though their lives are in mortal danger at times, Seth and Kendra come shining through in Indiana Jones style. Kendra is willing to risk her own life to save her friends and family.

383   Nix, Garth. *Above the Veil.*

Scholastic, 2001, pap., ISBN 978-0-439-17685-9. 248p. Series: Seventh Tower • Grades 5–7

☞ ACCELERATED READER ☞ READING COUNTS

In this fourth book in the series, Tal, Milla, and their Spiritshadows return from the planet Aenir, being chased through the castle by Sushin and his guards. They must rely on Crow, a rebel Freeman, to guide them through the lower corridors back to his Uncle Ebbitt. Tal and Crow must reach the red tower to steal the keystone so they can take it to the empress to prove Sushin and his Spiritshadows are preparing to conquer the kingdom. Meanwhile, Milla is on a mission to get back to the Icecarls to share with them the knowledge she has gained about Aenir and the Chosen. Will she be accepted or turned out into the ice to die for breaking Icecarl laws and for bonding with a shadow?

Gentle Criteria: This book is about honor and love for your family or clan. Milla has acquired her sunstone and knowledge about Aenir and the Chosen that will help her clan decide how to go forward. Tal is on a mission to acquire a keystone so he can acquire the knowledge necessary to free his enslaved family. As the journey continues, it appears that Milla and Tal may end up on opposite sides. Readers will want to find out who will prevail—family or friends?

384 Nix, Garth. *Aenir.*
Scholastic, 2001, pap., ISBN 978-0-439-17684-2. 233p. Series: Seventh Tower • Grades 5–7
☞ ACCELERATED READER ☞ READING COUNTS

The third book in the Seventh Tower series. Tal and Milla are now on the enchanted planet Aenir. They make a blood bond, swearing to support each other, which summons up two storm shepherds who must take a life because blood has been spilled on Old Hrigga Hill. Tal frees the storm shepherds from their eternal entrapment on the hill by making Odras and Adras their Spiritshadows. But Milla is so angry that she runs away, thinking she will never become a Shield Maiden—Shield Maidens are forbidden to have Spiritshadows. The Codex is trapped under a mountain and is sending messages to be found. Milla and Tal must fight against many new enemies. If the two succeed in rescuing the computer-minded Codex, they can ask it any question—including "Is Tal's father still alive"?

Gentle Criteria: As their journey continues, Tal and Milla learn more about each other's past and realize that they once shared a history.

385 Nix, Garth. *Castle.*
Scholastic, 2000, pap., ISBN 978-0-439-17683-5. 215p. Series: Seventh Tower • Grades 5–7
☞ ACCELERATED READER ☞ READING COUNTS

This is the second book in the Seventh Tower series, following *The Fall* (see below). Readers will want to read these books in order. Tal, one of the Chosen, has fallen out of the castle. He and Milla, an Icecarl, agree to help each other acquire the sunstones their families need. They are brought into the Shield Maidens' Ruin Ship where Milla's wounds—obtained from her fight with the one-eyed Merwin—are healed. The Shield Maidens give Tal a carved bone that shows them how to get into the castle. Milla and Tal must journey over ice and through the maze of tunnels to enter the castle. There they must find his Uncle Ebbitt who will help them create a plan to save his mother. Uncle Ebbitt tells them they must go to Aenir and retrieve the Codex, a machine that knows all. This will enable them to prove to the queen that Sushin is performing horrible deeds with the assistance of the royal guards. Once inside, they are captured; Milla is thrown into the nightmare chamber and Tal into a 30-foot pit. They must overcome the Spiritshadows and giant spiders, as well as the guards, to escape. First, however, Tal must teach Milla skills of the Chosen ones, and Milla must teach Tal how to fight—if they are to help each other.

Gentle Criteria: This book is about honor and love for your family, or clan. Tal knows he must find his own sunstone to save his family, and Milla needs one for the same reason—to save her clan. Throughout their lengthy journey, they save each other from certain death again and again, forming a bond of friendship that has never before existed between the two cultures.

386 Nix, Garth. *Drowned Wednesday.*
Scholastic, 2005, ISBN 978-0-439-70086-3; 2006, pap., ISBN 978-0-439-43656-4. 389p. Series: Keys to the Kingdom • Grades 5–9
☞ ACCELERATED READER ☞ READING COUNTS

This is Book Three in the Keys to the Kingdom series. Arthur receives an invitation from Wednesday, inviting him to lunch; transportation will be provided. Drowned Wednesday is one of the original treacherous trustees who is not abiding by the Will. Being a denizen, she has transformed her body into the shape of a whale. While Fern is visiting Arthur in his hospital room—after he broke his leg—an ocean wave crashes into the room, sweeping them both out to sea. Fern is mistakenly picked up by the ship sent to grab Arthur, and it sails off without him. Arthur is picked up by another ship, and he finds out that Wednesday probably doesn't want to invite him to lunch—she wants to *have* him for lunch. Wednesday has transformed into a giant whale that is more than twenty miles long, and she has already eaten most of her servants. He also learns that the third part of the Will has been hidden inside the whale by evil captain Feverfew who sails on a ship of bone. All of the trustees have second-in-command officers called Noon. Fortunately for Arthur, Wednesday's main officer Noon says Drowned Wednesday is willing to hand over the key to Arthur if he can retrieve the third part of the Will. Now Arthur must survive the dangers of the Border Seas, rescue Fern, and save a bunch of captured denizens inside the whale while battling Feverfew.

Gentle Criteria: Arthur continues in every book in this series to be a normal boy and a boy with a disability—considering his asthma—who does heroic things. He battles dangerous creatures in a magical other world without any magic of his own. The driving reason for this insanity is to save his family from harm and to correct an alternative world that has been altered by greedy caretakers of the Keys of the Kingdom. Along the way, he finds enslaved people whom he must help set free.

387 Nix, Garth. *The Fall.*
Scholastic, 2000, pap., ISBN 978-0-439-17682-8. 195p. Series: Seventh Tower • Grades 5–7
☞ ACCELERATED READER ☞ READING COUNTS

This is Book One in the Seventh Tower series. Tal has lived his whole life in the castle, a large structure with seven mysterious towers. It has never occurred to him that there might be a world beyond it. He is one of the Chosen who are served by their shadows and a hierarchy of people below him—at the bottom are the Underworlders. When his father mysteriously disappears and his mother becomes ill, it is up to Tal to find a new sunstone to support the family and make his mother well. Sunstones provide energy, light, and also healing powers. All his attempts to gain a new one fail, and he realizes that he will have to go outside and get one of his own. When he falls, he discovers a new people of Ice-carls and the animals that they live with. He is bound on a quest with a young girl named Milla, and together they try to reach the castle and get their own sunstones. Along the way they battle Selskis, giant animals who slam their way through the ice, and Shield Maidens.

Gentle Criteria: This book is about honor and love for one's family or clan. Tal knows he must find his own sunstone to save his family, and Milla needs one to save her clan. Even when Tal has a chance to get one without Milla, he knows he must do the honorable thing and stay by Milla as he has sworn he will do. The two of them are up against a larger evil than they know, but they stay true to each other, and doing so serves them well.

388 Nix, Garth. *Grim Tuesday.*

Scholastic, 2005, ISBN 978-0-439-70370-3; 2004, pap., ISBN 978-0-439-43655-7. 321p. Series: Keys to the Kingdom • Grades 5–8
⌒ Accelerated Reader ⌒ Reading Counts

This is Book Two in the Keys to the Kingdom series. Arthur is only home a few minutes from Book One, *Mister Monday*, when the telephone rings from the other realm. Grim Tuesday has found a loophole in the laws of the house and has laid claim to Monday's key. He has ruined the stock market so their family will lose their house if Arthur doesn't return to the house to claim Grim Tuesday's keys as well. If he succeeds he can right many wrongs. Grim Tuesday has stolen valuable artwork from the real world, and he continues to dig into nothingness that could soon destroy the foundations of both worlds. Arthur wants to free the slaves Grim Tuesday has been using and seal off the nothingness pits so no more damage can be done to his house or to his world. Arthur and Suzy seek the help of Captain Tom to sail them to a sun where Grim Tuesday has hidden the second piece of the Will in the form of a bear.

Gentle Criteria: Once again, even in the direst of circumstances, Arthur wants to help everyone who offers him a kind hand. At the end of the book, when he has the power of the key, he remembers and does elevate those who helped him during this mission. Arthur shows a strong love of family by placing his life on the line to save his family's fortune—and his family members aren't even aware that he has done it. Arthur is a kind, selfless individual.

389   Nix, Garth. *Into Battle.*

Scholastic, 2001, pap., ISBN 978-0-439-17686-6. 201p. Series: Seventh Tower • Grades 5–7

☞ ACCELERATED READER ☞ READING COUNTS

This is Book Five in the series. Readers will want to read books one through four first. At the end of book four, Milla was brought before the Crone's council. Instead of being put to death, however, she was made War Chief of the Icecarls. She has been chosen to lead the Shield Maidens and Icecarls into the castle to battle for the Spiritshadows and the Chosen to preserve the Veil that is in danger of being destroyed. If the Veil fails, then all sorts of unattached Spiritshadows can attack from Aenir and take over the world. Meanwhile, Tal has taken the Red Keystone, a source of magical powers, and its entrapped inhabitant back to Aenir to show the Empress proof that Sushin is trying to destroy the Veil. After reaching the Empress, Tal discovers that he has the Violet Keystone, the most powerful keystone of all. It was in the Shinestone, a ring people use for light, that he found lying on the ground in the tunnels. He must now return to the castle to use the ring containing the Violet Keystone to release his father and save the rest of his family. While Tal is busy with his agenda, Milla has left the safety of the war room to go out into battle to lead her troops.

    Gentle Criteria: This book is about honor and love for your family, clan, and friends. Milla must now lead the Icecarls into battle against the Spiritshadows and the Chosen. She is seeing for the first time that death isn't glorious, a tribute to her friend Tal. Tal is finally noticing the injustices that he has taken for granted by having less-advantaged people serve him, a tribute to his friend Milla. Will their friendships save them from attacking each other, and will they be able to join forces to battle the true evil at the center of this madness?

390   Nix, Garth. *Lady Friday.*

Scholastic, 2007, ISBN 978-0-439-70088-7. 305p. Series: Keys to the Kingdom • Grades 5–8

This is Book Five in the Keys to the Kingdom series. Arthur has defeated the first four caretakers of the keys who were wielding them for their own evil gains. Now he has given Dame Primus control over three of the keys, keeping one for himself in case he needs to use its power during his journey to obtain Lady Friday's key. Arthur wears a ring that shows how much mortality he has remaining. Whenever he uses one of the keys, he becomes less human and is at risk for becoming a denizen; once that happens, he can never become human again. Arthur has been tricked by Lady Friday into thinking she's abdicated her key and is in a race with the Piper and Superior Saturday to acquire it. Arthur has found a bit of the original material that was used to create the fifth Will, and a sorcerer changed it into a compass that will find the remainder of it. Lady Friday, a denizen already, favors capturing elderly humans and sucking out their memories so she can enjoy what it's like to be human. Can Arthur stop her by obtaining her key and taking away her power?

Gentle Criteria: Arthur, although at war with the Piper, Superior Saturday, and Lady Friday, always tries to minimize bloodshed. Arthur overrides Dame Primus' desire to extinguish all Piper children. Arthur also has compassion for those who help him accomplish his missions and often rewards them with better jobs or by returning them to wherever they came from. Each book in this series continues to amaze with new and highly creative ideas. For example, a river that will float anything with writing on it upstream is unique.

391 Nix, Garth. *Mister Monday.*
> Scholastic, 2003, ISBN 978-0-439-70369-7; 2006, pap., ISBN 978-0-439-85626-3. 361p. Series: Keys to the Kingdom • Grades 5–8
> ⌒ ACCELERATED READER ⌒ READING COUNTS

This is Book One in the Keys to the Kingdom series. Seven treacherous trustees have torn The Will, the binding power that runs a smooth world. It's Arthur's first day of school when the Physical Education teacher makes all students run before lunch. Arthur has an asthma attack and is dying when Mr. Monday and his butler appear from another dimension and give him a key to hide, saying they will reclaim it after he dies. Little do they know that the power of the key, actually a part of the Will, is enough to keep Arthur alive. Mr. Monday is furious and sends evil creatures after Arthur to retrieve his key, causing a sleeping plague and quarantines in the town. Now Arthur must enter another dimension to try to determine how to save his town from the plague. He is aided by a piece of the Will and Suzy, a girl he meets in the other dimension, through an amazing house that only he can see. There are all sorts of dangers he must face to solve the mystery of the key and his town's fate.

Gentle Criteria: All along the adventure Arthur sticks to the high road. He always wants to help someone in a crisis. He would rather restore people to their former nice selves with the power of his key than to destroy them. He shows a gentle kindness that the creatures he encounters do not. He does not crave the power he gains by possessing the key and would gladly give it up just to return to his normal mortal life with the plague gone.

392 Nix, Garth. *Sir Thursday.*
> Scholastic, 2006, ISBN 978-0-439-70087-0. 344p. Series: Keys to the Kingdom • Grades 6–9
> ⌒ ACCELERATED READER ⌒ READING COUNTS

This is Book Four in the Keys to the Kingdom series. When Leaf and Arthur try to return home, Arthur cannot leave because a Spirit-Eater clone has taken over Arthur's spot. Whoever the clone touches will eventually be able to mind-control. Arthur must send Leaf back alone to find the scrap of Arthur's clothing this

Spirit-Eater was created from and return it to Arthur, enabling him to destroy it and save his family. Meanwhile Arthur has been drafted into Sir Thursday's army and is sentenced to serve 100 years. Arthur must find a way to locate the fourth part of the Will and the fourth key to continue his claim to the kingdom. To make matters worse, Arthur's brain has been washed and he can't remember who he is. If that weren't enough, the Pied Piper, a son of the original architect, created a bunch of intelligent Nithlings and is threatening to take over the kingdom.

Gentle Criteria: Arthur continues to look for peaceful solutions to solve the kingdom's problems. Rather than punish Sir Thursday, Arthur orders him to be protected. And rather than continue fighting the Nithlings, Arthur tries to make a truce so lives will be saved and the kingdom will be peaceful.

393   Nix, Garth. *The Violet Keystone.*

Scholastic, 2001, pap., ISBN 978-0-439-17687-3. 233p. Series: Seventh Tower • Grades 5–7

⌒ ACCELERATED READER ⌒ READING COUNTS

This is Book Six in the Seventh Tower series. As Milla leads the Icecarls into battle to control the castle, she learns that Sharrakor, an ancient shapechanger, is behind the plot to lower the Veil. Tal is captured and thrown into the chamber of nightmares while giving spider antidote to his mother. Uncle Ebbitt sends Crow to rescue Tal and to tell him of the need to reach the Violet tower. Milla, Tal, Crow, and a few others must find a way to reach the tower before the Veil is destroyed; if that happens, shadow creatures will descend upon their world. They must put aside their differences and join forces to battle the one creature that can destroy their world.

Gentle Criteria: Several characters in this story learn how their actions affect others. At one point Milla mentions how she is an Icecarl who now often acts like a Chosen. Tal realizes that he is a Chosen who often thinks and behaves like an Icecarl. They both see how the Chosen have been treating the Underfolk like slaves. Crow, Tal, and Milla promise they will change the injustice of their current society.

394   Okorafor-Mbachu, Nnedi. *Zahrah the Windseeker.*

Ill. by Stephanie Cooper. Houghton Mifflin, 2005, ISBN 978-0-618-34090-3. 308p. • Grades 5–8

⌒ ACCELERATED READER

Zahrah was born dada, and has a green vine grows among her dreadlocks. Many of her classmates tease her, but her parents advise her to ignore them because to be born dada is a great privilege and means she will become wise. Zahrah has one true friend, Dari, who loves to explore and learn from books in the library. They both live next to the forbidden forest. When Zahrah reaches puberty, she discovers that she can levitate; Dari insists they enter the forest so she can practice flying. He is curious about it after reading an old book that encourages people to stop living in ignorance and learn about the forest. Once in the forest, Dari is bitten by a poisonous War snake, which puts him in a coma. The only cure is an unfertilized egg from the monstrous Elgort, located three hundred miles inside the jungle. Zahrah reenters the treacherous jungle in hopes of retrieving an egg to save her best friend. Will she be able to overcome the wild creatures in the jungle *and* her own fears?

Gentle Criteria: Zahrah is willing to risk her own life to save her best friend's life. By trusting in her inner self, she builds self-confidence and learns how to fly instead of just levitating. This story is a great adventure with a female heroine. Earth is referred to as another mythical place to visit. Readers will hope for a sequel!

395   Oppel, Kenneth. *Airborn.*

HarperCollins, 2004, ISBN 978-0-06-053181-2; 2005, pap., ISBN 978-0-06-053182-9. 321p. • Grades 7–9

⸙ Accelerated Reader ⸙ Reading Counts ⸙ Junior Library Guild

This is a wonderful Victorian Age fantasy. Matt Cruse is a cabin boy aboard an airship. The ship encounters a man in a battered hot-air balloon who, before he dies, claims to have seen strange and beautiful creatures in the air. A year later, the man's granddaughter Kate meets Matt and claims she can prove that her grandfather saw these creatures. Fierce storms, pirates, and some skeletal remains all come together to show that her grandfather was not hallucinating. But when they find the creatures, they aren't the beautiful, gentle beings they expected.

Gentle Criteria: Although pirates rob and kill in this story, it is an old-fashioned adventure and gives a good description of Victorian conventions. There is a lot of detail about how the ship works and a little romance. This book will appeal to both male and female readers. Also of note is the strong female character.

ꙮ   Michael L. Printz Honor Book, 2005

396   Oppel, Kenneth. *Skybreaker.*

HarperCollins, 2005, ISBN 978-0-06-053228-4. 369p. • Grades 7–9

⸙ Accelerated Reader ⸙ Reading Counts ⸙ Junior Library Guild

This sequel to *Airborn* (see above) is a fast-paced adventure in the tradition of Indiana Jones. Matt Cruse is continuing at the Airship Academy, and Kate is pursuing her studies at the Sorbonne. During a two-week training duty aboard the *Flotsam*, Matt glimpses the fabled *Hyperion*, an airship rumored to be loaded with strange curiosities and lots of gold, and obtains its coordinates. He and Kate team up with Nadira, a strange gypsy girl, and Hal, a captain with nothing to lose, to locate the airship and claim salvage rights. This page-turner is filled with Victorian Age inventions, romance, and adventure.

Gentle Criteria: Although there are a few gunshots, this is mostly a good old-fashioned adventure story with lots of action and a little romance.

397   Park, Linda Sue. *Archer's Quest.*
Clarion, 2006, ISBN 978-0-618-59631-7. 167p. • Grades 5–7
⌐ ACCELERATED READER

This is an entertaining fantasy filled with historical information about Korea. When a famous ruler and archer from 55 B.C. shows up in his bedroom, Kevin Kim must help him find a way home. Kevin, however, hates history! There is a wonderful moment when the myth of Chu-Mong crossing the river on the backs of turtles is played out in modern day as a tractor-trailer full of Volkswagen Beetles slides across the road and blocks the path of the person pursuing them. Lots of fun to read!

Gentle Criteria: This is an adventurous story in which a twelve-year-old boy does the honorable thing in helping a friend, and as a result, gains a greater understanding both of his family and the world around him. This book has many cross-curricular possibilities—in the areas of math and history, in particular. At the end of the book is a complete listing of the Chinese Zodiac calendar along with corresponding earth signs.

398   Pinkwater, Daniel. *The Neddiad: How Neddie Took the Train, Went to Hollywood, and Saved Civilization.*
Ill. by Calef Brown. Houghton Mifflin, 2007, ISBN 978-0-618-59444-3. 307p. • Grades 5–8
⌐ ACCELERATED READER

Ned Wentworthstein is the son of wealthy parents who do whatever they want. A picture of the Brown Derby restaurant in Los Angeles attracts both Ned and his father, and the family boards a train heading west. During a stop in Albuquerque, Ned visits an Indian shop where he is given a turtle carved from a mysterious stone. The turtle is said to keep the evil earth-god, Kkhkktonos, in check. When he misses the train in Flagstaff, he befriends the famous movie star Aaron Finn, his son, and a ghost. They decide to drive Ned to his parents. There is a robbery attempt but quick thinking keeps the turtle from being stolen. If the turtle ends up in the wrong hands, the Ice Age will return. When Ned hides the turtle in plain sight, however, it comes up missing. Will the missing turtle mean the end of civilization?

Gentle Criteria: This adventure story offers lots of entertainment for middle-school readers. They learn about ghosts and turtle mythology, and they meet interesting characters. Ned has no idea how he will defeat a coliseum full of wolves, saber-tooth tigers, and a huge earth-god, but he is willing to try to save the world. In the end, readers find out what a hero young Ned is.

399   Pratchett, Terry. *A Hat Full of Sky.*

HarperCollins, 2004, ISBN 978-0-06-058661-4; 2005, pap., ISBN 978-0-06-058662-1. 278p. • Grades 5–9

ॐ ACCELERATED READER ॐ READING COUNTS

This book is the sequel to *The Wee Free Men* (see below). Tiffany is eleven now and has been sent off to what her parents believe is an apprenticeship. They don't realize that Witch Weatherwax has set her up to learn witchcraft from Witch Level. Tiffany is surprised to find out that Witch Level is busy caring for all the residents of the mountainside. She helps deliver babies, attends to homebound people, and delivers meals. In return she gets a biscuit here and a bit of food there. Tiffany is shocked that she isn't learning more magic. Meanwhile, a disembodied demon, a hiver, has sensed Tiffany's power and is pursuing her, hoping to possess her body. The Wee Free Men learn of the hiver's presence and send a party after Tiffany to help defeat the hiver. While Tiffany is outside her body—examining it because she has no mirror—the hiver possesses it. The Wee Free Men enter her dreams and help her exorcise the hiver, but it is still stalking her, just waiting for its chance.

Gentle Criteria: When Tiffany asks Witch Level where she stores all the meat she's been given for her kind deeds, Miss Level replies, "I store it in people." Tiffany learns what it means to be part of a community: You are always helping people in need who may be able to help you someday when you're down on your luck. Tiffany applies that to her homeland as well, helping the sheep get delivered and picking up where her grandmother left off as the mother of the Chalk.

400   Pratchett, Terry. *Wintersmith.*

HarperCollins, 2006, ISBN 978-0-06-089032-2. 323p. • Grades 5–9

ॐ ACCELERATED READER ॐ READING COUNTS

In this third volume of the series that started with *The Wee Free Men*, Tiffany Aching is learning how to be a witch while serving under Witch Treason. Miss Treason takes her to the winter dance and warns her against participating, but Tiffany can't help herself and joins in, attracting the unfortunate attention of the Wintersmith, a.k.a. Old Man Winter, and upsetting the balance of the seasons. The Wintersmith then searches for Tiffany, finds her, and asks her to marry him. Tiffany has temporarily taken the place of Miss Summer and discovers that wherever she walks things begin to grow. The Wintersmith obtains the ingredients necessary to change into a man so that he can make Tiffany his queen. Meanwhile, winter is lasting too long, and Tiffany's sheep are in danger if she can't end it. The Wee Free Men come to the rescue.

Gentle Criteria: Tiffany Aching has a knack for doing the right thing and constantly demonstrates that it is better to give than to receive.

401   **Pratchett, Terry, and Lyn Pratchett.** *The Wee Free Men.*
HarperCollins, 2003, ISBN 978-0-06-001237-3; 2004, pap., ISBN 978-0-06-001238-0. 263p. • Grades 5–9
ACCELERATED READER *READING COUNTS*

Tiffany is the nine-year-old granddaughter of the great Granny Aching, whom many suspect is a witch. When her grandmother dies, Tiffany starts to see little blue men running around, but they are invisible to everyone else. Tiffany managed to clobber one with a frying pan and they believe her to be a witch, asking her to be their leader in Granny Aching's place. Meanwhile, her brother has been kidnapped by a fairy queen and taken to Fairyland. Tiffany teams up with the Wee Free Men to rescue her brother. They face many creatures and monsters, including dromes that can send them into a dream. Tiffany must constantly use her first, second, and third sight to analyze what is real. With the help of the Wee Free Men, she meets the queen for a final showdown.

   Gentle Criteria: The relationship between Tiffany and her grandmother is very touching. Tiffany says she does not mourn her granny because she never truly left her. The dialect of the Wee Free Men is fun to pronounce—a kind of Scottish-Irish-Elf-speak. The Wee Free Men provide lots of humor throughout the story—they fear no one except lawyers.

402   **Pullman, Philip.** *The Scarecrow and His Servant.*
Knopf, 2004, ISBN 978-0-375-91531-4; Gardners Books, 2005, pap., ISBN 978-0-440-86376-2. 229p. • Grades 5–7
ACCELERATED READER *READING COUNTS* *JUNIOR LIBRARY GUILD*

This is an old-fashioned comic fairy tale. When a bolt of lightning strikes him just exactly right, a scarecrow magically comes alive. The scarecrow and his servant Jack proceed to save the land from the evil Buffalonis with many adventures along the way. With humor that is both subtle and overt, this book will please many readers.

   Gentle Criteria: Its fairy-tale character and subtle underlying themes of good and evil will appeal to readers of many ages.

403   **Regan, Dian Curtis.** *Cam's Quest: The Continuing Story of Princess Nevermore and the Wizard's Apprentice.*
Darby Creek, 2007, ISBN 978-1-58196-056-3. 334p. • Grades 5–7
ACCELERATED READER *JUNIOR LIBRARY GUILD*

In this sequel to *Princess Nevermore* (1995), Cam and Princess Quinn change places. It is Cam who must venture to Outer Earth to discover his past and claim his future, and Quinn who must brave the expectations of picking her future husband. Quinn's tutor Ameka is getting married, and Cam is off on a quest to Outer Earth to discover who he really is and what are the contents of the box that the wizard Melikar has given him. Quinn is feeling lonely and realizes who means the most to her. When Cam discovers that he is not only nobility but that he also has ties to Outer Earth, it changes everything. Secret passageways, fairy protection, tools from Outer Earth, soldiers turned into squirrels and their horses turned into rabbits, walkie-talkies, and night goggles all help to save the day and enable Cam to finally claim his rightful bride.

Gentle Criteria: Cam proves that he is noble in both lineage and heart. He risks his own safety to save others. Quinn too proves true of heart. Readers are assured that in her future kingdom common sense will prevail over protocol and tradition.

404   Riordan, Rick. *The Lightning Thief.*
Hyperion, 2005, ISBN 978-0-7868-5629-9; Disney, 2006, pap., ISBN 978-0-7868-3865-3. 375p. Series: Percy Jackson and the Olympians • Grades 6–8
☞ ACCELERATED READER ☞ READING COUNTS

In this first book in the series, a modern-day take on the Greek gods, Percy Jackson—otherwise known as Perseus—finds out he is really the half-mortal son of Poseidon. When he ends up in a summer camp for other "half-bloods," he is sent on a quest to return a stolen lightning bolt to Zeus. There's no real blood-and-guts here. The monsters vaporize when they are killed and come back to life later; the Oracle is dressed in a sundress; Gladiola the pink poodle reads the signs and helps Percy and his friends on their way; and Hades complains about having to open a new subdivision for all the newly dead. But there is plenty of swordplay and other action. Fans of mythology and sarcastic middle-schoolers will adore this book.

Gentle Criteria: Percy finds his inner hero when he is on this quest. More than anything he wants to bring his mother—whom he believes is dead—back to life, but he will not sacrifice the good of the entire world—which may be on the brink of World War III—for selfish reasons. He stays true to his friends and his beliefs while still remaining the sarcastic young person he is.

405   Riordan, Rick. *The Sea of Monsters.*
Hyperion, 2006, ISBN 978-0-7868-5686-2. 279p. Series: Percy Jackson and the Olympians • Grades 6–8
☞ ACCELERATED READER

In this sequel to *The Lightning Thief,* Percy, the half-mortal son of the god Poseidon, is back with his friends Annabeth and Grover. On the last day of seventh grade, a game of dodgeball turns into a battle with cannibal giants. Annabeth appears and tells him that Camp Half-Blood is being poisoned and is no longer safe. Off they go on a quest to find the golden fleece and cure the camp, to keep it and the rest of the world safe. On the way there are some wonderful humorous adventures (demon pigeons attack but are repelled by Dean Martin music).

Gentle Criteria: Honor, courage, and loyalty overcome all. Scary monsters do no more than vaporize when they are exterminated. Percy finds the strength that resides inside him. He also discovers that people are not always what they seem, and that we he should not be quick to make judgments about other people—or beings.

406   Riordan, Rick. *The Titan's Curse.*

Hyperion, 2007, ISBN 978-1-4231-0145-1. 312p. Series: Percy Jackson and the Olympians • Grades 5–9

This is the third book in the series. If you ever wondered what the ancient gods would be like in modern times, this is the story for you. Percy Jackson is a demigod—his mother is mortal and his father is Poseidon. His friend Talia is the daughter of Zeus, and his best friend is Grover, a satyr. While trying to rescue two demigods from a school before the monster side claimed them, Percy's demigod friend Annabeth is captured. When Artemis disappears, an Oracle prophesies that five must go rescue him, but two of them will die on the mission, and one at the hands of his father. They must travel from New York to San Francisco, avoiding the skeleton creatures that are homing in on Percy's scent. Olympian gods help them along the way. They realize that if Talia sacrifices the innocent Ophiotaurus, or Sea Cow, she will bring down all of Olympia and become ruler. Will she join forces with the titans and fulfill the curse or stay true to her friends and father?

Gentle Criteria: It is impossible not to have death in a mythological setting where gods use mortals and semi-mortals to accomplish their goals. The two main characters who die in this book do so to save their friends. Their sacrifices also save all of mankind. When Zoe dies, she appears in the sky as a star constellation, the Huntress. She requests that they not try to save her because she's been alive for more than two thousand years. This is a book in which heroes selflessly battle any enemy to save their friends.

407   Scott, Michael. *The Alchemyst: The Secrets of the Immortal Nicholas Flamel.*

Delacorte, 2007, ISBN 978-0-385-90372-1. 375p. • Grades 5–9

Nicholas and his wife are keeping a low profile living in modern times when they are finally tracked down by Dee the Magician, who has been hunting them for centuries. He wants the *Codex*, a book that Nicholas possesses, so that he can unleash the dark Elders and rule the world. Fifteen-year-old twins Sophie and Josh are in the wrong place at the wrong time and are drawn into the battle. Nicholas suspects that it was divine providence because twins with Gold and Silver Aura are mentioned in the *Codex*.

Gentle Criteria: Many of the characters in this book are based on real individuals, makes the story even more fascinating. Nicholas Flamel actually did exist and was an alchemist. He did find the *Book of Abraham* (the *Codex*) and surprisingly became very rich. When his burial site was opened; his tomb was empty; maybe he really did discover the secret of immortality. This book combines the excitement of mythology, magic, and action adventure, and the twins demonstrate mutual love and loyalty.

408 **Shusterman, Neal.** *Everlost.*
Simon & Schuster, 2006, ISBN 978-0-689-87237-2; 2007, pap., ISBN 978-0-689-87238-9. 313p. • Grades 5–9
⌒ ACCELERATED READER ⌒ READING COUNTS

When Nick and Allie die in a car accident, they are sent down a tunnel of light together and find themselves in a land called Everlost, where all the lost souls hang out. Things that have been loved in life can pass over here, so these souls have possessions and even food, although food and breathing are not necessary anymore. They must keep moving or they will sink into the earth's core. They encounter a group of bullies, an amusing situation because they can't be hurt physically anymore. When they make it to the Twin Towers in New York, they meet Mary who cares for the needs of all of the orphaned, lost children. Nick and Allie notice that the children are in a rut and tend to do the same things every day. Nick and Allie believe there is more to afterlife than this and set out to find a way to reach the destination that was meant for them.

Gentle Criteria: This is a fascinating look at what happens to people who are in limbo. Mary, although her ideas are flawed, truly cares for the lost souls she finds and entertains them with TV, video games, and anything else she can find that has crossed over from the real world. Allie rescues her two close friends, who always find themselves prisoners of one bad guy or the other. Nick, who is the first to realize how the lost souls can get to heaven, delays his own journey so he can help the lost.

409 **Skelton, Matthew.** *Endymion Spring.*
Delacorte, 2006, ISBN 978-0-385-90397-4. 392p. • Grades 5–8
⌒ ACCELERATED READER ⌒ READING COUNTS

This story intertwines the lives of Endymion Spring, living in the 1400s, and Blake, a contemporary character. Endymion is Gutenberg's printing apprentice. He joins up with Fust, a rich, evil man who possesses a book of knowledge. The problem is that Fust can't read the book—all the pages are blank. He needs a pure soul like Endymion to unlock its secrets. Endymion realizes how dangerous the book could be in Fust's hands so he steals it and takes it to Oxford, hiding it in the library. In modern times, the book presents itself to Blake and his sister, but only Blake can read it. The book asks Blake to find its missing parts so it can once again be whole. And it warns him that someone is watching and they are in danger.

Gentle Criteria: The villains in this book are no worse than Cruella de Ville. Teachers will appreciate the author's style of stating that a person swore rather than giving the actual profanity. The book portrays life from the perspective of a child who doesn't really understand the adult world.

410   Stanley, Diane. *Bella at Midnight: The Thimble, the Ring, and the Slippers of Glass.*
Ill. by Bagram Ibatoulline. HarperCollins, 2006, ISBN 978-0-06-277574-0. 278p. • Grades 5–7
ACCELERATED READER *READING COUNTS*

Bella has been left at the wet nurse's house; her father no longer wants her after her mother dies in childbirth. Prince Julian also spends time at this kindly home and he and Bella grow up to be friends. Bella does not discover who her real father is until she reaches her thirteenth birthday, and then she must return to a house where she is not wanted—not by her father, her stepmother, or her stepsisters. This story is divided into three books, each about a magic token that Bella encounters: The Thimble, The Ring, and The Slippers of Glass. Along with the goodness of both Bella and Prince Julian, these three items demobilize two armies and prevent two kingdoms from warring. The prophecy of the Worthy Knight who will bring peace without carrying arms finally comes to life, and readers will be delighted to find out how it all came about.

Gentle Criteria: This is a delightfully constructed fairy tale. The most important story line in this book is the Worthy Knight who will bring peace to the two kingdoms with no weapons and no bloodshed. Bella and Julian are able to see through the petty squabbles of royalty to what really matters—the people who love us and the freedom to love them back.

411   Stewart, Paul, and Chris Riddell. *Fergus Crane.*
Random House, 2004, ISBN 978-0-385-75089-9. 215p. Series: Far-Flung Adventures • Grades 5–8

This is Book One in the Far-Flung Adventures series. Fergus Crane lives with his mother and attends school on a ship. His father disappeared on one of his sailing adventures years ago. Shortly after his mom's picture is published in the newspaper, Fergus starts receiving strange flying missives warning him he is in danger. These letters are being sent by his long-lost Uncle Theo. Uncle Theo sends a mechanical flying horse to pick Fergus up and explains that the school Fergus is attending is run by pirates. They plan to use the students to gather fire diamonds from a volcano that his father discovered. When Fergus gets home to warn his friends, they have already set sail to retrieve the diamonds. Now Fergus must save his friends from the pirates. He finds a shipwrecked sailor on the island. Could this be his dad?

Gentle Criteria: This book is full of invented gadgetry created by Uncle Theo. It is touching that Uncle Theo is aware that Fergus's mother resents his encouraging her husband to go sailing. So Uncle Theo has the vice presidents of his company send her little jobs to help make ends meet. The pirates' greed leads them to fall into the volcano. Fergus's rescue of his friends and reuniting his father with his mother are heartwarming.

412   Thompson, Kate. *The New Policeman.*
>   HarperCollins, 2007, ISBN 978-0-06-117428-5. 442p. • Grades 7–9
>   ☞ ACCELERATED READER ☞ JUNIOR LIBRARY GUILD

This story is a quirky fantasy. For her birthday, J. J. Liddy's mother wants nothing but time. What no one realizes is that time is leaking from J. J.'s world into the fairy's world. As he begins to investigate, he finds out more about his own family—a grandfather who disappeared long ago and a legendary flute that produced wonderful music. When he discovers that he really can stop the time leak, it is the magical charms of the Irish music that help save the day. This is a different take on the legendary sprites that belong to Ireland, and the harsh history that the Irish have endured. When J. J. realizes who his grandfather really is, he also realizes that it is the music and his family that will always get him through the difficult times.

   Gentle Criteria: The legendary Irish music and its fairies and leprechauns are on a collision course with the harsh religion of Ireland's past. When J. J. finds a way to let both worlds coexist, all is well. This is a story of family love, the warmth the music gives, and the ability to coexist peacefully.

413   Townley, Roderick. *The Constellation of Sylvie.*
>   Atheneum, 2005, ISBN 978-0-689-85713-3. 192p. Series: Great Good Thing • Grades 6–8
>   ☞ ACCELERATED READER

This is the third volume in the series. Sylvie and the other characters find the book they inhabit is now aboard a spaceship. They are frightened and in awe of the space that they glimpse as the book is held open. This is not the simple fairy tale that it first appears to be. While the astronauts argue and cause the spacecraft to go off course, Sylvie is tricked into marriage in order to save her precious animals. As the characters rearrange the letters to give the astronauts directions to save their lives, Sylvie and Rosetta manage to outwit the evil jester and save the day in their own world. Readers will be fascinated with the science fiction twist to the story as the astronauts become younger and younger in order to save themselves.

   Gentle Criteria: The characters in this book display qualities such as courage, love, and goodness. Not all of the astronauts are good people, but Sylvie has to deal with them in her own goodhearted way—she has no other choice. When Rosetta's two suitors argue and battle with each other, Sylvie and Rosetta find a way to make them work together. Goodness reigns in the end but not without some quick scientific minds. All kinds of readers will enjoy this one!

414   **Townley, Roderick.** *The Great Good Thing.*
Atheneum, 2001, ISBN 978-0-689-84324-2; Simon & Schuster, 2002,
pap., ISBN 978-0-689-85328-9. 216p. Series: Great Good Thing •
Grades 6–8
☞ ACCELERATED READER ☞ READING COUNTS

This first book in the Great Good Thing series is not your typical fantasy or fairy
tale. Sylvie, a princess, does the unthinkable: She looks at the reader. Once contact is made with the reader, characters are able to emerge from the book, visit
the reader's dreams, and explore new worlds. When the reader's brother sets the
book on fire, it is Sylvie's courage and sense of adventure that enable her to save
the day. Magical elements such as a huge invisible fish complete the fantasy.
Older readers will appreciate the multilayered fantasy, the complex fairy tale, and
the concept of crossing over in space and time.

    Gentle Criteria: Besides the fact that the basic concept for this book
comes from a good old-fashioned fairy tale, there are many good things about
this book. Sylvie has courage and believes in always doing the right thing—in
fact, that is the only way she can behave because it is the way she was created.
She fights for goodness in her own world and also helps both the reader and the
writer strive to do the right thing in their worlds.

415   **Townley, Roderick.** *Into the Labyrinth.*
Atheneum, 2002, ISBN 978-0-689-84615-1; Simon & Schuster, 2006,
pap., ISBN 978-1-4169-1392-4. 254p. Series: Great Good Thing •
Grades 6–8
☞ ACCELERATED READER

In this sequel to *The Great Good Thing*, Sylvie and the other characters find the
book they inhabit has become a bestseller, and they are going to be published on
the World Wide Web. This causes the characters great stress because—at any
moment—they could be safe in the gravity of the book or on a string to be
yanked anywhere in the weightlessness of the Web. The author, at Sylvie's
request, writes in a yoga instructor as a background character to help the characters deal with the new stress in their lives. Clever twists such as a rodent (a computer mouse) who can move them to any part of the story at a moment's notice
will keep readers entertained and curious for more. But three strong and intelligent young women—Sylvie, Laurel, and Rosetta, the yoga instructor—save the
day when the author's grandson introduces a virus into the computer. Some
mild language and higher-level story lines will entertain older readers.

    Gentle Criteria: The three strong young female characters, forthright
and good, are enough to promote this clever tale as a gentle read. The scariest
part of the story is the monster created from the virus that, in the end, is nothing
but computer code. Goodness and truth win out, but not without some language and scary moments, especially from the malicious grandson. This is not a
children's fairy tale but an older read for middle-schoolers who want more substance in their adventure.

416 Vande Velde, Vivian. *The Rumpelstiltskin Problem.*

Houghton Mifflin, 2000, ISBN 978-0-618-05523-4; Scholastic, 2001, pap., ISBN 978-0-439-30529-7. 116p. • Grades 5–7

☞ ACCELERATED READER ☞ READING COUNTS

The author poses the theory that the Rumpelstiltskin story makes no sense. Why would Rumpelstiltskin take any kind of payment for spinning straw into gold when he could spin all the gold that he needed? Why would the miller's daughter marry a king who threatened her with death if she didn't spin straw into gold? Inside this book are six splendid variations of the Rumpelstiltskin story—all with more plausible story lines. Each of the stories is amusing in its own right. A troll who wants a baby for dinner, a Russian domovoi who just wants his household to be happy, a daughter who teaches her father to stop bragging, and a beautiful girl who is taught that she may not always get her own way, all make for delightful reading.

Gentle Criteria: This story is a more logical version of the Rumpelstiltskin account, with goodness and love prevailing in the end.

417 Warner, Sally. *Twilight Child.*

Penguin, 2006, ISBN 978-0-670-06076-4. 223p. • Grades 5–7

☞ ACCELERATED READER ☞ JUNIOR LIBRARY GUILD

This book is a fascinating blend of fantasy and historical fiction. Eleni was born at twilight on the longest day of the year in Finland. Being a "twilight child" means that Eleni can see magical creatures. Set in the eighteenth century, this book gives a realistic feel of what life was like at that time as Eleni moves from Finland to Scotland to the New World. Along the way she is helped by magical creatures. The descriptions of the ships, the laundering process, and the desperation of the men all show a hard life, but there are many amusing moments. Eleni survives it all with her quick wit, her willingness to work, and her ability to find humor and goodness in many situations. Readers will like the exciting end to the book and its happily-ever-after feel, along with the amusing descriptions of fairies and other creatures.

Gentle Criteria: This book is full of hard working, honest people doing the best they can. The political unrest between Finland, Sweden, and Russia, and then later in the book between Scotland and England shows how people had to adapt to whoever was in control at the time. But they did their best to make a good life. Eleni perseveres and makes friends wherever she ends up. There is one fight scene at the end that is quite serious, but it is stopped by a dog.

418 Yarbro, Chelsea Quinn. *Monet's Ghost.*

Simon & Schuster, 1997, ISBN 978-0-689-80732-9. 151p. • Grades 7–9

☞ ACCELERATED READER

Geena discovers that she is able to throw herself into paintings at the museum. When it first happens she is frightened, but she finds that as long as she can back out of the painting in exactly the same way she got in, she can return home with no problem. When she walks into Monet's "Water Lilies," she finds that what used to be there keeps disappearing. The people in the castle tell her that a ghost haunts the area and keeps changing the scenery depending on the lighting that day. When she realizes that the boat she came on—and even the pond that she rowed across—is no longer there, she wonders if she will ever be able to return home. She sets out to track down the ghost and seek his help. The story is full of art references and descriptions of the world—France in particular—in 1893. It will certainly keep readers turning the pages.

Gentle Criteria: Adults may decide that this book is more appropriate for older readers because of a couple of "damns," but, all in all, this is an innocent book about a young girl deciding that she needs to save herself. Geena realizes that "if people only did the things they weren't afraid of, none of us would ever learn to walk." It is up to her to rescue herself, and she does a wonderful job. She also gets a rare perspective of the kinds of choices women had in the late 1800s, and she comes to appreciate the privileges she has.

419   Yolen, Jane. *Boots and the Seven Leaguers: A Rock-and-Troll Novel.*
       Harcourt, 2000, ISBN 978-0-15-202557-1; Magic Carpet Books, 2003, pap., ISBN 978-0-15-202563-2. 159p. • Grades 5–8
       ☞ ACCELERATED READER ☞ READING COUNTS ☞ JUNIOR LIBRARY GUILD

Troll Gog's best friend Pook can perform a little magic. When Gog's favorite band, The Seven Leaguers, comes to town, Gog's smarter little brother, Magog, suggests that Pook cast a spell on Gog and himself, making them look like humans instead of trolls. They can then become roadies who set up the band equipment in exchange for tickets. Pook puts a stay-put spell on Magog while Pook and Gog get hired for the job. They return to find that Magog has been kidnapped, and they track him deep into the forest where an evil huntsman is preparing to feed Magog to the dragon Wyrm. Gog and Pook must face the dragon, the huntsman, and other fierce creatures. When Pook is injured, Gog must continue alone to the dragon's lair, without any magic. Time is growing short and even if he finds his brother in time, will they have missed the concert of a lifetime?

Gentle Criteria: In fairy tales, people sometimes get eaten—as is the case with the huntsman who gets his just desserts when the dragon devours him. The gentle side of the story is how Gog is willing to sacrifice his concert and himself to find and protect his little brother. Even his best friend Pook is willing to go into the dangerous woods to save Magog.

420 Yolen, Jane. *Not One Damsel in Distress: World Folktales for Strong Girls.*

Ill. by Susan Guevara. Harcourt, 2000, ISBN 978-0-15-202047-7. 116p.
• Grades 5–9

⮑ ACCELERATED READER

Yolen presents thirteen folktales featuring heroic, fearless, strong, and resourceful females. From Greece comes the Huntress Atalanta who fells the boar that has been terrorizing the kingdom. Molly Whuppie is an English version of "Jack and the Beanstalk" in which Molly tricks the giant not once but four times. From Japan comes the story of the Samurai Maiden who defies the Emperor to search for her father who has been banished to an island. She not only slays a sea serpent but also ends a curse that has been making the Emperor ill, earning the Emperor's gratitude and her father's freedom.

Gentle Criteria: This book demonstrates that there are many ways of becoming a hero. Although Atalanta shows her fierce swordsmanship, it's not all about brawn. Molly Whuppie uses her intelligence to outwit the giant. The pirate princess outfoxes three different suitors to become wealthy beyond all measure and ends up becoming ruler of a kingdom. These stories leave us with a desire to discover more female heroines. It is good for both sexes to see the female shown in such positive leading roles.

421 Yolen, Jane, and Adam Stemple. *Troll Bridge: A Rock 'n' Roll Fairy Tale.*

St. Martin's, 2006, ISBN 978-0-7653-1426-0. 240p. • Grades 5–9

⮑ ACCELERATED READER

Moira, a classical musician, is late in arriving at the Trollholm Bridge, where she and eleven other girls are this year's "Butter Princesses." When she gets there, she sees a giant wave take all the girls over the bridge. She jumps in to save them but finds they have been taken by a giant troll. He can now capture humans because the new mayor has broken a pact. He forbids butter figures on the bridge for pollution reasons. Meanwhile the three Griffson brothers, also musicians, are on the road for a week's vacation. They stop at the bridge and are also swept over and captured for the troll's next meal. A Fossegrim in the shape of a fox assists Moira and the boys, and says it will free them and the princesses in exchange for the magic fiddle. The eleven princesses will marry the troll's sons in three days, so they must quickly develop a plan to save them. In Moira's and the boys' favor are the facts that trolls are slow and slow-witted and are enchanted by music.

Gentle Criteria: This book borrows from several different fairy tales, so when one of the boys fools one of the young trolls into taking his place hanging by the fire, the reader is not too surprised when the father troll accidentally eats his own son. The gentle part of the story is how Moira leaps into the river, forsaking her own safety to save the other princesses. The three boy musicians also do what they can to save the others. Readers also witness the mother-son bond when the three wives turn against their husbands so that their sons can learn music.

422   Zinnen, Linda. *The Dragons of Spratt, Ohio.*
   HarperCollins, 2004, ISBN 978-0-06-000022-6. 233p. • Grades 5–9
   ☞ ACCELERATED READER

Salt lives with his mom and dad who run the Wilds animal refuge in Ohio. Last winter a single dragon flew over and stopped to eat their zebras, and Salt and his parents are now in the process of hatching the nine dragon eggs she left before she died. Dragons have been an accepted species since Dr. Zhao discovered them in China. Salt's Aunt Mary Athena, a cosmetics scientist, unexpectedly pays a visit. Allison, a popular girl Salt has a crush on, can't stay away now that Salt's famous beauty-secret aunt is here. Salt's parents are called away to petition for more money to run the refuge and leave Aunt Mary in charge. But Aunt Mary has come for her own nefarious reasons: She wants to experiment on the dragons to find an ingredient that will stop skin from aging. She persuades Salt's friend Candi to show her where the recently hatched dragons are, and she drugs Blackie, a baby dragon. She then kills Blackie and uses his blood in her makeup. When Candi sees Aunt Mary again, she notices that she no longer has wrinkles—but her skin is turning green! Aunt Mary realizes that she has changed her own DNA and will turn into a dragon—unless she can find Salt and use his DNA to change her back.

   Gentle Criteria: Salt is infatuated with popular, good-looking Allison, and brilliant Candi acts dumb so that she'll be popular too. Through Salt's determination to hide the dragons from his aunt, and Candi's determination to protect Salt from his aunt, they realize they have much in common. Salt shows heroic qualities, and Candi realizes she doesn't have to hide her intelligence any longer. Salt decides to spare his dad's feelings by not telling him that his evil sister has turned into a dragon; rather, he tells him that she was suddenly called back to Paris.

Science Fiction

423   Alcock, Vivien. *The Red-Eared Ghosts.*

Houghton Mifflin, 1997, ISBN 978-0-395-81660-8; 1998, pap., ISBN 978-0-395-88394-5. 264p. • Grades 5–7

☞ ACCELERATED READER

From the time she was a baby in a pram, Mary Frewin has seen what she thinks are ghosts—sometimes as smudgy images and sometimes just parts of them, but always with red ears. When she tells her mother about it, her mother refuses to talk. One day Mary realizes that a ghost is following her with a large wolfish dog in tow. Finding herself in the middle of a "timequake," she discovers another world—an alternate universe. Will Mary find a way to return to the world she left?

Gentle Criteria: This is the story of a determined heroine. Shy and backward, Mary finds out that to make things happen, one must be willing to dig in and do the hard work. In an alternate universe, Mary grows up and learns to appreciate what she has. At the end, the two Marys—one from the present and one from the past—merge together and a new Mary is created. This new Mary is not afraid anymore. She has learned to trust people and take care of herself. She has also learned that even wicked people have glimmers of good about them, and sometimes you have to know when to ask for help.

424   Brockmeier, Kevin. *City of Names.*

Viking, 2002, ISBN 978-0-670-03565-6. 137p. • Grades 5–8

☞ ACCELERATED READER

When Howie orders *101 Pickle Jokes* from the book club, he is surprised to find that instead he receives a book called *The Secret Guide to North Melwood*. This book gives the real names of various locations around the town. It claims that if you knock three times on a portal and then say the "real" name you will be transported to that place as if by magic. If you say the name again within four hours, you'll be transported back. Howie shares this secret with his two best friends and they zip around town checking out all the places they can go. But using the magic too much has the bad effect of leaving the smell of rotten eggs. Howie ends up with a bully on his case when he transports into the video game hut and becomes the top scorer. He makes up with the bully by transporting him so he can reclaim his high-scorer status. But why was Howie sent this book? He transports into a room where Larry Boone is expecting him and finds the answer.

Gentle Criteria: When Howie transports into bully Mike Channering's room, he does so to gather evidence to use to make Mike stop bullying him. But he soon realizes that Mike has a tough home life. Instead of continuing to battle Mike, Howie arranges to set things right by taking Mike into the video game store where he can reclaim the one thing that makes him feel good: his status as the best video game player in town. During another transport, Howie meets his soon-to-be-born sister and champions her wish to be called Marie. This book is about seeing people for who they really are, not necessarily who they appear to be at first.

425   **Buckley-Archer, Linda.** *Gideon the CutPurse: Being the First Part of the Gideon Trilogy.*
Simon & Schuster, 2006, ISBN 978-1-4169-1525-6. 404p. Series: Gideon Trilogy • Grades 5–9
⌐ ACCELERATED READER ⌐ READING COUNTS

When Peter's father is unable to celebrate his birthday with him, Peter is sent to Derbyshire for the weekend. He meets Kate and they go with her father to his laboratory. In a bizarre accident they are transported back in time to the year 1763. They are befriended by Gideon, a reformed cutpurse (thief). Unfortunately, a local criminal named the Tar Man has taken possession of the machine that they need to return. They have many adventures as they try to reclaim the machine. Along the way they meet King George III, Charles Darwin's grandfather, and Samuel Johnson. They witness the differences between the common class and the noble life. When the Tar Man frames Gideon for a crime he did not commit, Peter and Kate save him by blurring. Readers will not be able to put this book down until they learn whether the three are able to return to modern times.

Gentle Criteria: There are lots of levels of goodness in this book. Peter and Kate promise they will not leave each other and will find the way home together. Gideon learns from them that the world is going to become a better place where children will be educated and people will not have to steal to eat. These children share true friendship with Gideon, but—even better—they give him the gift of hope for the future.

426   Clements, Andrew. *Things Hoped For.*
      Philomel, 2006, ISBN 978-0-399-24350-9. 167p. • Grades 7–9
      ᵔ ACCELERATED READER ᵔ READING COUNTS

This book is a sequel to *Things Not Seen* (see below). Through her grandfather's generosity, Gwen is living in his apartment building in New York City so that she can prepare for her violin auditions. When her grandfather disappears suddenly, she finds a message from him saying she should not tell anyone that he is gone and should continue as if he were still in the house. Her auditions are less than a week away, so she decides to do what her grandfather says and prepare for the auditions that may change her life. Her new friend Robert is able to mimic her grandfather's voice and to show her how to succeed at the auditions. But when a body is discovered in the freezer, it becomes clear to Gwen just how much the people who love her are willing to do to help her succeed.

      Gentle Criteria: Although a body in the freezer sounds like the makings of a morbid thriller, this story is really about Gwen's grandfather's determination to make certain that her auditions go through uninterrupted. Gwen sees the love and care that comes from everyone who is taking care of her. When it is finally her turn to play, it is the love of all of them in her heart that helps her to perform her best.

427   Clements, Andrew. *Things Not Seen.*
      Philomel, 2002, ISBN 978-0-399-23626-6; Scholastic, pap., ISBN 978-0-439-45620-3. 251p. • Grades 7–9
      ᵔ ACCELERATED READER ᵔ READING COUNTS

Bobby wakes one morning, stumbles to the bathroom to brush his teeth, looks in the mirror, and sees nothing. He has disappeared! What caused him to become invisible and how will he possibly get on with his life? His parents, both professors at the University of Chicago, swear him to secrecy because they don't want the government to find out and whisk him away. Things really become complicated when his parents are in a car accident and hospitalized. How will Bobby continue without anybody finding out about him? School authorities are looking for him, and the police suspect something sinister has happened to him. Desperate to get out of the house one day, he meets Alicia who is blind and does not know that he is invisible. When he tells her his secret, she helps him try to find a way to become visible again.

      Gentle Criteria: Bobby is a typical teenager whose parents drive him crazy. He knows this is because they love him so much. This book is a great read because the relationships ring true, there are many humorous moments connected with Bobby's invisibility, and it is all mixed up with the suspense of finding out if Bobby will ever become visible again.

428   DuPrau, Jeanne. *City of Ember.*

     Random House, 2003, ISBN 978-0-375-92274-9; 2004, pap., ISBN 978-0-375-82274-2. 270p. Series: Book of Ember • Grades 5–7

     ACCELERATED READER   READING COUNTS

This is Book One in the Book of Ember series. Lina and Doon live in the underground city of Ember; the city, however, is dying. The generator that provides their power is failing and the storage rooms are nearly empty of supplies. When Lina discovers an ancient parchment, she and Doon learn that there is a world outside the city. Will they be able to figure out the clues in time to save everybody? Set in a world where people don't know what trees or boats are, or that the sky is supposed to be blue, this is a fascinating look at the cultural clues that are left behind for future generations.

     Gentle Criteria: This is a story of brave people who save humankind on two levels. First there were the Builders who saved the people by creating the city of Ember. Now there are Lina and Doon who will try to save the people by leading them out of the city. Although there are doomsayers in the story and selfish people, this is a story of two clever twelve-year-olds and how they save their world.

429   DuPrau, Jeanne. *The People of Sparks.*

     Random House, 2004, ISBN 978-0-375-92824-6; 2005, pap., ISBN 978-0-375-82825-6. 339p. Series: Book of Ember • Grades 5–7

     ACCELERATED READER   READING COUNTS

In this sequel to *The City of Ember.* Lina and Doon and the rest of the people of Ember find their way aboveground and to the city of Sparks. Sparks is one of the few settlements in existence since the Great Disaster and the Plagues. There are only three hundred people in the city of Sparks, and they open their doors to the four hundred people of Ember, but it immediately becomes clear that there might not be enough food. The people of Ember are unskilled and must quickly learn the skills to survive. As resources dwindle, there is less cooperation. But Lina and Doon show them how the actions of a few troubled people can be fanned to violence, and that it takes a brave person to do good and stop the bad from happening.

     Gentle Criteria: This book could be a parable about how wars start and what it takes for people to prevent them. These people must learn to live together as neighbors and friends. This story emphasizes that bad deeds breed more bad deeds, but good deeds breed more good deeds.

430   DuPrau, Jeanne. *The Prophet of Yonwood.*

     Random House, 2006, ISBN 978-0-375-97526-4. 289p. Series: Book of Ember • Grades 5–7

     ACCELERATED READER

In this prequel to *The City of Ember*, Nickie is going to Yonwood with her aunt Crystal. Her great-grandfather has recently died, leaving his mansion, Greenhaven, to Nickie's mother and aunt. Nickie's father is off working with the government, and her mother is working in the city. Nickie is supposed to help her aunt clean the place and get it ready to sell, but Nickie has other plans. She has three goals on her list: Keep Greenhaven, fall in love, and help the world. How Nickie manages to accomplish all of her goals will surprise readers. A member of the town has a vision, and the town determines that the vision means they must rid the town of sin. Of course, Nickie wants to become part of the group of Good People, but she quickly finds that what goodness means is a matter of interpretation. In this simple story are some deep thoughts. For example, how can both sides in a war believe that God is on their side? How does one determine what is really good or bad? Nickie discovers that she must think for herself to find the answers.

Gentle Criteria: This book is a gentle read because it emphasizes how compassion, love, and forgiveness enable this town to survive. There are strong themes here about how people who can't get along can't survive, and what goodness really is.

431   Fardell, John. *The Flight of the Silver Turtle.*
Putnam, 2006, ISBN 978-0-399-24382-0. 233p. • Grades 5–8

This book follows the characters first introduced in *The 7 Professors of the Far North* (see below). Sam, Zara, Marcia, and Ben spend the summer helping Professor Ampersand and his colleagues build an electric airplane. They stumble across a cryptic message from Stribnek, a deceased scientist, that mentions his antigravity device. Now a sinister organization named Noctarma is trying to get the information so that it can create invincible planes that will rule the world. When some Noctarma agents try to apprehend the group, the children and an elderly lady manage to escape by plane, but the professor and Amy, an aviation mechanic, are captured. The elderly lady identifies herself as a pilot who used to work with Stribnek, and she guides them to Lady Clarissa, a friend who she thinks will help them. Unknown to them is that Lady Clarissa is part of Noctarma, and she captures the pilot. The children, however, escape again and fly off to try to recover the missing jewelry box that holds the key to antigravity before Noctarma finds it. But the box is in a sunken plane at the bottom of Lake Geneva!

Gentle Criteria: This story is filled with adventure and excitement. After one flying lesson from the professor's friend Gabrielle, Ben learns to fly and land the plane, a feat that will have many kids fantasizing. Although the agents of Noctarma are evil and trigger-happy with their machine guns, they are so inept that they never actually shoot any of the main characters of our story. It's a great family-oriented book because no one dies.

432   Fardell, John. *The Seven Professors of the Far North.*
Penguin, 2005, ISBN 978-0-399-24381-3; 2006, pap., ISBN 978-0-14-240735-6. 217p. • Grades 5–9
☞ ACCELERATED READER ☞ READING COUNTS

When eleven-year-old Sam gets to stay with Professor Ampersand and his grand-niece and grand-nephew, he's in inventor's heaven! Soon another professor arrives and tells Professor Ampersand to gather the others as he has something important to tell them. When six professors are all present, they are kidnapped by the evil 7th professor, Dr. Murdo. The children are not seen, but they overhear that the professors will be killed in four days. Now they must travel all the way to the North Pole using a secret underground railway to try to save the professors before Dr. Murdo destroys the world. Dr. Murdo has developed a perfect child by genetic manipulation. He has also developed a virus that when released will kill all life, and only he holds the antidote. Readers will be on the edge of their seats to learn whether the three kids get into the heavily guarded fortress and arrive in time to save the professors.

Gentle Criteria: This book will make a great movie. Although the kids should have gone to the authorities after the professors were kidnapped, they knew that no one would believe their story. So, with time running short, they acted with their hearts and set out to save the professors.

433   Fox, Helen. *Eager.*
Random House, 2004, ISBN 978-0-385-90903-7; 2006, pap., ISBN 978-0-553-48795-4. 280p. • Grades 5–8
☞ ACCELERATED READER ☞ READING COUNTS ☞ JUNIOR LIBRARY GUILD

The Bells decide they need to replace their robot, Grumps, when he begins to serve soup for breakfast. Mr. Bell contacts his professor friend who shares with him his latest invention, EGR3, a robot that has self-will and the ability to learn and reason. He is called Eager because he is so eager to learn. The Technocrats with the new expensive BDC4 robots have problems when their models start behaving strangely, ignoring their owners, exercising a mind of their own, and even partying. The Bell family and Eager find Professor Ogden and discover that the techno-scientists used real brains from dead people on the new BDC4s, and they are acting out their old memories. Meanwhile, Eager is constantly trying to become more human so that he can better serve them. Readers will contemplate what it is that makes us human as they read this entertaining speculation of the future.

Gentle Criteria: This book provides an interesting look at what the future might look like, such as walls in houses that change color or that move when the homeowner wants to redecorate. The robots are portrayed in a kind manner, and even when the BDC4s become corrupt, no one is in any danger.

This book allows readers to consider whether the positives of robot ownership will outweigh the potential negatives. Topics that a teacher may want to discuss include class separation, fuel shortages, and robot construction.

434 Gutman, Dan. *The Homework Machine.*

Simon & Schuster, 2006, ISBN 978-0-689-87678-3. 146p. • Grades 5–7
ᕫ Accelerated Reader ᕫ Reading Counts ᕫ Junior Library Guild

Four unlikely students become fast friends because of their secret Homework Machine. Genius Brenton has figured out a way to make his computer spit out his homework in blue pen. One day he lets the secret slip to class clown Sam ("Snik"), who doesn't realize how smart he is until he begins hanging around Brenton. Teacher's pet Judy overhears them. She knows she is smart but has trouble getting along with people. Then Judy mentions it to Kelsey, a slacker. And Kelsey realizes that brains and effort can benefit a person. The four finally decide the machine is more trouble than it is worth and throw the computer into the Grand Canyon with the help of Brenton's amazing catapult. Told in interview form, the book relates events leading up to the discovery of the Homework Machine.

Gentle Criteria: This book is about four very different students who discover that they are capable of doing good work on their own without the help of a machine. The four recognize that they have a good effect on each other, and they learn that being cool really means not being afraid to be yourself. And Brenton, the nerdiest of them all, is actually the coolest of all. The parents in this story are also inspiring people: One mother tells her daughter that she only quit smoking when she became pregnant with her, and Snik's father stops letting him win at chess so that he can experience losing.

435 Haddix, Margaret Peterson. *Double Identity.*

Simon & Schuster, 2005, ISBN 978-0-689-87374-4. 224p. • Grades 5–9
ᕫ Accelerated Reader ᕫ Reading Counts ᕫ Junior Library Guild

Two weeks before Bethany's thirteenth birthday her parents hustle her into the car and drive away, without explanation, dropping her off at "Aunt Myrlie's." Bethany is astounded because—as far as she knows—she has no other relatives! Her father sends her aunt a huge envelope stuffed with thousands of dollars in cash along with four birth certificates, all bearing the same birth date but with four different names and cities of birth. Bethany wonders who she really is when she encounters people who act like they see the ghost of someone long dead. How can Bethany find out who she really is and where she came from? Where did her parents go in the middle of the night? And who is quietly stalking her?

Gentle Criteria: This is a gentle read because it handles a serious subject (cloning) in the context of a loving family. Bethany's parents love her very much and will do anything to protect her.

436   Paulsen, Gary. *The Time Hackers.*

Random House, 2005, ISBN 978-0-285-90896-3; 2006, pap., ISBN 978-0-553-48788-6. 87p. • Grades 5–8

☞ ACCELERATED READER ☞ READING COUNTS

A new superchip has revolutionized history with the ability to look at events as they occurred. Dorso just got his computer back from the shop and weird things are showing up in his locker at school. Soon he and his friend Larry find themselves transported to places like Gettysburg and onto pirate ships where the action is real, evidenced by a flesh wound Larry receives during one trip. These real-life episodes have two things in common: the boys are always carrying Dorso's laptop around when they occur, and there is always a blonde computer geek with a laptop at the scene. Now, Dorso and Larry must work out what's happening before these hackers end up changing history, get them killed, or worse yet, destroy the earth!

Gentle Criteria: Dorso has his head on straight and realizes immediately the potential danger of changing the past. He doesn't run out and buy Microsoft stock, but instead tries to grab the hacker's computers before they destroy the world.

437   Paulsen, Gary. *The Transall Saga.*

Delacorte, 1998, ISBN 978-0-385-32196-9; Random House, 1999, pap., ISBN 978-0-440-21976-7. 248p. • Grades 5–9

☞ ACCELERATED READER ☞ READING COUNTS

Mark is camping in the desert when he witnesses a strange blue light. Upon examining the light, he is startled by a snake and accidentally jumps into the light. He is transported to a jungle with red grass and red leaves. Now Mark must live by his wits, avoiding dangerous beasts and eventually finding other human-like creatures. But no sooner is he accepted into one tribe when another tribe comes and takes them all captive as slaves. Mark escapes, but when he sees another tribe preparing to attack the village where his friend Leeta is, he runs back to warn the village. He is granted his freedom for his heroism; among the gifts bestowed upon him are a soda bottle and other artifacts that make him realize he has not been transported to another planet but has been sent far into the future after a holocaust has changed the world. Mark searches for the blue light so that he can return home and investigate the virus that caused the mutations in the human-like creatures.

Gentle Criteria: Mark remains constant in his belief that no one should be enslaved. He doesn't fight unless threatened or unless he is protecting his clan. He is willing to sacrifice himself for his village by leading an attacking army away from them. Once Mark discovers that a monkey virus is responsible for the conditions in the future earth, he becomes a doctor and commits his life to finding a cure.

438   Pearson, Ridley. *The Kingdom Keepers.*
Disney, 2005, ISBN 978-0-7868-5444-8. 325p. • Grades 5–8
⌐ ACCELERATED READER

Five middle-school students have been selected to become DHIs, which stands for both Disney Host Interactive and Daylight Hologram Imaging, for Disney World. Their images are computer-generated and serve as hosts for many of Disney's attractions. What they didn't know when they took the job is that they were hand-selected for their individual skills that might save the Magic Kingdom from an evil force led by Witch Maleficent. These kids must transport back into Disney while they are asleep and use their Daylight Hologram Images to find a solution to stop the evil Disney characters. They soon realize that the buzz-light-year lasers the pirates are firing at them are real, and they have actual burn marks when they wake up. Will this fearless five be able to save Disney for all of us?

   Gentle Criteria: This book reads like a made-for-Disney movie; it includes mild violence but the language is clean. The dialog is refreshing. One character, Finn, leads the others through the dangers of Disney at night. Goodness battles evil as the five students match with Maleficent and her minions to save the realm.

439   Seidler, Tor. *Brainboy and the Deathmaster.*
HarperCollins, 2003, ISBN 978-0-06-029182-2; 2005, pap., ISBN 978-0-06-440935-3. 311p. • Grades 5–9
⌐ ACCELERATED READER ⌐ READING COUNTS ⌐ JUNIOR LIBRARY GUILD

Darryl is orphaned when his entire family dies in a fire. While at a Keith Masterly-owned orphanage, he plays a video game that Masterly, the tycoon video game maker, has designed in hopes of finding geniuses. Masterly arrives and soon persuades Darryl to be part of his research team, saying he wants to adopt Darryl. Darryl is troubled by this because he has made friends with BJ, and hoped to be adopted by BJ's family. Unknown to Darryl, Masterly gives him a drug that makes him forget about BJ. Masterly is looking for a DNA bond that will reverse aging, and Darryl soon becomes one of his research scientists. Luckily for Darryl, Nina, another genius, tells him about the drug. They soon learn that Masterly has brainwashed them and is holding them captive in a lab with no windows. They must find a way to escape and free the other brainwashed scientists.

   Gentle Criteria: This is a story about the strength of friendship and love. Because BJ becomes Darryl's friend, he knows when something is wrong. He does not give up until he finds out what it is. Boris has lost his sister and refuses to give up looking for her. BJ and Boris never stop trying to find Nina and Darryl. Once

Nina and Darryl are freed from their drug-induced states they quickly remember the people they love and do everything possible to return to them. When they find out Masterly's evil intentions, they save all the other scientists as well.

440 **Woolfe, Angela.** *Avril Crump and Her Amazing Clones.*
Orchard, 2004, ISBN 978-0-439-65130-1. 212p. • Grades 5–7

In a freak laboratory accident, Avril Crump produces three very different clones: a talking dog, an eighteenth-century soldier who speaks like Shakespeare, and a little girl. Though the creation of the clones is a dark mystery, Avril loves these beings and knows she must protect them at all costs. It's a fast-paced adventure for younger readers.

Gentle Criteria: This story is a whimsical look at cloning. It's an entertaining mystery-adventure interspersed with lots of humor and action. This book is a gentle read because its underlying theme is that all life is precious.

Novels in Verse

441 Creech, Sharon. *Heartbeat.*

HarperCollins, 2004, ISBN 978-0-06-054022-7; 2005, pap., ISBN 978-0-06-054024-1. 180p. • Grades 5–7

☞ ACCELERATED READER ☞ READING COUNTS ☞ JUNIOR LIBRARY GUILD

Eleven-year-old Annie loves to run, but not on a team. She is a free spirit who does not want to be part of a crowd. Her grandfather's failing health is juxtaposed to her mother's pregnancy in this novel of self-discovery.

Gentle Criteria: This novel is vintage Creech. Strong characters pull at the reader's heartstrings as they work through their own particular passages in life.

442 Creech, Sharon. *Love That Dog.*

HarperCollins, 2001, ISBN 978-0-06-029289-8; 2003, pap., ISBN 978-0-06-440959-9. 86p. • Grades 5–7

☞ ACCELERATED READER

Jack lets his teacher know right away that he does not care for poetry—in his own free-verse poem. But his clever teacher, through use of well-known poems, draws him in. His devotion to the work of Walter Dean Myers comes to a high point when Myers visits the classroom. All the poems throughout the book are included at the end along with Myers's "Love that Boy."

Gentle Criteria: This is a warm story of a good teacher who succeeds in bringing to the surface a student's real potential. Students who are reluctant to read and write poetry will identify with Jack's hesitation.

443   Testa, Maria. *Almost Forever.*
　　Candlewick, 2003, ISBN 978-0-7636-1996-1; 2007, pap., ISBN 978-0-7636-3366-0. 69p. • Grades 5–9

A little girl gives her perspective of what is going on during her military father's one-year enlistment as a doctor during the Vietnam War. She mentions that when her dad opened his draft letter, her mommy sat down and didn't even finish decorating the Christmas tree. She recalls how they got to move to a crowded apartment building, but her mommy said, "At least it is free." She remembers how happy her mommy was taking them to the park and playing with them after receiving a letter from her dad. She thinks that her mommy must be in love with newscaster Roger Mudd as she stares at him every night. She hears her mommy tell the postman that she isn't getting any mail anymore, but she knows that isn't true because she sees the bills. Then her mommy stops playing at the park and cries at night in her room. Another letter arrives; what news will it bring?

　　Gentle Criteria: Written from an innocent child's perspective, the emotions are displayed on every page. But the book has a happy ending with the family reunited. This gentle read is an effective one because readers will feel their hearts tug all the way through the waiting for her father to come home, and will sympathize for the mother who struggles to keep the family safe while he is away. A little girl who just wants her daddy home makes it even more real.

444   Testa, Maria. *Becoming Joe DiMaggio.*
　　Ill. by Scott Hunt. Candlewick, 2002, ISBN 978-0-7636-1537-6; 2005, pap., ISBN 978-0-7636-2444-6. 51p. • Grades 5–9
　　ACCELERATED READER *READING COUNTS*

This is a collection of poems that when combined tell the story of a young boy who idolizes Joe DiMaggio. Before Joseph Paul was even born, his grandfather built him a chair. That small chair is where he sits with Papa Angelo and listens to Joe DiMaggio play. The poems share how he grows up with three older sisters, and how his father can't stay out of jail. The poems talk about kids at school who call him "Dago." But most of all, the poems show the love that he and Grandpa have for each other. In one poem, Grandpa points out the picture of Joe DiMaggio as a child with his parents and comments how Joe made his parents' hearts soar. When Joseph Paul tells his grandpa that he isn't going to seventh grade next year, his Papa Angelo jumps out of the chair, wanting to know why. He says because he's going to high school and wants to be a doctor. A few years later, they celebrate his high school graduation and his Papa Angelo's heart soars.

　　Gentle Criteria: This book shares the trying times when Joseph Paul grew up, amid prejudice against the Italian people. Even though his family has a hard time making ends meet because his father is frequently in jail and because of World War II, Joseph Paul never gives up his dreams.

445   Turner, Ann Warren. *Hard Hit.*

Scholastic, 2006, ISBN 978-0-439-29680-9. 167p. • Grades 7–9

⁀ ACCELERATED READER

This is a beautiful novel that illustrates the stages a family goes through when dealing with the terminal illness of a loved one. Mark Warren has everything a teen could want: he is star pitcher on his baseball team, has a great new girlfriend, has a best friend, and even has a great family. When his father is diagnosed with a hard-to-treat cancer, Mark begins to question everything he thought he knew about life. If he can just pitch a no-hitter, Mark thinks that will be enough luck to keep his father alive. Each poem takes the reader further along the road of his father's cancer treatment and eventual death. The last poems are a tribute to all the things his father taught him, and the love Mark realizes he can still feel even though his dad is gone.

Gentle Criteria: This is a story about family and friends standing together against a horrendous experience. Strong love from both Mark's family and friends is the constant theme. He gets through it because of the love and strong values that surround him. Readers experiencing a similar situation will find herein words of wisdom and sources for help. The book ends with a listing of support groups.

446   Yeomans, Ellen. *Rubber Houses.*

Little, Brown, 2007, ISBN 978-0-316-10647-4. 152p. • Grades 7–9

This book chronicles Kit's junior and senior years in high school when her little brother is diagnosed with and dies from leukemia. It is an accurate portrayal of the grief process that a family goes through when it loses a loved one, particularly, a young child. Disbelief and anger are very raw emotions here. Yet in the middle of it all, Kit is a typical teen girl who privately calls Buddy's doctor, "Dr. Hotness." The book is filled with instances of well-meaning people who don't say the right thing, doctors who make poor jokes in an attempt to lighten the situation, and friends who don't know what to do when Kit is no longer the strong one. Needing comfort for herself, dealing with visitors who wear her out, not being able to enter a room because Buddy was there before he died, putting up with friends who want her to join the world of the living again, feeling anger toward people who have never had anything bad happen to them, and watching her dad smash a fence to deal with his anger are all part of Kit's story. Yet, in the end, it is Kit who finds her way through by doing positive things with her life.

Gentle Criteria: This is a story about a typical teen in an untypical situation, trying to rise above the anger and grief that threaten to swallow her. Featured in this story are lots of well-meaning people, but it is Kit's strength that pulls her through and back into the world. She survives by giving of herself to help build houses for homeless people, and thereby becomes part of the world of the living again.

Short Stories

447   Asher, Sandy, editor. *On Her Way: Stories and Poems About Growing Up Girl.*
Dutton, 2004, ISBN 978-0-525-47170-7. 209p. • Grades 5–7
☞ ACCELERATED READER ☞ JUNIOR LIBRARY GUILD

This is a collection of stories about being a teenage girl, written by well-known young adult authors such as Angela Johnson, Margaret Peterson Haddix, and Marthe Jocelyn. Each story features strong female characters finding their way in the world. In "Rabbit Stew," for example, a younger girl turns the table on two older boys who think they are going to make a fool of her. These stories will make great read-alouds with listeners wishing that each story were a complete book!

Gentle Criteria: This book is a gentle read because it features positive female characters that will encourage female readers. The young girls in the stories show plenty of smarts and backbone as they make their way in the world.

448   Avi. *Strange Happenings: Five Tales of Transformation.*
Harcourt, 2006, ISBN 978-0-15-205790-9. 147p. • Grades 5–7
☞ ACCELERATED READER

Here are five clever tales of transformation by a favorite author of young adults. Each tale features an unexpected twist. In "Bored Tom," a bored young man decides to trade places with his cat. In "Babette the Beautiful," a vain young woman discovers that it is better to have flaws than not to be seen at all. Each story emphasizes that one should be happy with what life has given.

Gentle Criteria: In his own subtle and clever way, Avi shows the reader the pitfalls of greed, vanity, and laziness. Readers will chuckle at the amusing traps life has set for those who do not reach beyond themselves and become the best they can be.

449   Hausman, Gerald. *Castaways: Stories of Survival.*
Greenwillow, 2003, ISBN 978-0-06-008599-5. 165p. • Grades 7–9
ᴈ Accelerated Reader

A wonderful collection of survival stories, all based on fact, some more loosely than others. In "Turtle Island of Peter Serrano," Peter grows both a natural covering and uses shells to survive the elements on the little piece of land named for him. Spontaneous thinking saves the day in "The Modern Mariner and the Pilot of the Pinta," where cleverness makes the difference between life and death, and the people who survive go on to do good in the world. Readers of stories such as the well-known *Hatchet* will enjoy these quick reads about people who survived dangerous circumstances. Language arts teachers who use survival as a thematic unit will want to use these short stories to introduce the topic.

Gentle Criteria: These stories are good reading; each is about why humans need each other to survive in this world. Some of the stories are about loners who learn to appreciate the presence of another human in their lives. Others feature survivors who use the rest of their time on earth to do good for other people. All of the characters in the stories demonstrate that they are not afraid to use their wits, and their quick thinking makes the crucial difference in their survival.

450   Martin, Ann M., and David Levithan. *Friends: Stories About New Friends, Old Friends, and Unexpectedly True Friends.*
Scholastic, 2005, ISBN 978-0-439-72991-8. 186p. • Grades 5–8
ᴈ Reading Counts

Here is a collection of eleven short stories that deal with friendship, each written by a YA author. In "The Friend Who Saved My Life," Pam is a new kid in school who has been targeted by the class bully, Theresa. After one outdoor altercation, Mary Lou helps Pam clean up in the bathroom, telling her that she's got to stand up to Theresa or it's only going to get worse. As added incentive, Mary Lou tells Pam that if she doesn't, *she's* going to beat her up! So Pam fights back and puts an end to the bullying. Ironically, while Theresa and Pam are spending the next week on the time-out bench, Theresa invites Pam to go to the library with her. In "Flit," Monroe has moved for the sixth time in four years. He has an imaginary friend named Flit who helps him cope with not having friends. But Monroe's need for real friends wins out in the end as two people won't leave Monroe alone.

Gentle Criteria: Many of these stories deal with tough emotional times that young people go through. The common thread running through each story is that someone steps up, offering assistance or kindness that changes lives. It's reassuring to read these examples and learn that a simple act of gentleness can change someone's life forever.

451 Mercado, Nancy E. *Tripping Over the Lunch Lady: And Other School Stories.*

Dial, 2004, ISBN 978-0-8037-2873-8; Penguin, 2006, pap., ISBN 978-0-14-240624-3. 178p. • Grades 5–9

↗ ACCELERATED READER ↗ READING COUNTS

A collection of short school stories from ten YA authors. A superb example is David Lubar's "Science Friction." Four students have seven weeks to work together on a science project. They meet at Amanda's house once a week after school. They waste the first four weeks because they can't agree on anything. In week five they each share their best project ideas and put them to a vote. In week six their choice idea flops. Now, just one week away from the due date, they still don't have a project. As good fortune would have it, Amanda keeps a very messy room in which the kids hide the horrible snacks that Amanda's mom makes them each week. The hidden snacks include five weeks of moldy bread samples, five weeks of spoiled turkey, and five weeks of deteriorating carrot sticks. The kids receive an A for a well-thought-out mold project!

Gentle Criteria: These are amusing and insightful stories about school. In "How I Got My English A," a student in detention ends up getting an A on his paper after he hands his teacher the story about how they were kidnapped and the teacher married the criminal because he was a good speller. The language is clean and no one pulls any vicious pranks.

452 Pearson, Gayle. *The Secret Box.*

Atheneum, 1997, ISBN 978-0-689-81379-5. 119p. • Grades 5–9

↗ ACCELERATED READER ↗ JUNIOR LIBRARY GUILD

This book is a collection of five short stories centered around two girls and their older brothers. In "The Secret Box," one young girl discovers that her brother's friend is not the good guy that she thought he was, and she tries to find a way to make things right. In "Cousin Dolores," a girl goes to a funeral for a dog and finds out that her brother might possibly be a nicer person than she thought. "The Year of the Dog" takes readers through one brother's unrequited love. "Teacher of the Year" finds a young man struggling with the decision to do the right thing after one of his personal heroes falls from his pedestal. And in "Magic Boots," a sister teaches her brother a lesson after he does something unforgivable. Readers will find a lot to talk about as they peruse this collection of five thought-provoking short stories.

Gentle Criteria: Although people in these stories go astray, this book is about five individuals deciding for themselves what is the right thing to do. Honesty, love, and forgiveness are the themes in these stories.

453   *Shelf Life: Stories by the Book.*
Ed. by Gary Paulsen. Simon & Schuster, 2003, ISBN 978-0-689-84180-4. 173p. • Grades 5–9
ACCELERATED READER   READING COUNTS   JUNIOR LIBRARY GUILD

Gary Paulsen asked ten authors to contribute a story to this collection to raise money for ProLiteracy Worldwide. Each is an original piece that mentions a book within the story. Most of the stories are uplifting and make the reader think about the message being conveyed. In "Escape," Isabel is upset that her mamma spends their scarce money on books to send to her father who is in prison. They are constantly moving from shelter to shelter, so how can they afford to be buying books for her criminal dad? Then Isabel comes across a teen worker who is reading the same book that her mamma just sent her dad and asks, "Would you send that book to someone in prison?" The girl replies, "Why not, it's just escapist drivel." Then Isabel realizes that her mamma is sending a love letter to her dad, and the book is a means to escape the horrible daily routine of prison. She determines that she can make choices too, and she can pull herself out of her current situation.

Gentle Criteria: Each of the ten stories has a philosophical message. In "In Your Hat," jokester Daniel gets set up to turn in a fictitious book report and is shocked to find he can be played just like he plays most people. In "A Good Deed," girl scout Heather offers to read to a blind lady and is irritated when the neighbor across the hall, Risa, intrudes on their reading. But Heather's initial irritation soon fades when she learns that the younger Risa has great responsibilities as she cares for three younger brothers while her mom is away at work.

Mythology

454   Cadnum, Michael. *Nightsong: The Legend of Orpheus and Eurydice.*

Scholastic, 2006, ISBN 978-0-439-54535-8. 133p. • Grades 5–9

☞ ACCELERATED READER

Prince Orpheus, the poet singer, who is the son of a muse and a king, was given his lyre by Apollo himself. He meets Eurydice and falls instantly in love with her only to have her killed by a snake on their wedding day. After a couple of weeks of mourning, Orpheus decides to go to the underworld and retrieve her. He shudders at the horrors of Hades but is determined to convince Queen Persephone and Hades to let him take his bride back to the living world. After he wins them over with his poetry and song, they give him permission—on one condition. He must not turn around and look at Eurydice until they have left Hades. Will Orpheus be able to resist the urge to look back?

   Gentle Criteria: No human had ever dared to enter Hades to retrieve a departed loved one. Orpheus loves Eurydice so deeply that he is willing to risk his own life to have her with him. When poor Orpheus does glance back and loses his love for a second time, all hope appears lost, and he forsakes his lyre for months. Then a priest asks him to play, hoping the music will bring a young man out of a coma. When Orpheus plays, he is rewarded by hearing the voice of his lost love.

455   Cadnum, Michael. *Starfall Phaeton and the Chariot of the Sun.*

Scholastic, 2004, ISBN 978-0-439-54533-4. 124p. Series: Starfall • Grades 5–9

☞ ACCELERATED READER

In this first volume in the series, Phaeton has been told by his mother that he is the son of Apollo, but she is upset that Apollo hasn't claimed Phaeton as his own. With his mother's blessing, Phaeton sets off to find Apollo. He encounters a naiad who steals his food and money. Then he is confronted by a herd of centaurs and is rescued by Mercury who bestows upon him the gift of speed so that he can reach his father quickly. When Apollo asks Phaeton what gift he can give to prove his love for his father and mother, Phaeton asks to drive the chariot across the sky just one time. Apollo tries to dissuade him, fearing that no mortal can handle the mighty steeds. Phaeton won't take no for an answer and ends up damaging the earth and forcing Jupiter to strike him out of the sky with a lightning bolt. Mercury then visits Phaeton's grave and brings him back to life as the "wind," so that he can roam the earth.

Gentle Criteria: This book reads like a fable with the moral of the story being, "Be careful what you wish for." Phaeton is so proud that he can't stand a little teasing about his father's identity, so he gives up his comfortable life for a chance at glory. Even though Phaeton realizes how hard the horses will be to control, he believes Apollo will be able to save him if things go wrong. When he loses control of the horses, he regrets his decision, finding out the hard way that he is mortal after all. He has accomplished his mission but lost his mortal life in the process.

456   McClaren, Clemence. *Aphrodite's Blessings: Love Stories from the Greek Myths.*

Atheneum, 2002, ISBN 978-0-689-84377-8. 202p. • Grades 7–9

ACCELERATED READER

A trio of love stories from the Greek myths, based on the strong female characters of Atalanta, Andromeda, and Psyche. Each story gives an account of the character's marriage—from the girl's point of view. These stories are cleverly told and are a refreshing change from the typical popular romance.

Gentle Criteria: Based on Greek myths, this book provides good historical retellings that feature the wry humor of a female point of view.

457   Yolen, Jane, and Robert J. Harris. *Atalanta and the Arcadian Beast.*

HarperCollins, 2003, ISBN 978-0-06-029455-7. 245p. Series: Young Heroes • Grades 5–9

ACCELERATED READER   READING COUNTS   JUNIOR LIBRARY GUILD

Atalanta is a wild girl who is hunting with her adopted father when they are attacked by the Arcadian beast. Her dying father tells her that she was raised by a she-bear and that she was found with a ring tied around her neck. After burying her father, Atalanta is confronted by a huge bear. This grown bear is the cub that was raised with her. She names the bear Urso, and he becomes her only friend. She next challenges the great hunter Orion to a race whose victor will be allowed to join the hunt for the Arcadian beast. She wins the race and is eager to exact her revenge on the creature that killed her father. Along the journey she has a dream that explains the reason behind the beast's curse. Atalanta also discovers who her real parents are and why she was raised by wild animals. She learns much about herself and what justice and mercy mean. This fictional book takes famous mythological characters and writes about their lives as children.

Gentle Criteria: Atalanta has been guided well by her adoptive parents. She has been taught to respect the earth and to hunt only for food and not out of malice or for sport. She responds well to those who show her kindness and is brave beyond words. She is willing to risk her own life to avenge the life of her father.

458   **Yolen, Jane, and Robert J. Harris.** *Hippolyta and the Curse of the Amazons.*
HarperCollins, 2002, ISBN 978-0-06-028737-5. 248p. Series: Young Heroes • Grades 5–9
ᜑ Accelerated Reader ᜑ Reading Counts ᜑ Junior Library Guild

The law of the Goddess Artemis requires that Amazon Queen Otrere's second baby boy be sacrificed. The queen tells her daughter Hippolyta to take the baby to his father, and the Amazon tribe is then cursed for breaking the rules. Hippolyta has the idea of sacrificing her half-brother in place of the newborn baby to lift the curse. Along the way she begins to have feelings for her half-brother and to understand her mother's view that they should not have allowed the gods to guide their lives. When Artemis commands her to sacrifice her half-brother, she refuses and a whole flock of gryphons descends on her. She fights gallantly but is about to tire out when her father, the god Ares, saves her. Ares forces the god Apollo to call off his pet gryphons, and he convinces Artemis to cancel the curse and allow the mortals to choose their own destiny.

Gentle Criteria: Hippolyta, a well-trained Amazon, can't understand why her mother refuses to follow the law and sacrifice the baby. She loves and honors her mother enough to follow her instructions even though it will cause her mother to be removed from the ruling party. With the guidance of her war-god father, Ares, she learns the proper place for war. During her journey with her half-brother, she also learns that she loves him and will fight to the death to protect her family. This is a story of family love and of doing the right thing.

459   **Yolen, Jane, and Robert J. Harris.** *Jason and the Gorgon's Blood.*
HarperCollins, 2004, ISBN 978-0-06-029453-3. 246p. Series: Young Heroes • Grades 5–8
ᜑ Accelerated Reader

This is the fourth volume in the Young Heroes series. Jason has been adopted and trained by a half-horse-half-man creature, or centaur, named Chiron. Chiron has also been in charge of training five other boys—two of whom are royalty. When Chiron is attacked by a group of renegade centaurs, they steal his

Gorgon's blood; with this blood they will be able to wipe out the kingdom of Iolcus. Chiron tells Jason that he is the rightful future king of Iolcus and must lead the other boys to retrieve the blood before the centaurs poison the water of Iolcus. Prince Acastus overhears that Jason is a threat to his future position as king and decides to get rid of Jason. The six boys set out to catch up to the centaurs and encounter dangerous harpies and other obstacles. These Young Heroes books project the lives of heroes when they were young.

Gentle Criteria: As adults can imagine, one boy trying to lead five other adolescents—each with a mind of his own—could be an impossible task. But Jason, by listening to the teachings of Chiron, assigns each boy with a leadership task so that each feels important and in charge of some aspect of the mission. Jason also wins over Prince Acastus by assuring the prince that he is no threat to his future kingdom, and that they together must save the kingdom from the poisonous Gorgon blood.

460   Yolen, Jane, and Robert J. Harris. *Odysseus in the Serpent Maze.* HarperCollins, 2001, ISBN 978-0-06-028735-1; 2002, pap., ISBN 978-0-06-440847-9. 248p. Series: Young Heroes • Grades 5–9
 ☞ Accelerated Reader ☞ Reading Counts ☞ Junior Library Guild

This first volume in the Young Heroes series that describes an adventure Odysseus had as a child. While traveling by ship to his father, Odysseus and his friend Mentor fall overboard only to be rescued by pirates. On board the pirate ship they meet two other captives, Helen of Troy and her cousin Penelope. They escape and borrow a satyr's boat only to have it begin leaking and sinking. They luckily encounter a mechanical ship designed by Daedalus that takes them to Crete. Here they find Daedalus's workshop and a key that will open all locks. They are captured by King Deucalion and Penelope is thrown into the maze, and Mentor and Odysseus into the dungeon. Helen, using her beauty, frees them, and Odysseus enters the maze to save Penelope from Ladon, the multi-headed serpent. Odysseus slays the serpent and with the assistance of the key, frees his former crew members and rescues Penelope and Helen. Goddess Athena visits Odysseus and informs him of her part in his successful adventure.

Gentle Criteria: Odysseus lives by the code with which he was raised: "Any danger averted is an adventure." Odysseus, although young, is still a hero. He puts himself at risk several times during the story.

Poetry

461   Grimes, Nikki. *What Is Goodbye?*
Ill. by Raul Colon. Disney, 2004, ISBN 978-0-7868-0778-9. Unpaged •
Grades 5–9

☞ Accelerated Reader ☞ Reading Counts

Anyone who has experienced the tremendous feelings of loss caused by a death
in the family will appreciate this book. In alternating poems, a brother and sister
tell about their lives from the moment they learn of their brother's death to one
year later. The stages of grief—denial, anger, memories, and acceptance—are
realistically illustrated in the poems. Each person in this family finds a way to
work through the grief and still cherish memories. When their parents are simply
too grief-stricken to talk about it, the brother and sister find a way to express
themselves through drawing and writing. In the end, they learn to appreciate an
ordinary day and to hold on to the good memories they have.

Gentle Criteria: This book is a true treasure that can help children who
are suffering because of the death of a loved one. These poems will tug at the
reader's heartstrings. Without being graphic in any way, they express the emotions that people go through when dealing with death. The possibilities for discussion are endless. The whole point of the book is to show readers positive
ways to deal with loss. At the end of the book is a short piece by the author
about dealing with death, emphasizing that it is acceptable to deal with it in any
way that feels right to you—everyone feels different emotions at different times.

462   Nye, Naomi Shihab. *A Maze Me: Poems for Girls.*
Ill. by Terre Maher. HarperCollins, 2005, ISBN 978-0-06-058190-9.
118p. • Grades 5–9
☞ ACCELERATED READER ☞ READING COUNTS

In the introduction the author states how at age twelve she was stuck in a strange place. While her friends were jumping into womanhood by wearing lipstick and stuffing their bras, she realized how great she had it as a child. Naomi could see that adulthood meant balancing checkbooks, doing daily chores, navigating complicated relationships, and maintaining cars; she didn't want to take on those responsibilities. Included are Naomi's poems from childhood to adulthood, giving readers glimpses into Naomi's feelings about the world at each stage.

Gentle Criteria: Naomi's father says that a stick and acorn were his only toys growing up. He carved the acorn into a wooden top and wrote in the dirt with his stick. He said that is what made him the man he is today. In "Feeling Wise," a lady is quoted in the newspaper as saying that it's not hard to feel wise—just think of something dumb and then don't say it. These are just two examples of the wisdom and insight that are reflected in Naomi's poems. The author's purpose is to gently reassure young girls making the move from childhood to adulthood, and to remind them to stop, take note, and enjoy the ride.

463   Williams, Vera B. *Amber Was Brave, Essie Was Smart: The Story of Amber and Essie Told Here in Poems and Pictures.*
Greenwillow, 2001, ISBN 978-0-06-029461-8; HarperCollins, 2004,
pap., ISBN 978-0-06-057182-5. 52p. • All ages
☞ ACCELERATED READER ☞ READING COUNTS

Two sisters learn to depend on each other when their father goes to jail and their mother has to work even harder to support the family. Told in verse, the two sisters lovingly describe what each can do to help the other. One is brave; the other is smart. One can make toasted cheese sandwiches; the other can talk the grocery man into giving them a container of milk and letting them pay later. But they have to push the front door together to get it open. These two girls learn to hold each other up through hard times, until the day when the door opens and their father walks back in their lives.

Gentle Criteria: At first glance this seems to be a book for the very young. But when readers start traveling through the touching verses, they will see there is much here to absorb. This is a family in crisis that finds positive ways to get through it. Families that have gone through hard times will sympathize with and admire these wonderful sisters.

Biography

464   Bolden, Tonya. *Maritcha: A Nineteenth-Century American Girl.*
Abrams, 2005, ISBN 978-0-8109-5045-0. 47p. • Grades 5–9
☞ Accelerated Reader ☞ Reading Counts

This is a short scrapbook-like biography of Maritcha Lyons, an amazing African American woman. Born in New York in 1848, twenty-one years after the state abolished slavery, she was the granddaughter of Frederick Douglass. Her aim was "to do the best for myself with the view of making the best of myself," and she did. When her family attended antislavery meetings they were not there to agitate but to learn their duty—get instructions for the Underground Railroad. When her family moved to Providence, Rhode Island, after the terrible Draft Riots of 1863, Maritcha spoke to the state legislature about the fact that there was no high school for African American children and won her case—all at the age of sixteen! She spent nearly fifty years as an educator, eventually becoming an assistant principal in Brooklyn. Besides discovering a wonderful life story, readers will get a taste of New York City at that time and the situation of African Americans—even in free states—before the Civil War.

Gentle Criteria: This story is about the honorable life of Maritcha Lyons; she and her family quietly stood for what was right and helped wherever they could. Maritcha is a young person eager to help make the country an enlightened and equitable place and her achievements are considerable.

☙ Coretta Scott King Author Honor Book, 2006

465   Cooper, Ilene. *Jack: The Early Years of John F. Kennedy.*
Dutton, 2003, ISBN 978-0-525-46923-0. 168p. • Grades 7–9
☞ Accelerated Reader ☞ Reading Counts ☞ Junior Library Guild

This is a biography focusing on John F. Kennedy's childhood and youth. Readers learn about the chronic and painful childhood illnesses that Jack endured, which taught him that life can be unfair. Focus is placed on the strength of the Kennedy family unit and its poor Irish beginnings. Although Jack's father was far from perfect, nothing was more important to him than his family. He encouraged his children to win at whatever they did and to always stand by their family. Readers may be shocked to read about the prejudice the people of Boston had against the Irish and the Catholics. One of the essays Jack wrote during his junior year illustrates his recognition that justice does not always prevail—one can simply be born in the wrong place and time. This understanding may have contributed to President Kennedy's greatness.

Gentle Criteria: Although readers will see that Jack and his father were both far from perfect, their confidence in their abilities bred success. Family was very important to both of them, and they recognized that unfairness exists in the world. Readers will see a strong family unit that served the Kennedys well.

466   Fleischman, Sid. *Escape: The Story of the Great Houdini.*
HarperCollins, 2006, ISBN 978-0-06-085095-1. 210p. • Grades 5–9
* READING COUNTS

This book describes the life of Erich Weiss, the son of a poor Jewish rabbi, who became the most famous escape artist of all time—Harry Houdini. Houdini's drive, ego, and knowledge of publicity made him famous when other headliners failed. In 1897 Houdini challenged the Chicago police to lock him in shackles and put him in jail. He instantly became famous when he managed to free himself. Houdini took great pride in fooling people, but he would not tolerate the spiritualists who pretended to speak for the dead, making grieving people think they could communicate with their deceased loved ones. He made it his mission in life to expose these frauds. Harry died of a ruptured appendix on Halloween night, 1926. He promised his wife he would communicate from the other side, but no spiritist could ever reveal the secret words they promised to share with each other.

Gentle Criteria: The author shares the facts of Houdini's life in a chronological format that reveals both his accomplishments and his personality. He had the ability to create legends and attract publicity. This is a revealing look at a self-made man.

467   Freedman, Russell. *The Voice That Challenged a Nation: Marian Anderson and the Struggle for Equal Rights.*
Clarion, 2004, ISBN 978-0-618-15976-5. 114p. • Grades 5–9
* ACCELERATED READER * READING COUNTS * JUNIOR LIBRARY GUILD

This is the true story of Marian Anderson, a world-class singer who was not permitted to sing at Constitution Hall in Washington, D.C., because she was black.

But with the influence of people like Eleanor Roosevelt, her concert was rescheduled to be held at the Mall in front of the Lincoln Memorial, and more than 75,000 people attended. Her talent was inspiring and her class and dignity prevailed at all times.

Gentle Criteria: Students, parents, and teachers dread the annual biography assignment. But this book is a good one for such an assignment! Rather than being a story of prejudice and hatred, it is a story of true grace under pressure. Marian Anderson is presented as *not* just another girl, but a girl with an amazing voice who did not let the prejudices of the day stop her. She is a positive figure from the civil rights movement and this is a book that students will enjoy reading.

⅏ NEWBERY HONOR BOOK, 2005; ROBERT F. SIBERT MEDAL, 2005

468 Jimenez, Francisco. *Breaking Through.*
Houghton Mifflin, 2001, ISBN 978-0-618-01173-5; 2002, pap., ISBN 978-0-618-34248-8. 195p. • Grades 5–9
⌐ ACCELERATED READER ⌐ READING COUNTS ⌐ JUNIOR LIBRARY GUILD

This sequel picks up where *The Circuit* (see below) leaves off, with an immigration officer arriving in Francisco's classroom to deport him and his family to Mexico. However, Francisco and his older brother are able to make it back to Santa Maria where they try to support themselves and continue through school. One of their bosses takes them out to a restaurant for the first time; the brothers teach each other how to dance; and once again kind teachers help them get through difficult circumstances. Professor Jimenez wrote this sequel to pay tribute to his family and teachers and to voice the experiences of children who confront obstacles in order to "break through" and become the butterflies they are capable of being.

Gentle Criteria: Although there are some rough spots in the lives of these family members, their perseverance, courage, hope, and hard work are a testament to what is possible. The combination of their efforts and the kindness of the wonderfully generous people they encounter help them to survive.

469 Jimenez, Francisco. *The Circuit: Stories from the Life of a Migrant Child.*
University of New Mexico Press, 1997, ISBN 978-0-395-97902-0; pap., ISBN 978-0-8263-1797-1. 134p. • Grades 5–9
⌐ ACCELERATED READER ⌐ READING COUNTS ⌐ JUNIOR LIBRARY GUILD

Twelve short episodes make up this story about a migrant child, based on the life of the author. The prose is very matter-of-fact. The conditions described may be harsh but the tone is never one of self-pity. Many kind teachers make a difference in this child's life, from the teacher who submits his drawing for a blue ribbon, to the one who finds his older brother a job as a janitor. His parents work so hard to simply give their children a bag of candy for Christmas, and they want their children to have a better life than they did. When a fire destroys the house they are renting, the boy realizes that nothing is lost because it is all saved in his heart and mind. Jimenez, now a professor, shares the knowledge that anyone can overcome his life circumstances.

Gentle Criteria: This is a collection of stories that reminds readers that people are capable of anything they put their minds to. Any one of these twelve stories will serve as a discussion starter.

470 **Kehret, Peg.** *Small Steps: The Year I Got Polio.*

Whitman, 1996, ISBN 978-0-8075-7457-7; 2000, pap., ISBN 978-0-8075-7458-4. 174p. • Grades 5–7
☞ ACCELERATED READER ☞ READING COUNTS ☞ JUNIOR LIBRARY GUILD

This well-known author describes the year she turned thirteen and battled polio. While many students today are not familiar with polio, their grandparents and parents will likely remember standing in line to receive polio vaccinations. Peg Kehret's polio came on rapidly, progressing from a headache to paralysis from the neck down. Writing from the perspective of a teen, she relates what it was like to spend one of her teen years unable to move. Pictures are included, one showing Peg in the iron lung in which she spent some of her illness. Luckily, she was one of the patients who could be rehabilitated. This edition updates the original 1996 version.

Gentle Criteria: This is the inspiring story of a thirteen-year-old who faces great adversity. Students will relate to her feelings about being a teen and will have great respect for how positively she survived that terrible year. This book is an excellent choice for students looking for stories about real people.

471 **Kraske, Robert.** *Marooned: The Strange But True Adventures of Alexander Selkirk, the Real Robinson Crusoe.*

Houghton Mifflin, 2005, ISBN 978-0-618-56843-7. 120p. • Grades 5–7
☞ ACCELERATED READER ☞ JUNIOR LIBRARY GUILD

This true story of Alexander Selkirk proves that truth really can be stranger than fiction. In 1705 Alexander was marooned on an island in the South Pacific for four and a half years. Selkirk had been second in command of a ship, but was preparing to lead the men to mutiny. As his punishment, the captain of the ship abandoned him on the island. Read how Selkirk survived debilitating loneliness, and actually ended up enjoying his own company, the fresh air, and the efforts it took to find food and shelter.

Gentle Criteria: This is a detailed and wonderful record of how one man survived by himself in the wild. Selkirk's strength of spirit is an inspiring story.

472   Lawlor, Laurie. *Helen Keller: Rebellious Spirit.*
Holiday House, 2001, ISBN 978-0-8234-1588-5. 168p. • Grades 5–9
⌐ Accelerated Reader ⌐ Reading Counts

This book does a remarkable job of telling not only the story of Helen Keller, who was deaf and blind, but also the story of Helen's teacher, Annie Sullivan. The story explains what was happening in the world socially, politically, and financially at that time, and how Helen was affected by all that was going on around her. Not only did Helen learn how to read braille, sign, and read lips, but she also learned how to type and talk. This biography details her relationships with well-known people such as Alexander Graham Bell and every president who was in office during her adult life. Helen, having studied religion and philosophy, formed her own opinions about what was happening and wasn't afraid to speak them. She championed equal rights for women and blacks even though her actions were in direct conflict with her family's values. After graduating from college, she lectured, became part of a traveling show, and was a fund raiser for the American Foundation for the Blind.

   Gentle Criteria: Helen Keller continued to strive to communicate with the world despite all the hardships she endured. Her story is one of determination and success, and will be an inspiration to all who read it.

473   Lekuton, Joseph Lemasolai, and Herman Viola. *Facing the Lion: Growing Up Maasai on the African Savanna.*
National Geographic, 2005, ISBN 978-0-7922-8328-7; pap., ISBN 978-0-7922-7297-7. 127p. • Grades 5–9
⌐ Accelerated Reader ⌐ Reading Counts ⌐ Junior Library Guild

Lekuton does a wonderful job describing life growing up as one of the nomadic Maasai people in northern Kenya, and then being immersed into Western culture when he entered school. The Maasai family picks the least important child to go to school because the others are needed to watch the herds. The hardships are described very matter-of-factly—walking twenty miles, searching for his family for two weeks after school ended because the tribe had moved to find new grazing ground, undergoing the ceremony of circumcision, and licking the sweat off the cows' noses when there was no water. When called to interview for a scholarship for school in the United States, Lekuton rode on a cattle truck, standing inside with the cows and caring for them for two long days. Now he teaches at a private school in Washington, D.C., and spends time each year helping the Maasai villagers.

   Gentle Criteria: Here is the real-life story of a man who has made a positive impact on the world. It illustrates why we should not assume that people are ignorant because they live differently. This book is a great biography to use in the classroom or with a book club. Lekuton would be a great person for young people to interview.

474   Paulsen, Gary. *How Angel Peterson Got His Name: And Other Outrageous Tales About Extreme Sports.*
Wendy Lamb Books, 2003, ISBN 978-0-385-90090-4; Random House, 2004, pap., ISBN 978-0-440-22935-3. 111p. • Grades 7–9
☞ ACCELERATED READER ☞ READING COUNTS ☞ JUNIOR LIBRARY GUILD

Gary Paulsen relates tales from his youth about what we now call extreme sports. Paulsen grew up in the 1940s and 1950s, long before bungee jumping and skateboarding were mainstream sports. He and his friends made their own versions, which were often dangerous but always amusing. Skiing behind a car on a winter road, hang gliding with an old World War II target kite, and staying in a circus ring with a live bear for sixty seconds are just some of their stunts. Readers will wonder how Paulsen and his friends survived. Fans of Paulsen's other books will want to read this autobiography.

Gentle Criteria: This book tells the story of kids trying to have fun with the materials they had. Paulsen describes at length how hard and long they had to work for the little bit of money they earned. There's no vandalism or bad behavior in this story, but some of their poor judgments make for amusing tales.

475   Sowash, Rick. *Heroes of Ohio: 23 True Tales of Courage and Character.*
Rick Sowash, 2003, ISBN 978-0-911861-12-9; 1998, pap., ISBN 978-0-911861-13-6. 146p. • Grades 5–7

One of the best parts of this book is the introduction in which the author tells readers that what heroes do is "not easy, not required, and not selfish." Kids, for example, are heroes when they refuse to put down other kids. People are heroes when they help someone without expecting anything in return, and so forth. The author goes on to describe the ways in which twenty-three people from his home state of Ohio are heroes. Reporter Januarius MacGahan helped to liberate Bulgaria when he let the world know the terrible things happening there. Granville Woods could not attend school but read and worked in many jobs to eventually become the black Thomas Edison. John Parker helped to free slaves even when it meant sneaking into the overseer's bedroom to rescue a baby hidden there to keep the parents from trying to escape.

Gentle Criteria: These are all inspiring stories of people who took care of others first and tried to make the world a better place. The story of Januarius MacGahan is difficult to read because he discovers an entire hill of skulls during his reporting.

Nonfiction

476   Bausum, Ann. *Freedom Riders: John Lewis and Jim Zwerg on the Front Lines of the Civil Rights Movement.*
National Geographic, 2006, ISBN 978-0-7922-4174-4. 79p. •
Grades 5–9

 ACCELERATED READER READING COUNTS

In the summer of 1961, Freedom Rider buses carried blacks and whites together into the deep South, defying the segregation laws in force at the time. This inspiring account is told from the viewpoint of two riders, Jim Zwerg and John Lewis. The book follows each through his childhood and young adult years leading up to the summer of the bus rides. Jim Zwerg encountered little racial diversity in his hometown, but when he realized his college fraternity was segregated, he turned in his pin. John Lewis believed that with education and determination he could change the wrongs he perceived in the world. In the statement of purpose for the Nashville Student Movement they wrote that love "matches the capacity of evil to inflict suffering with an even more enduring capacity to absorb evil." Together they changed transportation and other rules through nonviolent protest, confronting life-threatening mob hatred with peace.

Gentle Criteria: The Freedom Riders were a group of people following the teaching and leadership of Mohandas Gandhi and Martin Luther King, Jr., who believed that they could change the world positively in a nonviolent way. The first two pages of the book are enough to inspire any reader to follow his or her heart and do what is right. Jim Zwerg and John Lewis each speak to the importance of finding what makes one passionate.

 ROBERT F. SIBERT MEDAL HONOR BOOK, 2007

477 Beller, Susan Provost. *The History Puzzle: How We Know What We Know About the Past.*

Lerner, 2006, ISBN 978-0-7613-2877-3. 128p. • Grades 6–9

☞ ACCELERATED READER ☞ READING COUNTS ☞ JUNIOR LIBRARY GUILD

This book tries to help the reader make an informed decision about how to judge history. The reader should first be aware that a reporter may be biased. For example, there are two different accounts of the battle of Little Bighorn—the army's account and the Native Americans' account. The author also points out that historians tend to believe written history that was published immediately after an event more than accounts written several years later. Such is the case with Judith McGuire, who was a diarist during the Civil War. Her writing is considered more truthful than that of diarist Mary Boykin Chestnut, who waited several years before publishing her account. The book goes on to explain archaeologists' insights into many historical places and events and looks into such questions as who was King Arthur; was there really a Noah's Ark; and what happened at Pompeii?

Gentle Criteria: This book is a great educational tool to help students become savvy investigators of what is real history versus what has been slanted to serve a particular agenda. Although it contains a photograph of a field of dead Civil War soldiers, its intent is not to shock but to demonstrate how photography is useful in helping to accurately report history.

478 Borden, Louise. *The Journey That Saved Curious George: The True Wartime Escape of Margret and H. A. Rey.*

Ill. by Allan Drummond. Houghton Mifflin, 2005, ISBN 978-0-618-33924-2. 72p. • Grades 5–9

☞ ACCELERATED READER ☞ READING COUNTS

This is the moving, true story of Hans and Margret Rey, both German-born Jews, and their escape from Europe in 1940. Hans and Margret were friends who eventually married and honeymooned in France. They later made their home in Paris. In May 1940, two million people attempted to leave the city fleeing the Nazis. The trains were no longer running, so Hans paid a month's rent to buy parts to build two bicycles. They bicycled out of Paris as five million people were leaving the city—the largest motorized evacuation in history. They were assisted along the way by farmers and other kind people. Eventually they made their way to New York with their precious manuscripts, one of which would later become *Curious George*, selling 27 million copies and loved by readers all over the world.

Gentle Criteria: This is a stirring story of two clever people who escape a dangerous situation. Readers will be on the edge of their seats as they read about the terrible situation of millions of people, especially Jews. The Curious George stories are still endearing to read, and readers will appreciate them even more when they realize what their famous authors endured to bring them to publication.

479 Bowen, Asta. *Wolf: The Journey Home.*

Bloomsbury, 2005, ISBN 978-1-58234-689-2. 276p. • Grades 7–9

This is an updated version of a book originally published in 1997, *Hungry for Home: A Wolf Odyssey*. The author takes readers through the life journey of an alpha female and her alpha male, describing what happens to them as they become part of the wolf relocation project in Pleasant Valley in northwest Montana in the late 1980s and early 1990s. Although this is a vivid survival story with wolf hunts, ranchers, and poachers, it is an even stronger demonstration of what these intelligent animals are capable of. Wolves have strong familial instincts. The process they use to find a mate, make a home, and teach their young to survive is deliberate and highly intelligent. Although Marta, the alpha female, is killed by poachers in the end, it is the legacy of her tenacity, intelligence, and love for her pack that will enable her offspring and their future generations to survive. Readers will be engrossed in this tale of family love and survival.

Gentle Criteria: Although harsh at times, this book can still be considered a gentle read because of its strong message of hope. Proponents of wolf relocation will find this an inspiring story of how, with human tolerance and a little bit of help, these intelligent animals can survive. Students of endangered species, the environment, and survival will quickly become engaged in this story and hopeful for the future of these animals.

480 Covey, Sean. *The Seven Habits of Highly Effective Teens.*

Simon & Schuster, 1998, pap., ISBN 978-0-684-85609-4. 168p. • Grades 7–9

Written by the son of the author of *The 7 Habits of Highly Effective People*, this is a positive read for teens in much the same vein. Divided into sections, this book covers private victories—being proactive, practicing good habits, having goals; public victories—being positive, creating synergy with other people, and understanding other people's actions; and renewals—keeping your body and mind healthy and refreshed. It emphasizes that positive habits build up while negative habits tear down. It also discusses how to have a positive attitude. Teens are reminded that they cannot change all the things in their world that aren't right, but they can change how they react to them. Not letting one's fears make one's decisions, letting kind words warm your world, understanding others' (even your parents') point of view before reacting, and creating synergy (the process of making one better idea out of two different ones) are just some of the topics addressed. Full of positive quotes and stories, this book is certain to be one that teens dip into frequently.

Gentle Criteria: This book is full of suggestions about how to create a positive world—both within and outside oneself. Looking at the world positively, being proactive instead of reactive, and seeing others' viewpoints are consistent themes throughout this book. It's a good tool to promote conflict management and positive living.

481   Dendy, Leslie, and Mel Boring. *Guinea Pig Scientists: Bold Self-Experimenters in Science and Medicine.*

Ill. by C. B. Mordon. Henry Holt, 2005, ISBN 978-0-8050-7316-4. 213p. • Grades 5–9

ACCELERATED READER *READING COUNTS* *JUNIOR LIBRARY GUILD*

The authors share the stories of ten people who used their bodies for the purpose of helping mankind. Physician George Fordyce subjected himself to very hot conditions to find out if his body temperature would rise. He found out that humans can withstand temperatures of 260 degrees dry heat and 122 degrees humid heat if they are well hydrated. He discovered that perspiration cooled his body. Horace Wells and William Thomas Green Morton performed experiments on themselves using laughing and other gasses to lessen dental pain; the results were later applied to surgical procedures. Dr. Jesse Lazear proved that the mosquito caused the spread of yellow fever in Cuba and unfortunately died of the disease himself. The selflessness of these people saved millions of lives.

Gentle Criteria: Although death does befall some of the heroes in this book, it is written in a manner that highlights their sacrifices for the benefit of others. Students who like reading about extreme measures will enjoy this book.

482   Freedman, Russell. *Freedom Walkers: The Story of the Montgomery Bus Boycott.*

Holiday House, 2006, ISBN 978-0-8234-2031-5. 114p. • Grades 7–9

ACCELERATED READER *READING COUNTS* *JUNIOR LIBRARY GUILD*

This is an account of the key personalities and events that contributed to the Montgomery Bus Boycott, an event that lasted 381 days. Although Rosa Parks and Martin Luther King, Jr., are the names that most people recognize, there were many other courageous individuals who believed in the justice of their cause, such as Jo Ann Robinson, Claudette Colvin, E. D. Nixon, and Ralph Abernathy. This book does an excellent job of describing the quiet dignity, discipline, and dedication that thousands of black people had to possess in order for the boycott to work. They were proud to be arrested; they met hate with love; and after winning their court case, they did their best to exhibit love and goodwill at all times.

Gentle Criteria: This is an amazing example of what peaceful demonstration can accomplish. Although some of the more violent episodes of the civil rights movement are mentioned, including Emmett Till and the church bombings, the point of this book is that a large group of people can accomplish its objective by simply doing what the group believes is right.

483   Giff, Patricia Reilly. *Don't Tell the Girls.*
Holiday House, 2005, ISBN 978-0-8234-1813-8. 131p. • Grades 5–9
⌐ ACCELERATED READER ⌐ READING COUNTS ⌐ JUNIOR LIBRARY
GUILD

Giff, who is known for works of historical fiction based on her family, including
Maggie's Door and *Nory Ryan's Song*, now offers this memoir. While telling of
the hard times that both sides of her family went through, Giff reminds us of her
Nana's constant focus on the good times. Readers will share the author's desire
for answers to questions: Did Grandfather Michael really disappear mysteriously
instead of meeting his wife at the ship, or did his wife send him packing after he
gambled away her money? Who was Mary Redfern, and what was her connection to Giff's family? And why did Nana cut her face out of some pictures and
not others?

Gentle Criteria: The focus on remembering the pleasant times and recognizing common bonds such as love, illness, and death is comforting. Especially
charming is the fact that the author shares her grandmother's traits of clumsiness
and making mistakes. Children often think adults are perfect, but Giff's grandmother proved otherwise. When Giff confessed to a mistake, her grandmother—
rather than scolding her—always told her about an incident when she herself
made a similar or perhaps worse mistake. This book is a great tool for use in
classes doing family history projects. Readers will want to go to libraries and
look at city directories and birth, marriage, and death certificates pertaining to
their own families.

484   Gourley, Catherine. *War, Women and the News: How Female
Journalists Won the Battle to Cover World War II.*
Atheneum, 2007, ISBN 978-0-689-87752-0. 198p. • Grades 7–9
⌐ ACCELERATED READER ⌐ READING COUNTS ⌐ JUNIOR LIBRARY
GUILD

An amazing group of women journalists are highlighted here. These women
went beyond the society pages and talked about real-world issues. They proved
that women wanted to know more than just the latest hem length. These
women did not need rescuing, but they showed the world the people who did.
When First Lady Eleanor Roosevelt held weekly press conferences that only
women reporters could attend, they talked about much more than society.
When Dorothy Thompson was expelled from Germany for calling Hitler a small
man, her fellow male journalists saw her off with bouquets of red roses, even
though they knew they could be in serious trouble just for their show of support. Anne O'Hare McCormick wrote that women had the soul of the nation in
their keeping. Therese Bonney's photograph of German tanks coming across a
serene cow pasture speaks as loudly as any words ever could. These were courageous women who believed what they were doing could make a difference.

Gentle Criteria: This book is about a group of women working to change deplorable conditions. They showed the human side of suffering through their photographs and news stories. Teachers can use this book to show how one person can have an influence and how journalism can effect change.

485   Govenar, Alan. *Extraordinary Ordinary People: Five Masters of Traditional Arts.*

Candlewick, 2006, ISBN 978-0-7636-2047-9. 85p. • Grades 5–9

This book describes five very different masters of traditional art. Each has received the prestigious National Heritage Fellowship, which recognizes individuals who have mastered culturally defined art forms. From Qi Shu Fang who performs Beijing opera to "Tootie" Montana who designs and sews the elaborate costumes worn by Mardi Gras Indians during their annual celebration in New Orleans, these are truly talented and amazing artists. One of the highlights is the detailed photographs showing the process of creating these art forms. Costuming, weaving, beading, boat building, and more are featured. Art students and teachers alike will be inspired by these talented people who are preserving their cultures.

Gentle Criteria: This book profiles five people who are preserving the beauty and dignity of their cultures. This book has many aspects, including respecting the multicultural dimensions of our lives, preserving art forms, and admiring our diversity.

486   Greenwood, Barbara. *Factory Girl.*

Kids Can, 2007, ISBN 978-1-55337-648-4; pap., ISBN 1-55337-649-8. 136p. • Grades 5–9

Facts and fiction are interwoven in this story about the young girls who worked in the factories of the early twentieth century. Emily Watson is ready to move on to Continuation School when her father is laid off and leaves the family to look for work out West. They do not hear from him for several months and Emily's family is evicted from their home. Emily must quit school and go to work. The only job she can find is in a shirtwaist factory snipping loose threads. As readers continue with the story, the author inserts pictures and facts about child labor in the big cities in the early 1900s. These images and the information about reformers of the time (some as young as seventeen) are both interesting and disturbing. When Emily's immigrant friend Magda, whom she has taught to read and speak English, perishes in a factory fire, Emily decides it is time to speak to the reporter who has been trying to get information from her.

Gentle Criteria: This is a book about bravery and goodness. Emily understands that she must get a job to help her family survive. Her desires for her future do not matter. Her teacher, who recognizes her potential, gives her a graduation certificate of distinction even though she did not take her final exams.

Emily's friend Magda risks and loses her own life in order to save the little girls from the fire.

487   Grogan, John. *Marley: A Dog Like No Other.*
HarperCollins, 2007, ISBN 978-0-06-124034-8. 196p. • Grades 5–9
This adaptation of John Grogan's best-selling book was written just for kids. From the time that John and his wife pick out the puppy to the day they must decide to end his misery, this is the story of Marley—one bad-mannered but thoroughly lovable dog. Nicknamed the Labrador Evader (instead of Retriever), Marley is off to a bad start when the teacher kicks him and his embarrassed owners out of dog obedience school. But Marley is much loved in spite of it all. Marley gets cast in a movie where he promptly drives the cast crazy, unlocks the bars of his cage with his tongue, and makes friends with everyone, both human and animal. Dog owners will understand every antic and every bit of love exhibited in this heartwarming story of a dog and his family.

Gentle Criteria: Money can't buy a dog waiting by the door for your return every day, only love can. This dog may have been the worst-behaved dog in the world, but he certainly was the author's best friend. Marley gave his family loyalty, devotion, and total, complete love. It's a heartwarming story.

488   Ketchum, Liza. *Into a New Country: Eight Remarkable Women of the West.*
Little, Brown, 2000, ISBN 978-0-316-49597-4. 135p. • Grades 7–9
⌐ Accelerated Reader ⌐ Reading Counts
A fascinating set of stories about eight strong and independent women of the West. When these women saw that something needed to be done, they took action; they did not wait for someone else to do it. Klondike Kate, who "wasn't built for going backward," made it through the wilderness of Alaska to work with the miners, set up a restaurant, and help the mounted police. She also dog-sledded one hundred miles to find and help a sick miner. Bethenia Owens-Adair not only got a divorce when divorce was unheard of, but she also made sure her son received an education, and she then went on to get a medical degree, believing that education was the key to her survival. Biddy Mason freed herself from slavery and went on to become one of the richest women in Los Angeles, sharing her wealth to help countless others. She believed, "If you hold your hand closed, nothing good can come in. The open hand is blessed, for it gives in abundance, even as it receives."

Gentle Criteria: Not everything in these stories is gentle, but this is a positive book about women who persevered and did not let hard times embitter them. They overcame the racism and sexism of the times. They held firm to the idea that helping people was the right thing to do, and because of that they are revered and respected to this day.

489   Loewen, Nancy, and Ann Bancroft. *Four to the Pole: The American Women's Expedition to Antarctica, 1992–93.*

Linnet, 2001, ISBN 978-0-208-02518-0. 84p. • Grades 5–9

*ACCELERATED READER

This is the amazing account of the American Women's Expedition (AWE) across Antarctica to the South Pole. Told through both journal entries and narrative, this slim book relates an awe-inspiring journey by a group of four women and how they withstood Antarctic conditions as they skied 660 miles, dragging supply sleds behind them. They learned both to be leaders and to know when to ask for help. Melancholy, injuries, and illness plagued them, but they never gave up. Preparations for the trip included making plans for what to do if they didn't survive it; for example, all of them chose to have their bodies left in a crevasse if they died. Blistered heels, greasy hair, sore bodies, and infection were among the problems they faced. The women kept in touch with more than 250,000 schoolchildren through group e-mails and recorded messages. AWE still exists and holds yearly events recognizing the achievements of girls and women.

Gentle Criteria: There are many reasons why this is an inspiring read, not the least of which was the purpose of the journey itself: to focus attention on the achievements of women; to teach children about the continent of Antarctica; to make people aware of environmental issues; to assist in research relating to women; and to encourage people to take on new challenges. One of the women said that when she became discouraged she thought of the snow sparkles as all of the people at home who were encouraging them on their way. Inspirational indeed!

490   Marcus, Leonard S., compiler and editor. *The Wand in the Word: Conversations with Writers of Fantasy.*

Candlewick, 2006, ISBN 978-0-7636-2625-9. 202p. • Grades 5–9

*ACCELERATED READER *READING COUNTS *JUNIOR LIBRARY GUILD

A great book for readers who love fantasy, this volume presents thirteen well-known authors of all ages and backgrounds, who talk about their lives and their work. An interview, a photo of an original manuscript page, and a book list are included for each author. Several of the authors discuss World War II and how it affected their families. All of the authors share the sentiment that doing what you like for a living is a wonderful gift. Their stories express the need to believe in oneself—that sometimes you just have to dare to believe and not worry about what other people think. Lloyd Alexander talks about fighting in World War II and realizing it was not the glamorous life he expected. Tamora Pierce talks about how she and her two sisters tried to run away from a less-than-perfect home life. Franny Billingsley talks about how her father sang two ballads to each one of his five children every night. These interviews reveal the lives of great writers, their varied backgrounds, and their commitment and success. They read and wrote fantasy even before it became such a popular genre, as a way of coming to terms with negatives in their world. Not only was their writing wildly successful, but so were their personal lives.

Gentle Criteria: This book is a gentle read because the authors show such courage and honesty. All the authors express the need to persevere—whether it is to grow up and escape from a bad situation, or to work hard at something even when you are not certain you will succeed.

491   *The Nobel Book of Answers: The Dalai Lama, Mikhail Gorbachev, Shimon Peres, and Other Nobel Prize Winners Answer Some of Life's Most Intriguing Questions for Young People.*
Ed. by Bettina Steikel. Trans. by Paul De Angelis and Elisabeth Kaestner. Atheneum, 2003, ISBN 978-0-689-86310-3. 254p. • Grades 5–9
⮑ Accelerated Reader ⮑ Junior Library Guild

Twenty-one Nobel Prize winners answer intriguing questions. When asked "What Is Love?" the Dalai Lama says that we were not born into this world to harm others. Mikhail Gorbachev, writing about winning the Nobel Peace Prize, says that those who bring peace to others receive it themselves. Shimon Peres admonishes readers not to be as small as themselves but to be as big as their hopes. Kenzaburo Oe answering, "Why Do We Have to Go to School?" says that we need to experience all the languages of the world to find the one that speaks to us, for example, the language of mathematics, music, art, and so forth. "Why Can't I Live on French Fries?"; "Why Are There Boys and Girls?"; and many other chapters make for entertaining and educational reading.

Gentle Criteria: There are whole passages in this book that readers will want to remember. Teachers looking for nonfiction passages to use will find all twenty-one of use in one subject area or another. Book clubs looking for discussion starters can use these questions. The answers to the questions are inspiring and thought provoking.

492   Osborn, Elinow. *Project Ultraswan.*
Houghton Mifflin, 2002, ISBN 978-0-618-14528-7; 2006, pap., ISBN 978-0-618-58545-8. 64p. • Grades 5–9
⮑ Accelerated Reader ⮑ Reading Counts ⮑ Junior Library Guild

This book tells the story of a wonderfully inspiring project to reintroduce a migrating swan population to the Atlantic Coast. It has been 200 years since trumpeter swans lived naturally in the eastern part of North America; their population was wiped out by hunters. Unlike ducks, swans and geese learn the migration route from their parents. Because there are no parent birds available to teach the new cygnets imported from Alaska, dedicated scientists in the Trumpeter Swan Migration Project are taking on the parents' role, teaching the young birds to follow ultralight aircraft.

Gentle Criteria: There are many dedicated humans trying to rectify some of the damage done to the environment by mankind, and this fact-filled odyssey profiles such an effort. The scientists involved in the project will persist in this process for at least ten years as they try to ensure the swans know the way and will survive. Future scientists and students doing research will find this an inspiring and rewarding read.

493   Paulsen, Gary. *Caught by the Sea: My Life on Boats.*
Delacorte, 2001, ISBN 978-0-385-90025-6; Random House, 2003, pap., ISBN 978-0-440-40716-4. 103p. • Grades 7–9
☞ ACCELERATED READER ☞ READING COUNTS

Gary Paulsen presents an excellent example of how not to learn to sail. He bought a boat and started sailing without any previous experience. On the first day he had three near-misses with other craft, bumped into a yacht and then a Coast Guard boat, and was ticketed for not having a bell. He was then caught out at sea and ended up sailing all the way to La Paz, Mexico, before making it back to shore. He speaks candidly of his ignorance and his near-death experiences. He also shares the stories of other sailors who were not so fortunate. This is a thoroughly entertaining read.

Gentle Criteria: Despite all of the author's ignorance of sailing, he survived to write about his many potentially disastrous near-misses. His writing describes the beauty and serenity of the open sea, and readers will understand his burning desire to sail. Readers will definitely be persuaded that it's worth learning about sailing before getting on a boat and setting out to sea.

494   Perry, Susan K. *Catch the Spirit: Teen Volunteers Tell How They Made a Difference; Stories of Inspiration from 20 Remarkable Recipients of the Prudential Spirit of Community Award.*
Franklin Watts, 2000, ISBN 978-0-531-11883-2; Scholastic, pap., ISBN 978-0-531-16499-0. 192p. • Grades 5–9

The young people profiled in these stories—twenty teens who won the state-level Prudential Spirit of Community Award—are truly remarkable. They include fifteen-year-old David Levitt, who realized that people have to eat every day—not just on holidays; Jenny Hungerford, who went from being a young cocaine addict to talking to kids about how easy it is to become addicted; and Marcus Houston, a teenage football star who shoveled snow to raise money for an essay contest he created to convince kids that getting an education was the most important thing they could do. These are outstanding young adults who took it upon themselves to change their world instead of waiting for others to do it for them. Appended at the end of the book are lists of more students and the community services they performed, along with organizations to contact if teens would like to join a volunteer group.

Gentle Criteria: These are positive stories about kids with the character and willpower to make the world a better place. Students looking for ideas will find this an inspiring read.

495 Revkin, Andrew C. *The North Pole Was Here: Puzzles and Perils at the Top of the World.*
Kingfisher, 2006, ISBN 978-0-7534-5993-5. 128p. • Grades 5–7
⇒ ACCELERATED READER ⇒ JUNIOR LIBRARY GUILD

Readers will be fascinated by this look at the North Pole and how it inspires people to go beyond what seems humanly possible. Andrew Revkin, a *New York Times* journalist, travels with a team of scientists to the frozen north. He is the first reporter ever to file stories and photographs from the top of the world. Interspersed between his newspaper articles are compelling accounts of journeys made to the North Pole throughout history. He tells stories of Russian tourist parties complete with champagne and caviar; of the great scientist Karl Weyprecht, who in 1874 convinced eleven countries to come together to collect data at the pole, being asked to stop walking because the ice might melt underneath him; of the noise and grinding of the great slabs of ice; and of a moment where three broken bolts threaten to undo a year of scientific research.

Gentle Criteria: For readers who are intrigued by the prospect of journeying to the North Pole, these inspiring anecdotes about people who faced hardships to travel there to do research will not disappoint.

496 Rubin, Susan Goldman. *Art Against the Odds: From Slave Quilts to Prison Paintings.*
Random House, 2004, ISBN 978-0-375-92406-4. 50p. • Grades 5–9
⇒ ACCELERATED READER ⇒ JUNIOR LIBRARY GUILD

Herein are descriptions and examples of art created against all odds. Included is artwork done by prisoners and artwork created in the ghettos. The book's author believes that many of these artists would never have ended up in prison if they had discovered their artistic talent beforehand. The quilts made by slaves represent expression in color by many who didn't even know how to read. Quilts hanging on clotheslines with arrows going three directions in one color and one in another color showed the path of the Underground Railroad. Examples of Outsider art—done by individuals who are mentally ill—include some amazing creations. Also included are a few examples from artists who were prisoners of war, such as Robert Knox Sneden, a prisoner of the Confederates, whose drawings help us to understand the Civil War.

Gentle Criteria: This book is tactful in that it does not include details of the crimes perpetrated by the artists, nor the sights witnessed by the prisoners of war. The book emphasizes that humans always try to express themselves through art regardless of their circumstances. For example, during a trip to Kenya, a doctor witnessed children creating toy snakes from bottle caps and boats from old sandals amidst a village suffering from drought and famine.

497 Sandler, Martin W. *America Through the Lens: Photographers Who Changed the Nation.*
Henry Holt, 2005, ISBN 978-0-8050-7367-6. 182p. • Grades 7–9
☞ ACCELERATED READER ☞ READING COUNTS ☞ JUNIOR LIBRARY GUILD

This book offers wonderful examples of how the art of photography and talented photographers have changed the world and made it a better place. Photographers profiled include Mathew Brady, whose pictures of the Civil War brought its grim realities to the American people; Frances Benjamin Johnson, who documented the dignity of African Americans as they strove to better themselves once they were freed from slavery; Lewis Hine, who forced child labor laws to change; William Henry Jackson, who was instrumental in creating the national parks system; and Dorothea Lange, who brought relief to millions during the Depression. This book is a testament to the many artists who had a positive influence on the world.

Gentle Criteria: A great photographic essay about people who used their talents for good, and about the history of our country. It could form an effective base for collaboration between a history class and an art class, looking at why images are more successful in producing positive change than text, and what could be brave about taking a picture.

498 Schwager, Tina, and Michele Schuerger. *Gutsy Girls: Young Women Who Dare.*
Ed. by Elizabeth Verdick. Free Spirit, 1999, pap., ISBN 978-1-57542-059-2. 261p. • Grades 7–9
☞ ACCELERATED READER ☞ READING COUNTS

Part One of this book profiles twenty-five amazing young women who share their experiences climbing mountains, playing college football, drag racing, building houses for Habitat for Humanity, researching Antarctica, and more. Especially noteworthy is their ages, from fourteen to twenty-four. Part Two takes the reader through setting goals, getting in shape, and building confidence. At the end of each story are suggested readings, Web sites, and organizations to contact.

Gentle Criteria: This book is full of stories of young women who have found the courage and determination to do amazing things. Inspiring and positive, this book encourages readers to go out and try new things.

499 Sidman, Joyce. *This Is Just to Say: Poems of Apology and Forgiveness.*
Ill. by Pamela Zagarenski. Houghton Mifflin, 2007, ISBN 978-0-618-61680-0. 47p. • Grades 7–9

Classroom teachers and book clubs will enjoy this book. A sixth-grade class creates a slim volume divided into two sections: one of apologies and one of responses from the people who have been wronged. Some people are forgiven while others are not. Prompted by the poem by William Carlos Williams "This Is Just to Say," this book contains apologies for stealing jelly doughnuts, getting hit in dodge ball, making a comment about someone's dress, pulling a fire alarm, and more. In the responses, parents, teachers, and friends alike tell the other person that the blunder was not as big as it seemed, that they are still loved, and that sometimes life is just that way. Readers will be prompted to write their own poems of apology.

Gentle Criteria: Although one responder says that he is still "pissed off" at the person who wronged him, these are poems about people who have made mistakes, the people who still love them, and the fact that both sides are willing to open the lines of communication to make things better. Some children learn that their parents were not really mad after all, and the incident is long forgotten. Readers will see that sometimes acknowledging a wrong and asking for forgiveness is enough to begin to make things better.

500 **Thimmesh, Catherine.** *Team Moon: How 400,000 People Landed on the Moon.*
Houghton Mifflin, 2006, ISBN 978-0-618-50757-3. 80p. • Grades 5–9
☞ Accelerated Reader ☞ Reading Counts ☞ Junior Library Guild

This is an inspirational account of the 400,000 people who enabled Apollo 11 to land on the moon. This number included seamstresses who sewed together twenty-two layers of fabric for each space suit; engineers; flight directors; camera designers; software experts; suit testers; aerospace technicians; navigators; and many others. Readers will find numerous intriguing stories here. For example, the photographs taken during the mission were of extreme importance and could not wait for the film to be decontaminated before being developed. So film engineers developed a substance that would kill the germs without harming the film. Five hundred feet from the moon the astronauts had only sixty seconds of fuel left. Readers can follow the frenzied calculations the scientists performed to determine whether the spacecraft would make it.

Gentle Criteria: Rarely does a book come along that shows so clearly what can be accomplished when people work together. Teamwork is the theme here. The mission could not have been accomplished if just one person had failed to do his job correctly or to take ownership of the project. What a great message to send!

Author Index

References are to entry numbers, not page numbers.

L

LaFaye, A.
Edith Shay, 234
Strawberry Hill, 89
Worth, 235

Lalicki, Tom
Danger in the Dark: A
Houdini and Nate Mystery,
236

Larson, Kirby
Hattie Big Sky, 237

Lasky, Kathryn
Christmas After All: The Great
Depression Diary of Minnie
Swift, 238
Dreams in the Golden Country:
The Diary of Zipporah
Feldman, a Jewish Immigrant
Girl, 239

Lavender, William
Aftershocks, 240
Just Jane: A Daughter of
England Caught in the
Struggle of the American
Revolution, 241

Lawlor, Laurie
Helen Keller: Rebellious Spirit,
472

Leavitt, Martine
Keturah and Lord Death, 364

Leeuwen, Jean Van
Cabin on Trouble Creek, 242

Lekuton, Joseph Lemasolai
Facing the Lion: Growing Up
Maasai on the African
Savanna, 473

Levine, Beth Seidel
When Christmas Comes Again:
The World War I Diary of
Simone Spencer, 243

Levine, Gail Carson
Cinderellis and the Glass Hill,
365
Ella Enchanted, 366
Fairest, 367
Princess Sonora and the Long
Sleep, 368
The Princess Test, 369
The Two Princesses of Bamarre,
370
The Wish, 371

Levithan, David
Friends: Stories About New
Friends, Old Friends, and
Unexpectedly True Friends,
450

Lieberg, Carolyn
West with Hopeless, 90

Lin, Grace
The Year of the Dog, 91

Littman, Sarah Darer
Confessions of a Closet
Catholic, 92

Loewen, Nancy
Four to the Pole: The American
Women's Expedition to
Antarctica, 1992–93, 489

Lombard, Jenny
Drita My Homegirl, 93

Look, Lenore
Ruby Lu, Empress of
Everything, 94

Love, D. Anne
The Puppeteer's Apprentice,
244

Lowry, Lois
Gossamer, 372
Stay! Keeper's Story, 95

Lubar, David
Sleeping Freshmen Never Lie,
96
Wizards of the Game, 373

Lupica, Mike
Heat, 97

M

McCaughrean, Geraldine
Cyrano, 98
Peter Pan in Scarlet, 374
The Pirate's Son, 245

McClaren, Clemence
Aphrodite's Blessings: Love
Stories from the Greek Myths,
456

McCully, Emily Arnold
Beautiful Warrior: The Legend
of the Nun's Kung Fu, 2

McCutcheon, John
Christmas in the Trenches, 3

McGill, Alice
Molly Bannaky, 4

McKay, Hilary
Caddy Ever After, 99
Indigo's Star, 100
Permanent Rose, 101
Saffy's Angel, 102

McKissack, Pat
Nzingha: Warrior Queen of
Matamba, Angola, Africa,
1595, 246

McNamee, Eoin
The Navigator, 375

Madden, Kerry
Gentle's Holler, 247

Louisiana's Song, 248

Malcolm, Jahnna N.
Perfect Strangers, 103

Many, Paul
These Are the Rules, 104

Marcum, Lance
The Cottonmouth Club, 105

Marcus, Leonard S.
The Wand in the Word:
Conversations with Writers of
Fantasy, 490

Martin, Ann M.
A Dog's Life, 106
The Doll People, 376
Friends: Stories About New
Friends, Old Friends, and
Unexpectedly True Friends,
450
The Meanest Doll in the
World, 377

Martin, Rafe
Birdwing, 378
The World Before This One: A
Novel Told in Legend, 379

Mass, Wendy
Jeremy Fink and the Meaning of
Life, 107
A Mango-Shaped Space, 108

Matthews, L. S.
Fish, 109

Mazer, Harry
The Wild Kid, 110

Meehl, Brian
Out of Patience, 111

Mercado, Nancy E.
Tripping Over the Lunch Lady:
And Other School Stories,
451

Mills, Claudia
Alex Ryan, Stop That! 112
Lizzie at Last, 113
Makeovers by Marcia, 114

Morgan, Clay
The Boy Who Spoke Dog, 115

Morgan, Nicola
Chicken Friend, 116

Morgenstern, Susie Hoch
Secret Letters from 0 to 10, 117

Morpurgo, Michael
The Amazing Story of
Adolphus Tips, 249
Kensuke's Kingdom, 118

Morris, Gerald
The Lioness and Her Knight,
380
The Quest of the Fair
Unknown, 381

Title Index

References are to entry numbers, not page numbers.

C

D

E

F

G

H

I

J

O

P

Q

R

S

Subject Index

References are to entry numbers, not page numbers.

Family life—Fiction

Series Index

References are to entry numbers, not page numbers.

Appendix

Listed here are titles that are included in the Accelerated Reader and Reading Counts programs, followed by a list of Junior Library Guild selections. References are to entry numbers, not page numbers.

Accelerated Reader

The Abernathy Boys (Hunt), 226

Above the Veil (Nix), 383

Across the Wide and Lonesome Prairie: The Oregon Trail Diary of Hattie Campbell (Gregory), 209

Aenir (Nix), 384

Aftershocks (Lavender), 240

Agnes Parker . . . Girl in Progress (O'Dell), 123

Airball: My Life in Briefs (Harkrader), 71

Airborn (Oppel), 395

The Akhenaten Adventure (Kerr), 356

Al Capone Does My Shirts: A Novel (Choldenko), 183

Alex Ryan, Stop That! (Mills), 112

Alida's Song (Paulsen), 256

All the Way Home (Giff), 69

Alphabet of Dreams (Fletcher), 337

The Amazing Story of Adolphus Tips (Morpurgo), 249

Amber Was Brave, Essie Was Smart: The Story of Amber and Essie Told Here in Poems and Pictures (Williams), 463

America Through the Lens: Photographers Who Changed the Nation (Sandler), 497

The Antarctic Scoop (Bledsoe), 30

Aphrodite's Blessings: Love Stories from the Greek Myths (McClaren), 456

Aquamarine (Hoffman), 351

Archer's Quest (Park), 397

The Arrow Over the Door (Bruchac), 179

Art Against the Odds: From Slave Quilts to Prison Paintings (Rubin), 496

At the Sign of the Star (Sturtevant), 278

Atalanta and the Arcadian Beast (Yolen), 457

The Babbs Switch Story (Beard), 175

Backwater (Bauer), 24

Bambert's Book of Missing Stories (Jung), 87

Bandit's Moon (Fleischman), 194

Basketball (or Something Like That) (Baskin), 23

The Beasts of Clawstone Castle (Ibbotson), 352

Beautiful Warrior: The Legend of the Nun's Kung Fu (McCully), 2

Because of Winn-Dixie (DiCamillo), 59

Becoming Joe DiMaggio (Testa), 444

Bella at Midnight: The Thimble, the Ring, and the Slippers of Glass (Stanley), 410

The Big Burn (Ingold), 227

The Birchbark House (Erdrich), 192

Birdwing (Martin), 378

The Black Canary (Curry), 328

Blizzard's Wake (Naylor), 253

Bloomability (Creech), 51

The Blue Djinn of Babylon (Kerr), 357

Blue Fingers: A Ninja's Tale (Whitesel), 284

The Boggart and the Monster (Cooper), 323

The Book of Story Beginnings (Kladstrup), 363

The Book Without Words: A Fable of Medieval Magic (Avi), 302

Boots and the Seven Leaguers: A Rock-and-Troll Novel (Yolen), 419

Boston Jane: An Adventure (Holm), 218

The Boy Who Saved Baseball (Ritter), 135

The Boy Who Spoke Dog (Morgan), 115

The Braid (Frost), 198

Brainboy and the Deathmaster (Seidler), 439

Breaking Through (Jimenez), 468

Cabin on Trouble Creek (Leeuwen), 242

Caddy Ever After (McKay), 99

Cam's Quest: The Continuing Story of Princess Nevermore and the Wizard's Apprentice (Regan), 403

The Canyon (Cole), 45

Reading Counts

Junior Library Guild

About the Author

DEANNA J. McDANIEL is a Library Media Specialist, Genoa Middle School, Westerville City Schools, Ohio, with more than 25 years' library experience; and a freelance researcher for *Web Feet*.